HOW HEAVY IS THE MOUNTAIN

HOW HEAVY IS THE MOUNTAIN

▼

An Alaskan Tour Manual/Novel

Tim Rundquist

Writers Club Press

San Jose New York Lincoln Shanghai

How Heavy Is The Mountain
An Alaskan Tour Manual/Novel

Writers Club Press
an imprint of iUniverse.com, Inc.

For information address:
iUniverse.com, Inc.
620 North 48th Street, Suite 201
Lincoln, NE 68504-3467
www.iuniverse.com

ISBN: 0-595-13120-4

Printed in the United States of America

DEDICATION

—To Neil Young: whom, for years and years, I
thought was the only person who understood me.

—To Heather: who **does**.

CONTENTS

Part One: Please Don't Shoot The Tenants

Part Two: The Backwards Parade

Part Three: How Heavy Is The Mountain

Part Four: Hunkering Down

PART ONE: PLEASE DON'T SHOOT THE TENANTS

▼

"I was standin' by the side of the road,
rain falling on my shoes…"
—bob dylan

The Fog Woman: A Tlingit Fable

▼

One day in the early autumn, Raven went out fishing in a canoe. It was a chilly, misty day, and as he paddled out from the shore the fires of the village quickly faded and disappeared. Soon, a fog set in, blurring the familiar contours of the forest and the mountains. As it thickened, the shore vanished altogether. The waves died down, and it grew deathly still and quiet on the water.

Raven felt fear. All of his bearings were confused by the dense fog and the silence. How could he hope to find his way back to the village? The strong currents of the passage could sweep him far out to sea if he paddled in the wrong direction. Raven stared at the grey, murky sky, at the depth of despair—but as he did so, an apparition appeared before him: a strange woman now sat in the canoe. Her solemn brown eyes offered no explanation as she removed her conical cedar-bark hat, held it in her left hand and began to gesture with her right hand. There was a barely discernible movement in the fog, and as Raven watched in amazement, the woman directed the fog into the hat with her hand movements, at first slowly, and then with increasing speed. Within minutes, the fog was gone from the water, vanished into the mysterious woman's hat. She replaced the hat on her head and said nothing.

Raven began to paddle back towards the now visible shore, relieved and bewildered. As he approached the village, however, he realized that he had still not caught any fish. The clan would go hungry if he came back with an empty canoe.

As a new wave of despair hit Raven, the Fog Woman stirred from her meditations and sat up in the canoe. She held up four fingers before Raven, dipped them into the water and beckoned to Raven to fetch his gaff hook. Where the Fog Woman's fingers had been in the water, there were now four live salmon. These were the world's very first salmon. Raven stared in amazement once again at the unusual fish, but he recognized dinner and swiftly gaffed the four fish into the canoe. The Fog Woman dipped her fingers into the water again, then several times more, and soon Raven had a canoe full of salmon, and was at last ready to return to the hungry village.

The people of the village were impressed with the bounty that Raven had brought to them. Raven accepted their praise and, knowing a good arrangement when he saw one, put the Fog Woman to work creating more and more salmon. She did so without complaint, and shortly the drying racks of Raven were full of fish.

As a result of his new-found wealth, Raven quickly became the most powerful and influential figure in the village. In a potlatch ceremony, the most lavish the village had ever witnessed (more than 100 blankets and woven baskets were given away), Raven wed the Fog Woman, to ensure his continued good fortune. Once this had been done, of course, Raven had more drying racks built and ordered the Fog Woman to create more and more salmon. For a period of time, the village worked virtually non-stop, constructing racks for Raven, and the Fog Woman providing salmon as quickly as the racks went up.

Easy times lay ahead for the village. Their drying racks were full to capacity, they could exchange their wealth for the goods of other clans, and everyone was growing fat and prosperous. Raven was perhaps the most pleased with his new-found fortune; as the most powerful individual in the village, he could come and go as he pleased, live in the best enclave in the cedar clan house, eat the food and take the wife of anyone else, if he so desired. And, he did all of these things accorded his privilege. The Fog Woman remained at his fire, silent as always.

After a time, Raven grew very boastful about his powerful position. He took to swaggering about the village, wealth protruding above his beltline, ordering others about, talking in a loud voice about his personal attributes that had made such a lifestyle possible, and the shortcomings of others which mired them in their inferior status. The villagers began to shy away from Raven's approach, lest they become the targets of his scornful attention.

One day in the Spring, Raven heard voices in his head and began to chase his wife, the Fog Woman, around the village, shouting insults and trying to hit her with a dead salmon he had taken from one of the racks. At the water's edge, the Fog Woman suddenly turned and stopped Raven in his tracks with a look in her eyes that stilled the mist drifting down the mountainside. She held up two fingers, whistled through them three times and beckoned with her other hand. At the sound of an approach, Raven turned back towards the village, and watched in stupefaction as all the salmon that the Fog Woman had created came back to life, left the drying racks and began to make their way back to the ocean. Thousands upon thousands of fish marched past Raven and the Fog Woman, at her direction, jumped into the water, and swam off. Within minutes, all the salmon had departed the village, and Raven's huge drying racks were completely bare.

The Fog Woman turned and, without a word, walked back up the hill, into the cedar trees, along the stream. Raven began to stumble after her, calling out her name, but soon lost her trail. She was gone.

These days, salmon are born in the fresh-water streams and rivers of the coast, but migrate out to sea as soon as they are old enough to do so. After a period of several years, they swim back to the same streams in which they were born, produce their offspring, and die there. We cannot fully explain this phenomenon. Perhaps they return because they wish to visit the Fog Woman.

TANGLED UP IN BLUE

▼

Predawn blues and greys, covering the sleeping college dormitory. A hasty cup of instant coffee, the honk of a car horn: my ride to the Seattle-Tacoma airport. A brief pause by a dumpster, to dispose of a term's worth of class notes. I won't need them for this trip; I won't need that Class of '86 diploma.

What am I getting myself into? I have no idea; I am a blank slate, I am jumping into a glacial river.

The lights of the airplane are muted, humming tunelessly. On board, there are two classes: one for the suits and sport-coats, balancing coffee and briefcase on alternating knees; one for the flannel shirts, Levis and miniature liquor bottles. The luggage crew loads equal parts Samsonite and Coleman ice chest, held together by duct tape.

Morning comes at last as the plane lifts out of the Northwest fog, into the pink-and-blue early summer sky. The tallest peaks of the Cascades and Olympics are sharp, snowy islands in the rolling grey.

Weather patterns: mostly fifties and cloudy up North, this time of the year. Other patterns: yellow is the colour of my true love's hair, in the morning. Green is the colour of...

One can smell the rain clouds before the plane actually enters them: cedar pitch, smokehouse, various legends, the red-brown earth being washed away by coastal torrents. A descent, and all is dark again. The Alaskans reach for their carry-on totems, preparing for arrival.

Out of the blue, into the black...

Into the rain. Kris Westerberg picked up his backpack and guitar from the baggage claim area, shifted the weight onto his back, and stepped outside. A ferry waited at the bottom of the hill, loading airport traffic and passengers to take over to Ketchikan. Ketchikan: founded in 1887 as a fish cannery site, according to Kris' tour manual. Home of the chief Kitcha; the place where the creek *Kitsch-khin* flowed into the sea; Tlingit for Place Of The Eagles, who waited on the stony beach for spawned-out salmon to be carried down the creek. Ketch-as-many-fish-as-you-Kan.

Kris shivered at the front rail of the ferry, longish blonde hair tucked into his denim jacket. Even though the channel crossing was not a long one, the opposite shore was not clearly apparent until the boat was nearly at the city dock; the sparse cars and trucks on the landing area seemed to be melting in the mist. As the ferry docked, a white van caught Kris' eye with a familiar logo: identical to that on the button he wore on his lapel.

A man emerged from the van. His movements resembled those of a bulldog: tenacious, deliberate, low to the ground, strong. The man did not wear a raincoat, but carried a blue blazer over one arm and stood out in the rain in his shirtsleeves. He squinted in the direction of the off-loading ferry, as if he were a skipper looking for the breaking fin of a salmon. Apparently satisfied, he pursed his lips, took a comb out of his back pocket and quickly ran it through his slicked hair.

"Roy Haverman," said the man as he took Kris' hand in a strong grip. "Welcome home." He smiled: a squinty, late middle-aged bulldog smile. "I'm your boss, but don't let that change your opinion of me. Come on, let me drive you to the hotel. I'll show you around town later."

Kris loaded his gear into the company van and clambered onto the front seat beside Roy. The inside of the van was cluttered with cases of motor oil, some fishing gear, boxes of tour brochures. "There are three of you guys coming up from Seattle," commented Roy. "You're the first one to make it up; we're starting with a whole new crew. Don't know why, but this year we had the damndest time finding local tour guides from town here. The fishing must be too good."

They drove along Front Street into town, past the old canneries, docks and waterfront bars. Kris took it all in, made small-talk about the flight up, and studied the lines on Roy's face. They were good lines: a lot of smile creases, crow's-feet from years of squinting through mist and fog, a few taut lines of rough times: some late nights, some conflicts.

"This street was a lot tougher when I was police chief here," commented Roy. "Especially back in the early days: the fishermen, the shady ladies, all that money and nothing to spend it on but trouble. Things sure changed when we got statehood; before that, this was like its own little nation. But you can still feel it here sometimes: when all the boats are in, or when its been raining for a couple weeks on end." Roy looked thoughtful, momentarily out of place behind the wheel of a tour van. "Got out of the department a few years back; Tish made me do it 'cause my heart was acting up. Guess I'm taking it easier these days. Sure don't feel like it." Almost imperceptibly he winked, in old uncle fashion—and Kris decided that he liked Roy.

In front of a sputtering neon sign, Roy pulled up and motioned for Kris to hop out and grab his pack. "Here's the Ingersoll: your hotel. I'll meet you and the others here in a couple mornings, and we'll talk about work, then I'll show you around, drive the tour route. In the meantime, you'll need to find a place to stay for the summer: the company will put you up for the first two nights, then you're on your own."

Even though he had known of this arrangement, forty-eight hours suddenly seemed like a very short time to Kris. "Will there be much of a problem finding a place? Where should I start?"

Roy didn't seem overly worried. "Fishing season hasn't really kicked in yet: should be plenty of places. I'd start just by walking around. You'll have this town figured out in no time. See you in the morning." He waved goodbye, rolled up the van window and disappeared down the wet street.

Kris checked in, went upstairs to his room, surveyed at a glance the twin beds, white towels, a television that the housekeeper must have left on, blaring out MTV. He pushed the window open wide, breathing in the salty air, and told himself that the immediate past of college was far behind. How long had he been dreaming about coming to Alaska: since his first Jack London story? How many ski trails had in his mind turned into frigid Alaskan sled tracks? Now he was there: just barely across the southern border, in a modern (albeit slightly seedy) hotel, television tuned into the 1980's—but he was there. *I wake up along some roadside, dreaming of the way things sometimes are...*

About an hour later, Kris' music-video musings were disrupted by the sound of someone fumbling with a room key outside the door. He rose from the lumpy bed, opened the door, and there was another backpack, another dripping raincoat, another person very much like himself.

"Hey, Kris!" grinned Peter Helgeson as he pulled his gear into the room. "They said it would be wet here, but they didn't quite say it was going to be quite like this." He dropped his sopping pack on the floor, shook Kris' hand. "At least in Seattle, the rain sometimes **stops** for a while."

"That's about right, buddy. It hasn't stopped since **I've** been here. C'mon, let me help you with your gear." Kris and Peter had been friends throughout their time at the University: crew teammates, roomies for Kris' final year in the dorms. If it were at all possible, Peter was even more Scandinavian-looking than Kris: blonde curly hair, glacier-blue eyes, a little shorter than Kris' 6'4" but more strongly-built. People often made joking "Ole and Sven" comments around Kris and Peter, noting the obvious fact that the two looked just like brothers.

But if they were Norwegian twins, Kris had preceded Peter in birth by just a few minutes: he was one year ahead in school, had done a fair amount of traveling, had been around the block a few more times, and was perhaps a bit more inclined to seek out new experiences. Kris was the one who had spotted the ad for Alaskan summer work in the student newspaper, and broached the subject of heading up North together. Peter did not take too much convincing: he had several cousins who had spent summers fishing in Alaska, and had returned to Seattle flush with funds and tall tales. Both had passed the initial round of interviews and completed the bus-driver training unscathed, and were accepted into the hiring pool of Driver/Guides.

Over the Spring, through the last hellacious/ soporific round of Final exams, their conversations had increasingly turned in a northerly direction: in particular, speculation as to where they might be stationed. Neither had been to Alaska before, but Kris had hoped for the interior, from what he had heard of its mountains and wide-open tundra; Peter, from the outset, had favored Southeast for the tall trees and water. Once they had learned of their mutual assignments to Ketchikan, Kris, Peter and another college friend, Dan Vanderwal (who would be arriving at the start of June), had agreed to room together. Kris and Peter figured that locating a suitable residence should be the major task for the next couple days: then, they could begin to explore.

Meanwhile, outside the hotel window, it was still pouring. For the few people on the street, galoshes (locally known as "Sitka Sneakers") and Helly-Hanson ponchos were the fashion of choice. "My cousins told me," said Peter, "that the locals don't use umbrellas in Ketchikan. For one thing, the wind here is often such that you'll do a Mary Poppins down the street if you try to open one. Not to mention, it means you're a **weenie**, anyway. You're supposed to just throw on your gear and go with the weather."

"Guess I'd better get rid of my umbrella, then. Can't be a weenie in Alaska." Kris raised an eyebrow, smiled at his friend. "Got your heavy-duty rain gear?"

"You bet. Got all my fishing stuff, too. Got that 'local' look going." Peter flopped into an easy chair and returned Kris' grin of camaraderie. "We're **here**, buddy. There's no going back."

On the hotel TV, a Cars video had come on. Lead singer Ric Ocasek, to impress some MTV chick, had turned into a fly, then into King Kong. The nighttime entertainment in Ketchikan surely would get much better than this. At some point, this might even begin to feel like home.

MOVING IN

▼

the only things standing straight in this
neighborhood are the totem poles,
serving as touchstones, reminders,
places to tie up one's psyche outside
 the houses reside at crazy
 angles, corresponding to the
 pitch of the forested slopes
 rising woodsmoke meets mountain fog and
 becomes indistinguishable; the din of
 children and cultural clashes are
 sharp but muffled,
 even the most exultant cries are lost
at the base of deer mountain is the
ketchikan ballpark, with its two
possible field conditions: mud or dust,
no in-between
today it is a muddy lake, and bawden st. is
a spawning-run river
 the old hospital building at
 347 bawden is the foundation of

the neighborhood: grey-whale stolid, wide
like the prow of an abandoned schooner
its wooden steps ascend saint-like among
salmonberries and wild rhubarb,
   a jacob's-ladder covered with water
from the top of the stairs the
neighborhood makes more sense,
simply a cut in the bluffs off the ocean;
the fisheries play out their
life-and-death only blocks away,
boats huddle in the narrow harbor
   we moved into the old
   hospital building, despite the
   ghosts of gurneys and aura of north-
   country fishermans-blues coating the
   walls and cupboards;
   an ammonia cleanser, selected for its
   simple violence, made the place
   livable; all that we need are
   blankets, food, some kind of christening:
   perhaps a missionary

HAIDA WAYS

▼

Fun Tour Fact #42: in downtown Ketchikan, at the base of a dead-end street, resides a relatively short but very significant totem pole. Modeled on an historic design, the pole's characters are buttressed by a stout, smiling Buddha-like figure. According to local legend, one who rubs the protruded tummy of the totem figure in a certain way will have money within 24 hours.

The company van split the multicolored slick that washed down from the creosoted front steps of the Bawden Street Apartments. "I've been **here** a few times before," commented Roy as Kris and Peter piled into the van. "Usually under somewhat more pressing, police-type circumstances."

"It's a bit gnarly in there," admitted Kris. "But it cleaned up all right. Anyhow, it's my first apartment, ever. Pete's, too. You gotta start somewhere."

"We're paying $600 a month for that place," complained Peter. "Can you imagine what they charge in the **upscale** part of town?"

Roy chuckled as they drove away. "Rents are high all over Southeast: too many mountains, not enough flat places to build apartments. The girls in the office can't believe you guys are living here. But I reckon you'll make out fine. They're looking forward to meeting you."

The apartments were just a short distance uphill from the Ingersoll Hotel, site of the company office. However, the only direct route between the two was a very long wooden staircase, a finger-like extension of a downtown street. The closest driveable route slithered circuitously out of the neighborhood, depositing the van at the hotel in about five minutes time.

Jacqui, the office manager, smiled warmly at Kris and Peter from behind her desk in the hotel lobby. A Ketchikan native of 33 years, Jacqui had the easy-going, brown-eyed look of someone who moved with the rain, rather than against it. "You should know that Ketchikan can do better than that old hospital building," she told the boys as she shook their hands. "Just give this town some time—it'll grow on you."

"Yeah: just like the moss," cracked a tall, raven-haired woman who was leaning up against the wall. "Like the mildew on my boat. Like the 'magic mushrooms' up on Deer Mountain."

The boys were introduced to Sylvia, another local woman who would be working as a part-time guide. Sylvia had slung fish at the canneries, waitressed in the tough waterfront bars, and generally done whatever it took to scrape by in Ketchikan for the past decade or so, living out of her old cabin-cruiser moored just south of town. Sylvia was the first of what would be several local part-time hires, signed on to help with the busiest cruise-ship days.

"Why are there no local full-time guides?" wondered Kris. "One would think that the company could find all the people it needs around here, rather than having to recruit down in Washington."

"Good question," replied Roy. "In fact, I've been pushing for years for exclusive Alaskan hiring. Nothing against you guys," he added quickly. "Believe me, I tried to find an all local staff—but this town is too busy in the summers. It's either feast or famine: during the winter, there's not a heck of a lot to do for a living, but this time of year, there's almost too much."

"That's me," said Sylvia: "makin' hay while the sun shines—if 'sun-shine' is what you could call this. I'm hanging on to my barmaid gig: this is the prime season. Those fishermen, when they come in, are about the best tippers in the world. I'll try to get out fishing myself as much as possible. Most everybody I know here has at least two or three jobs during the summer."

"So here you boys are," smiled Jacqui, "instant Alaskan experts from Seattle. Or, soon-to-be experts."

Kris, Peter and Roy took leave of Jacqui and Sylvia, and left the hotel lobby. It was time to begin the "fam tour": the first familiarization with Ketchikan, following the tour route, that Kris and Peter would receive. They loaded into the van, and Roy drove the short distance from the hotel to the old Spruce Mill dock: the downtown site where the cruise ships discharged their passengers for day excursions. The dock was very long, lined with huge concrete posts (or "dolphins") for tying up the ships. As many as three cruise ships could dock right alongside downtown; when there were additional ships—or if a ship was too large to come all the way into port—they moored in the inlet and ran passenger dinghies ashore.

"The ships come up here to Southeast for five or seven day cruises through the Inside Passage," began Roy. "If the passengers have begun their trip from the south, rather than starting up in Skagway, this will be their first port of call in Alaska. And, they pretty much take over downtown when they're here. All those tourists, coming endlessly down the gangplanks: we—us and 'Brand X', that is—scoop up a fair amount of them in our buses, the rest hit the souvenir shops, the ice-cream stands. Some even wind up in the bars, accidentally-on-purpose."

"Are the ships here every day? And what do you mean, 'Brand X'?"

"We're now seeing at least one cruise ship four or five days a week. Some days, there are two or even three big ships in port. It's gotten a lot busier over the past few years—and it's just going to keep growing.

" 'Brand X', of course, is our competition: we're not the only game in town. There's one other big, Seattle-based touring company here in

Ketchikan, and we go head-to-head with them all over the state, in every port. There are a few other, smaller local companies who pretty much pick up our 'leftovers': the folks who aren't pre-booked on any tour package, but just up and decide they want a totem-pole tour. Of course, we get a few of those walk-ins, too."

"So, does this mean we'll be working only when the ships are in: like, regular five-day weeks?" wondered Peter.

"Hell no: there's plenty of work to be done, every day. There's airport transfers: picking up and dropping off independent travelers. Ferry transfers. Lots of baggage delivery: you'll be glorified bellboys at times. Lots of good old-fashioned grunt work: washing buses, oil changes, lube jobs. We'll find plenty to keep you busy."

"Were you ever in the Army by chance, Roy?" Kris wanted to know. Roy said nothing, grinned, gunned the van engine and drove off the dock, back onto Front Street.

"So, if I were beginning a tour right here—as you almost always will—I would start off something like this." Roy moved a small boom microphone into position, turned it on, and transmogrified into tour-guide mode.

"Folks, welcome to Ketchikan, Alaska's First City and salmon capital of the world. Population: usually, about twenty-five thousand, making it the fourth largest city in Alaska; today it's about twice that, what with all the ships in port. Usual weather: plenty of 'liquid sunshine': an average of one hundred sixty inches of rain per year. My name is Roy, and I'll be your guide on today's three-hour Ketchikan City Tour.

"We will be making three stops today. The first will be at the Totem Heritage Center, where you'll view artifacts from the Tlingit and Haida peoples, and hear a brief presentation on local native history. From there, we will walk next door to the local hatchery, where you'll see young salmon fingerlings gearing up for their trips down-river to the sea. Then, we'll drive down to Creek Street and Dolly's House, the historical heart of Ketchikan's colorful red-light district. Finally, we will drive a short distance north of town to Totem Bight, site of the largest collection of contemporary totem poles in all southeast Alaska."

Roy paused for a moment. "Of course," he said, "that's all pretty plain-sounding. Lesson number one of tour-guiding is: do not be boring. Do not sound as if you've just memorized something from a Chamber of Commerce flyer. You should be able to communicate the basic facts that I've just told you, but do it in your own words. You may be a little wooden-sounding at first, but give it some time: you'll come into your own way of saying things.

"What do I do? Personalize everything. Try to weave the town into real-life stories. Believe me, I've got plenty of stories of my own. As the summer goes by, you'll pick up your own personal folklore. Trust me: you can't help but do so, if you have any kind of life for yourself around here."

While Roy had been talking, the tour van had wound its way through Kris and Peter's neighborhood, following a creek up to the edge of town. Just before the creek ducked into a stand of tall hemlock trees, they saw two long, low wooden buildings. The one in front had ornate totem figures carved on the facade.

"This is the Totem Heritage Center," explained Roy. It hasn't quite opened for the season yet, but you'll see it soon enough. I highly recommend that you spend a good deal of time in here: as much as possible while you're starting out as guides.

"Have you read up much on the local Native peoples? They're a big presence here—about one-third of Ketchikan's population, an even higher percentage in outlying areas—and you'll find that the native culture provides probably the most interesting, well-received information on the whole tour.

"You have two major tribes here in Southeast: the Tlingit—pronounced 'Klink-it'—and the Haida. They're cousins of the coastal tribes south of here, in British Columbia and Washington; much more in common with them than with the Athabaskan and Eskimo peoples of mainland Alaska. But despite the similarities, you don't see a lot of fraternizing between the tribes; they were historical enemies and all. Even to this day, a Tlingit man will get **really** upset if he finds his wife in a Haida-bed."

It took just a moment for the inexcusable pun to register. Kris and Peter turned to Roy at the same time, saw the almost imperceptible old-uncle wink. "Lesson number two," thought Kris: "there ain't no joke too corny to use on tour."

"Anyhow," concluded Roy, "you'll be talking about the Native culture a lot more once you're on the way out to Totem Bight. Let's check out the hatchery now.

They paused on a small footbridge that passed over the creek. "You wouldn't know to look at it now," said Roy, "but in a couple weeks this creek will be filled with salmon, from bank to bank. Four separate runs—some of which will overlap—head up this way.

"About half of these will be the hatchery fish. They'll swim up into the pens there; the females will be harvested for their eggs; the males will be 'milked' of their sperm. As the summer goes on, you'll be able to watch the fingerlings grow up, from being barely visible to pretty good-sized smolts: ones that stand a pretty good chance of making it out to sea.

"The rest are the wild runs: we get kings, pinks, silvers and chum in this creek. The kings are my favorites to watch: they're about as noble a fish as there is. That gravel bar just upstream is a major spawning bed: you'll see forty-pound female kings—'hens,' they call 'em—flop onto their sides and shimmy their tails up and down, blasting out nests for their eggs in the gravel. A single male, one who has been tailing each hen upstream (and probably fighting off a bunch of romantic rivals), will come along and spray the eggs. That's about it: both fish will just drift away downstream, soon to die.

"And, you can see the whole drama from up here. You'll have a hard time tearing the tourists away from this bridge once the salmon are in: people are mesmerized watching 'em. You can impress your guests with your considerable knowledge of the salmon's life cycle: the birth-to-death anadromous story, the uncanny way they find their way home. I bet you'll even have a few fishing stories of your own to tell, after a while.

"It's the same deal in Thomas Basin, the little bay at the mouth of the creek. The salmon will congregate out there, gathering up strength and numbers, changing into their colorful, misshapen freshwater forms: getting up the gumption to head upstream. They'll work off all that nervous energy by putting on about the most spectacular jumping displays you'll see: they're real acrobats. Every few seconds, a big fish will perform some impossible, twisting leap. It's the biggest show in town: people will gather there for hours on end."

"Who needs TV, when you have all this?" mused Kris.

Roy led Kris and Peter past the fingerling holding pens, back towards the tour van. "As a consequence, you'll find that folks around here have a serious case of 'fish on the brain'. For instance, there's this local artist, guy name of Ray Troll: you'll see some of his stuff in the downtown studios. He draws these elaborate, dream-like illustrations of salmon, halibut, and about every sea-dwelling critter—often, taken quite a bit out of context. Take a look at his 'Humpies From Hell' gang portrait sometime. He's got quite a local following."

They drove away from the mountainside, towards the south end of the Ketchikan waterfront. They met the shoreline and followed it for about half a mile, to a street lined with tiny, 1920s-era cabins—which, upon closer inspection, was actually a street of water.

"Welcome to Creek Street." said Roy. "The place where both the fish and the fishermen came to spawn."

Kris and Peter, having taken careful note of the more prurient aspects of Ketchikan's history while studying the tour manuals, knew all about Creek Street: historically, the most notorious red-light district in all southeast Alaska. They knew about the boom-and-bust economy that had drawn mostly-male hordes of fishermen, loggers, and other seekers of fortune: men who, in the good times, had money to burn and nowhere else to go; who, in the bad times, still took solace in some of that negotiable affection. They knew about Dolly, the greatest self-styled entrepreneur on the street: an imposing figure at six feet tall and well over two hundred grand-opera pounds; an extremely shrewd businesswoman who came to own most of the street and a good deal of downtown (not to mention the city council); a woman who took absolutely no guff from anyone.

But they didn't know anyone who had actually seen Creek Street in its heyday, and arrested people on it, until now.

"Creek Street was hopping well into the 1950's," began Roy. "Of course, Dolly herself was long since retired—she was an old lady by then—but the trade was still going strong. Guys would be lined up on the boardwalk, most every weekend night. As the line moved forward, you'd see a trickle of guys sneaking out the back doors of the cribs: the married men, mostly.

"In a way, it was a shame to shut down such a going concern: talk about a recession-proof industry. But, you've got to remember that the world was changing pretty quickly back then: television and radio were here, statehood was on the way, and the city fathers now wanted a modern, civilized community."

"Somebody told me," said Kris, "that during Prohibition they made trap-doors in most of these crib-house floors: so that skiffs loaded with booze could slide up the creek in the moonlight and hand-pulley their goods up into the houses. I kind of like that idea: I mean, the creativity involved."

Roy chuckled. "Yep: folks here were pretty ingenious at dodging the law. Still are. Anyhow, you'll see all this for yourselves—and get the full story, many times over—when you'll stop by Dolly's House on your tours. They've made it into a little 'museum of commerce': fixed it up and replenished the antique furnishings. They've even hired some local girls, decked out in the costume of the day, to give the tour spiel."

Again, Kris and Peter's prurient young minds flashed to...teddies, negligees, Yikes!—before reality checked in and reminded them that the girls' attire certainly would be conservative enough so as not to provide fresh cardiacs to elderly tour passengers.

Kris, Peter and Roy clomped up the boardwalk, peered through the drawn, slightly musty-looking lace curtains into Dolly's, and strolled back past the gift shops that would be re-opening in a few days. "From whore-houses to knickknacks and curios, in less than thirty years," commented Peter. "Imagine that."

"And now," said Roy, "to the north end of the road." They got back into the van, skirted downtown along Front Street, passed the Alaska Marine Highway and airport ferry terminals, cleared the semi-industrial outskirts, and left Ketchikan proper.

"How far does this highway go?" asked Peter. "My understanding was that the road dead-ends a ways out of town, rather than connecting up with anything."

"Right you are. Almost all the towns in southeast Alaska are isolated from one another—and are cut off from any road access to Canada and the lower 48. They haven't figured out a way yet to build highways over glaciers. There's a turnaround about 30 miles up the road: when you're here, you're **here**.

"Besides, we're on an island, anyway. It's good to remind your guests of that, since they may be a little shaky on the geography and think they're on the mainland, just a few miles outside of Vancouver. The full name of the island is 'Revillagigedo': named after some Spanish viceroy. Go figure. People around here call it 'Revilla' for short or, more simply, 'the Rock'."

The highway curved around the shoreline rocks, dipped back inland, emerged from a grove of tall firs, and burst upon a scene from Tacoma, or Cleveland, or Hoboken, New Jersey.

Roy grimaced upward at the smoke stacks. "The Ward Cove mill. Ketchikan Pulp. They've got a sweet deal with the U.S. Forest Service, for logging big timber on surrounding islands—places that have never seen logging before—and paying only a fraction of the market price for the trees. Now, I'm no tree-hugger, but that's pretty shady, in my opinion."

Kris took a whiff of the airborne effluent: indeed, there was a strong essence of Tacoma about it. "What do people around here think of this?"

"The usual high-spirited ambivalence. People hate what's being done to some of the old stands of forest around here: places that have been clear-cut, wiped out overnight. No one really knows for sure—maybe they don't want to know—what the mill is doing to the water in Ward Cove. On the other hand, there are lots of jobs at Ketchikan Pulp: most folks in town either work there themselves or know someone who does. And, no one has given up using paper products yet. There's hardly a quicker way to gain attention in a bar in town than to bring up the subject of the mill."

"What I want to know is: how do we talk about this to our passengers? How can you pass by here without getting into some kind of big political discussion—which I'm guessing is death to a tour?"

Roy recognized Peter's concern. "It's not easy. I'm not asking that you not care, or not take some kind of stand, on the pros and cons of the mill. All I ask is that you keep your tour on track, and let your guests come to their own conclusions."

The nightmare of the pulp mill was quickly obscured by the deep woods. "We're just a few miles away from Totem Bight," said Roy. "Tour-wise, I would recommend that you give your folks a little 'quiet time' here. It gets to be too much if a tour guide is yakking away constantly: especially when there's not a whole lot to say at the time."

"The more you say," posited Kris, "the less value your words have. Kind of an 'economy of speech' idea."

"**Deep**," commented Peter.

"Whatever," said Roy. "All I know is, folks need a rest. There's a lot to do and see around the totem poles. You'll be busy, too."

Finally, they pulled into Totem Bight. At the parking lot's edge was a dense, dark stand of hemlock and red cedar, into which a single pathway disappeared. Two twenty-foot totem poles stood guard at the head of the path: one of which was simply a smooth, squared-off trunk, with a large flatfish skewered on top.

"Any guess why they built **that** one?" queried Roy. "Just for the halibut."

Kris and Peter, filing yet another pun into their memory banks, followed Roy up the path. "Seriously: you'll really want to set the tone of things as you head up this way: the big trees, the rain, the Native families toughing it out through the long winters—on this actual site, by the way. The mythologies, and the way that they played an important role in the peoples' everyday lives."

They came out of the woods, and beheld a grassy clearing, about the size of a baseball field. Within the clearing and ringing it, like players and spectators in some surreal, brightly-colored ballgame, were about twenty-five totem poles. Frogs, beavers, salmon and other neighbors cavorted, glowered, hung suspended in time and space, up and down the poles' lengths: arranged in precise legendary order. They were crowned with eagle's wings, raven and bear heads, beasts unknown (except to the maker), and even Abraham Lincoln on one. Some of the poles towered over fifty feet high.

Roy stood next to Kris and Peter, admiring the spectacle. "I never get tired of this first view of the poles from the forest: the day you do, it's time to hang it up. Anyway, all of these are quite recent in origin, but carved in the traditional style: some, in fact, are replications of old poles. Each one has a story associated with it: the Fog Woman, Kats and His Bear Wife, Raven Steals The Sun. Of course, you'll need to learn all of these stories, in at least Reader's Digest form, to tell your guests as you walk them around."

"Spectacular," said Kris. "But, why don't they have the old-time, authentic poles out here?"

"A couple of reasons. First, things made of wood don't last in this climate. Remember some of the antique poles you saw back at the Heritage Center? They only dated back to the 1920's or so, and they'd just about had it. Very seldom nowadays will you see poles from before the turn of the century. So, the older poles wouldn't hold up to the weather for long, and aren't much to look at anyway.

"Second, there's been a real revival of the craft in recent years. A local native man, name of Nathan Jackson, almost single-handedly brought pole-carving back from the dead. He began turning out new but traditionally-based poles a few years back, and now he serves as a 'master carver,' with apprentices studying under him. So, it's good that there's a forum like this for their work. There's nothing inauthentic about these."

At the far end of the clearing, a long, low cedar building perched at the water's edge. Roy, Kris and Peter crossed the clearing, followed the building's length, came around the front side and stood before the gaping maw of the Raven.

"This, of course, is the Clan House: where thirty to fifty people would live. All of the inhabitants would be closely related, like an extended family, and of either the Wolf or Raven clan. This one is a Raven house, as you can tell from the design on the front entryway: built as Winter lodging, in the Haida style."

"Making it a pleasant little Haida-way, no doubt," commented Kris.

Roy was momentarily surprised by Kris' punnage one-upsmanship. Then, he broke into a hard grin-squint as he whacked Kris on the behind with a rolled-up tour brochure, driving him into the clan house.

"Anyhow," Roy continued, "the natives lived here communally, with no partitions between the immediate families, and did all their cooking and socializing around that big fire pit in the middle. The pit, by the way, is the best place to stand when you're telling all this to a crowd: kind of appropriate, don't you think?"

The house was about fifty feet long, thirty feet wide, and very dark except for the light allowed in by a smoke hole. "You may want to bring your tour groups together here. It's the perfect time to close your tour with a bang, wow your guests—and guests from other tours, who will also have gathered around—with your expert story-telling abilities."

"This all sounds like fun," said Kris. "But, there's so much new information to swallow. I have a hard time seeing how we'll be able to do this, solo, in just a few days."

"I've been thinking about this, too," said Peter. "People pay big bucks to come up here; they won't want to see some kid from Seattle passing himself off as a real Alaskan: an 'instant expert', like Jacqui said. What kind of credibility can I hope to have?"

"It's a basic problem," admitted Roy. "The tourists will ask where you're from, and all that. It's OK to say you're originally from Washington: about half of Southeast is anyway, especially during the Summer. But, they don't need to know you're fresh off the boat, so to speak. Your guests should not know that you have only been in Alaska for several days as of your first tours." ("Rule #3," Kris noted).

"But, as time goes by this Summer, it won't be a problem anymore. The tour rap will come: you're already more articulate than any number of people who have tried it. Some of them are even still in the business." Roy smiled kindly. "And just watch: you'll make that gradual transition from Guide to Native before you even realize it. It happens to everyone, like it or not. No exceptions, if you stick around here long enough."

First Morning

▼

I am up first, rising from sagging army-surplus cot to slap on company duds, grab leftover danish and cold coffee, and walk down silver-brown stairs to the busyard. it's not far, nestled in the trees between rows of empty crab-pots and other fishing detritus. the buses are quiet, dewy, almost hopeful from a distance; i get closer and see the telltale school-yellow from under the new paint job. 18-inch legroom and sharp-elbow stop signs on the sidepanel are further past-life giveaways. but it's ok, it's only a three-hour tour, just like the gilligan theme song. vehicular homeliness will surely be obscured by natural alaskan beauty.

will guidely nerves be similarly obscured? will my tongue vapor-lock; will I be a mute totem-pole behind the wheel?

back in bus training class we learned the ritual of the pre-trip checkoff: the means by which we catch all impending mechanical failures and thus ensure that we do not break down in our fancy motorcoaches on the fairbanks highway, armed with only swiss army knives and duct-tape to repair them. but this is the rock, and these are only schoolbuses. i pop the hood, look around at the mess of wires, see no loose ends or electrical fires; pull the dipstick, tap the tires; checkoff complete. ketchikan is like the hotel california, these buses can check out but never leave.

Roy rolls up in his weathered datsun pickup, the one in which he drives all over town, at almost all hours, as if he were still on patrol. his wife tish, whom we met over backporch barbecue the other night, says it keeps him sane and out of her hair. roy sent me out early today to do an airport transfer before the tours. we all take turns with these he said, winking; why not get yours out of the way for now. oh well, a couple less hours sleep, a couple less hours trying to memorize the tour manual.

now the rest of the gang files into the busyard: peter, sylvia, a couple of part-timers borrowed from 'brand x' for the day. they pop the hoods of their buses, dive in like mergansers. after a while they finish and line up in front of their buses like fighter pilots before a mission: i expect only half of you to return from this mission says commander roy, concern wrinkling his brow.

pete looks out of character in white shirt, slacks and company tie. they actually gave us diagrams on how to tie a tie; what are we, hicks? i reckon so. but why not let guides deck out in flannel, jeans and boots, like the locals? do tourists really expect ivy leaguers and prepsters out here? at least they let us wear raincoats instead of blue blazers in ketchikan.

I look up and see clouds sliding off the mountaintops; the rain has stopped. might even be a clear day—the first one yet.

in a while roy will go to the dock with his radio and call in each driver, one by one, to pull up to the ship and take on guests: kind of halfway noah's ark in reverse. when i return from the airport i'll jump right in, open my portals to the gangplank, welcome those 42 strangers to my new hometown.

THE MAN WITH THE BEAR-HAT HEAD

▼

"Back, back, back..." The deckhand kept waving Kris' bus up the ramp, off the airport ferry, which had been too full to ride that run—despite Kris' sixth sense that told him he was running out of roadway. Ultimately, the deckhand's frantic motions, plus a gentle reminder from the concrete buffer, told Kris that he could stop now.

At least there are no passengers aboard. Still embarrassing. Aren't these ferry guides supposed to know what they're doing? Didn't feel like much damage was done, though—surely nothing to endanger the sacred Safety Bonus.

When the next ferry came in, Kris reloaded without incident. He called Roy on the shortwave radio once he was on the other side, letting him know that he was on the way to the dock. He inched through the stop-and-go traffic along the waterfront, and heard a fair amount of honking, saw people pointing to his bus. Figuring that the townspeople were just being friendly—owing, no doubt, to the continuous goodwill that Roy had generated for the company—Kris smiled and waved back.

"Boy's sure got a fucked-up fender," commented one bystander, referring to the moustache of metal that curled, in Snidely Whiplash fashion, around the rear of Kris' bus.

The surging crowd, from Kris' immediate view, was just barely restrained by the concierge on the gangplank. Finally, at some imperceptible signal, the dam broke, and a sea of windbreakers, cameras, tote-bags and comfort-clad pairs of legs swam towards the bus door.

"How are you doing, good morning, are you having a nice cruise?" Kris' natural politeness (*Where is **this** coming from?*) successfully concealed his butterflies for the time being. His thoughts were fleeting as he set about the business of collecting tickets, counting heads, finding the last available seats and checking out with Roy. Then, as he eased into the line of traffic heading off the dock, he had a moment or two to collect himself.

*This reminds me exactly—I mean, exactly—of being in a Lutheran church congregation, somewhere in the Midwest. Fairly elderly folks, mid-Fifties and up; neatly dressed, orderly, nice as pie. And eager: to learn? To **follow**? Yikes.*

Well, here goes nothing. "Hello everybody, and welcome to Ketchikan, Alaska, the gateway to the North. My name is Kris, and I'll be your guide throughout this morning's excursion. This is my…"

"Are you from Alaska, young man?" interrupted a passenger, from somewhere near the back.

"Well, um…" *What do I say?* "Y-you know, it doesn't take real long to become a 'native' around here. All it takes is a full year—covering all the seasons, from the first snowfall through the spring thaw—to be considered an official Alaskan sourdough. Uh, let's just say I'm a 'sourdough in training'.

Kris took a deep breath. "And so are all of **you**, in fact. Our goal today is to get you folks well started down the path to sourdough-hood." *Whew.*

Kris gave the rest of his introduction, citing the pertinent facts and figures (fourth largest city in Alaska, 160 inches of annual precipitation), previewing the various stops and points of interest, and inviting questions "…at any point. Go ahead: test my knowledge." *Maybe a preemptive approach will help ward off the unanswerable questions.* When he had finished, he glanced into the rearview mirror at his passengers, to see how things were going over. Most were simply gazing out the window, at the colorful flora and fauna of downtown Ketchikan. A few passengers towards the front met his glance and smiled at him. Kris reflected a smile back at them in the mirror.

So far, so good. "Next, we have a typical residential neighborhood. As you probably can tell, function tends to prevail over form in much Alaskan architecture. Some of these homes may not look like much from the outside, but I can almost guarantee that they keep out the rain."

"Where do **you** live, driver?"

If only you knew! "Well, right in this neighborhood, in fact. Too bad we've already passed my place: I could invite you up, cook you all a nice gourmet lunch. Some of my special peanut butter and jelly, or maybe even some delicious macaroni and cheese: generic brand, of course." *More laughter, more smiles.*

Before Kris could digress much further, the bus arrived at the Totem Heritage Center parking lot. He gratefully turned his group over to the museum guide, a Tlingit girl in native dress, and retired to his idling bus to regroup and reflect on the tour's beginning.

I feel like I've hardly said a thing of substance: rattled off some statistics, made a couple joking references. I've almost entirely blanked on the tour manual: instead, I see places and things through the windshield, and make comments about them. So far, I seem to be keeping everyone more or less happy. But there's much more to go.

Clearly, I can't keep skating by on personal charm all summer. But maybe Roy is right: the overall tone of the tour matters much more than the orderly recitation of facts.

Kris' guests emerged from the museum, and he walked them over to the hatchery. There still wasn't too much happening in the fingerling pens, but the season's first run of kings was just getting underway. The wooden footbridge over the spawning stream soon became packed with spectators. True to Roy's prediction, Kris nearly had to resort to desperate measures to draw the group away from the fish, in order to resume the tour.

"Plenty of time to watch the salmon, once you're back downtown. Come on, we've got a date at Dolly's House." *I hate to be a Tour Nazi—this is truly a very cool sight. But enough is enough.*

It's no longer Sunday church: it's now kindergarten. Stay together, watch out for anyone wandering off, stop that dawdling. Hold hands while crossing the street.

It took a while for the excitement to wind down, giving Kris only minimal time to explain Creek Street and Dolly's. *Geez—I wonder if some people think we're actually going to visit a whorehouse.* As they strolled up the boardwalk, a crowd involvement/ embarrassment idea suddenly occurred to Kris:

"OK, who wants to revisit history? Which of you gentlemen would like to go knock on the door and ask for Dolly?"

There was some chuckling, some slightly-nervous twittering. Then, a man of about seventy-five, with a humorous Grandpa-type expression, stepped out the crowd, earnestly knocked on the door. He cleared his throat as the door opened just a crack:

"Ahem: might the lady of the house be at home?"

An attractive young woman, in 1920s flapper headgear and silky chemise, peeked her head through the doorway, reached out with her right arm, gestured coyly to the man to come closer and, once he was within range, quickly pulled him inside. There were some audible gasps, but then everyone laughed as Sue, the summertime "proprietress" of Dolly's House, reappeared and welcomed them for a 15-minute visit.

Kris leaned up against a low 1890's doorframe (he always had to remember to duck while at Dolly's), looked on as Sue entertained the crowd with her slightly-risqué history of Creek Street. *This touring is not a one-person gig, by any means. While we're on the bus it's my "show," but at the stops I feel like I'm simply facilitating things: encounters with a variety of people who have something unique to offer about Ketchikan—and, most importantly, have done this before. That takes away a lot of the burden.*

After they left Dolly's, Kris took a few minutes to sketch a history of the region: from Russian fur traders to fisheries and gold to timber to "…you folks. Tourism is the latest major economic boon to southeast Alaska. So thanks for coming—and keeping me in a job." Then, after clearing downtown again, Kris piloted his bus towards the northeast, giving his guests a taste of a very hilly part of town. Kris' bus was a vintage double-clutch model—which, after about three months of training, he was able to operate adequately, but with a minimum of grace. Several retired-farmer types in Elks Club jackets grimaced visibly whenever Kris ground the gears. *Sorry, guys.*

About ten minutes out of town, just past Ward Cove, there was a crackle of static, and Roy's voice came in over the radio:

"Base to Kris. How's it going out there?"

Kris looked back at his passengers: most were looking out the windows at the forest scenery, a few were catching a quick nap. "Things are just fine: much better than I expected, in fact. I can't believe how smoothly things are going."

Roy chuckled. "That's great. Glad you're enjoying yourself. All days won't be quite as smooth as this. Which reminds me: Peter pulled into Totem Bight a few minutes ago; you'll be the last ones there. Would you run a sweep of the place, make sure that no ship passengers are left out there—and that Peter's doing OK?"

"You bet: no problem. Over and out." *What's up? Is Peter having a somewhat different first-tour experience?*

By the time Totem Bight rolled around, the sun had vanished. A torrential downpour began just before Kris began to unload his group. Luckily, almost everyone had heeded the cruise director's advice and brought plenty of raingear. "Here we go again," said Kris, cheerfully. "You know what they say: if you don't like the weather here, just wait fifteen minutes."

Kris and his group caught up to Peter on the other side of the path through the woods. It was readily apparent that he was not having such a fun day: his passengers had been caught in the rain, and were soaked. Their expressions ranged from grouchy to cold-and-indifferent to get-me-out-of-here; Peter was struggling to keep their attention, and looked flustered. Kris arrived just in time to hear him say something like,

"And here on this pole we have, uh, The Man With The Bear-Hat Head. Um, I mean, the bare wife. Uh…"

Kris saw the problem, read the underlying expression of angst, took Peter aside. "Let's merge our groups. Less pressure, less waiting in the rain at each pole."

Peter shook the water out of his ears. "Tour From Hell. This rain is just the *coupe de grace.* Anyhow, forget the poles. Let's just get 'em inside the clan house. And you talk, I'll act. That's about all I'm capable of right now."

"'Raven Steals the Sun' will be far more effective with stereophonic effect, anyhow." Kris gave his friend a reassuring grin, and they joined forces.

When everyone had packed into the clan house, Peter came back to life, and he and Kris entertained their audience. With carefully-practiced movements, they acted out the ancient Tlingit tale of Blackskin and his feat of tearing a giant, evil sea-lion in two. They amused in their depiction of married life with a bear, in telling the story of Kats and his Bear Wife (the totem pole that Peter had been trying to describe). They concluded with "Raven Steals the Sun," mystifying all as to the impregnating powers of humble hemlock needles. The stories ended, everyone applauded, Peter looked relieved; a stubborn sunbeam gave rise to a tropical-looking mist that rose from the bight as people emerged from the maw of the doorway.

When Kris and Peter got back to the parking lot, with their smiling, chattering passengers, Kris saw, for the first time, how truly messed-up the rear of his bus was. And he laughed.

"A little trauma brings out the best in everyone," said Kris.

"Tell me about it," said Peter.

Did You Know

▼

That western red cedar, the most majestic denizen of the southeast Alaska rainforest, has always been the most valuable tree to Tlingit and Haida craftsmen. Its size and density provide the perfect medium for gigantic totem poles; its insulating and water-repellent qualities made for weather-proof clan houses and sweat lodges; its highly aromatic and odor-absorbent properties lent livability to the rather close living conditions. Thus, cedar wood has probably contributed as much to local civility of life as any other Alaskan resource.

Kris sniffed the apartment air like Smokey the Bear. "Mmmm **mmm**, smells like your specialty again, Pete: Carboniferous Potatoes."

Peter emerged from the tiny kitchen, holding a heavily-smoking skillet of what looked like sliced charcoal briquettes. "Dang, I just can't get these to come out right. It **must** be the pan."

"Black on the outside, raw on the inside: just like Ma used to make." Kris grabbed a plate, scooped up some smoldering spuds, laid a fried egg on top, doused on plenty of ketchup. "My turn to cook tomorrow, all right?"

"I can hardly wait, Mr. Macaroni King."

"Okay okay **okay**." Kris took a bite, grimaced slightly, slathered on more ketchup. "At least when Dan gets here, we'll get some variety in our diet."

"That's right: isn't he coming in a few days?"

"Day after tomorrow. I have an airport drop-off, so I'll just hang out there and wait for him."

Peter pensively chewed his home cooking. "I wonder what he'll think of this place. I don't think he's ever lived anywhere like this before."

"Do you mean like this apartment, or Ketchikan?"

"Both. He's from a pretty upscale part of Seattle. And, he's kind of clean-cut: definitely more so than you or me. It's all rather funky, compared to what he's used to. But I also know that he's all psyched about the fishing—whenever we manage to get out in a boat. He actually chose Ketchikan as his base, for just that reason. I think he'll be fine."

"Probably so." Kris paused. "And do you know what? I think we're doing okay, too. In an odd way, this is all starting to feel pretty comfortable: the living situation, even the tours."

"Yeah, now that we have a few tours under our belts, and a couple weeks in town. I wouldn't care to repeat that first tour fiasco: it was just out of control. I had no confidence, and I'm sure that people picked up on that. It would be great if we could spare Dan from a similar experience." Peter smiled at the memory. "And I'm definitely starting to feel like I **live** in Alaska now: like I want to explore, become involved with the place, rather than just standing around in awe of it all."

"Me, too."

Please Don't Shoot The Tenants, Part One

▼

One day in early June, Kris met Dan Vanderwal, the third roommate, at the Ketchikan airport. It was pissing-down rain, as usual.

"What am I getting myself into?" asked Dan, as they shook hands. Dan was about five-ten, with sandy brown, neatly-cut hair, dressed conservatively in sweater and khakis. His face was calm in nearly all situations, including the present strange and new circumstances. But as Kris and Peter had learned, through their time together in bus training, Dan's mellow demeanor masked a subtle, intelligent wit that had a way of coming up with unexpected profundities.

Kris just smiled as they loaded Dan's gear into the company van and drove down the ramp to the ferry dock. "Well, there's a lot to learn; I'm only now beginning to get a handle on it all. For starters, there's the problem of the ferry. Whenever a bunch of people come in at the airport, or need to be dropped off, we have to take one of the buses over. Ever tried to drive onto a small ferry with forty senior citizens providing directions? And the deckhands **really** try to pack the vehicles on when it's busy; sometimes, there is literally an inch to spare on either side or end to end. I already have personal knowledge of this, believe me."

At a signal from the deckhand—the very same one who had previously wrapped the bus fender—Kris drove down the ramp. As they neared the boat, the pitch of the ramp dropped very sharply, so that as the front wheels of the van touched the deck, the trailer hitch in back scraped with a loud grating noise.

The deckhand looked up at the sound, then turned back away. Dan blinked his eyes. Kris shrugged and continued: "The tide here is another factor. If you come over to the airport during high tide, no problem; the loading ramp is almost horizontal. However, when you get a low tide, like right now, you're in real danger of bottoming out—especially with a full bus. In fact, during the real extreme 'minus tides,' they can't load any vehicles at all: the ramp is at about a 45-degree angle." Kris paused as the ferry lurched into motion. "Ketchikan is about the only place I can think of where you have to worry about the ocean tides when going to the airport."

The Ketchikan skyline slowly came into view through the rain as they approached the opposite shore. "As you can see," explained Kris, further flexing his emerging guidely skills, "the town is about seven miles long, seven blocks wide. See those stairs above downtown, the ones going straight up the mountainside? Those are some of the city streets. Richard Brautigan wrote about them: 'The Silver Stairs Of Ketchikan'."

"Looks like a town built for eagles instead of people," commented Dan.

They disembarked from the ferry and began the slow crawl south along Front Street. "Another thing about Ketchikan," said Kris, "is that this street is basically the only way to get through town. With 15,000 people, and nearly one car per capita, it makes for some dandy traffic jams, especially on cruise ship days. Plus, they just got their first stoplight here a couple months ago. It was a major event, according to Roy. Some folks are still trying to figure out how to deal with it."

"Speaking of Roy, there he goes." The old Datsun truck inched by, going slowly enough for Roy to wave, smile, and in sign-language welcome Dan to Ketchikan. "He's **everywhere** in that truck. You want to find out what's going on in town, Roy is the one who knows. Nothing, I mean nothing, gets past him."

"That's cool," said Dan. "Still the cop on the beat."

They came into downtown, past the strip of bars along the waterfront. "Of course, no shortage of beverage here," said Kris. "Probably the most important thing I've learned since I've been in town is this: hit the bars just when the fishing boats come in—say, after a halibut opening. If you're lucky, or simply wait around long enough, one of the fishermen will ring the bell at the bar. That means he buys the whole **house** a round. You'll just be sitting there, minding your own business, RING! goes the bell and before you know it, the bartender opens another beer and plops it down in front of you." Kris looked over at Dan, smiling, trying to gauge his reaction.

Dan had been quiet, almost half-dozing while taking everything in. His eyes opened all the way as Kris finally steered the van up Bawden Street and pulled into the parking lot near the wooden steps. He gazed at the peeling tarpaper of the old hospital building, the boarded-up windows, the high weeds growing up through cracks in the stairs, the empty bottles strewn about. "Is this where we live?" he finally asked.

"Welcome home," said Kris. "Welcome to the low-rent district. Come on in, it's not so bad." They picked up Dan's luggage, hiked up the stairs, stepped into the dark, spaghetti-smelling corridor and entered the apartment.

Dan's first culinary act, that very night, was to break out a cache of Spam and Wonder bread. When Peter came home from work to the delicate aroma of frying Spam, he gently urged Dan to pursue an alternative dinner menu. Dan shrugged it off, toasting up some Velveeta sandwiches instead, and thereafter kept his special meat products to himself, in the cupboard with his Captain Crunch and other goodies.

And in time, Dan came to like the apartment. Kris and Peter had especially saved for him the room at the end, which was by far the largest in the whole place. It had a commanding view of the harbor, the inlet, downtown, the wooden steps—and, unfortunately, the chorus of winos who gathered nightly across the way. To alleviate impromptu social calls by the latter, Dan nailed his windows shut and placed cardboard over the glass. Consequently, his room came to be known as "The Cellar." It was here that he laid out his deepest plans, designed his board games, placed his various, mysterious maps and illustrations on the wall.

In time, the boys even got to know, or at least recognize, their immediate neighbors. Across the hall was a large family, very poor, with interchangeable kids. The parents worked down on the waterfront, at one of the processing plants; their yellow rubber coveralls and boots frequently lay in fishy heaps before the doorway. Their kids were always in and out of the place, riding Big Wheels or skateboards, tearing up and down the hallways as if they were bowling balls in an alley. Frequently, the boys were nearly traffic fatalities.

Next door was a middle-aged man who lived with a teenage boy. The two were almost identical in their attire: slicked-back Duck's Ass hair and long sideburns (the old man had probably found their hairdos on sale at the Goodwill store), beat-up leather jackets, jeans, construction boots. The boys didn't see much of them during the daytime, but they would sometimes hear the clomp-clomp of their boots in the hall at 2 or 3 AM, just as the sky was getting light. They presumed that the two were father and son, but they never knew for sure the true nature of the relationship. Perhaps, they didn't want to.

Towards the end of the hall, at the top of the stairs, lived an older, larger Filipino woman. Her door was usually open just a crack, so one could frequently smell the aroma of exotic cooking as one walked past. The view into the apartment, though, was blocked by a large bookshelf, loaded with ceramic Virgin Marys, gory crucifixes, and other colorful religious knickknacks.

One time, Kris paused by the Filipino lady's door, trying to get a closer look at all the paraphernalia. Soon, he noticed a pair of angry eyes staring back at him. "What's the matter with you? Shoo! You a Peeping Tom?" The Filipino lady slammed the door in his face.

Directly above them was a family of Tlingits, one of many such families who lived in the old hospital building. In a way, the apartments were a microcosm of the town, as far as the state of the natives was concerned: some success stories, some sad circumstances, a lot of in-between, a lot of drinking. The boys' upstairs neighbors fit all of the above categories. At times, when Kris, Peter and Dan were coming home from work, some of the large brood, especially the two teenage girls, would lean out of the window and talk to them. At other times, especially on weekends, the television set upstairs would be going all night: at full volume, to the accompaniment of footstomps, singing and strange, unintelligible bellowing—possibly, matching the action on the TV.

"Sounds like a great party," Peter once commented, after having been awakened for the umpteenth time, "but I'm afraid, if I were to go up there, I might never leave."

Other neighbors would sometimes reveal themselves: in the laundry room, on the wooden steps, sleeping in the hallway in front of their apartment. Occasionally, the boys would have to step over one of these neighbors as they entered their front door at night or left in the morning.

One thing they noticed over the course of the summer was that the cast of neighbors, except the aforementioned holdovers, was continually changing. Somebody was always either moving in or being kicked out, and the "Vacancy" sign in the front office window was never taken down.

"Why is there such a high turnover at the apartments?" Kris once asked Brad, Jacqui's boyfriend. "I can see why people are clamoring to get in, but why would anyone voluntarily choose to leave such a fine establishment?"

"Hey, don't knock it," retorted Brad. "I was **born** there. So was this whole town, practically."

Indeed, the building did retain something of the hospital about it— from the huge, wide hallways (suitable for runaway gurneys, frisbee games, Roller Derby) to the lingering aroma of Pine-Sol mixed with mothballs. Most of the time, though, it resembled something else altogether. Sometimes at night, the boys would hear a noise that sounded like a single gunshot, coming from the depths of the building. It may have been some old machinery or pipes protesting their working conditions (long hours, low pay), but to their vivid imaginations it was of course gunfire: perhaps ritual executions of recalcitrant, threatening or non-paying tenants.

In time, the boys took these occurrences in stride. BANG! "There goes another one," they would say to each other, rolling their eyes. Finally, out of compassion or artistic inspiration, it was hard to say which, Dan drew a sign on some cardboard and stuck it on their front door. The sign said, simply,

"Please Don't Shoot The Tenants."

HALIBUT LIPS

▼

sittin in the north country
faces in the rain
on the rock you get to know them all.
the indian in the library who never moves
we call him halibut man
the yes lady in the laundromat
oh yes yes yes yes
yes yes yes she said to
no one in particular
the little girl on the rocks
at mountain point
daddy i ain't eatin no
humpie she said
but her daddy knew she would
don't forget the professor
the professor does nothin but walk
we've seen him on both ends of town
just walking and smoking
in his green polyester castoffs
    the professor looks a little
    too much like me

THE SAILORS, PART ONE

▼

"Sailing hard ships through broken harbors
Out on the waves in the night..."

—Neil Young

The ocean was always within Kris' consciousness as he walked and drove through the streets of Ketchikan. While the Tongass Narrows did not exactly conjure up the high seas, the constant flow of waterborne traffic in and out of town, not to mention the aroma of fish everywhere, made the water impossible to ignore. From the beginning, Kris felt that he should get to know southeast Alaska by its most distinguishing feature.

But this was not easy. He didn't feel quite right strolling onto the docks and gawking at the boats: that was for tourists. Nonetheless, he found himself increasingly drawn to the docks and the waterfront: walking around, trying not to look too wistful. Occasionally he was successful in seeking out ocean-centered conversations, but that was about as far as it went.

Work sometimes provided similar chances. One of Kris' job duties was to meet the Alaska State Ferry as it came into port and expedite any tour passengers who might be disembarking. In contrast to the chaos of cruise ship days, the ferry dockings were actually quite leisurely: nothing to do but hang out on the terminal wharf, shooting the breeze with anyone handy while watching the ship slowly advance like a floating city in the crystalline night.

One of the regulars on the ferry dock was a security guard: the non-threatening variety, just another middle-aged guy with a paunch and a tin badge. However, the guard, who introduced himself as Ed, proved to be quite approachable and friendly, always up for conversation. Ed soon became a familiar figure to the boys as they would make their ferry pickups.

From their initial perceptions, Ed had a fairly conventional Ketchikan thing going: he had half-intentionally come to town about twenty years prior, had survived on odd jobs and salmon runs at Mountain Point until landing a guard job from Louisiana Pacific on the old Spruce Mill dock. He lived in a trailer just south of town when he was not out on his boat somewhere. Upon mention of the word 'boat,' the boys subsequently discussed the ways in which they might finagle a trip on the inlet with Ed sometime soon.

Broaching the subject proved surprisingly easy. "Sure boys, I go out almost every weekend. Could use some company, and there's plenty of fish out there. I'm going out after cod this coming weekend; why don't you talk to Roy and see if you could get some time off work?"

Back at the office, Roy raised his eyebrows. "Fishing? With Ed?" He smiled and shook his head, but would not elaborate. A rendezvous was set up for the following Friday. Peter decided to go over to Ed's place early to help load up on gear; he would meet the others at the small-boat harbor downtown.

But when Peter came down the gangplank to meet Kris and Dan, he was alone. He looked pale and flustered, hands in his pockets. "Guys, I've got some news about Ed. He, uh, likes young men. A **lot**. Sorry, I just don't feel like being on a small boat with him."

"Hmmm," said Dan. "How did you find out?"

"I got to his place, was expecting the stuff to be ready and waiting, or at least in a shed somewhere. But Ed calls to me from his trailer, which looks like this total rust-bucket, kind of sad-looking but somehow...I don't know, **hazardous**, almost toxic. So I went inside, with some reservation. We're in this tiny little trailer, smells like a mushroom cellar, looks like a bachelor tornado. I see an opened, crusty can of beans on the edge of the sink, some cheesy-looking novels and magazines lying around. Anyway, he asks me if I would like a beer, I say sure, he hands me a six of Hamm's, says 'Help yourself...' and then **drops trou**. Right in front of my nose. Says he's trying to decide what to wear for the big fishing trip, then takes off **everything**. He's strolling around that trailer, tallywhacker flapping in the breeze, gabbing about halibut, ling cod or something. I clear my throat, am starting to think about getting out, and then he is there, right in my face; he shares some interesting tidbits about how he and his buddies like to go camping on this little island, and maybe you could come around some weekend, and by that time I remember a crucial dental appointment that, tragically, prevents me from going fishing with Ed—and I'm sorry about the canceled trip, guys. Things were a little too wacky. I thought you would understand."

"Somehow, I'm not real surprised," said Kris.

"**Raspy**," commented Dan.

Back to the drawing board. Kris resumed his tantalizing but futile forays to the waterfront. He had just about given up hope when, one day on the docks, Kris nearly bumped into a burly man tying down his boat. The man's face was wide and red, with thick black hair permanently sculpted by the wind. His initial expression was not one of anger, only surprise, and this quickly gave way to a rough-edged smile. With a huge, water-softened hand he gestured towards a full crab pot that Kris had nearly punted into the ocean. "Been out crabbing, for fun. Got more than I can use. Want some?"

In Kris' mind, there was no quicker way to make friends. He borrowed a bucket, scooped up the scrabbling, live crabs, called out "Hey, thanks,"

and started to make for the apartment. But on the way home, he got to
figuring that, to balance out the deal somewhat, he'd better try to scout up
a suitable treat for Charlie. A bottle of Chivas Regal appeared in an inspirational vision; he had received a couple of paychecks and some gratuities,
and was feeling somewhat flush with funds. The Chivas strategy proved to
be right on the money: Charlie popped the bottle top, gave it an apprecia-
tive sniff and told Kris, "Go get some buddies." And within the hour, the
boys were introduced to their first 'real' Alaskan friend.

The Scotch flowed freely, passing from hand to hand as the boys and
Charlie lounged on the freshly-scrubbed deck of the fishing boat. There
was plenty of drink and conversation for everyone. After a time, the party
more or less evolved into a monologue from Charlie about nautical life,
the cosmos, everything.

"Yeah, sometimes you get lonely if you spend too much time at sea by
yourself. Makes you do funny things, seek out funny companions. I tried
pets. Some guys are real superstitious about animals, or even plants on
board: they say it makes the boat want to seek out land, like the bottom
of the sea, or the rocks. But I didn't give a shit about that. Anyway, I had
this pet mynah bird for a while. Some drunk in Dutch Harbor had anteed
him up in a poker game, and I won. Lucky me. That bird was funny,
smart as hell, but a pain in the ass. Used to jabber all the time. Knew a
choice variety of cuss words. Also, someone taught him to say, 'Birds can't
talk…that's **preposterous**!' Except he couldn't quite pronounce
'preposterous;' it came out sort of a garbled mess towards the end. He used
to shit everywhere on the boat, speaking of messes. Used to steal stuff,
mostly shiny or colorful things: coins, fishhooks, playing cards, a .22
bullet. Finally the bird just vanished at sea; went overboard with some
rotten herring or something. Glad to get rid of that damn thing.

"There've always been all kinds of birds hanging around the boat: gulls,
cormorants, pelicans, ravens. Especially the ravens: damn, they're pests,
but they're about the smartest birds around. Did you know that they've

cataloged a vocabulary of some 73 different raven calls? Hell—I've **worked** with some guys who didn't have a vocabulary of 73 words."

Charlie paused, cleared his throat, drained another shot of Chivas, looked thoughtful. "After a while, I decided I'd better find a wife, start a family. If you want a challenge in parenting—try having a little kid, or two kids, on board. We would all live on the boat when I was in port, or in some bay set-netting. When the kids weren't potty-trained, we would pack fifteen dozen diapers on long trips out of town. We had to wash the diapers overboard, and hang 'em out to dry. The block lines and riggings were covered with all these white cotton diapers. After a while, we came to be known up and down the coast as 'The Sailors'; we must have looked like some 18th Century clipper ship, with all those sheets to the wind.

"Later, there were some summers where my daughter and a friend would come fishing. For about six weeks or so I wasn't trying to highline; we were dropping an occasional seine, sometimes just set-netting on shore. It was like vacation, for all of us. The girls really had fun with it. They even figured their own system of calculating a fish's worth: in terms of Haagen-Dazs ice cream bars. A humpie or a chum was worth about a buck and a quarter, enough to buy one fudge bar. Now a king, that was worth three or four Haagen-Dazs. "I caught a four!" they would call out to each other as they would pull in their little set-nets, and could hardly wait till the trip to the buyer, so they could cash in on their ice-cream bars."

The boys had long since memorized the five varieties of salmon in Alaska, and the two names for each of them: king, or chinook; silver, or coho; sockeye, or red; pink, or humpie; finally chum, or 'dog salmon'. "I've noticed that most Alaskans are real salmon snobs," commented Dan. "Most people Outside can't believe that Alaskans turn up their noses at an entire salmon species and feed them to their dogs.

"Damn straight," said Charlie. "Why eat a fuckin' chum, when I can feast on all the sockeyes I want?"

"I see nothing wrong with chum," interjected Kris. "They had 'em at the salmon bake in the city park a while back, and I saw nothing wrong with it. They tasted pretty good."

"That's just cause nobody else wanted 'em around here, Bozo," said Peter. "That's why they were **free**."

Charlie took a long pull off the Chivas bottle, looked thoughtful, and started off on yet another tack. "You know, oftentimes out there, I get to thinking about **water**. Hell, I'm totally surrounded by it: around me, below me and above, when it's pissing-down rain, as usual. You know, I almost feel sorry for the raindrops that fall right back into the ocean and never make it to land. Just think of all the great adventure they could've had if they'd only landed on shore somewhere: down fast gullies, off the tip of a cedar bough, in the fur of a big grizzly, riding up and down the mountains.

"You know that old sailor's nightmare—'Water, water everywhere,' *et cetera*? Well, it's even true in Alaska. You get stuck out in the Aleutians somewhere, the islands are tens, maybe hundreds of miles apart, if you can even find 'em in all the fog. You start getting concerned when you're onto some crab or something, but you're way the hell out by Attu or Kiska and you're just about out of potable water. It's hard to imagine that here on land, especially in such a rainy place. So what we did was to look for icebergs in the water—just the little ones, 'bergie bits,' as my wife called 'em—when we were heading out that way. We'd winch the sucker on board, stick it down in the hold or something until things got on the lean side. Then we'd just haul it up on deck, let it melt, catch the runoff. Funny thing is, it's about the sweetest, purest drinking water you could ever imagine. No way for it to go bad when it's all froze up like that. And it's **old** water, too: maybe some snow fell on top of a mountain a couple thousand years ago, and took all that time to work its way down to the bottom of the glacier and calve off."

"What a potential marketing scheme," commented Dan. "10,000 year-old, pure drinking water from the Arctic. I can see it becoming trendy, given the right Yuppie sales pitch. 'Mastodon Lite'."

"Yuppies," mused Kris. "Not many around here; not many of anyone, for that matter. Even this corner of the state seems huge and empty. Still, I can't help but wonder about the impact of development in Alaska: new people, new industry. Have you noticed this, or thought about it much?"

"That's the biggest thing I'm worried about," admitted Charlie. "For someone generally without any causes, that's my number one. This is a tough land. Has to be, make no mistake. But it's also fragile. God, I hate to think of what could happen if there ever was an oil spill in Alaska. All those virgin shorelines, especially around Prince William Sound, where the big tankers go.

"I remember fishing off Santa Barbara in '72, the year of the big spill there. Just a mess. I remember seeing some of the birds and marine critters that had been hit by the oil. They had set up a rescue center, where they would take 'em in and try to clean 'em up. But they still lost about half of what came in.

"My favorite places in the state, by far, are the ones that haven't been 'discovered' yet: the places you can't drive to, or boat to unless you know exactly where you're going. They say that only one percent of the state is accessible by road. You can't drive anywhere into Southeast except Skagway, Haines and Hyder. You get further North, on the mainland coast, and it's even more isolated: you can't drive to those places at all. That's where you find the real Alaska, in my book: towns like Yakutat and Cordova..."

"Cordova.. isn't that the place where they keep threatening to complete the highway, punch it through to town?"

"Yeah, that's it. Real ornery place. The state sent 'em some troopers once—since, technically, they do have a chunk of Alaska Highway 10 in their possession. So what if it ends at that earthquake-damaged bridge a few miles out of town? Anyway, the locals didn't take to the troopers too well. The local kids would set out dummies along the side of the road: a little fabric and stuffing, somebody's old flannel shirt and jeans, strung out along the shoulder to look as if someone had been smacked by a car. I think they even swiped a mannequin from somewhere, used that, made it all gory. Drove the cops nuts, all those false alarms. Last I heard, in fact, the troopers were on their way out. You want a place where the real Alaska lives, is likely to for quite some time, try Cordova. God, I hope that road never goes through.

"Word of advice: get to know this state, while you can. Know it before the Feds, or the developers, or whomever get to all of it and ruin everything. Know it through the sea and the land—but especially through its people. Let their experiences shape your dreams, and **your** subsequent experiences, of Alaska."

Charlie was a little embarrassed by his eloquent speech. "Here, take some more of these crabs, get the hell out of here: I've gotta set sail. They go good with sourdough bread and White Zinfandel," he added.

"Maybe we could tag along sometime, help you out for a day?" began Kris hopefully. But Charlie laughed, not cruelly, and waved off the question.

"Yeah, it'd be fun to take you guys out, tour you around," said Charlie. "But this ain't no pleasure boat. Strictly business here—I'm making my living.

"But why don't you talk to my nephew here in town? Mike, big, tall skinny kid, just turned eighteen: works at the airport. He's got a little Boston Whaler that he takes out for halibut all the time. I bet he's looking for some company."

Peter was leery. "Man, where have I heard **that** before?" He and the others swiftly told Charlie the tale of Ed and the aborted fishing excursion, with three-part harmony and orchestration. When they had finished, Charlie roared with laughter and said,

"Hey, Mike's a good kid. Kinda provincial, but a good kid. He needs somebody to make a gentleman out of him—or, at least, to believe his fishing stories. Just be sure, when you go, to take along a big bag of Snickers bars. Take some when you ask him too, just in case. That's about all he eats, I guess."

Tattoo Concert Review

▼

the venue: the foc's'le bar, just another rain-soaked place over on front street, a short downhill stroll from the old hospital building. a place inhabited on most nights by seagulls, grizzly bears and genetic variations thereof (just act normal, says kris to peter and dan, they can smell fear). but tonight is different, because of

the band: formerly "buck nekkid and the tattoos" until buck jumped ship somewhere near sitka, now simply "tattoo." current members are: ma kitty, singer and guitarist, an easy-chair of a woman, makes you want to climb into her lap; dresses like the mother of kansas and cherokee nations, voice like a ship's bell lined with quilts. wheatgerm, vocalist and trombonist; arlo guthrie's lumberjack brother, hard to tell where hair stops and flannel begins; battle-starred trombone held loosely in one beefy flapjack hand, suspenders held up with the other (what a **zook**, says dan, approvingly). henry the multi-instrumentalist, fluent in banjo, mandolin, tin kazoo and who-knows what else. the twin brothers jim and carroll, on washtub bass and 60's hammond organ, respectively; jumping mid-song between instruments for stereophonic and visual effect. finally dr. science, playing drums like someone stirring soup, a fine democratically scientific long-haired beat and a campbell chicken noodle-o smile.

the tunes: "come on in my kitchen, **mmm**-hmmm, 'cause there's going to be rain outside," ma kitty's most-welcome invite; baked-bread harmonies bringing the audience to a place where something good is always cooking. then "don't be cruel," wheatgerm exhorts as elvis, sliding his trombone round the dangerous curves, bending a bit at particularly tight hairpins; jim, carroll and dr. science are loyal jordannaires, bop-bopping at appropriate places; ma kitty picks up the pieces and weaves them into her aural quilt. for interlude purposes, an occasional crazed bluegrass sprint, lasting a minute or less. then the finale, a song written especially for them in some parallel universe, greg brown's fellini-dream folk tune "rooty toot toot for the moon," celebrating motorcycles and kissing someone under a green-cheese kerosene-burning moon; the crowd's awe rises and condenses then pours down in adulation as wheat-germ lets loose with his most joyous 'bone solo of the evening (that trombone player's **partying**, shouts pete to kris); this is what it's all about, folks says wheatgerm as the song ends; he sets down his spent, battered instrument and grabs a bottle-a something.

the promise: don't go and leave the rock now, says dr. science, we'll be back in august. thumbs up, say kris peter and dan.

CALLING FOR EAGLES

▼

"Stupid sharks," said Mike the baggage boy, Charlie the fisherman's nephew. "I hate 'em. You get one on your line, feels like a nice halibut. Then, it starts spinning in the water, and it's one of those 3-foot sand sharks. Get 'em up close to the boat, that rough skin'll saw your leader right in half—you lose all your gear. When I can land 'em, I like to cut off their noses with my buck knife. Messes 'em up: they get dizzy and die."

There were no sharks in the back of the dinghy this time: only a slew of rock cod and two nice forty-pound halibut. The halibut both had bullet holes between their eyes; Mike had taken his .22 pistol and shot the fish as they were being landed. "Instead of a monster loose in the boat that can break your leg," he had explained, "they'll come in more like a sheet of plywood." Halibut, especially the bigger ones, could make a wreck of boat and angler if one didn't take such precautions. Still, the first one had not been entirely quieted by Mike's pistol shot: with its tail, it had knocked over Mike's candy and pop lunch. M&M's were now strewn about all over the bottom of the dinghy, becoming a salty, chocolatey mess.

Dan, Kris, Peter and Mike were in a little cove out from Knudson's Marina, letting the tidal currents carry them over the halibut hole. There were no other boats around; this was a secret place, discovered by Mike and his little brother a couple summers ago. Several times, Mike had regaled the others with tales of landing a 225-pound "barn door" halibut in this spot the past July. Dan, Kris and Peter were still trying to decide whether he could even have fit such a fish into his tiny Boston Whaler, let alone land one. Oh well, it was a good story.

The tide was going back out again, meaning that feeding time was almost over. The fishing action had dropped off considerably: only a couple halibut nibbles here and there, and the occasional rock cod or non-keeper fish (true cod, the nightmarish turbot) that they customarily threw back. Which was OK: the bait herring were thawing and getting mushy, the beers had given up the ghost and it was starting to rain.

Dan pulled in a little rock cod as they passed the point of the cove. He had reeled up the fish so fast from the bottom that it had gotten an air embolism: the rock cod's swim bladder protruded like a balloon out of its mouth as it drifted on the water's surface.

"Kind of takes the sporting challenge out of it," commented Dan, "when they **die** on the way up."

"Watch what I do with Rocky here," said Mike. He pointed to the shore, where a single bald eagle stood guard in a tall, dead cedar snag. He gave a whistle through his teeth: a shrill "Eeee, eeee," then took the rock cod off Dan's hook and threw it high into the air. It landed with a splash about twenty feet off the bow of the Boston Whaler.

"Give him a minute," said Mike. "You **know** that he saw it. They don't call them 'eagle eyes' for nothing. He's just making up his mind. I know this eagle, he lives here."

They kept drifting for a little while. The rock cod kept pace in the current with the boat: not a bad clip, for a dead fish. Then, they heard roaring air above their heads. With an ear-splitting "**Eeee!**" the bald eagle swooped over the boat, dipped to the ocean's surface and snatched up the rock cod in his talons, hardly disturbing a drop of water. He quickly veered back to the shore, dropped the fish onto the beach and stood towering over it, flapping his wings, deciding what to do next.

"See you later," Mike called to the eagle. "Enjoy your snack." He started up the outboard motor and turned the dinghy back towards the marina.

Please Don't Shoot The Tenants, Part Two

▼

The halibut lay like a manhole cover on the rickety wooden steps. Mike stood over the fish, long thin Rapala knife held loosely in his hand, ready to perform the ritual. "Well, let's get cutting," he said.

Slice, slice. Slop, slop. Drip, drip, blech. Save those cheeks, they make the best eating of all. Look at all the meat on those suckers: nearly forty pounds of solid muscle. No wonder they can hurt you with those tails.

Unwittingly carrying on the traditions of the old hospital building, Mike performed the surgery, periodically handing off fat strips of meat to Peter, who put them into a pan filled with cold water. The meat was firm and fine-grained, so pure in its uncooked state as to be translucent: a very pale, gelatinous pink. The halibut cleaning attracted a minor crowd: two tiny, skinny cats, who stared longingly at the tasty fish guts, and one of the little Tlingit girls from upstairs. She wore a grimy red parka, with white fake fur around the collar; wide, opaque brown eyes looked out from an unwashed, un-noseblown face. She silently watched the spectacle, as if such events were routine or removed from reality, like a Saturday morning cartoon.

They gave a big slice of halibut to the girl. She held the fish like a Jell-O accordion, staring at it for a moment as if to figure out how to play it. Then, she ran off up the stairs, to take it to her mama.

The ritual done, the four fishermen lugged the meat up the stairs. The entrails had been swept off to the side, into the salmonberry bushes, where the cats were having a go at them. At the scene of the carnage was a large, slick, slimy spot.

"Didn't we leave kind of a mess?" asked Dan.

"Don't worry," replied Kris, "the rain will take care of it."

"Looks like we'll have a freezerful again," said Peter as he began to load the fridge. "I feel like I'm laying in firewood for the winter."

"That's the way they do it up North, out in the Bush—with fish, I mean," said Kris. "I read that the Natives catch salmon in their fish-wheels during the Fall, and just stack them up outdoors when it starts getting cold. The fish last the whole Winter that way: they just chip 'em off the pile and thaw them out as they need them. Interior Alaska: Nature's Icebox."

" 'Honey, throw another fish on the fire, it's getting cold in here' ," said Dan.

"Speaking of salmon," said Peter, "does anyone want some of this humpie? It's been in the fridge for quite some time now. It's getting kinda ripe."

"Is that one of the fish you caught in Ward Lake? One of the spawners? You've got to be kidding."

"I know," admitted Peter, "I'm ashamed. It's just that there were so many of them, and they were so fun and easy to catch. Most were in such sad shape that this one looked pretty good in comparison. But it's still disgusting: look, nothing but mush. That'll teach me, I guess."

Dan opened the apartment window about halfway. The faint effluvium of fish-guts had given way to the normal smells and sounds of early evening on Bawden Street: Chinese and Filipino cooking, woodsmoke, laughing, talking, arguing, the loud television upstairs, the fishing boats coming home into port several blocks away. "Roof Shot?" asked Dan.

The roof of the apartments next door had, for some reason, become a favorite target for the boys in their more easily-amused moments. The goal of the game was to try for the peak of the roof, the projectiles being any handy objects; it took a substantial, well-placed throw to attain such a feat. Among the current collection on the next-door roof were some Dungeness crab shells, an empty tuna fish can and a half loaf of moldy Roman Meal bread, flung piece by piece.

"Sure, why not?" said Peter. "It seems like a deserving fate." He took the long-dead pink salmon, which had adhered to the bottom of an aluminum pie pan, walked over to the window, made sure no one was looking, and gave the pan a good fling. It frisbeed high over the wooden steps and skidded to a halt about two-thirds of the way up the roof.

"Not a bad shot," commented Kris. "Somewhat lacking in distance, but nice form."

"It's all in the wrists," explained Peter.

"Uh-oh, looks like you had an audience," said Mike, as he watched from the kitchen window. One of the neighborhood's multitude of starving cats had been crouching in the eaves of the roof; he had witnessed the commotion and was now sneaking up on the pie pan to investigate.

"He'll be sorry," murmured Dan.

The cat reached the pie pan, peered into it, gave it a sniff, made sure no one was looking, and pounced on it, face first. With his teeth he grabbed the salmon, but it was stuck so securely to the pan that when he picked up the fish, the whole thing came along with it. The cat tried to escape, but he would not let go of the salmon. He staggered about the roof in vaudevillian fashion, pie pan in his face, trying to shake it loose, before finally disappearing over the rooftop.

As soon as they had sufficiently recovered from their laughter, the boys sat down to platefuls of halibut cheeks and other choice cuts from the day's catch. Mike had taken the fish and simply sautéed it in butter, with lemon and a dash of pepper. As they clinked their beer bottles together in a toast, each was acutely aware that this was a special occasion. Even though they had enjoyed similar meals in the past, even though they would be eating halibut from the freezer for the next two weeks or so, very seldom would it taste this good again.

"Beats the hell out of Spam," said Dan, after he had taken his first bite of halibut cheek.

The Only Day Of Summer

▼

We set off to climb deer mountain in the endless daylight that occurs once maybe twice per month, the sunshine quota; life in ketchikan leads one towards quiet acceptance of the surreal until the only day of summer comes. plunging into the crooked mansion-cathedral of the uphill trail, striving to travel light; we shift our packs, unburdening our mental rain-coats and respective totems. the layers of fog and vegetation grow thinner, the purity of the air intensifies until thorny tropical brooding devil's-club gives way to spongy moss and clean-scrubbed blueberries; we stop to graze as grizzlies might, pausing by a late snowfield, viewing the peak for the first time.

A scramble for the summit, as warm and dry as any sierra nevada out-ing; a new sensation not precipitation not mildew but sweat, honest sweat; feels good to earn it. we come out on top and find peace of mind, sun-splayed boulders, post-illumination signs of mountain-goat, eagles stretching wing in dry dry blue sky; far below the inlet is an azure plain, the silver stairs of ketchikan are today a brilliant emerald-green.

A pause before the return trail; think i'll just drift down and stay above the rain forever i said, spreading my arms to soar

OVER THE HUMP

▼

On July 16, Kris was earning his daily $52.50 by standing around on the Alaska Marine Highway dock in the wee hours, waiting for a much-delayed ferry from the south. Roy was being paid nothing whatsoever for doing very much the same thing, was there for the pleasure of it. They had just watched the sun dip below the horizon, to the far north. If the ferry was another several hours late, they would see the sun pop up again, in nearly the same spot: only a few degrees east.

Kris and Roy were passing the time, shooting the breeze, hanging out. Roy had gone through half a dozen cigarettes: Camel Straights. "I know they're not good for me. Tish hates 'em. But I figure, if I've lived **this** long..." Kris declined the cigs, but tried to emulate Roy's seaward squint. It would take him decades more practice.

They had been talking about how the season was going, and how things looked for the immediate future. "Well, you boys are 'over the hump' now," said Roy. "We just passed the midway point of the tour season. Another eight weeks, and things will have shut down altogether."

"I suppose if Ketchikan was going to drive us crazy," said Kris, "it would have done so by now."

"Either that," replied Roy, "or we've **all** gone crazy, and have no way of knowing it." He chuckled. "Anyhow, the summer has gone well. You boys were pretty green when you first came to town. Now, you're about as good guides as there are in Ketchikan—all fender-bending aside."

"Gee, thanks, I guess." Kris enjoyed Roy's deadpan ribbing. "And by the way, whatever became of my Safety Bonus appeal? The company never got back to me on that."

"Yeah, I was going to tell you: I just got the word a couple days ago. You've been acquitted. The bosses in Seattle figured that, since the ferry deckhand directed you back into that post, you weren't at fault. I put in a good word for you on that one. So, your bonus is still alive. You just better be careful from here on out: don't make me look bad, now."

"I'll be careful. That extra four hundred bucks is nothing to sneeze at."

Kris and Roy were silent for a moment, watched as ship lights came into view down the inlet, grew brighter, then ducked into the downtown docks. False alarm.

"You know, I'm already thinking about next summer," said Kris. "This is a pretty good gig: I like the work, and the money is way better than I expected. I'll probably manage to sock away about three thousand bucks. Tell me, Roy: how many of your Seattle drivers usually come back here for a second year?"

"Almost none, in fact."

Kris was surprised. "Really?"

"Yep: in this division, at least. Most guides figure that one summer in Ketchikan is enough. It's not that they don't like it—most people manage to have a pretty good time here—it's just that there's so much more to see in Alaska. This is only the beginning."

"I think I understand. Why not keep getting paid to see Alaska—the whole thing—for a few summers?"

"That's right. The typical guide sticks around for at least two years, more often three. A four-year guide is getting a little long in the tooth: not only from the guide's standpoint, but also the company's. They stop giving annual raises after the fourth season."

"Why do you suppose that is?"

"I don't know. Maybe you lose some kind of edge, some freshness. Maybe your patience with the tourists starts to wear out. Maybe a little sarcasm starts to sneak into your tours."

"It's hard to imagine; the touring business still seems new and fresh to me. But I guess I can see how it might happen." Kris was reflective. "So, where would you recommend going after Ketchikan, if such a thing were to be?"

"Why not work your way north, along the Panhandle? Juneau is a fun town: it's got great scenery, a big glacier right outside of town, and about twice as many people as Ketchikan: a lot is going on there in the summer. But for my money, I'd try Skagway. A classic small Alaskan town, loaded with Gold Rush history: has all the benefits of Southeast, but is a real gateway to the rest of the state, not to mention the Yukon." Roy paused, took a drag on his cig, looked thoughtful. "If I were a young man in your situation, that's just where I'd go next."

TOUR TIDBIT #77

▼

A halibut begins his life looking like an ordinary fish: swimming right-side up, skinny-side down; one eye on each side of his head. But then, as a halibut smolt begins to mature, something very strange happens: one eye begins to creep, Picasso-like, from one side of his head to the other. Then, once the eye has traversed his nose, the halibut begins to swim on his side, so that both eyes are on the upper half. Eventually, the halibut's body metamorphoses to fit this drastic change: he perfects an up-and-down swimming motion, so that he is no longer floundering (all bad puns aside) but scooting like a manta ray; the sunny-side up turns the same mottled, murky color as his bottom-feeder surroundings; the over-easy side fades to fishbelly white (ever wonder where the expression came from?) and is seldom thereafter exposed.

When you flop over a freshly-caught, mature halibut—first ensuring that he is dead or otherwise indisposed—you can actually see the dark spot and empty socket where the juvenile eye formerly was located, before it crossed the Great Divide.

Imagine the personal crises that would ensue among human teenagers if, around eighth grade or so, their left eyes began to migrate towards the right sides of their faces (or vice-versa).

LUTEFISK BREATH

▼

One rainy morning in late July, Kris, Peter and Dan were hanging around inside Peter's schoolbus at the yard, shooting the breeze while the defrost fans worked at full blast. One had to take preemptive measures against rapidly-forming moss and fungus on such wet days: i.e., about 95% of the time. High-powered fans notwithstanding, Ketchikan Defoggers (Brawny double-ply towels) were generally vital throughout morning tours.

There was a knock on the hinged double door. Kris pulled the handle, and there was a woman covered head-to-toe in a pink rain-slicker and matching boots, looking all of twelve years old, ready for school. All she needed was a Brady Bunch lunch-box.

"Morning, boys." Gini smiled sweetly as she stepped up into the stair-well. "I've got a favor to ask you." Gini had been hired around the first of the month, as a part-time guide for the remainder of the summer. She was in her late thirties, freshly divorced, very attractive, and had come up to Ketchikan from Seattle with her new boyfriend, a timber subcontractor. *She looks just like a character from a Brautigan story: fragile-pretty, wrong-side-of-tracks but winsome, firmly indebted to the Welfare Department. Formerly the best-looking woman in the honky-tonk (still not too far off), now girlfriend of ex-logger: the "sweetheart and darling of all mud puddles."*

"Anything for you, Gini." The boys were not immune to her charms.

"Well, it's like this. My two sons, John and Bobby, came up here about a week ago. They're good kids, really—but, uh, it turns out my boyfriend doesn't really like kids. Especially teenagers. And, he and John had a little falling-out last night. Nothing happened, really—but now my boyfriend doesn't want John back in the house, at all." Gini twisted a long black curl around her finger, looked up at the boys from the stairwell. "Do you suppose you could take him in? I mean, for the rest of the summer? I'll pay his share of the rent for him. He has nowhere to go."

There was no resisting such an entreaty. After the morning's tours had ended, Gini borrowed a company van, disappeared for about twenty minutes, returned and deposited on the boys' doorstep a beat-up Army duffel bag and a skinny, sullen-looking kid of seventeen, with a wild mop of brown hair. "Boys, this is John. I hope he won't be too much trouble. Thank you **so** much."

Gini turned and left. John stood there in the doorway, arms hanging loosely at his side.

"Uh, how you doin', John? Welcome."

"This really **sucks**, man." John shoved his duffel bag into the room with a booted toe. "Old man kicks me out, no money, no way to get back to Seattle…but thanks anyhow." John's pout suddenly bent upwards into a lightning smile, that was gone as quickly as it had come.

Well, what the hell, the boys thought. John's pile of teenage hubris fit more-or-less into a corner of the Cellar, and life at Bawden Street was already chaos: no problem to work a little more in.

And, John was definitely a more chaotic individual than his mother had been led to believe. His entrances were dramatic, his exits furtive, and he had way too much energy for the sodden streets of Ketchikan. The boys scarcely believed that even Seattle could have contained John, until they discovered his primary voltage outlet:

"This town sucks," said John, for the zillionth time. "No fuckin' music. I miss Seattle. I miss my band."

"Oh?" This was something new. "What kind of band?"

"Punk band. Over in Ballard."

"What's the band called?"

"Lutefisk Breath."

Kris and Peter subsequently explained lutefisk[1] to the non-Norwegian Dan, and its ubiquity in the teeming Scandinavian ghettoes of Ballard: "Hmmm. Sounds pretty punk, all right."

Their only clue as to the repertoire of Lutefisk Breath came when Kris arrived home one day to the sound of industrial, thrash-metal power chords being strangled from his acoustic nylon-string Epiphone. "My James Taylor songs will never sound quite the same from **this** guitar again," Kris thought as he bade John to take it a little easier.

Ultimately, the boys alerted John to the fact that there were all kinds of head-banging opportunities in Ketchikan, "...if you only had a fake ID. Someone as enterprising as yourself ought to be able to score one of those."

John's face lit up, looking (for a split second) just like his mother. He rapidly left the apartment and, within a couple days, was more or less out of their hair.

"I haven't seen John for quite a while," commented Gini one morning on the docks. "I hope he's finding something to do."

Later that morning, a report came that the company luggage van was AWOL. Roy said nothing, hopped into his pickup truck, signaled for Kris to ride along. Together they set off in Starsky and Hutch-style pursuit through the streets of Ketchikan.

After numerous high-speed chases and merciless interrogation of reluctant suspects, Roy and Kris found themselves putting along on the

---

1.Lutefisk: a traditional Scandinavian dish in which fish, usually cod, is prepared by using caustic lye in a key part of the process. Served mostly on holiday occasions, one theory is that lutefisk is eaten in modern times only to remind Norwegians of how bad things formerly were.

outskirts of town. Gazing down the highway, Kris thought he saw a lone, wild-haired figure walking along the shoulder towards them. As a car came by in the opposite lane, the figure stuck out its thumb in the universal hitchhiker's gesture, and was quickly engulfed in the rainy wake of the car's passage.

"Looks familiar," mused Kris.

Roy merely squinted and nodded. In a few seconds, the truck pulled up in the gravel next to the hitchhiker, who of course was John.

"Ran out of gas," said John, by way of explanation. "Van's up the road a little ways." He slid into the front seat next to Kris, slumping down into his hooded sweatshirt so that only his eyebrows were visible.

Amazingly, Roy said scarcely a word to John, instead confiscating his forged set of car keys and giving him a look seldom encountered outside of boot camp.

After the van incident, John was not nearly so mobile as before, and was forced to take up a more sedentary pastime: one which kept him at home much more often.

"Dammit," said Peter, "I'm tired of it smelling like **pot** in here all the time. If he wants to go smoke out with his own stoner buddies, fine. But this is getting out of control. I'm tired of finding those soggy roaches in the bathroom sink."

"I can hardly wait 'till the Ketchikan vice squad busts down our door," commented Dan, almost wistfully.

"What would they want with **us**?" said Kris. "It's not as if there's a lack of misdemeanor activity in this building. But I think you're right, Pete: enough is enough."

It was time to lay down the law. These days, John was mostly giggly and eating a lot of Cheetos. Finally, the boys were able to communicate with him in a comprehensible manner: John, lips orange with Cheeto dust, was contrite, even remorseful, swore it wouldn't happen again. But the very next night, the boys returned home to find John's apartment keys on the kitchen counter and suspicious, pungent *cumulonimbi* dissipating in the bathroom.

An hour or so later, John came back. POUND! POUND! "Shit! Goddam door's locked. Where the hell's my key? Anybody home?" POUND! POUND!

"I don't hear anything, do you?" asked Dan.

"Nope, not a darn thing," said Kris.

"Well, we warned him," said Peter.

POUND! POUND! "Anybody home? Aw, let me in, man." POUND! POUND!

Then, the huge Tlingit family upstairs began to pound. At first the boys thought there might be some kind of synchronicity at work: some kind of primal call-and-response. But the blaring television soon revealed that it was just the normal, critical media commentary.

After a while, there was no more pounding, from upstairs or outside. Kris thought he heard a sigh, then the sound of someone lying down in the spaghetti-smelling corridor. Then silence.

Around 1:30 AM, Kris felt kind of guilty. He was the one berthed closest to the hallway, so he crept out of bed and softly opened the door, intending to let John inside. But then he saw the angelic face (no doubt whose son this was), peacefully sleeping, cozied-up on some drying Carhartt duck-brown coveralls. Utterly content. Kris smiled and closed the door. *Anyhow, this won't be the first time the neighbors step over someone in the morning...*

DOCKSIDE CONVERSATION: 8/2/86

▼

Everything was happening at once in downtown Ketchikan the morning of August second: sun and shower, multiple ships in port, the United Nations on the streets of the city. Standing calmly amidst the hoopla were Kris, Peter and Dan, winding down from their morning tours and gearing up for the PM extravaganza.

"I like these 'double-shot' days," commented Kris. "A concentrated eight-hour burst of work, over with before you know it. A lot of energy, from all the chaos. Gratuities up the yin-yang."

"It almost takes this kind of day to get me going anymore," commiserated Peter. "The single-tour days have gotten pretty mundane; airport transfers are downright snooze-fests. Know what, guys? In terms of work, I'm getting just a little bored: there's only so much variety you can give to a three-hour city tour."

The early days of acute tour anxiety were well behind them; the basic problems of crowd management and providing passable answers to the myriad of tourist questions were old hat. Peter was now able to joke on his tours about the Man with the Bear-Hat Head. Kris had memorized the full name of the Spanish viceroy after whom the Rock was named: "Don Juan Vicente Pacheco de Padilla, Comte de Revillagigedo y Viceroy de Mexico," he liked to get out in one breath, to the amazement of his guests.

Dan had taken to telling his groups that yes, it was very true that Ketchikan received 160 inches of precipitation per year: "…and that's thirteen feet of water, folks. But the amazing thing is, it happens **all at once**. This year, it is scheduled to arrive at 12:00 noon, **today**."

The three friends continued to watch the unloading of ship passengers, the loading of provisions and gear, the arrivals and departures of shore dinghies, float planes and just about all of the buses in town. "This still beats hell out of 'real' work, though," conceded Peter. "I've been thinking about it, and now I'm pretty sure that I want to come back and do this again next year. Maybe not Ketchikan—probably not, in fact—but somewhere in Alaska."

Kris and Dan figured that, barring unforeseen life circumstances, they would be back as well. Juneau, Skagway, Fairbanks, Anchorage? Kris reflected back on his late-night conversation with Roy.

"The question now is, how to pass the time for the rest of the summer," said Dan. "I'm starting to climb the walls in that apartment: it's too much of a soap opera for me to deal with much longer."

Peter agreed: "Yeah, the bar scene here is really getting old. And we can't go fishing **every** day."

Kris smiled mysteriously. "Well, I've actually been working on that. Remember how there was that ad for volunteer DJ's at the NPR station? I stopped by there the other day, and I might have gotten a radio show for the remainder of August; they seemed pretty interested in me. If I got the gig, that's definitely where I'll be hanging out. And, I don't see any reason why you guys couldn't, too."

THE MUSKEG MESSENGER

▼

At 1:58 p.m., the Reverend Romanoff pulled off his headphones, grabbed his cassock, flipped on the fade-out music for his weekly talk show and left the studio. Kris, waiting on the other side of the window with an armload of records from the KRBD music library, dashed into the studio, set up his first musical selection, grabbed a plastic recipe box full of odd slips of paper, and prepared for his radio show.

Kris had gotten the show simply by walking into the station, announcing his availability, showing that he could run the sound board and, when asked whether he had radio experience, saying "Yup." He did not add that his only such experience had been in high school, spinning records for a station that "broadcast" over the campus loudspeakers between classes and at lunch.

As the second hand swept past the twelve, at exactly 2:00 p.m., Kris' show began.

"And now...the Muskeg Messenger. Every Monday and Wednesday, KRBD-FM is proud to present this public service for our listeners in out-lying areas. To have your message read on the air, simply call in to this station, or drop us a line in the mail. Some messages may be edited for length and/or appropriateness. No commercial messages, please." Kris opened up the recipe box, picked out the first message and began to read:

"The purse-seiner **Heather M.** is looking for an experienced crew hand ASAP. We'll need you for as long as Marty is laid up; at least two trips. Departing for Prince William Sound within the week; inquire on the docks or care of KRBD."

Kris wouldn't have minded the kind of money that the fishermen made, at all; he had a friend back at the U. of W. who had paid for an entire year's tuition from just six weeks of fishing. It was the occupational hazards, though, that were frightening: anything at all could happen out at sea—or, in the bars back on dry land.

"All of us from Tattoo would like to thank everyone for their support of our concert at the Foc's'le Bar. Special thanks to the guy who straightened out my trombone for me, says Wheatgerm, and of course thanks to all those highlining bell-ringers who kept the rounds coming. We're hitting the Marine Highway for our 'Humpie Heaven' tour; see you back in town next month!"

Kris had considered bringing in his bootleg Tattoo tape from the Foc's'le concert, to expose it to some much-deserved air time. However, upon extensive review, Kris had decided that it wasn't quite up to snuff, radio-wise; the tape was about 90% beer-bottle-against-something collisions and what sounded like the barking of harbor seals. You could sure hear the bent trombone, though.

"As a result of our Skookum's repeated rendezvous with certain unsavory types around the Spruce Mill dock, we now have seven puppies of indeterminate national origin to give away. Guaranteed to be full of personality. 710 Tongass Avenue."

Occasionally, some spontaneous editing was necessary by Kris to keep the show within suitable bounds for a family audience. This one was a borderline case.

"Knut: sorry we didn't show up in Klawock—we got held up at the gas station and missed the ferry. See you next Monday? Jim and Burt."

Presuming, of course, that another such untimely robbery did not occur.

"Sheila: please come back; all is forgiven. I promise to put down the seat on the head if you stop drying socks and undies on the stove. I need you; it's almost chum season. Where are you, honey? Steve."

This one had to be a work of creative writing—an occasional occurrence. Kris put his hand to his head; he could almost feel the station manager's footsteps coming up the stairs. "Hey, I just read 'em, I don't write 'em," Kris would have said, shrugging innocently. But this time, for some reason (must have been the manager's coffee break), no official station disclaimer was forthcoming.

There were a couple of school-related announcements, a plug for the upcoming Blueberry Festival, a yard sale or two (despite Ketchikan's general lack of yards), and finally Kris closed the recipe box, thanked the listeners for their support, started his first record and eased into the afternoon jazz and blues show. Kris felt fortunate to have been handed the responsibility for the Muskeg Messenger: it was great extemporaneous speaking practice, the messages were often entertaining, and he was getting a glimpse into the lives of those people who lived beyond the end of the road—an understanding of the small, true to life events and concerns that somehow grow larger out in the Bush. Out there, Kris, felt, was where Alaska truly began.

And, as Willie Dixon's "Back Door Man" knocked at the thresholds of cabins all across Prince Of Wales and Revillagigedo islands, it occurred to Kris that radio, and modern telecommunications in general, was one of the very few ways in which the great distances and rugged isolation of Alaska could be brought closer together. From the listing of far-flung Alaskan NPR stations on the wall of the studio, to the fact that every Alaskan community above population fifty had at least one satellite dish, Kris realized that the state could truly be thought of as a community in this electronic sense—not to mention the rare linkage provided to the out-side world by such technology. The sociological benefits of North Slope residents being able to tune in to MGM classics were not to be scoffed at—nor, even more importantly, access to Chicago Cubs games on the WGN superstation.

"Eskimo Appreciation Day, Wrigley Field…alert Harry Caray." Kris jotted down this note onto some KRBD stationery, thought better of it, and deposited the memo into the circular file for safekeeping.

Kris decided that, having helped to bring together a substantial portion of Southeast Alaska via the airwaves, he would love to see the rest of the state—starting next summer. Glennallen's NPR station had the "Caribou Clatters;" North Pole (just outside of Fairbanks) had "Trapline Chatter," and there were other, similar shows all over Alaska. What were those places like?

Less rainy, probably.

The odd nights when Kris would substitute on the station-closing late night rock show were interesting, too: fulfilling, perhaps, a different type of societal need. He liked to jettison the conventional format, such as by playing back-to-back rockabilly, reggae and soul-funk tunes, or sometimes different versions of the same song for a while ("Louie Louie" and "Johnny B. Goode" seemed to work best). The request line was always open, and Kris fielded calls from all over Southeast. The music suggestions were eclectic, ranging from old favorites like Neil Young, Bob Dylan and the Grateful Dead to emerging artists like R.E.M. and the Replacements, to the timelessly odd/ oddly timeless (Captain Beefheart's "Trout Mask Replica" had a small but very devoted following). Kris acquired a deeper appreciation of all these musicians.

He also brought in Peter, Dan and even John as guest DJ's. The show evolved into an on-the-air party at times: a six-pack or two, stacks of records, plenty of inspired, pointless chatter until 2 am or so.

"This, uh, song is Juice Newton's 'Queen Of Hearts.' My mom really likes Juice Newton. This one is for **you**, Gini!"

As the show wound down in the wee hours, Kris often wondered how many listeners were left out there. Three or four? Were they somewhere in Ketchikan (probably the old hospital building, if anywhere), or out on a distant reach of Prince Of Wales? Regardless, his closing tune, in honor of these last few listeners, was always the title track from Donald Fagen's "The Nightfly." In giddier moments, Kris was apt to improvise lyrics to this tune, merging Fagen's storyline with that from the famous, disgusting movie "The Fly":

"I'm Brundle the Nightfly, hello Baton Rouge,
I've got plenty of donuts, and a mouthful of bile;
Oh, you may not believe this, but
once there was a time,
when I didn't have compound eyes..."

Ad nauseum. At these times, Kris fervently hoped that old Steely Dan devotees were not tuned in to his show.

Somewhere between 2 and 2:30 am was the only shot of true darkness that Ketchikan received during midsummer. Towards August, it was the darkest part of the lengthening nights. That was when Kris would flip the switch on the turntable and cue up the mike once more:

"Good night, Ketchikan."

"We've got provisions, and lots of beer,
The key word is 'survival' on the New Frontier..."

—Donald Fagen

THE SAILORS, PART TWO

▼

fisher of men
lolling in the lush waves, like
ophelia's afterthought
an apple: round waxy-red perfect
hungry, a man stoops in shallows for
the fruit, wipes away
saltiness and takes a bite
    cool crisp sweetness, thoughts of
    autumn and horses then searing
    pain as barb pierces lip,
    a cruel hook, blood on snowy apple-flesh and
    a tensing of line
final sensation: pulled
from shore, dragged off struggling sand into
pale-blue shadows then the deep
    "**Brrrrr**," said Kris, closing the old notebook. "I'm glad Charlie has some company while at sea now."
    "Kinda morbid, but pretty good," admitted Peter.
    "My uncle, the literary fisherman," said Mike, shrugging. "Best to leave that stuff alone out here, I guess."

The Boston Whaler held a full coterie that day: Kris, Peter, Dan, Mike and John. Even though it was late August, there was a discernible promise of autumnal weather in the air; this would in all likelihood be the final fishing excursion. The boat rode low in the water as they crossed the inlet towards Mike's halibut hole.

Hands turning blue in the stiff southerly wind, they hooked on the frozen herring and plunked their heavy-duty gear overboard. But the "barn doors" seemed to be in hiding that day: after a good thirty minutes traversing the grounds, they'd had no substantial bites. "Screw this," said Mike. "Wanna try for salmon? They might be running on the other side of the island, out in the open water."

The boys were up for this, so the Boston Whaler putted around the north end of Gravina. And there they ran into a challenge: if the sheltered waters of the Narrows had been relatively rough on this day, the actual surf they encountered was a surprise. The low-riding boat bobbed like a cork as the boys struggled to ready their salmon gear.

"Now **this** is Alaska fishing," commented Peter. "Gotta hit the surges, gotta get a little wet..."

"Gotta get a little green around the gills," commented Dan, pretending to "feed the fish" as he let out a salmon trolling line.

The luck was much improved. There was a late coho run streaming in from the deep sea, and the boys found the tail end of the comet. They laughed in the salt wind, hauling in the dancing fish, easing them over the scant gunwale, nearly filling the rear footspace in thirty minutes as Mike continued to direct the boat into the wind.

"What a ride!" shouted Peter. John, his line in, stood in the tiny bow like a punk-Viking figurehead, grasping the hitching ropes and broncoing the boat up and down. This was wild, fun, exhilarating adventure...for about thirty more seconds, until the waves began to come in over the gunwales and the bow nearly submerged.

"Knock it off," said Kris, apprehensive for the first time. "Are you fucking crazy?" John, slightly chagrined, retreated from the bow and reseated himself as Mike tried to come about hard in the increasingly choppy water.

Then, there was a splintering sound, a thunk, and a splash. Without knowing quite how or why, Peter's hand darted out of the boat and caught the outboard motor by its gas line, as it broke off from the stern, fell into the water and sputtered to a halt. "Gawd, that's never…that's **never** happened before," stammered Mike. Efforts to restart the motor were useless, as the plugs and points had been flooded with salt water. The Boston Whaler, caught by the wind and the current, began to drift north, back towards the open sea.

It took them a short time to realize the immediacy of their situation. Then Kris spoke up: "Remember those early mornings with Crew, out on the lake? Remember thinking about tipping your boat, about how cold and bottomless the water always seemed? Well, this is pretty damn similar, but worse: it's always Winter in this ocean. If we do go down, we'd better be real close to land…we just wouldn't have much time."

"I remember freezing my ass off when we dumped a scull, more than once," said Peter, gripping the side of the rocking whaler. "I know that I don't want it to happen again. But, I was always able to see the campus or a bridge from where we were on the lake. This is different. Much different."

"We should steer towards one of those islands down there," offered Dan. "If we can make it to the head of the big one…A lot of boats go by here. They'd be sure to find us if we can land."

"Actually," said Mike, "if not that island, the next stop is probably around Wrangell somewhere. No place to land between here and there, hardly—especially with the way the current is running. I sure hope somebody will find us, one way or another."

"You all can cut the doomsday shit," said John. He grabbed an oar and begin pulling hard towards the headland of the larger island. The others were set back momentarily by surprise, but Mike grabbed the other oar and joined him, while Kris, Peter and Dan began to bail with whatever was at hand, trying to buy time against the waves that were beginning to wash over the stern.

Peter reached down into the legspace and picked up a salmon. "These won't do us much good right now, I guess." He looked at his friends, and no one said a word as he dropped the fish overboard to lighten the load. The others followed suit, and as dinner disappeared over the gunwales, the boat began to ride a bit higher.

The headland came and went. The bank of the narrow island was like the median on Interstate 5, at slightly-over legal speed limit. On the lee side they could see the nexus of the competing currents, where the bore tides stacked up on one another like an endlessly breaking wave. There was no way to breach the fast water, despite their hard paddling. They would have to try the next island—if there was one. The open water loomed ahead.

About then a tattered fishing boat, one that looked as if it had made a few rocky landings, hove into view. The boys stood up and waved. Instinctively sensing trouble, the boat pulled up beside them within a few minutes.

A deck hand threw a rope to the boys, and an angry-looking man stepped out of the wheelhouse. "What the fuck are you doing out here, with all of you in that little whaler? Are you nuts?"

The boys were silent, but accepted the tacit offer of help—and even that help's conditions. "We'll have to go all the way back in to Larsen's, then back out here again before we get on our way. That's a bit of fuel. About ten bucks worth, I figure. For each of you."

The boys drew in their breath. "But they got us by the short hairs," thought Kris. "And they're right: we don't have any business being out here like this." Sheepishly they tied up and fell into the wake of the seiner as they were towed back to town. And thus the summer fishing season ended.

Fun Fact #34

▼

One of the true oddities of fish behavior is the sad saga of the 'jack salmon'. Jacks are immature kings that have been out to sea for only two or three years, rather than the usual five, but nonetheless show up at the spawning grounds with their mature brethren. The jacks are not physically ready to spawn yet, but something, no one knows what, draws them in early. They get into the fresh water, and their bodies change like the other fish; they go upstream with the others, but when it comes down to brass tacks, they can't perform. They aren't able to mate, and since there's no going back to the sea once their bodies have changed, they die anyway. Ultimately, it's a fruitless, even pointless adventure: not unlike those of the poor souls who used to come visit the ladies on Creek Street in Ketchikan.

THE WOMEN OF KETCHIKAN

▼

"To all the girls I've loved before…"

—Julio Iglesias

"There ain't no nookie like Chinookie."

—Ray Troll

"Yep, Ketchikan is a tough town to get **laid** in," said Charlie the fisherman, during a typically frank conversation on the city docks. "Unlessin', of course, you're a **salmon**."

Indeed, the summer's prospects for romance had slipped by with every progressive salmon run. The humpies and the chum had good reason to go up Creek Street. But, since the boardwalk's crib houses and "ladies of negotiable affection" had been put out of business by Ketchikan's finest, the odds were not favorable on the street for the boys, in their endless, 21-year-old quest for good, honest Chinookie.

There was only Dolly's House, and Sue, the girl who gave the little tour spiel there. "Dolly's House was the most no-**tor**-ious place on all of Creek Street," Sue would explain, standing there in her slightly-daring 1920's taffeta dress. "Dolly, a statuesque woman, over six feet tall and well over two hundred pounds, was sometimes known to entertain some **twenty** gentlemen per evening." Sue would sigh and roll her eyes, looking exceedingly innocent. "The married men's entrance was to the rear...of the **cabin**," she would finish hurriedly, blushing prettily as Kris, Peter or Dan would shoot her a quick glance.

The tourists, oblivious to such subtleties, would poke about the tiny cottage's upper floor, looking at the antiques; Sue would turn in mock exasperation to whomever was giving the tour, laugh, and chat for the two minutes or so of free time. Then, Sue would flash a nice smile and wave goodbye with a white-gloved hand as the tour departed.

From such a highly-charged setting (about the only interesting aspect of the city tour that remained by August), certain thoughts and fantasies about Sue naturally evolved as the summer wore on.

"It's about midnight," said Dan, "and it's pissing-down rain, as usual. You're walking past Creek Street, and you see a soft, white light glowing through a part in some curtains up the boardwalk—at Dolly's, in the upstairs bedroom. As you approach the crib, there is, through the window, the flash of a gartered leg..."

"...One can sense, tangibly, the sighs of loneliness, unfulfillment: a longing to, somehow, recreate **history**," continued Kris. "The pitter-patter of the rain, the tiny wooden trundle bed, creaking like an old boat..."

But, it was all talk. During the mid-tour chit-chat, Sue had upon several occasions made thinly-veiled references to some young man she knew, owner of a small plane as well as a boat: probably large and hairy, from the sound of things. Sue had also at times extended vague half-invites to local parties: usually nestled in the deep woods at the north end of the road, or on someone's boat in an obscure harbor—always, impossible to find.

Late one Sunday morning, Dan returned from the AM city tour. "Saw Sue down at Dolly's early on," he said. "She was looking kinda rough. I think she made it to work just before I got there, probably had just gotten up out of bed; I'm sure she'd had a long night. Her hair was a little lopsided, liable to catch sail in a good wind...and she even had a **bald** spot." Dan's eyes were wide; thus was a formidable local talent demythologized.

The other truly good-looking girl in town was Theresa. A late, part-time addition to the intrepid Tour Guide staff, Theresa had just graduated from college on the East Coast, and was on a hiatus back in the hometown.

"You should have seen Theresa in high school here," said Roy once in an aside to the boys. "Long, long auburn hair, full of life, nice dancer's legs under that cheerleader's skirt. She was the talk of the town, yes sir. You just couldn't see how such a pretty girl could've come from Ketchikan. Half the boys in town were ready to marry her at the drop of a hat." Roy paused, pursed his lips and looked thoughtful. "I sure don't recall her giving any of them the time of day, though."

And Theresa did seem slightly out of place in Ketchikan. "Damn, where did she get that haircut? And that purple streak?" grumbled Mike the baggage boy. To the boys (for whom her hair was not such a drastic event) she was friendly enough, and they all agreed that she would stand out from the crowd even back in Seattle. Her friendliness, however, did not extend as far as a visit to the old hospital building for brews and Roof Shots.

Peter, who had taken a definite fancy to Theresa at the outset, had the following story to tell one day:

"Last night, I was walking up towards Mike's house, and I decided to pass by Theresa's place on the way over: just to see if, by chance, she was outside, or otherwise visible—and, in the best of all possible worlds, to be invited inside. Well, I was coming up the hill below her house, and as I got closer I could see someone in the lit window nearest me. Sure enough, it was Theresa; it looked like she was in the kitchen, washing dishes or something. About thirty feet from the house, she raised her head and looked right at me, making direct eye contact. But before I could even lift my arm to wave hello, in a millisecond she was gone. VOOP! She disappeared from the window, as if she were trying to hide. I just kept on walking. Couldn't believe it.

"This morning, when I saw Theresa at work, she made no mention whatsoever that she'd seen me. I didn't say anything, either." Peter sighed and shook his head, looking, suddenly, a lot like Roy.

Theresa's behavior suddenly made more sense one day in mid-August when, without warning, she quit the tour company and bought a one-way ticket back to Boston. Kris, having volunteered like a gentleman to give her a lift to the airport, managed to divine intimations of a leather flight jacket, Ralph Lauren "Chaps" and three-day facial stubble on the ferry ride over.

"So long!" Kris waved as Theresa vanished through the airline gate. "Keep in touch," he added, somewhat gratuitously.

So, it was back to the drawing board for the boys: back to the crusade amongst the general public. By this latter stage of the summer, though, their forays into Ketchikan's watering holes had become more sporadic. The rough, pungent ambience had become less intriguing—partially due to Tattoo's glaring absence from town, partially due to Kris and John (equipped with fake I.D.) nearly having the bejeezus stomped out of them one night at the Alaska Bar:

"Hey, I think yer lookin' at my **woman**. Stop lookin' at my woman."

"Excuse me?"

"Don't liketha way yer lookin' at my **woman**. Gitcher eyes off her, asswipe."

"What the hell are you talking about, man?"

SHOVE!! Kris went flying into John, who banged against the bar, causing their draft Buds to water the sawdust. The woman in question suddenly appeared, wearing a sweatshirt with cutoff sleeves, involuntarily flexing her mastoid muscles, and watched impassively as Kris and John gave up the diplomatic solution, opting for Peace With Honor (backwards, out the door).

Besides, as they had figured out, the woman-to-man ratio was none too good in such places, anyway. One could expect to find one or two fisher-women to every fifty fishermen in the more colorful locales. Those ladies possessing the gumption to risk such instant, enmasse popularity generally either boasted a phalanx of testosterone-laden bodyguards, or else seemed quite capable of self-defense.

As Big Sue (not to be confused with Bald-Spot Sue) put it one day, in yet another frank discussion:

"Yep—it's this way all over the state. If yer a woman, the odds are good. But the goods are **odd**."

As a very-local driver/guide, Big Sue added an interesting dimension to the tourism industry in Ketchikan. There was nothing small about Big Sue: big Ben Davis coveralls (serving as her all-purpose off-duty attire), big hair (a towering, red Aqua-Net creation, borrowed from Priscilla Beaulieu-Presley circa 1962), big voice, a big laugh. Although at age 39-again she was well out of eligible range for the boys, she nonetheless had ways of making her availability known when they were around.

"Hey, lookit that cop on the corner there," bellowed Big Sue one day while everybody was riding in the company van. "I'd sure liketa go over there and pinch him right in the **butt**!"

The boys thence kept their posteriors under guard whenever Big Sue was around—but she was still a good friend; they were never at a loss for colorful conversation when they were together. Rather than address the boys by their real-life Seattle names, though, Big Sue (in keeping with the habits formed during her shadowy Peterbilt past) made up new "handles" for each of them: Kris became "DJ," by virtue of his part-time occupation; because of his curly blonde hair, Peter was "Gorgeous George" ("That pro wrestlin'…really gets me **goin'**," commented Big Sue); Dan, due to his still clean-cut appearance (for Alaska), became "Preppie."

Where Big Sue went after work, or how she conducted her social agenda, was a mystery to just about everyone. As for the remaining women in the lives of the boys that summer, though, there was really no mystery to speak of. Sylvia, when she wasn't threatening to go off and clobber someone, could usually be found with Jim, one of the tour directors off the cruise ship: identifiable by his pointy sideburns and omnipresent "Gilligan" hat. Gini, the "sweetheart and darling of all mud puddles," was interesting to fantasize about, but basically unrealistic—especially since John had moved into the apartment. Jacqui and her likable beau, Brad, were just about a perfect couple, in their minds.

However, one night after work, on Labor Day weekend—the final weekend of the tour season—DJ, Gorgeous George and Preppie found themselves in the company of the aforementioned three women, for a final fling at the Foc's'le.

Tattoo had returned, just like they said they would. Many drinks were consumed, many dances were danced, everybody had fun. That was just about it.

Epilogue to "The Man With the Bear-Hat Head"

▼

Passing time at totem bight, on the last tour of the season: not really summer anymore but some kind of interminable existential rainstorm

a series of realizations from behind the wheel: one, i shouldn't have turned off this poor old bus, cause now the battery's dead, good thing there's a phone booth out here; two, that tour director's getting restless, he's the middle-aged guy with the umbrella from the cunard princess who needs entertainment rather than a simple over-there-on-your-right tour; three, while waiting for a jump start i've been entertaining, digging deep into my repertoire for stories about each and every totem pole, including the famous "man with the bear-hat head"; four, as far as the passengers are concerned, this is appropriate, fun, planned, part of the program: look at that fine young man up there, he sounds like a real alaskan to me

PART TWO: THE BACKWARDS PARADE

▼

"the circus burns in carnival flame
and for a while, you won't know my name…"
—tim buckley

FOURTH OF JULY, 1898

▼

"The streets are gay with miles of bunting and acres of flags and rockets, with firecrackers and popping six-guns, with exploding dynamite and blaring bands and marching men. Down Broadway the procession advances, and at its head, mounted on a handsome dapple-grey, is a pale-faced man with the eyes of a poet and the beard of a Mephisto, who waves his spotless white sombrero in greeting to the crowd. And the crowd waves back and cheers as Jefferson Randolph "Soapy" Smith, the marshal of the parade and the dictator of Skagway, goes riding past."

—Pierre Berton, **Klondike**

"Like all successful dictators, Soapy was all things to all men. He was courteous to women, kind to children and started a campaign to feed and care for all the stray dogs in town. He contributed generously to churches and itinerant preachers. He was something of a friend to the downtrodden. He was also a sleight-of-hand artist who parted suckers from their money."

—Archie Satterfield, **Chilkoot Pass**

After The Gold Rush

▼

The twin-prop Cessna, the commercial airline in those parts, dipped its wings to either side, as if saluting a glacier. In reality, the plane was sniffing the air: testing the thermals, gauging its handling power vis-a-vis the arctic blasts from the icefields. By Alaskan standards, it was a nice, smooth flight.

Kris' knuckles were a delicate shade of white for most of the flight from Juneau. However, the scenery along the way, up the Lynn Canal, was so spectacular that he was occasionally able to disregard the precarious circumstances and stare down at the incredible vistas: the white-capped, jagged peaks, recently dusted by a late-Spring snowstorm, nudging each other like retired dignitaries on a park bench; the places where the silty river deltas fanned out into the ocean like Marilyn Monroe's skirt; the innumerable glaciers that carved the narrow valleys and sipped the sea.

One of the narrow valleys to the north began to show signs of human settlement: tiny square grids and boxes, some boats, a puff of smoke up on a ridge. **Skagway**: "Home Of The North Wind," in some derivation of Tlingit. Kris' new division manager, Norm Devereaux, had sent him a campy postcard featuring local residents being blown by the famous wind down the length of the business district. According to Norm, the town's primary thoroughfares had just been paved, for the first time ever. Thus, the upcoming tour season would usher in a new era: After The Dust Bowl.

Skagway, for a number of years now, had been in an era of After The Gold Rush: the great stampede of 1897-98 that had permanently put it on the map. The two valleys at the northern end of the Lynn Canal provided narrow slits through the Coast Range to the Yukon interior's lakes and plateaus—and, nearly ninety years previously, the gold fields of the Klondike. Consequently, the twin valleys gave rise to Skagway and its sister city, Dyea. The boomtowns attracted all the flotsam and jetsam of a gold rush for about three tumultuous years: all the wild spirits, bad karma, cheap whiskey and big hearts that chased around the West like whirlwinds throughout the 1800's. After things had died down in southeast Alaska, Dyea was left to sink into the tidal flats, but Skagway survived: hunkering down against the wind, building a stone City Hall and a railroad—and, eventually, moving its crazily-leaning Gold Rush-era buildings to stand together in ragged glory, along a newly-paved Broadway.

Finally, the airplane banked into Skagway's glacial cut, swooped down low over the town, flew to the far end of the valley, made a sudden U-turn, narrowly avoided clipping a mountain (from Kris' perspective), and landed. The plane braked just short of the sea, and Kris pried his fingers away from the armrests. They were home.

Some kind of fanfare wafted briefly in the air, then was quickly swept away by a stray Taku wind. On the runway, Kris spied a lone figure in a blue squall jacket. "*Deja vu*," thought Kris as the figure strode towards the plane. At first he thought it had to be Roy from Ketchikan, the appearance was so similar—but, as the man reached the plane and tapped the window, Kris saw that he was much younger.

"Norm Devereaux," said the man, sticking out a bear-like paw in introduction. Kris' first impression was that of an Native wrestler, like one of the Swinomish he had grown up with in the Skagit Valley: a sturdy Alaskan, someone not to mess with. However, he quickly saw someone who could also be a friend: dependable, concerned, not above sharing a story and a beer or two.

"Ever heard of Soapy Smith, the great Gold Rush con man?" asked Norm, leading Kris and his pack to the company van. "He used to run this town, living off the miners as they passed through. Someone like you, just arriving in Skagway, would have found himself 'befriended' at the outset by one of his gang. They'd take you into a saloon, buy you a shot or two, show you the ropes, so to speak. Maybe they'd even take you to the telegraph office, urge you to send a wire home to your worried family—on Soapy's private line, which ended about a city block into the harbor. Or, they might just use the more direct approach: fleece you at the gaming tables, knock you on the head and rob your boots. So **welcome**, Cheechako." Norm laughed, with a note of mock malice.

"Anyway, Soapy still colors this town. He's the wind on the ridge; the moss on the tombstone; the onion in the Hot Red Onion. Probably even stalks the halls of the Portland House. If you haven't read up on him already, you'll learn all about Soapy soon enough."

As they left the airstrip and entered Skagway proper, Kris felt more Ketchikan *deja vu*. The town's outskirts, like Ketchikan's, were somewhat haphazard: here a gingerbread Victorian, there a leaning wreck with dismembered Maytags in the front yard. It was another long, skinny town, clinging to life against the mountains. The primary differences, from Kris' eye, were fewer and smaller trees (owing to Skagway's position in a "rain shadow," behind the seaward mountains) and the orientation of the town: Skagway was perpendicular to the sea. Only the very foot of town was exposed to water, with the other end pointing inland, tapering out on the road up to White Pass.

Then, as they rounded a corner and beheld the Portland House, the tour staff's summer residence, Kris' *deja vu* experience was completed:

Like a Time-Life book collection on historical hats, or a three-story heirloom Christmas fruitcake, the Portland House grandly occupied the southwest corner of Fifth and State. It looked as if it had been planned by an inspired but eclectic architectural committee, partially torn down during its construction and hastily slapped together again. The front side was a towering, tarpaper faux-Frontier façade (from the set of a spaghetti western, filmed in Hoboken), while around the back a stairway of questionable structural integrity shakily ascended to the second floor rooms. Creaky, old-ship sounds and a one-armed sofa greeted Kris and Norm at the front door.

"I think I've lived somewhere like this before," commented Kris. "Like, last summer."

"Pick a room, any room," said Norm as they carefully stepped across the threshold. "Most of the gang is here now, but there's plenty of space left. That big room on the ground floor should still be open. Only problem is, there's a big water leak in the ceiling of the room right next to it. You'll **know** it when someone upstairs is showering or flushing. But I found a big plastic bucket, so no worries."

Norm led Kris into the large room, and he saw its potential, despite the scattered old newspapers, empty paint trays and quiet pitter-patter from next door. They unloaded Kris' gear onto the floor. "Someone will train you on the Skagway and Dyea local tours in a couple days," said Norm. "Then, I'll take you up to Carcross, just across the Yukon border: that's where we run our all-day excursions." They shook hands, and Norm left the Portland House, waving goodbye as he clomped off down the boardwalk.

Somewhere upstairs, a toilet flushed. Kris heard a cascade into the plastic bucket. "Sounds like it needs to be emptied," he mused to himself.

Later in the afternoon, the smell of unidentifiable but good cooking captured Kris' attention. He left his room, rounded the corner of the hallway and found himself in a kitchen, decorated about halfway between Early Alaskan and Modern Fraternity: old pots and pans hanging from nails in the log wall, cans, bottles and vegetable refuse everywhere. Four guys and a young woman formed a casual, leaning tableau around a stove and a kitchen table.

A tall, thirtyish man with long brown hair, round glasses and a grad-student look peered up from his vegetable-chopping. He wiped his hand on his sweats and shook Kris' hand. "Name's Mark. Welcome to the Slob Kitchen. Pull up a chair, we're doing some stew in here."

"Yeah, it's Peasant Stew night," said another man, a blue-collar type in jeans and suspenders. "Delivery day at the grocery is tomorrow. So on nights like this, we generally make up a stew from whatever is left in the produce section."

"Kind of a pseudo-chowder tonight," said a tall, lean, young Clint Eastwood look-alike from where he was slouching against the counter. "Caught a ling-cod off the ferry dock yesterday, and we found some old carrots, onions and potatoes at the store. Smuggled some High-Test across the border from Whitehorse when I came to town. That should help it down some."

There was a re-distribution of High-Test (O'Keefe's Extra Old Stock beer), and introductions were made all around: Mark, the former grad student from the University of Washington English Department; blue-collar Llary, from rural Oregon; Brian, the Eastwood-esque artist from Michigan; Séan, a self-described "black-sheep Business student" from Pacific Lutheran University in Tacoma; Tami, an itinerant waitress-turned-bus-driver from everywhere. This was the group that had commandeered the kitchen, and more or less formed the present core of the Portland House.

"A little history on this place," said Llary. "It's been at various times a hotel, a restaurant, a brothel, vacant, maybe a secret meeting place. I don't know what the hell you'd call it now: maybe it's like Steinbeck's Palace Flophouse and Grill in **Cannery Row**: a center for the working indigent. Anyway, it's ours."

Kris described his room for the kitchen crowd: the panorama of high-country snows out the window; the nice rough-hewn beams beneath the tacky, peeling wallpaper; the built-in waterfall next door. The others promised to exercise due caution while bathing, lest one of them plummet through Kris' ceiling.

"The house is finally filling up, and so is the town," commented Séan. "But they still haven't convinced many tourists to visit Alaska before May. Actually, it's real pretty here in the late Spring: that first greening-up comes fast. I got here two weeks ago, and there were still patches of snow on the ground: you'd never know it now." Séan paused. "I guess that's why I'm here: to go through some changes."

"Now **this** guy," said Tami, pointing to Mark, "I don't know what the hell he's doing in Alaska. Nice place in Seattle, in tight with the UW English department, girlfriend—almost **settled**, even. I never did catch the story: how is it that you wound up here?"

"Well," began Mark, "back in high school, "my Civics teacher asked our class what two goals we wanted to accomplish within the next five years. Most of my classmates stated the usual, reasonable goals: go to college, get married, become a yuppie, what have you. When it was my turn, I said that: number one, I want to go to Alaska. Number two, I want to drive a Porsche. "Forget it," said my teacher, in front of everybody. "You'll never do it." So much for positive reinforcement at one's impressionable stages.

"When I got up to Anchorage in April, one of the first things I did was to go to a sports-car dealership and rent a Porsche for the day. I drove up to the foothills, and had a friend take a picture of me with the Porsche, with Mt. Flattop in the background. In the photo, I'm flipping off the camera. I mailed it to my Civics teacher."

"Anchor-Town," said Brian. "You made it to the Big Wicked City. How was it?"

"Urban Alaska," replied Mark. "Both positive and negative. On one hand, it's not much different from being in Spokane or somewhere during the winter. Kind of a dead downtown, suburban sprawl, movie theaters, McDonald's. On the other hand, they tell me that the moose come out of the woods and graze on your rose bushes when the snow is high. The inner-city youth in Anchorage are a bit different, too—rather than toting around loud boom boxes, they carry portable space-heaters."

"Hey, I resent that," called a voice from the other room. "We're a modern major city. Don't need no **steenk**-ing space-heaters." In a moment, a slight, athletic-looking man of about thirty-five walked into the kitchen: sandy hair, rather clean-cut except for a fine handlebar moustache. This was Derek, a schoolteacher from Anchorage who, like many others of his profession, supplemented his income with summers of touring. This was his seventh year with the company, and all but his first season had been in Skagway.

Derek was fond of referring to the parallels between elementary education and the cruise-ship crowd. When Kris commiserated as to this connection, Derek shrugged and smiled. "The basic principles are just the same. Keep all your information simple and understandable, make sure everyone looks both ways before crossing the street, and leave plenty of time for naps after lunch."

They all figured that the rest of the tour drivers would be in Skagway by the end of the week—including Kris' friend Peter, who was just finishing up at the University. But, among the existing cast, there was one notable exception from the present kitchen gathering.

"You haven't met Kevin yet," said Brian. "You will soon enough; he's just off on some voyage right now. Real funny dude, a nut: squirrel bait."

"Been in the state for a week now," said Llary, "and already on his tours he calls himself 'Captain Alaska'."

"How to describe him?" said Mark. "Well, he's kind of like all the male characters on 'Gilligan's Island' rolled up into one. Sometimes, he's the slightly-obnoxious but appealingly hedonistic Mr. Howell—you know, 'Let's have Gilligan bring us another drink, Lovey.' Sometimes, when he's having one of his periodic bursts of warped genius—like when he tie-dyed his underwear in the bathroom sink with grape Kool-Aid mix—he's the Professor. In rare moments, he's the bumbling, paternal Skipper. But most frequently, he's Gilligan himself: floppy sailor's cap and sneakers, full of goofy non-sequitirs, inexplicable but beloved—somehow, never quite managing to escape the desert island. Get the picture?"

But when Kris finally saw him, at about ten the next morning, he was reminded more of the "love child" of Bill Murray and John Belushi, freshly out of hibernation.

"Hey, you must be Kevin. Mornin'."

"Huh? Grruuummm." He arched his substantial eyebrows and made directly for the fridge.

It was to be weeks before Kris saw Kevin with his eyes fully open. This only occurred after Kevin, walking around on the city docks after his birthday party, half-voluntarily plunged into the harbor. Any sighting of Kevin before nine p.m. or so generally featured what Llary dubbed a "squirk:" a sleepy squint combined with a perpetual smart-ass smirk—which from an early age had drawn the ladies like flies and made most guys want to wipe it off his silly face.

After everyone had finally arrived, shortly before the first work day, the official After The Gold Rush picture was taken at the photo/costume studio next door. It soon occupied a place of honor in the office window, and was gaped at in awe by passersby all summer long.

Interestingly, the old-time outfits donned by the Portland House crew for the sepia-toned classic matched their Alaskan *personae* in some way. Julia, a Skagway local working as a tour expediter (or "expie"), was the big-hearted but savvy dance hall girl. Tami was a similar, more world-wise version of the same. Kevin found a convict's uniform, complete with iron manacles and black-and-white stripes. These he wore with his inscrutable "squirk." Kris stood behind Kevin with a hand on his shoulder, resplendent in red Mountie uniform, thrusting out his chin and grinning insipidly (the only one smiling in the photo) ala Dudley Doright. Off to the side, Brian slouched in a preacher's frock, with a Bible in his hand, twenty-dollar bill marking the proper place. Eastwood, circa *Pale Rider*, was the obvious role model.

Derek, the schoolteacher, the mock-serious purveyor of mind-candy, posed as the local bartender: "Name yer poison." Séan posed as a boozy, befuddled-looking but crafty gambler (Derek's best customer), expression somehow bringing to mind the dirty-raincoat brilliance of Lt. Columbo. Peter Helgeson (who arrived a couple days after Kris) was the earnest Seattle college-boy, ripe for a fleecing by Soapy Smith and his minions. Llary was the hardscrabble goldpanner, weary but with a telling glint in his eye. Susan, another Pacific Lutheran alumnus, was the Victorian matron who, after a few months of the Gold Rush, somehow found herself acting as a local "madam." Mark was the fanatical, round-spectacled sea captain, who had somehow piloted the leaky tugboat up from Seattle, through religious fervor and sheer willpower: Captain Ahab meets Ulysses Grant.

Finally, Norm dominated the center of the photo: decked out in suit, string tie and cane, watchful and impassive, about to break his somber expression into either a reprimand or a hearty laugh. Bear-like, but balancing his infant daughter on his knee. The man who somehow held the picture together.

Bigger Hammer

▼

"Dorm food," said Peter, tucking into his Prospector's Breakfast of sour-dough hotcakes with blueberries, reindeer sausage and eggs over-violently, "was **never** like this."

Kris nodded in commiseration as he knocked off the last of his Kitchen Sink omelet and homefries. "Yeah, man—no more dorms for you, no more **college** ever. This is the place to be." The two friends occupied a rear booth at the Bigger Hammer Cafe, home to the best kick-ass Alaskan breakfast in town. Vicki the waitress, upon seeing the boys come in, had smiled and simply put a whole pot of java on the table; the place was already a tour guide mecca.

Kris and the newly-arrived, freshly-graduated Peter were waiting for their "official" Skagway orientation, courtesy of Derek, the Oldest Living Tour-Guide. Derek would be joined by his younger brother Karl, an ex-rugby player who was about halfway through the process of becoming a "Skagpatch" local: holding down a variety of jobs during the Summer, holing up in his riverside trailer through the Winter. The effect of the brothers' joint presentation was, according to Kevin, something like listening to the play-by-play and color commentary on Viking dwarf-tossing. This, as far as they could tell, connoted an interesting camaraderie of sibling opposites.

Due to Karl's late bouncer shift at the Red Onion, Skagway's very hip, semi-dubious watering hole, the morning mood was moving in Molasses Standard Time. But this was okay: coffee was plentiful, and Kris and Pete had a bit of catching-up to do.

"So, what about our old roomie, Dan Vanderwal?" inquired Kris. "I kind of lost touch while I was being a ski-bum last Winter."

"I guess he's doing the conventional Dan thing," replied Peter. "Graduated a semester early—in the top ten percent of his class, no less— turned down a Big Eight accounting job to design his own house. Drew up a hell of a set of plans, decided that he needed more cash to finance his dreams and headed back up to Alaska. But he'll be working tours out of Anchorage this Summer; I guess he didn't want to be a Rainbird again, just like us."

"Have you heard anything of the Ketchikan locals? I can't see them leaving town any time soon."

"Well, Roy is like the downtown totem pole: he's a local institution. I actually heard from him a couple of times over the Winter: he's doing great, supposed to be slowing down a little bit, but that's probably Tish speaking more than him. Roy hasn't seen Charlie around at all, but thinks he's seen his boat out and about."

"How about your buddy, Big Ed?"

"Didn't ask. Didn't want to know. But Mike is still around town: still living on Snickers and soda pop, figuring out what to do with his life. Supposedly wants to go a police academy, down in Oregon. Roy just does-n't see it."

"Do you suppose he would have to come after our favorite juvenile delinquent ex-roommate?"

"You mean ol' Lutefisk Breath? Nope: John's already been taken care of. You wouldn't believe what's happened to him: apparently he was in San Francisco over the winter, hanging out with some buddies; was joy-riding in somebody's stolen car one day, got going a little too fast, jumped it off one of the hills; wrecked the car and smacked a pedestrian, to boot. Last I heard from Roy, John was, uh, proceeding through the criminal justice system."

"No kidding. Well, I thought he could have gone either way: basically not a bad guy, but self-destructive as hell. Poor Gini couldn't be too happy about this…"

As Kris and Peter mused over John's fate, the cafe door swung open, and the doorway was filled by a broad set of shoulders, a New Zealand All-Blacks rugby jersey, 6'4" of bar bouncer/ short-order cook/ tour guide. Karl was followed through the door by his much smaller, yet strangely similar, older brother.

Karl, though he had never met Kris and Peter, recognized them and made straight for their table. "Coffee and indolence, gorgeous women waiting on you…" His eyes gave an affectionate sideswipe to Vicki, who arched her eyebrows in response. "I'd say you've got the Coach Commander style down pat." He held out a ham-like hand in welcome.

"My little brother," said Derek. "Doing his best to win the hearts and minds of all Skagwegians. Just think: they have to deal with him in the **winters** now." Derek wore his customary half-resigned, half-proud expression.

Kris and Peter, on the verge of being swept away by coffee floods, rose from the table. They joined the brothers in piling into the company van, conveniently double-parked just outside the swinging cafe door, and drove off in the general direction of the harbor.

"I figured," said Derek, "we'd start with the basics first: the city tour. But of course, you'll be doing much more than this: you get increasing variety as you get your feet wet. There's the Gold Rush tour, which takes you a little ways out of town, to the old Dyea townsite, and generally takes up an afternoon. Then, there are the excursions to Carcross, about 130 miles up and back. That one's a big deal for the tourists, because they get to cross the Yukon border, have a camp lunch and show, check out the town, see some of the more important places in the Klondike history."

"Us guides like Carcross too," said Karl, " 'cause you can stretch out some in your Road Rap: lay on the history, the corny jokes, the whole shebang. Plus, it's one of your few chances to split town for a while. Unless you do what some of us have done in years past, which is to go in together on some old beater car—maybe five hundred bucks, tops—for the all-important runs into Whitehorse."

"Those 200-mile pizza-and-movie expeditions," verified Derek, "do take on major sanity-keeping significance."

They reached the waterfront. The old, massive wooden pier hugged a rocky cliff on the south side of the inlet's head. High above, on the flat rock faces, intrepid crew members had painted their ships' insignia: a couple dozen logos competed for the most precipitous view.

"The adventure begins here," said Derek. "People will come streaming off the ships for all the local land excursions: similar to what you saw in Ketchikan, no doubt, but even more dramatic, due to the difference in scale. Several Skagways could fit aboard some of the larger ships. And there's always this 'welcoming committee…' "

"I think we've seen it already," said Kris. "On the way to catch a ship's arrival yesterday, we followed this group of people in costume: kind of a 1890's-meets-1960's thing. They were riding in carriages, on horseback, in an old Model-T. When the ship's passengers disembarked, they cheered, whistled, sang, made noise. A little disorganized, but definitely friendly."

"Way funkier than anything Ketchikan ever had," added Peter. "But they seemed to go over real well."

Derek turned the van around, drove back towards downtown. The Skagway skyline, punctuated by the onion domes of the Golden North Hotel, was tiny in comparison with the surrounding mountain ridges. "One of the major issues that prospective guides raise," said Derek, "is that this is a **very** small town. How in the world does one pad out a city tour to two and a half hours, without driving around in circles or otherwise being boring? The answer is, of course…"

"**Personality**," interjected Karl with a flourish. "Rather than merely reciting facts, infusing the tour with a little zip, a little mustard. Chutzpah. Local color."

"Which my brother has, in spades," finished Derek. "We will elaborate on this further. But first, the main drag."

They turned up Broadway, into the heart of downtown. "One immediate change for this year's City Tour," said Derek, "is **pavement**. Through all the years of this town's history, it was mud or dust, no in-between—and once upon a time the **railroad** even ran down the middle of the street. This Spring, over the course of a week, the asphalt trucks came and made history.

"Now, for the first time, the shopkeepers will not cringe at our buses' approach. Our guests can get the front-row view of the hubbub, the chaos, all these great old Gold Rush buildings. The AB Hall: the old Arctic Brotherhood meeting place, with that 10,000-piece driftwood facade. The Red Onion, of course, where they never have taken down the red lights in the upstairs windows or the lurid portraits of the old 'hospitality' staff. The Eagles Hall, where they run the Days of '98 show: equal parts Klondike can-can and Greek tragedy. All these old 'cribs'—tiny Houses of Negotiable Affection—where they now sell popcorn and toy train whistles."

"That is something that struck me right off the bat," said Peter. "It seems as if the real history of this place has been sanitized. Things seem almost too tidy...too **cute**. My understanding of Skagway is that the actual history is a little rougher than what we see now. Are they trying to present a Disneyland version of the Gold Rush?"

The brothers were silent for a moment. "Well, yes and no," Derek finally said. "On one hand, there is a certain, superficial, unrealistic picture of Alaska that is presented here. But figure: these are cruise ship passengers, most of whom are here to be entertained, not educated. The marketing for these trips caters to folks who want an escapist holiday, some luxury, some scenic sights. The ports of call can be almost incidental. Anything too far beyond the stereotypical image of Alaska would be disappointing, if not jarring."

"But on the other hand," said Karl, "the real Alaska is always just below the surface—for those who want it. That's another function of the 'local color' aspect: it offers the first clue that something else is goin' on. And, the curious have a way of finding it."

"That's the tradeoff for a town like Skagway," finished Derek. "How much of ourselves do we reveal, without selling our collective soul? How far can we go in catering to a certain market: a market sufficient to keep the town going in otherwise lean times, to keep the 'local color' in bread, boots and beer—but not enough to make life here not worth staying for."

"Living here over the summer," said Karl, "will give you much of the inside scoop: the who's who, the real doings. The rest of the knowledge takes a winter or two in town."

They had pulled into the parking lot of Skagway's museum, an impressive stone building which also doubled as City Hall. "Speaking of who's who," said Peter, "I've seen this gigantic, bearded guy around town. Usually just strolling down Broadway, weaving in and out of the shop doors, lingering, chatting, never seeming to be doing very much. Yet, he somehow seems in charge of everything."

"That would be Wheatgerm," said Derek knowingly. "Larger-than-life figure. Hell of a trombone player. De-facto leader of the Bigger Hammer Marching Band—and hence, unofficial mayor of Skagway."

"Wheatgerm..." mused Kris to himself. "Now where have I heard that name before?" Then a certain evening at the Foc's'le Bar in Ketchikan replayed itself in his mind. Kris smiled and, for the moment, kept the revelation to himself.

"The Bigger Hammer Marching Band," continued Karl, "leads the most shadowy of existences—but emerges publicly every July 4th for the big downtown parade. Or, more accurately, the real **small** parade. It's so small that, after everyone has passed through, they all turn around and do it again, only bass-ackwards. You haven't lived until you've heard Wheatgerm play 'Sweet Georgia Brown' backwards on the trombone."

"And how, pray tell, are you privy to all this inside scoop, Karl?"

"I'm an apprentice, Bro." Karl stood up straight and saluted. "I'm a Hammer-in-training. They might even let me march in the parade this year: as the Pooper-Scooper."

Kris and Peter learned that they had probably already attended a couple Bigger Hammer meetings without realizing it: while hanging out in front of the Eagles Hall, watching some barefoot guys pitch horseshoes; while eavesdropping on spirited academic discussions around the Red Onion's pool table; while standing on the docks amongst the "welcoming committee."

"Who do you think is behind all the hoopla here," asserted Karl, "those 'spontaneous' beach parties you'll see at the Onion this summer, those 'impromptu' hootenannies out at the point? It seems that most small towns in Alaska—at least, any town where you'd care to live—have some gang like this, who don't seem to be doing very much but really ruin (oops, I think I met 'run,' Freudian slip there) the show. In form and attitude, kind of the 'Anti-Rotarians'; in function, not too different."

"But remember, buddy," Derek admonished his little brother, "if you think you can **explain** the Bigger Hammer—you probably don't really get it."

Karl looked down at his size 13 boots, momentarily abashed.

They left the museum parking lot, driving along a creek's edge. "The suburbs," said Derek, "begin about two blocks from here. Scattered houses and trailers, some overgrown lots, some interesting surprises in the woods."

"Who knows what you may find in there?" said Karl, mysteriously, as they turned off the main drag into a dirt alley. "Sometimes a horse, grazing away: or a sauna, or somebody's moonshine still. Sometimes, merely rusty 55-gallon oil drums. Sometimes, even...*voilà!*"

A row of antique railroad passenger cars emerged from the trees and tall grass. They were patiently lined up on an abandoned railroad spur, like a pack train of mules. Derek idled the van, to have a closer look.

"Here is what is left," said Derek, "of the White Pass and Yukon Railroad. Popular acronym: WP & YR. Alternative acronym translation: Wait Patiently and You'll 'R'rive. The narrow-gauge rail track heads straight up the Pass from here, on the opposite side of the canyon from the highway."

"The idea," said Karl, "was to make your life a little less hellacious, by providing transport over the worst of the route to the Klondike gold fields. In the old days, the railroad took you all the way to the shores of Lake Bennett, from where you could continue by water the rest of the way to Dawson. They began building it in 1898, the peak year for crossing the passes.

"There's a great quote from the chief engineer in charge of the project. 'Give me enough snoose and dynamite,' he told his doubters and naysayers, 'and I'll build you a railroad to Hell.' "

"And it was quite an engineering feat to punch the railroad through," said Derek, "for its time, for **any** time. But of course, it wasn't finished until 1900, after the Klondike gold rush had just about had it. The railroad was still used for many years: for early tourism, to haul goods into and out of the Yukon. It shut down once the highway opened in 1977, and has been sitting dormant ever since."

"They talk about rolling the WP & YR for tourists again," said Karl, "running trains up to the Pass and back. But they'll have to do something about the track first. I've walked it quite a ways, up past the Denver Glacier overlook, and there are some spots on the trestles where you're looking down at an awful lot of blue sky. Till then, these old cars are just camping out in the Skagway suburbs, biding their time."

As they drove slowly past the line, they saw that the railcars were named for the great lakes of the Yukon and northern British Columbia: Kluane, Tagish, Tutshi, Atlin, Teslin, Dezadeash. Through the dusty windows, they could see straight-back, pew-like wooden benches. In their minds' eyes, they saw the benches lined with Levis, hoop skirts, wool and buckskin britches.

"So you see," said Derek, "what we're doing is more than merely padding out a City Tour: it's more like a treasure hunt. Another example of what we mean is our next stop: the local **cemetery**."

They rejoined the main street briefly, turned off onto the cemetery road. The road snaked dustily through the old WP & YR railyard, clung to the east ridge's bottom edge for a quarter-mile, narrowed and finally gave up at a big rockpile. A well-worn footpath led up into spruce and lodgepole pine.

Derek led the way into the cemetery grounds. "Now, you might think of this as kind of a downer for part of a vacation tour—especially since most of the folks you'll be taking here are a wee bit closer to death than you are. But this, once again, gives you a chance to inject some local color."

"And maybe even act out some real-life dramas," said Karl. "For example: that final duel on the Skagway docks between Soapy Smith and Frank Reid, the 'local hero' who finally did him in. Derek and I used to have the duel choreographed out pretty well—and guess who got to be Soapy about every time? It was a role I relished: but I don't do it nearly as well as Jim Richards, the guy in the Days of '98 show."

They came upon the famous headstones of Reid and Soapy. The monuments stood only twenty feet apart, but were exact opposites in grandeur: Reid getting the hero's mini-mausoleum, Soapy a forlorn, yellowing slab surrounded by a leaning picket fence.

"Here is yet another central mystery of Skagway:" said Derek, "the role that Soapy plays in the town's collective psyche. We know that Reid was lionized in death, credited with 'civilizing' the town and all that. We know that Mr. Smith, the great bunco artist, the former medicine-show soap salesman, was responsible for about a year of complete lawlessness in Skagway: murder, mayhem, you name it. But who does Skagway remember more vividly—and affectionately? Who gets star billing in the show at the Eagles Hall?"

"Who generates the most debate," said Karl, "as to the what, and why, and how, during those snowy, profound midwinter afternoons at the Red Onion? It's Soapy, hands down."

The two brothers instinctively lined up back-to-back between the two headstones, took ten martial paces, wheeled and fired with blazing index fingers, slowly collapsed to the cold ground.

"Damn you, Reid: you're at the bottom of all my troubles. I should have got rid of you three months ago."

—Soapy Smith's final words

Upon rejoining the highway from the cemetery road, the van crossed the Skagway River bridge. After another quarter-mile, a dirt road doubled back up the north ridge above town. As they turned up this road, Derek glanced back at the highway, which inclined sharply from the turnoff.

"There it is: the only way out of town, planes and boats aside. Straight up the big hill, over 3,000 feet elevation in less than 30 miles. Once over the summit, you're in Canada—and it does look and feel totally different. You'll be going that way on your Carcross tours."

"Remember what it was like before there was a road?" mused Karl. "Prior to '77, when you were here, you were **here**. Skagway folks used to entertain a pretty nasty local strain of cabin fever in those days: they called it 'Skagwacky'."

"It explains things," chimed in Derek, "like snowshoe softball, Hot Red Onions,[2] moving the downtown buildings around, and other wintertime diversions."

---

2. The house specialty at the Red Onion: mulled, spiced brandy with cranberry juice and a splash of Cointreau. Very warming

"And I suppose," said Kris, deductively, "it explains the Bigger Hammer: kinda, sorta."

Derek and Karl each clapped Kris on the shoulder.

"Bingo."

"Yup."

"I think he's gettin' it."

As they passed from sight of the highway, Karl once again grew reminiscent. "Sometimes, when the pass is all snowed in, it feels like the old days: the ol' cabin fever. At times like that, we used to go out and chop wood. Nowadays, people just rent videos."

Heading up the ridge, they passed the city landfill, a scenic overlook, a trailhead for AB Mountain, and a sign which said "Dyea, 7 Miles."

"Speaking of still more local color," said Derek, "you'll meet Dyea Gary when you run your Gold Rush tours out this way. He's kinda the last of his breed: part of a gang of bushers who migrated to the Taiya River valley about ten years ago, tried to revive the old township. But almost everyone else has picked up and moved back to town."

"So, how does he entertain the tourists out there?"

"Well, Gary just acts like himself, mostly," said Karl. "He welcomes people to his homestead. He shows them around the place, explains its history: the fact that it's right across the river from the old Chilkoot Trail, and the cabin actually dates from that era. Talks about Dyea. Teaches them how to pan for gold. Lays on the bullshit, thick or thin, depending. Gives folks a taste of the sourdough thang: and he doesn't even have to change his clothes to do it."

"And people like it?"

Derek grinned. "Oh yeah, they eat it up. Literally. Even those who don't get into the outdoorsy, Gold Rush stuff: why, they'll just hang out under a tent awning by the campfire, stuff themselves with his hot biscuits and homemade jam."

"And some folks will get utterly **wrecked**," winked Karl, "on this evil brew that he calls 'Dyea Hooch': André champagne and Yukon Jack. Yee-haw, as Gary would say."

"So the ride back from Dyea," concluded Derek, "can be either really loopy, or really sleepy. Or really **green**, if you take the curves a little too fast."

"I can hardly wait," said Peter.

Moving in, Part Two

▼

the peasant stew died an
ancient death long ago said peter, and
the urban take-out-the-trash band has
yet to arrive on the ferry
    i hear archaeological rumors of another
    kitchen in portland-house forbidden annex
    said kris: it is key to our long-term survival

back we went to rehab the second
kitchen: the patient needed ammonia,
sponges mop and broom, but mostly
screwdrivers and our own bare hands

    someone long ago stapled tacky
    bile-green wallpaper, now dangling in
    tattered untenable rasta-dreadlocks
    grab and rip, here it comes, yuck!

but what is underneath? old newspapers:
must've been cold scarecrow winter to

slap these on the wall, must've been
bachelor hermit newsboy living here

digging down
1943: aleutian campaign
　　continues dutch harbor bombing many
　　lives evacuation unabated by

　　　　　　　　1936: harriet pullen leaves
　　　　　　　　　　skagway hotel burns to ground nothing
and down

　　　　　　　1927: yankees win pennant ruth
　　　　　　　and gehrig bronx bombers face
　　　　　　　cards in series managed by

　　　　　1921: president harding to visit skagway now
　　　　　in talkeetna after golden
　　　　　spike ceremony rumors of

at dig's end we find bare log-
cabin settler's wood: rough-hewn
and square nails: now here's a
pioneer kitchen says kris, soon
steamy vapors of soup, bread and
sheepherder's coffee will grace these beams
　　probably more like top ramen and
　　kraft macaroni if i know you, says pete

let's do my room next i said,
plenty of history under them thar walls

THE MEN WHO DON'T FIT IN

▼

"He's a rolling stone, and it's bred in the bone:
he's a man who won't fit in."
—Robert W. Service

"Inspirational" was the only apt word for describing the early-summer Skagway morning. Sunshine glinted off the high snowfields; the valley was humming with fresh foliage, wildflowers, energy. Kris and Peter arose early, their vision automatically drawn to the crystal-blue sky above the mountain passes.

The crystal vision was splintered as Norm roared up to the Portland House in an incredibly rusty, weather-beaten Ford Pinto. "New, official house wheels. Three hundred bucks. Whaddya think?"

Kris thought that a new muffler, new tires, a bucket of spackle and duct tape, maybe a frontal lobotomy, were about right. But the fake-wood exterior paneling was very cool, and regular road trips to Whitehorse were now more than a pipe dream. *And, weren't Derek and Karl just talking about this?*

Norm pushed open the driver door, with considerable protest from the hinges, stepped out and gestured chauffeur-like for Kris, Peter and Llary to enter. "We could, of course, take a company van for a training run, but I figured a shakedown cruise was in order. Anyway: Carcross awaits."

Norm settled into the driver's seat, clutched the steering wheel. He looked like a big kid driving a Go-Kart. "I swear: it feels like my rear end is dragging the ground, driving this thing after sitting up so high in a bus. But this'll be fun."

Indeed, Norm's sense of fun had far outweighed his stern side, in the short time that Kris and Peter had known him. Driver training sessions had carried an air of informality, often digressing into jokes and story-telling; evening staff meetings had a way of migrating to the Red Onion after a time. The work always got done, but a good time was had in the process. The Portland House gang all figured, correctly, that Norm must have been one hell of a tour guide.

They caught the main road, cleared Skagway's suburban tents, Quonset huts and horses, and were out of town. Just shy of the Skagway River bridge, off to the right (on the way to the Gold Rush cemetery) was the company busyard. Mark and Kevin, in matching grease-stained coveralls, waggled their bus-washing brushes and squeegees in the direction of the Pinto as it passed.

"Bus detailing day," commented Norm. "Our fleet mechanic, Klaus, is here from Fairbanks, so we're taking this opportunity to get everything ship-shape for the season. Don't worry, guys, your turn will come soon— like **tomorrow**, in fact. So I definitely hope you enjoy today's trip."

After the Dyea turnoff, the highway turned sharply upward, plunging into deep aspen and alder. The Pinto downshifted into a plodding but determined 30-mph groove. "How could we not?" replied Kris. "This might sound corny, but I woke up this morning, saw what it was like outside, and felt absolutely **alive**: like I had to get outside, breathe the air, seize the day. Touring up the highway or scrubbing buses, it didn't really matter."

"But it's **not** corny," said Norm, "it's the absolute truth. I feel—and I'm by no means alone on this—that you've got to treat every glorious day here as if it were the 'Only Day of Summer'. Alaska's summers are so short, and so intense, you've got to treat each day of this weather as if it were the **only one** you will get all year. Try spending a Winter here sometime, and you'll really know what I mean."

"I sure felt like dancing in the streets whenever the sun managed to peek out in Ketchikan," said Peter. "The weather here is bound to be a lot better, from all I've heard. But everything I've seen so far tells me that people here feel the same way."

"Skagway is definitely a party in the Summer," said Llary. "No doubt about it."

The Pinto was not having a party occasion, beginning to groan as it continued lugging up the winding highway. "Fourteen miles to the summit," said Norm, "an average seven-percent grade, all the way up to 3,200 feet elevation. If you don't get one of the new, fancy 'turbo' buses for your tour, your speed up the pass will closely approximate the pace of this fine vehicle.

"Luckily, there is a ton of Gold Rush history to talk about here: the old White Pass trail parallels the highway, down in the ravine there, and you can see the railroad on that opposite ridge. There's so much history, in fact, that you'll probably want to pick and choose your favorite stories, rather than trying to squeeze it all in. It's all in your tour manuals, of course—plus that big stack of books I left in the house. The Pierre Berton is especially good."

"What did **you** like to talk about when you were a guide on this route?"

"I always enjoyed comparing the White Pass route with the Chilkoot Trail: the pros and cons of Dead Horse Gulch versus the Golden Stairs. Both were about equally insane, in my book, but they offered very different experiences: a long pack train from Hell, or a short hump up a 40-degree vertical cliff.

"And, in any event, neither route offered particularly favorable odds. Historians figure that about 100,000 people departed from some point on the West Coast—Seattle, Portland, San Francisco—for the Klondike gold fields. Of those 100,000, only about 40,000 made it as far as Dawson City, the Gold Rush boomtown—whether by our two trails or by routes originating elsewhere in Alaska that, by all measures, were even worse. Of the 40,000 who made it to Dawson, only half, about 20,000, actually staked a claim in the goldfields: not only were all the good spots long since taken, but plenty of people went there just to engage in far less risky, typically more lucrative commercial activity. Of those who staked a claim, one fifth, about 4,000, found any gold at all. And of those 4,000—indeed, of the original 100,000 who set out for the gold fields—only about 400 people actually can be said to have 'struck it rich'. "

Llary whistled: "Whew: you had to be one determined individual to make it up the trail. And even then, that wasn't usually enough."

"Did you ever try hiking the Chilkoot yourself, Norm?" Kris wanted to know.

"Nope, never got a chance—although I would have loved to. You've got to understand, I was always a long-haul driver when I passed this way. We would drive down from Whitehorse in the morning, drop off our passengers at the ships, wait around a couple hours, load up again and come back up the pass. There wasn't much time to explore around Skagway." Norm looked wistful for a moment. "Unlike what you guys will be able to do. These mountains are full of incredible trails: day trips to Upper and Lower Dewey Lakes and AB Mountain, a lot of longer hikes. I probably wouldn't take too much convincing to give you enough time off to do the Chilkoot, at some point this Summer."

Kris and Peter looked at each other. "Thanks—we'll **definitely** keep that in mind."

They cleared the timberline, broke out into alpine boulders and snow, and finally could see the top of the grade. As the Pinto approached the summit, the needle on the temperature gauge began to twitch as if it were having a seizure: fidgeting into the red zone, then jumping back out again. Norm and Peter, from their front-seat vantage, could see the first telltale steam curling out from under the hood.

"**Easy** there, Old Paint: we're almost up top." They reached a fortu-itously situated turnout on the White Pass summit, and Norm reined the car over, to cool down and graze a while.

Llary stepped out, studied the panting and wheezing Old Paint. "Well, I reckon you've just officially named our house wheels, Norm."

"I reckon so."

The others unfolded from the Pinto and stepped out onto the snow-covered highway shoulder. "Welcome to Canada," said Norm. "The international border runs right along the crest of the Coast Range. Believe it or not, there are benchmarks delineating the boundary on top of most of the major peaks. The border was hotly contested for a time, after Alaska was purchased from the Russians in 1867: if Canada had gotten its way, in terms of border surveying, Skagway and Dyea would not have been part of the United States. The U.S. resolved the issue with a little 'gunboat diplomacy,' however, and the boundary was set at its present position."

They gazed around the mountain panorama. The young, sharp-faced peaks of the Coast Range, covered in icefields and deep snow, sniffed the bright air. The narrow ribbon of highway plunged away towards Skagway: snaking across a one-lane suspension bridge, back over the timberline (about 2,000 feet elevation) and down to the green glacial valley, barely visible far below.

"What an incredible change, in such a short distance," commented Kris.

"That's one of the things I love about this Carcross trip," said Norm. "You pass through four distinct land types in just 66 miles: from the tem-perate coastal valley to this alpine landscape, then some lake country and, finally, semi-arid terrain. The weather changes considerably, too: since it is so much drier on the leeward side of the mountains, Carcross and Whitehorse get much hotter than Skagway in the summer—and much colder in the Winter."

At Norm's gesture, the three guides turned their attention towards a waterfall in a nearby mountain saddle. "Something else interesting about this pass," continued Norm, "is that it's a continental divide. These snowfields to our left drain into the Skagway River, while those on the right actually form the headwaters of the Yukon River.

"I always liked to illustrate the significance of this with a hypothetical bucket of water. If one were to empty the bucket on the west side of the pass, the water would wind up in the Lynn Canal, just twenty miles away as the raven flies. However, if one were to empty the bucket just a few feet to the right, on the east side of the pass, that water would enter the Yukon River system, flow five hundred miles north, take a sharp turn at Dawson and then flow west across the entire width of Alaska—traveling a total distance of more than two thousand miles before winding up in the Bering Sea."

At length, Old Paint seemed sufficiently rested to resume the journey. They piled back inside and descended from the pass. "And by the way," said Norm, "this is still British Columbia: we haven't crossed into the Yukon quite yet. This gives you some sense of what a huge province B.C. is: consider that the next border south of here is Washington state."

Rather than taking them back into a gentler region, the road down the east side of the pass put the Pinto and its occupants into a lunar landscape: a broad, volcanic alpine valley. Craggy rock outcroppings stretched across the valley floor, concealing tiny, cold lakes twice as deep as they were wide. Gnarled, low bushes and shrubs were the only survivors.

"Torment Valley," said Norm: "named not only for the way it looks, but also for how it felt on the feet. Imagine, after you and your horses had somehow survived the hell of the White Pass trail, looking forward to some kind of respite, but instead having to deal with this terrain. These volcanic rocks would slice your boots, and your horses' hooves, to ribbons—and don't even think about trying to drive something with wheels across. People quickly learned that the only realistic way to traverse the valley was to wait for Winter, when the high snows smoothed things out somewhat. Those who failed to yield to such common sense gave this place its name."

"Actually," said Kris, "I think it's beautiful here. It's just as rugged and wild as I would expect this country to be."

"I agree," said Norm. "There's nowhere else quite like this. And the grayling fishing in these little lakes is killer in the late Summer."

About two-thirds of the way across Torment Valley, they rounded a corner and, unexpectedly, came upon a small cluster of forlorn but official-looking buildings.

"Fraser, British Columbia. Canadian customs. Even though we crossed over at the top of the pass, they have the station down here. The Canadian government is slightly more forgiving now than they were during the Gold Rush days, when they placed the officers right on top of Chilkoot Pass. As bleak as those dormitories look, at least here they don't have to dig out from fifty feet of snow every winter."

As they pulled up to the kiosk, the Customs agent's eyes grew wide at the sight of Old Paint, plugging away into international terrain: seldom did such a steed traverse the pass. Then, recognizing Norm, he gave the most cursory of interrogations, waved them on through.

"Another difference from the old days," continued Norm, "is that Customs no longer checks whether you have a year's worth of provisions upon entry."

"I read something about that," said Peter. "You had to show the Mounties that you had 2,000 pounds of food and gear, which they would mark off against a checklist, before they would let you continue on to the Klondike."

"That's right," said Norm. "The idea was to avert famines in the gold-fields—which, according to the records, were pretty severe the first couple of Gold Rush years. Imagine: all those men, some of them already wealthy, but with nothing to eat but gold nuggets. Anyhow, the 2,000 pounds requirement was a good solution, but it imposed considerable hardship upon those who actually had to lug that stuff all the way from Skagway or Dyea to Dawson."

"OK, then," said Llary: "If you chose the Chilkoot Trail as your route, you had to go quite a ways on foot: the Golden Stairs were impassable any other way. Obviously, you're not going to carry a ton of gear on your back, all at once. So, how many trips up the Stairs would that mean?"

"Do the math," replied Norm. "Figure that most men could carry no more than fifty pounds at a time up the Stairs—and remember now, this was in the days before REI and fancy-schmancy backpacking gear. That pencils out to, let's see, some **forty** trips, back and forth, before you and all your gear were together at the top of the Pass, and you could go on your way. That's probably why, to this day, you can find all kinds of stuff along the Chilkoot Trail that the Stampeders ditched along the way: stuff that was unnecessary, frivolous or just too heavy."

Norm thought for a moment. "There was just one exception to the fifty-pound 'limit' that I'm aware of: a Native called 'Skookum Jim'. According to the legends, ol' Skookum—which means 'strong' in the Chinook jargon—once hauled a 150-pound box of bacon, strapped to his back, over the Golden Stairs."

"Gee," commented Kris, "next time I think I have a backpack that's too heavy, I won't complain quite so much."

"Speaking of trails and such," said Norm, "Here's Log Cabin Crossing: where the Chilkoot Trail comes out."

They had finally left Torment Valley, and had dropped enough in elevation for trees and wildflowers to reappear. Where the abandoned WP & YR railroad tracks crossed the highway was a dusty gravel parking lot. "These days, most people hike the trail as far as Lake Lindeman, then follow these tracks back to the highway. When the trail is passable again, in a couple weeks, you'll start seeing tired, grubby backpackers trying to hitch a ride back to civilization."

"Could be **us** in a month or two," Kris thought to himself. "I'll be as kind to the hitchhikers as possible: might as well build up some positive 'trail karma'."

Past Log Cabin, the highway roller-coastered through spring-green hills, crossed a multitude of tiny snowmelt streams that, as they now knew, would not taste salt water for more than two thousand miles. They came to the crest of a large hill and, looking below, saw a long, dark blue ribbon of water, kicked up into whitecaps by the wind.

"We are now in the third distinct geographical region of the Skagway-Carcross run," said Norm. "Just behind the Coast Range is this belt of glacial lakes: each of which is at least twenty miles in length and hundreds of feet deep. This one, Lake Tutshi,[3] runs so deep and cold that the southern Tutchone were afraid to venture out onto it. They even had some legend about a Loch Ness type monster living in the lake."

Indeed, the lake was very imposing-looking. "Hey, do you suppose we could talk the monster into making special cameo appearances for the tourists?"

"Probably not. I hear he's too shy."

Norm's punning play on the lake's name went over everyone's head. (But late that night, at about 3:00 am, Kris sat upright in his bed. He filed the pun away for future reference.)

Peter's eyes appraised the wild, rocky lakeshore as they drove past. "Just look: all this shoreline, and not a single cabin, condominium or high-rise casino. Only a single boat launch. Looks like fishing heaven."

"Yeah, isn't it beautiful? I know of some people who have caught thirty to forty-pound lake trout in Tutshi. And of course, they had the whole lake to themselves."

They traversed a small ridge and came down to the shore of another, highly similar lake. "This is the Windy Arm of Lake Tagish," said Norm. "The reason for its name should be fairly obvious. It looks huge, but this

---

3. Pronounced "Too-shy."

is only a small portion of a sixty-mile lake. Of more immediate interest, once we round this next corner, is..."

"WELCOME TO THE YUKON TERRITORY," said the large wooden sign. "We're **here**," said Norm. "The Yukon: one of Canada's two official territories. 25,000 people, spread out over an area the size of Texas—and more than half of them are in Whitehorse, the capital. This border lies at 60° North latitude: two-thirds of the way to the North Pole from the Equator.

"But you already should know all that." Norm gave a meaningful look to his passengers. "You'll spit out the facts and figures to your groups, and maybe half of them, at the most, will remember the specifics. I want you to impress upon them something more than that: namely, the fact that this border is also a real **psychological** frontier, just like Alaska's.

"A whole new set of rules—some would say, hardly any rules at all—apply here. The people who came to the Yukon wilds and survived, with most of their toes, fingers and mental faculties intact, were and are truly a special breed. Robert Service wrote all about them: the 'Men Who Don't Fit In' anywhere else. A more recent work in the same genre is 'The Colourful Five Percent,' by Jim Robb: all about the hardy breed of bushers who, in their own 'colorful' but oddly pragmatic ways, have thrived here."

"I don't know about the 'five percent' or not," said Llary, "but back in Oregon there's this small portion of the population who have moved back to the land, or never left it in the first place, really. Some have more 'color' than others—some have maybe a bit **too** much—but one thing they all have in common is that they're tough as nails, as resilient as the blackberry bushes."

"Same general idea," said Norm. "But the difference is that, with the exception of the Tutchone, everyone here originally came from somewhere else, chasing some kind of dream. And as we well know, not every whacked-out Yukon dream came true: think of all the unsuccessful Gold Rush stampeders. Think of the man responsible for all this mining debris above us on the mountainside: Colonel Joseph Conrad."

"Huh? Joseph Conrad, as in 'Heart of Darkness'?"

"Not exactly." Old Paint stepped gingerly onto a narrow, steep shoulder, on the Lake Tagish side of the highway. "Colonel Conrad's dream was the Venus Mine, a hard-rock operation he opened here in 1912. Like a number of places around here, gold-bearing quartz veins run through this mountain. Conrad's men tapped into what looked like a nice vein, drilling mine shafts and building a tramway to the lake, for hauling the ore down." Norm pointed up at the still-visible shafts, and traced with his finger the path of the old tram. "The ore came down to a storage building: that's the big wreck by the lakeshore, the one that looks like a slant-wise grain elevator. From there, the rock was barged to an ore crusher, the remnants of which we will see a few miles down the road.

"However, Colonel Conrad failed adequately to consider that he still had to get all of that crushed ore out of the Yukon, to be refined. Unlike placer gold, which is mined in nearly pure form, and much more easily transported, this type of hard-rock deposit must be very rich in order for a mining operation to pay off. Back in 1912, the only expedient way out of this part of the Yukon was our friend the White Pass railroad—which, unfortunately, ran along Lake Bennett, some distance to the west of here. The colonel had gambled that the Venus Mine would be a rich enough strike to warrant development of another major route out of the Territory. After this had been done, he could become a wealthy man, at last—or the operation would at least pay for itself. Ultimately, he lost the gamble: it was a pretty good strike, but not a great one."

"Interesting," commented Kris, "how you always hear about the big bonanzas, and the abject failures, but never the **mediocre** gold strikes."

"Conrad was definitely a bonanza kind of guy," replied Norm. "A little clue as to his character may be found in the name of that little stream across the way: Big Thing Creek. The colonel was always going on about the 'Big Thing': that huge strike that he spent the best years of his life looking for, but always eluded him."

"'Colonel Conrad was always looking for his Big Thing.' **Hmmm**. Might that be taken by our guests as some kind of interesting euphemism?"

"Oh, probably," Norm laughed. "Some of those seniors are a little friskier than you would think."

Mooseheads and Caribou Racks

▼

"A bunch of the boys were whooping it up in the Malamute Saloon;
The kid that handles the music-box was hitting a jag-time tune..."

—Robert Service again

Several miles past the Venus Mine, Lake Tagish took a hard dogleg to the left. Kris, Peter, Llary and Norm stopped briefly at the Bove Island overlook, to stretch their legs. Then, Old Paint began a long descent into yet another distinct type of terrain.

"Believe it or not, we're entering an actual **desert**," said Norm. "There are now several high ranges between here and the Gulf of Alaska, which collectively do a great job of scraping away the precipitation. Consequently, this valley receives less than ten inches of rainfall per year."

The lush lakeside vegetation was giving way to tall lodgepole pines, scraggly kinnickkinnick bushes, and not much in between. "Reminds me a little of eastern Oregon," commented Llary.

"A little further on, it looks more like Saudi Arabia," replied Norm. "Just on the other side of Carcross are some serious **dunes**. A long time ago, a glacial lake covered the lowest part of the valley, and when it disappeared it left behind all the sandy lake-bottom material. Over time, the winds coming off Lake Bennett have whipped up about one square mile of big, rolling dunes: about the last thing you'd expect to see at this latitude. Carcross likes to boast that it has the 'World's Smallest Desert'."

"Which reminds me," said Kris: "I'm still trying to figure out where the name 'Carcross' could have come from. Could you fill us in?"

"Of course—but this is strictly hearsay, as is so much of the Yukon folklore." Norm smiled enigmatically. "According to the story I've heard, there used to be a fair amount of caribou that migrated through here: no thundering herds, just a few extended families. You know: uncles, second cousins, shirttail relatives. No one knows what happened to the caribou—they just up and vanished—but they were around long enough for the impromptu tent community that formed at the head of Lake Bennett to be called 'Caribou Crossing.' Unlike most of the Gold Rush campsites, this one survived long enough to warrant real-town amenities, such as postal delivery. One problem, though: in those pre-postal code days, there were several different places in the north country with the name 'Caribou Crossing'. Lots of caribou, lots of crossings, and therefore lots of mixed-up mail delivery. So, in order to end this growing problem—and to give the new town its own identity—the founding fathers shortened the name by combining the first two syllables and chucking out the rest. *Voilá*, 'Car-Cross'.

"And speaking of founding fathers, here's where our friend Skookum Jim comes back into the story. Originally, he was from around here: one of the southern Tutchone. Later on, he was a member of the party that made the first big gold strike in the Klondike. Some even say that ol' Skookum himself was the one to make the actual discovery, rather than George Carmack. Anyway, even though Jim grew quite wealthy, he never forgot his roots: he ended up settling down in Carcross, came to own a lot of the town, and finally passed away there. One of his properties was the Caribou Hotel—which we can now see off in the distance."

At the bottom of the hill was a small community of box-like dwellings, clustered against the shore of Lake Bennett and divided by the Nares

River. Two structures stood out among the huddled cabins: the Caribou
Hotel, a gray, three-story box, and a very large wooden boat.

"That's the S.S. Tutshi," said Norm. "One of a fleet of steam-powered
paddlewheelers that plied the big lakes and the upper Yukon River. This
one and the S.S. Klondike, up in Whitehorse, are the only two intact
boats left of their kind."

"The tallest building in town is a **boat**," commented Peter. "Kind of
like Ketchikan on cruise-ship day."

Right where the sand dunes began on the valley floor, they turned off
the highway and entered Carcross. "The population here is two hundred
or so, about half-Native," said Norm. "The only town for fifty miles
around. It's got a school, a health center, a Mountie station, even a curling
rink—but as you can see, there's nothing fancy about the place at all.

"And, that's the chief appeal of Carcross: you **really** feel like you're in
the Yukon here. That's why we bring our guests up this way."

They pulled into a large, swirling-dust parking lot, between the S.S.
Tutshi and the "downtown" boardwalk. In the middle of the lot was an
old, decrepit stagecoach. The coach drivers, and their horses, had long
since turned to dust, but two entrepreneurial Native children had set up a
table and were selling old Yukon license plates as souvenirs. •

"Only a buck apiece," said one of the children. "Are you the tour-bus
guys?"

Kris, Peter, Llary and Norm made their day by picking up one
rusted, dented plate apiece. "Perfect Portland House decor," Kris
thought to himself.

They strode across the lot, walked into the middle of the main street
and looked around. Traffic was not a problem.

"You guests will spend about two hours here," said Norm. "First, you'll
take them on a little spin around town: takes about ten minutes. I'd suggest you stop for a moment by the lakeshore, so they can see the old cabins and hear about the Gold Rush 'armada': the fleet of 7000-plus
homemade boats that sailed down Lake Bennett in May 1898, on the first

navigable day after Spring breakup. It's quite something to visualize as you're sitting there, gazing across the lake.

"Then, you'll come back here and have lunch. Your guests will get beef stew, biscuits and apple cobbler, plus a little entertainment: a 'Gay 90's' revue, with can-can dancers, a musical saw player, and other hoopla. After lunch, you'll turn 'em loose on the town for an hour or so; then, you'll round 'em up, put 'em on the bus and, I guarantee you, they **will** fall asleep on the way back to Skagway."

Norm looked at his watch. "We're supposed to meet Mia, our Carcross expie, at the Caribou in a little while. What say we head over there and check it out?"

They crossed the street, stepped down into an Arctic entryway (a depressed threshold, to help keep cold air from getting inside), and into a Yukon time-warp. The plank floor of the saloon rippled like a tarpaulin in the wind, held in check only by a heavy, dark-wood bar that looked as if it had been carved from a single old-growth log. The bar was pockmarked with chips, head-sized dents and pre-Columbian graffiti. Behind the bar, a hundred different colors, flavors and viscosities of booze twinkled like ragtime piano; against the opposite wall, a barely-electric icebox complained about modern times, hoarding its collection of off-sale sixpacks, cartons of Players cigarettes and authentic Gold Rush-era hoagies. Scattered tables, chairs and customers rode the ripples on the floor.

For some reason, Kris felt as if he were being watched. His eyes drifted above the bar, and locked into a set of glassy, elliptical-pupiled eyes: those of a Dall sheep ram's head. Next to the sheep was a full-racked bull caribou, with eyes equally as expressive. The severed-head procession stretched all the way around the room: another ram, several more caribou, a mountain goat, a huge moose, a rather surprised-looking black bear. A couple of faded, desiccated lake trout feebly flapped 40-year old varnish fumes on either side of the door transom.

"Gee, nice wildlife display," commented Kris.

"Tami will have a hard time dealing with this place when she runs tours up here," said Llary. "She has this major phobia about stuffed animal heads in public places: they genuinely freak her out. Even 'Myrtle', that ancient moosehead hatrack at the Onion, gives her the willies."

"I thought that only **male** moose had antlers," said Peter. "So why 'Myrtle'?"

"I dunno: why **not** 'Myrtle'?" retorted Llary.

"Transvestite moose?" offered Kris.

With the mystery of Myrtle still unresolved, they walked all the way inside, found a relatively sturdy table and sat down. A murmur was generated amongst the fair-sized midday clientele, as the Carcross locals eyeballed the four Skagwegians.

"I think maybe **we're** the 'Men Who Don't Fit In'," Kris astutely pointed out.

"Relax," said Norm. "Have a Moosehead. Have two. The liquid kind, I mean. The cultural differences will blur: trust me."

Peter was dispatched to the bar for a round of beers. A fortyish woman sitting on a nearby barstool looked him over. "I like yer **hair**," she said. "Y'look just like that wrestler guy on TV, what's-his-name...Gorgeous George?"

Peter confirmed the uncanny resemblance, politely excused himself, and retreated to his table of bemused colleagues.

"Congrats," said Llary. "Looks like you've found a friend."

"**Uff** da," said Peter.

"I understand," said Kris, "that you've have had some interesting experiences up in Dawson, Norm. Was the local ambiance anything like this when you were a tour guide there?"

"Just like this," said Norm, "only even more so. And to me, that was the fun of it: putting myself into that Yukon mind-set, doing my best to interact with the locals. Of course, there were often unintended consequences: several sticky situations, but one that, well, ended a lot better.

"In my long-haul days, I would pass through Dawson about twice every two weeks, staying there for two nights at a time. I definitely did my best to check out the local color: at times I was pushing the envelope as to the 8-hour 'bottle to throttle' rule. Anyway, one night I found my way to Diamond Tooth Gertie's—the only saloon in town where gambling is still legal—and I saw this beautiful croupier there. Went over to her table, was sufficiently moonstruck to lose about twelve hands of blackjack in a row. Cleaned me right out. I don't think she was particularly impressed with me.

"But I kept going back there, whenever I was in town. Kept dropping all my Canadian money at her table. I shrugged off the losses, said it was only play money anyhow. She scolded me in this wonderful French-Canadian accent. It was love, of course. Eventually, I left Dawson with something more than loose change."

Many times already, the Portland House gang had seen the interplay at work between Norm and his lovely wife René, late of Quebec and Dawson City, now dividing her attentions between overseeing the company's Skagway expediter staff and caring for one-year old Josey. Kris, Peter and Llary hadn't heard the full story before, but readily agreed that Norm had done very well by his Yukon experiences.

"Speaking of exotic foreign women," said Norm, "here comes Mia."

A halo of white-blonde hair brightened the visual din of the hotel bar. A woman looking to be in her late twenties, of medium height and skier's build, crossed the uneven floor, smiled and sat down to join them. Kris saw a wide, full mouth, bright teeth, and blue-blue eyes that were almondine in shape, giving her features a slightly Eastern cast.

"How do you do," said Mia, in a charming but unidentifiable European accent.

"Mia's originally from Finland," said Norm. "She's here for the summer from the Toronto area, and will be our local liaison here in Carcross, making sure that everything is ship-shape for this end of our tours. Other days, she'll be up in Whitehorse, helping out our expie staff there."

"And other days, I will be down to see **you**," said Mia. "A girl can't stay all alone in her cabin **all** the time." The boys learned that Mia had rented for the summer one of the vintage cabins by the lakeshore; in return for their offer of Portland House hospitality, they were invited to stop by the cabin "…**any** time you're in Carcross." Mia smiled again, and even the glassy eyes of the critters on the wall seemed to shine in assent.

DOCKSIDE JOURNAL ENTRY: 6/14/87

▼

It's hard to wake up with the sun these days, since it's light pretty much all the time this close to the solstice. This morning, I was woken up by a **shadow**: a large shape looming behind the curtain on my bedroom window. I rose from the bed, tiptoed over to the curtain and yanked it open. Of course, it was just a couple of tourists: fooled again by the deceptive, antique-storefront appearance of the Portland House. They jumped back several feet from the tall apparition in underwear.

"Well, it looks like there should be **something** here," I thought I heard the woman say as they walked away.

I slapped my uniform on, navigated through the crusty pots and pans in the Slob Kitchen, found that my Honey-Nut Cheerios had once again made it through the night. In a few minutes, we piled into Old Paint and made it to the busyard.

Since I'm only going to Dyea, I got #602, one of the older buses: doubledy-clutch, doubledy-clutch, as Neal Cassady would have said. This was OK, except the thing really reeked when I stepped inside: somebody had forgotten to dump the shitter. So I went back to the "Blue Lagoon" (hip Coach Commander lingo for the on-board head), popped the window hatch; Norm happened to be standing there, and he volunteered to pull the plug while I ran the hose inside the hatch to rinse and refill.

Unfortunately, he was wearing a nice, charcoal pinstripe suit—so he could schmooze with the cruise ship officers on board—and dumping can be a messy job if you don't jump out of the way in time. Of course, he splattered himself: horrible brown-green specks on his suit jacket. Norm cussed a blue streak as I apologized like hell, grabbed some Handi-Wipes and helped make him presentable again.

We got to the waterfront just in time to hurry up and wait. Turns out that hackysack is the thing to do while waiting on the docks. I'd only played it a couple of times before coming up here, so the learning curve has been steep—even though there are only three basic rules to remember. First, do not catch the sack with your hand; second, don't serve to yourself; third, never, ever say "sorry" for a lousy shot. You get "hacked"—the sack is flung at you, hard—if you break any of these rules. My chest and arms bear the imprints from numerous violations.

So we stood in our little circle for about ten minutes, focused like a wagon camp on this little beanbag we were bopping around with our feet and shins—and in Brian's case, with his head as well. He must have been a halfway decent soccer player in some prior incarnation.

We broke off the hackysack when mass human activity around the gangplank became apparent. The chaos was fascinating to view from our distance.

"Note," said Mark, scientifically, "the symbiotic relationship at work here. The mother ship, tied umbilically to the life-sustaining pier, people and goods flowing in and out. It's **interdependency**, by George."

"Like mistletoe and oak trees," said Tami, romantically.

"Wile E. Coyote and the Roadrunner," said Kevin, helpfully.

"Lichens on the boulders," said Llary, purposefully.

"Alice Algae and Freddy Fungus took a lichen to one another…" began Derek, lapsing into elementary-education mode.

"But their marriage was on the rocks," Karl finished for him.

The strands of passengers, like strands of DNA (see, I'm not immune to all this scientific metaphor) are now curling in this direction. It's my first solo run out to Dyea: hope I can keep all my Gold Rush history straight. But Gary will charm their socks off, regardless.

Speaking of Gary: he and Norm were hanging out in the Onion not long ago, drinking Duck Farts (Kahlua and chocolate milk; **where** do they come up with these drink names?). Gary thought it might be fun to have the drivers, plus the Whitehorse expies, over to his place soon for a sauna party. Norm was hip to this, and of course so were we. Gary seems very cool, from what I've seen so far: a genuine Alaskan character. The party will be sometime next week.

Gotta go.

COCKTAIL HOUR

It was midnight in the
red onion saloon and
the sun was blazing
soapy smith slumped onto a
glass table face landing
in a beer-ring atoll
beneath his eyes there
was a parallel universe
in which men were hunting
dall sheep on a mountainside
during a spring snowstorm
      he'd heard of this universe before but
      never knew it personally

SAUNA, SVIM (PART ONE)

▼

The big bend around Middle Bay; the steep switchback; the twisty part by the big boulders, just barely wide enough for a bus. If you take the Dyea road much over twenty or twenty-five, the ride is bouncy and dusty for those unfortunates sitting in the back, over the wheel wells. However, Kris (the driver) and his several passengers were not overly concerned with a smooth ride. Norm, amazingly, had lent the Portland House gang one of the buses for the sauna party at Gary's homestead. "Tomorrow's a real quiet day; no ships in town. Just be back by dark (it was barely past the Summer Solstice). I don't want to know what goes on out there, now." Norm had winked, looking a little nostalgic.

The Chilkoot trailhead, the old bridge over the Taiya, the tumbledown Gold Rush-era foundations, the almost imperceptible turnoff to the homestead. The little cabin, unmowed yard and beginning-to-explode garden—and the welcoming committee. Dyea Gary was scarcely any different in real life as he was *en costume* for the tourists. Wide-brim hat, overalls, faded flannel, big grin of welcome and amusement playing about his lips. "Damn: I hardly recognize you without your polyester. Whole shitload of leftover biscuits and hooch over there. We're about to spark up the sauna; why don't some of you guys help with the chopping."

Some of the driver/guides had been out there all day, getting a head start on the festivities. People milled about Gary's cabin and garden, munching biscuits, sipping hooch, playing horseshoes, picking strawberries. Kevin walked up to Llary, who was splitting logs for the sauna fire, paused for profundity purposes. "If a tree fell on you in the wilderness, and no one else was around—would it really have happened?"

"You, Kevin, obviously demonstrate the effects of trees having fallen upon you. Many trees. Yet, you're still walking among us. Go figure."

Others shortly gathered around and reduced the woodpile to chippings and whittlings. They picked up armloads of split logs and toted them down to the riverside sauna, to the tune of an corrupted Led Zeppelin riff (led by Kevin): "Got a whole lotta logs...**BWOWWW**...Got a whole lotta logs..."

At the river's edge sat a squat, hand-hewn structure, like a low-slung storage cache. On the inside, the history of a thousand good sweats radiated sweetly from the cedar beams. In one corner sat the homemade sauna stove, representing possibly the highest use (of the innumerable uses) for the 55-gallon oil drum. The boys stuffed the woodstove like a Thanksgiving turkey—except instead of sage and toasted breadcrumb aroma, it would exude **heat**: the type of heat that cleansed and purified.

Another dust cloud filtered up from the driveway. The Whitehorse expies had arrived, having successfully commandeered a company van. Like the female Gold Rush entrepreneurs who made a fortune by serving apple pie at the base of the Chilkoot trail, the expies were a highly welcome sight: in addition to providing their delightful company, they had been charged with bringing the ciders, smokies and High-Test. The van lurched to a halt in the yard, nearly knocking over the half-moon door on Gary's privy, and a giggling Annabel, Kara, Yvette and Mia burst out, partially-consumed supplies in their arms. The Dyea sauna population was now complete.

"And when we got on the ship
he brought out something for the trip
said 'it's old but it's good…'
Like any other primitive would…"

—Neil Young

Everybody was present, the sauna was rapidly heating up, but…

"Hold it," said Brian. "Think we'd, uh, better go test the altitude first."

"Altitude Test," said Mark and Kevin in unison, looking at each other knowingly. The three sauntered back behind Gary's cabin, by the giant lilacs and berry patch, with a curious Kris in tow. Gary emerged from the cabin, with some rather suspicious altitude-testing paraphernalia.

"Alaska homegrown is the **best** shit," said Gary. "All those long hours of daylight. Fertile glacial river-bottom soil. You know how the flowers up here seem that much more intense, that much more vivid in color? Well, the same thing applies here. This is a particularly potent strain of local herb: they call it 'Matanuska Thunder-Fuck'." Gary filled his pipe and lit it, the space wrangler, the psychedelic sourdough. "And in Alaska, growing your own, for home use, is absolutely **legal**."

Kris briefly paused to consider the logistical problems of enforcing the "War On Drugs" in rural Alaska: the great distances, the likely potshots taken by angry homesteaders at DEA planes flying over the bush, the pointlessness of it all. Then he stopped being so damn analytical as the pipe was passed to him.

Very shortly, cruising altitude was reached. The treetops seemed tiny, far below. In the stratosphere they found many interesting things. The lilacs were intensely purple, white, fragrant. The strawberries were ripe and delicious. They became hungry bears, savaging the leafy growth for treats. Primitivism prevailed. But eventually, through the time and space distortions they realized that the sauna was ready and waiting.

Their progression to the riverside was deliberate and dignified but festive, like the House of Lords marching in the Tournament of Roses Parade. Everyone else had gathered around the sauna, waiting to see who would be the first to enter. But there was never a doubt about Mark's intentions. "Reckon I'll go European, here," he commented, and in accelerated autumnal fashion he shed his clothing. The rest of the boys instantaneously decided what the hell (Dyea Gary was already naked, trotting over from his cabin), and blue jeans and t-shirts littered the forest floor. A parade of full moons disappeared one by one into the darkness of the sauna.

Mia, being a good Finn, was delighted, and joined in the clothing-optional frenzy without a moment's hesitation. The other Canadian expies looked at one another with slight trepidation, the Skagway boys tried not to hope too hard, but higher instincts prevailed, and a more graceful lunar progression filtered into the hut, occupying the rest of the bench space.

It was dark, humid, and very, very warm. The heat began to build, began to crawl over their bodies, into their lungs—but it was a welcome guest. The first beads of sweat emerged. "In Finland, this is ritual time," said Mia. "Cedar or birch boughs are a must. Your partner spanks you on the shoulders and back with the branches—the green fragrant parts—to get your blood going. Cleanses and rejuvenates. Then, when you've had enough, you go running out bare nude into the snow, roll around—or, someone chops a hole in the lake and you dunk. I like this last one better. All winter long, it's nothing but 'sauna, svim, sauna, svim…' "

These last words she spoke reverently, like a chant or a mantra. Kris looked at the glistening silhouette of Mia against the glow of the fire, and dreamed of being stranded for a winter in Scandinavia, saunaing and svimming with such a creature.

Every few minutes, buckets of water were dumped on top of the wood-stove; the groans of "**Yessss!**" matched the hissing on the glowing-red iron plate. As persons reached the boiling point, they would pop out the buck-skin door flap, pick their way barefoot down to the river's edge, and lower themselves in, hanging onto a guiding rope to avoid being pulled away by the current. Those remaining inside the sauna could hear the painful/pleasurable cries as someone dunked. The angel-food cake screams of Annabel generated a minor exodus, as several of the boys felt compelled to assist her *au naturel* river entry. Kevin was the one who detached the rope from the riverbank, tied it to a tree limb and created an impromptu swing, hurtling out Tarzan-style into the middle of the glacial flow and dropping into the chilly water. When glaciation began to set in, all one had to do was jump back into the sauna and thaw. This cycle went on for a surprisingly long time.

The final, lasting image was that of a shimmering circle: the Skagway boys and the Whitehorse girls seated on the benches in a concentric chain, administering backrubs to the lucky person in front. "Squeak, squeak" went their hands upon perspiration-slick flesh, snap-crackle-pop went the fire, "Oohh, ahhh," went Annabel as she vocalized her pleasure. Kris, working contentedly on Mia's smooth shoulders, did not see how any Alaskan summer evening could better culminate. The Dyea riverside was home; the sun refused to go down.

THE BACKWARDS PARADE

▼

4th of july lies like a llama down
main street skagway, expectant airplanes

buzzin the town like mosquitoes, banners,
red firecrackers, smokebombs, thunderclouds even

dragged from the midwest for the occasion
soon the bigger-hammer marching band sounds its

stolen-airhorn signal, the parade begins;
trotting out trolleys, warhorse mayors

emeritus, clowns you don't remember,
old engines made orgasmic by new steam

dodging water-balloons, cool-whip,
fruit, vegetables and other havoc, the

slow-bicycle race ambles aimlessly till
nudged aside by wheatgerm and his brigands

the true descendant of soapy, toilet-plunger
raised proudly in hand, leading the bigger-hammer

a marching-band from mars, a riot of
false noses and obscene brassy sounds, their

antarctic formation carries the day as
skagway cheers its home-baked heroes and

their cloud of dust; child pipes up
oo mama, can this really be the end? but

it isn't, as the parade goes backwards too
marching in reverse, prolonging the dog-day

"that's why time's goin so slowly
son, you see, the clock's stopped"

afterwards wheatgerm stumbles back
into the fray, his beard is parted like

the red sea, "well i never askd
t be yr **mountain**," he tells those

gaping upwards in awe, but soon proper attention
is focused on the city's finest pie-eaters,

from all warped boardwalks of life, united for
mere minutes to swinomishly consume coconut-

creme; norm emerges as the winter, flashing
the crowd imitation of meringue santa—

claus, ho ho ho, let's have a beer
norm retires to the red onion for

duck-fart chasers while others sense a fatal
attraction to the portland house roof where

indeed the la brea tar pits have
resurfaced in the form of a party; guests

in imported beach-chairs sink into the
roof like so many sabertooth tigers, albeit

tall cool ones, laughing and
spitting watermelon-seeds at their fate

DINNER BELLS

▼

The Only Day Of Summer was swept away with the empty bottles, saber-tooth tiger skeletons and other glacial debris from the Rooftop Party. Skagway turned gray and windy; the suspension footbridge shrieked and swayed over the river. The Dyea road was almost deserted as Kris rode a mountain bike out to Gary's homestead: in some places, creeping into the headwind at a standstill, in others, nearly parasailing.

Kris found Dyea Gary down by the sauna, sawing up a windblown cottonwood. "Damn stuff's hardly worth burning, it's so soft," grumbled Gary. "But it's a freebie from Ma Nature. Thanks for coming by to help out."

Kris was glad to get away from the Portland House hubbub for the day, and didn't mind helping replenish the woodpile. All those campfires for the tourists—plus past and future riverside saunas—ate up a lot of fuel. An extra chainsaw grinned like an alligator at Gary's feet. Kris fired it up, and together the two men whomped through the latest casualties of the wind.

After all the logs were bucked and hauled over to the woodpile, they fell to splitting. Ordinary, manly conversation once again became possible.

"What **I** wanna know," leered Dyea Gary, "is what's up with you and this Finnish lady, this Mia."

"I don't really know how, or why. But something got started at that sauna session. One nice friendly backrub, and now I notice her every time I get up to Carcross. She sidles up, makes some innocuous reference to birch or cedar boughs, and slips away, laughing."

Gary whistled. "Whew: sounds like my ex-wife. Of course, she was Finnish, too: long and blonde, big mood swings, a sauna fiend. Learned all about the wild side of saunaing from her..." And Gary elaborated at some length, with five-part harmony and full orchestration.

Kris had never heard Gary's personal saga before. He learned that Gary had grown up in Southern California, in stark contrast to his current hatred of crowds and hot weather; that, despite his current non-academic demeanor, he had held an early interest in field biology, and was on the verge of some kind of academic career; that this had run headfirst into an early marriage in particular and the 1960's in general; that, after the marriage ended, there was a "lost decade" of drifting through construction work, park rangering and other survival mechanisms that kept him mostly outdoors; that this had led to the cultivation of, by his early forties, a strong environmental ethic, as well as budding curmudgeonly tendencies; that a gradual drift towards Alaska became inevitable; that his first winter instate had somehow resulted in another marriage, to a moody Finnish woman, whose recollection made him simultaneously glow and shudder.

As to Mia, Gary concluded that Kris had to ride it out, to see where the trip was going—and that an impromptu, neighborly visit to Mia's Carcross cabin, followed by an invite to the riverside sauna, was in the offing. Kris was inclined to agree.

By woodpile reckoning, and by way of mood swings, the subject of bears somehow came up next.

"What most people can't get used to," began Dyea Gary, "is the notion that, in Alaska, they're not necessarily at the top of the food chain. Practically anywhere you go in the state—even at the very edge of Anchorage—there is an active predator-prey relationship. We are the prey:

or, at the very least, we are subject to the whims of bears while on their home turf."

"The naturalist in me says 'amen' to that: kind of puts us humans in their place, as just another species." Kris hesitated. "But, at the same time, that primal fear, the fear of being eaten, is highly disturbing."

Gary nodded. "And that's as it should be. What you do out in the woods should always be oriented towards this basic concept: that the bears are **always** out there. With this in mind, the precautions that you take are actually fairly basic:

"First, most bears will shy away from you, if they have fair advance warning. The major exceptions would be when you've come between a mother and her cubs, or have stumbled onto a kill or food stash. If you're way up north, any encounter with a polar bear also would be excepted; they're active predators of humans...

"Anyway: let any bears that may be out there know that you're human. You do this by making people-type noises whenever passing through high brush or other suspicious areas. Clap your hands, yell 'hey bear,' tell it you don't taste good, sing it Country-Western songs,[4] whatever. If there's no perceived threat—and if a bear's basic fear of humans is still intact—he would just as soon stick to berries and ground squirrels rather than hassling you.

"When you're in a group of some kind, ordinary conversation generally does the trick. But you have to make a conscious effort to make noise when hiking solo. Alaska is one of the few places where you can stomp around in the woods, talking to yourself, and people won't think you're crazy."

---

4. Dyea Gary's famous Country-Western joke. Q: What happens when you play a C&W record backwards? A: You get out of jail and get your house, wife, dog and pickup truck back.

Kris was intrigued. "I understand that some folks in bear country tie a cowbell, or even sleigh bells, to a backpack: to serve the same purpose as talking, with less hassle."

Dyea Gary leaned on his splitting maul, grinned knowingly. "And there, my friend, is one of the bigger myths around. Hikers think they're buying protection when they pick up those doodads. I call such devices 'dinner bells.' Want to know why?

"Sure, you're giving notice to a bear that someone, or something, is out there—so the surprise factor is eliminated. The bear can hear you, all right, but that fear of humans ain't triggered by a few jingle bells. Furthermore, bears are **curious** critters. Santa Claus aside, those bells aren't a sound that occur in nature. Mr. Bear may actually come sniffing around, just to see what the hell you are. In my humble, bear-chawed opinion, you may as well be ringing a come-n-git-it triangle."

"Point well taken. But, uh, what do you mean, 'bear-chawed'? You're just being facetious, right?"

"Nope. I'm not kidding. Several years ago, up at Russian Lakes, on the Kenai Peninsula, I was batted around pretty good by a coastal brownie. Bear even gave me a few licks, a couple love bites. But he spit me right out: guess I didn't agree with him."

"Holy shit."

"Yeah, that's what I said, too, plus a few other things. I can laugh about it now, but at the time I remember thinking, 'Jesus, just let me get through this without losing an arm or a leg...' Actually, I wasn't thinking much at all: pure survival instincts were kicking in. Luckily, I happened to have the right instincts. How I survived was like this:

"First, when you make that initial close-up contact with a bear—after all your warning tactics have failed—you've got to fight your urge to run like hell. You see, when a bear first spots you, it still may not know what you are; if you cut and run, the bear's predatory instincts kick in, as it figures that you must be something tasty if you flee. And it **will** catch you: it doesn't look much like a jackrabbit, but it can hit 30 miles an hour.

"Anyway, after you've made your stand, there's still time to convince the bear that you're human. What you do is stand up straight, raise your arms above your head—to make you appear larger—and talk to the bear while slowly backing away. If this goes right, the bear should eventually figure out what you are, and go on about its business.

"If, by some chance, this doesn't work, the bear may charge. But realize that about 90% of these are false charges, meant to intimidate: the bear may come to a screeching halt just feet away from you, growl, sniff at you, then stalk off. Amazingly, you should still stand your ground in these cases—but you also should have dropped to the ground, curled up in fetal position, with your hands behind your neck. Leaving your pack on helps protect your back, too."

"So, how do you **remember** all this stuff, in such a panic situation?"

"Like I told you: I'm not thinking, I'm acting instinctively. All of this information is so firmly ingrained by now: all those solo walks in the woods, thinking about bears, and what I would do if I saw one...I tend to border on the paranoid sometimes." Dyea Gary laughed. "But I'm sure it's saved my ass, on more than one occasion.

"Anyway, there's another key variable to keep in mind: whether it's a brown or black bear that's after you. If it's a brownie or grizz, you're still supposed to stay in that fetal position until the last possible moment: when you know that the bear is serious about attacking, is giving you more than love taps. Only then do you begin fighting back. But with a black bear, it's different: you begin fighting back right away, as soon as it comes charging. They're more dangerous, because they're even less pre-dictable; the odds are more favorable if you fight them at the git-go."

"So, if you're not one of these professional bear-wrasslin' types, how exactly does one fight off a bear?"

"Well, as Malcolm X used to say, 'by any means necessary.' "Gary apol-ogized: "Sorry, 60's flashback. It happens. Seriously: there are many schools of thought on this. Your Big White Hunter type, the mentality that curses Alaska more than almost any other place, will of course be packing his gun. But it takes a pretty serious cannon to do much more than piss off a bear, and you usually get only one shot. Given the pain-in-the-ass of toting such metal around—not to mention the substantial odds of blowing off your own foot—this doesn't seem like a very good idea. I used to pack a gun in the woods, but no more.

"Lately, I've been seeing more people carrying these industrial-sized cans of mace or pepper spray. They're supposed to be good up to fifteen or twenty feet away—plus, they have the advantage of not killing or seriously injuring a bear. But once again, you get only one shot. And what if the wind is a bit strong that day, and your pepper spray goes wide to the right?"

Dyea Gary split his final log, threw it onto the woodpile. "Me, I take kind of a Zen approach anymore: if it comes, it comes. Carrying around those massive weapons creates bad vibes, a mind set that wholly detracts from one's enjoyment of wild places. But I still keep my eyes peeled for good, sharp walking sticks while in the woods: I figure a good poke in the nose or eyes would discourage a bear that wasn't intent on eating me. Otherwise, what can you really do?"

"But, all of this bear talk has been about **confrontation**." Gary leaned back against a tree trunk, pulled out a pint flask of Jack Daniels from deep within his overalls, and took a good slug: quittin' time. "So long as I'm in this yakking mood: I've got some pretty amazing stories from my ranger-ing days out in Katmai, that are all about a different kind of human-bear interaction. Care to hear some?"

"Well, of course. Fire away. Gimme a shot of that J.D. first."

Dyea Gary's eyes glowed as he took on his Alaskan sourdough/ story-teller persona. "Well—first of all, you've got to get a sense of what Katmai is like. Way out in western Alaska: the Valley of 10,000 Smokes, the Brooks River and other rivers and streams which, all summer long, are chock full of spawning salmon. Rolling hills covered with blueberries, lowbush cranberries and about twenty other kinds of berry. Hardly any people around at all. In other words, Bear Paradise.

"With all this food, and hardly any worries, the bears get fat and sassy. I've seen 'em lying on their backs in a berry patch, shoveling in the berries with their front paws—yet, they're dainty enough so that they don't take in hardly any leaves and twigs with the fruit. When they go fishing, all they need to do is walk out to the middle of the river, just above the falls, and stand there with their mouths open: AHHH…" Gary tilted his head to the side, opened his mouth; his beard parted to reveal grizzly-sized incisors (or so it seemed to Kris). "Literally, the salmon leap right into their mouths. The bear walks off with his fish, the next one in line takes his turn, and so on: it's quite a set-up.

"And what's best about Katmai is that people haven't screwed up the system. The bears go on about their business as if you weren't there. The summer populations of both bears and humans are constant enough so that everybody gets familiar—and to an extent, comfortable—with each other. You recognize the all personalities, all the eccentric characters: just like any small town.

"One of my more surprising discoveries was that some of the bears seemed to have a sense of humor. I was riding my bike along this mountain road on a real foggy morning: one of those mornings when you can hear a pin drop, somebody crunching their cornflakes a quarter-mile away, and…footsteps. The kind that sound like something big, with very large feet, is following you—but trying, in vain, to be quiet about it. I could hear this 'FLAP, FLAP FLAP' while riding, then no sound when I was still. Then there were **two** sets of tiptoeing, flapping large feet…and they seemed to be picking up their pace.

"Well, by this time I was gettin' a little paranoid: didn't want to be a Meal on Wheels. Yet, I couldn't figure out why a bear, or a couple of bears, would follow me. They'd seen plenty of bikes before, so it was probably more than simple curiosity. Seemed more likely that these bears knew who I was—and, if I could have seen 'em, I may have recognized 'em—and they were just trying to freak me out in the fog. Decided this was the ticket: and, of course, it was working. Ditched my bike in the middle of the road, went off into the bushes a few feet away, to see who would come.

"Sure enough, a couple of young brown bears, teenagers probably, came loping and flapping out of the fog. Still could barely see 'em, but I sure could smell 'em: those bears get pretty stanky from all that rolling around in fish guts, just like a big old dog, only worse. Anyhow, I'm sure they smelled me in the bushes, too, knew I was there—but of course they were more interested in the bike. They were tapping the pedals with their paws; I wouldn't have been at all surprised if the bears had gotten onto my bike and rode off together, tandem. After a while, they just loped off into the fog again, probably laughing at me."

Gary shook his head. "Another story, another early morning: way late in the tour season, because it was actually dark. I was sittin' in the camp shitter, doin' my business. Same thing as the other time: heard this FLAP, FLAP of footsteps, then eerie quiet. I took my sweet time in the can, of course, waiting for the footsteps to go away, but every time I thought the coast was clear, I would hear something again. Well, I couldn't sit there forever: after I while I just poked my head out the door, couldn't see nothing, couldn't hear nothing, seemed that the coast was clear. Stepped outside into the dark, walked forward a few feet and WHUMP! I had run into a pillow. A six-foot tall pillow. In the dawn's pale glow I saw that the pillow had blondish-brown fur, and a head: a **big** one. I had walked into the ass end of a huge boar grizzly.

"The bear turned his big old head, seemed to regard me kind of sadly, shaking it from side to side. Other than that, he didn't move an inch.

"But I sure did. I turned around, tiptoed back into the outhouse and locked the door. I waited a long time, until it was good and light, before I ventured out again. My buddies, wondering what I'd been doing all that time, figured I'd taken about the longest dump in history."

Dyea Gary roared with laughter at the memory, and Kris joined him. Finally, wiping the tears from his eyes, Gary had one final thing to say:

"I guess all of this has shaped my outlook towards the bears, wherever I go in the state. What I always remember, above everything else, is that it's their home, much more than it is mine. Out in the bush, I am their guest; I know it and they know it. In places like Katmai, sometimes you get lucky enough to know 'em socially, to a degree—but you still respect 'em and give 'em their space. And if bear-human interaction is to be inevitable in Alaska, that's just how it should be."

INDIAN SNOW

▼

The morning came too early, as usual. "Wake up!" shouted Norm as he walked down the Portland House hall, banging on a dirty pot with a spatula. "Rise and shine! You play, you **pay**!"

Eventually everyone was rousted, shuttled to the busyard and given their vehicle for the day. They drove back through town to the waterfront, parked their buses in a neat row on the dock and, in honor of Norm's disciplinary endeavors, lined up and saluted him as he passed by. Norm laughed, waved them off, and readied himself at the gangplank for the day's tourists.

Here they come, filing off the ship runway. The guy with the umbrella, breaking them off into orderly strands, steering them towards all us Alaskan experts. They've probably paid a bundle for this—but they've got the bucks for it. Probably carrying plenty of small change from all those gift-shop purchases. Might be about a hundred-dollar day tipwise, if I'm lucky.

Here comes my strand. Light-colored cardigans, windbreakers, a few L.L. Bean outfits mixed in. Lots of cameras. They look lively, receptive, ready for fun. Climb aboard, watch your step, welcome to Skagway. Beautiful day, isn't it? Bet you had a wonderful cruise: all those glaciers. See any whales?

Perfect weather: sunny, should get up to about seventy today. Up towards the summit, I can see the mountains all the way to their tops. Things are looking good.

Kris had been dispatched to Carcross for the day, but had been given the rust-bucket of the bus fleet: poor old oil-belching #602. The passengers packed inside to the gills, chattering, oblivious to the relative lack of luxury—possibly expecting, perhaps wishing, to rough it a little in Alaska. And the Perfect Tour began.

"Local Lingo Lesson #1. Pass yourself off as a real Alaskan. Impress your friends. Be the hit of parties back home. Here we go:

"Up in these parts, you're going to hear people described in one of two ways. The first word is one you've likely heard before: 'Sourdough.' Maybe you've had sourdough bread, here or elsewhere: tough, tangy, made from the only strain of yeast which, in the old days, could survive the rigors of the North. It was that or eat flat bread. The way the early stampeders kept their yeast starter going through the winter was to store it in a little leather pouch, which they kept next to their bodies, in the warmest possible place...um, the **second** warmest: their armpits. Towards springtime, right about the time they'd change their underwear, things certainly got a little sour. So a Sourdough is one who has actually survived at least one Alaskan winter, without too severe a case of cabin fever.

"There is, however, an alternate explanation: Sourdoughs are simply those who've been up here through a full winter, and are all sour because they haven't got any dough left." Kris paused, to allow for sufficient pun reaction.

"Then there are those who have not suffered such rigors: those who may not know quite what they are in for. These are the ones staring about dazedly at the first October snowstorm, wondering what to do. These are fish-in-a-barrel for old Soapy Smith: the newcomers, the rookies, the greenhorns...the **Cheechakos**. C-H-E-E-C-H-A-K-O. It's a lousy thing to be called, but it may be true of many of us. Perhaps all of you. Certainly me.

"Reputedly, the specific origin of the word 'Cheechako' comes from the Haida packers, who were charging those exorbitant prices to the newcomers. They say that our present-day term comes from those Natives trying to pronounce the word 'Chicago.' To them, everybody from Outside was automatically from Chicago. So now, whenever you are called a Cheechako, you at least know what it means—whether or not you are actually from Chicago."

The Skagway River rushed glacially under the highway bridge, down to the inlet, paralleling the airport runway. "Cheechakos and Sourdoughs. Which one are you? During the Gold Rush, there were plenty of both. Doesn't take long to become an **honorary** Sourdough, though. That's our goal for today."

Kris punched the accelerator as the bus rose above the river valley, past the shantytown campground, into the trees, to the Customs station just below the first big grade.

"U.S. Customs. A border crossing doesn't get much more laid-back than this. We know these guys: there are just two of them, and they live right in town. If you make a run up to Canada for the day, it's good to be back across the border by midnight—that's when they go home. But if you come in after hours, you're supposed to go up to the porch there and explain yourself to the video camera. It's like Uncle Sam becomes your video dad: 'Where have you been? Don't you know what time it is?' "

Around the bend, up the narrow valley, a sheer wall of white.

"The Denver Glacier. Part of a contiguous system of icefields, covering the majority of the northern Coast Range. Every river and stream sipping the sea between here and Juneau is glacier-fed. In fact, this one's other end is in the mountains just above Juneau—some eighty miles away, as the raven flies. Many's the time I've considered hiking up there, to the head of the Denver Glacier, strapping on my skis, having a nice run across the ice-cap before finally unfurling my backpack to reveal a parachute, or better still, a hang-glider, shooting off the tip of the glacier and sailing into downtown Juneau."

These last sentences were spoken quickly and breathlessly. If Kris got the words out right, the tourists would feel like they were whooshing right off the end of the Denver Glacier with him.

They took a quick picture stop at Pitchfork Falls, then began the serious climb. At the steepest grade, right above Deadhorse Gulch, Kris had found that one had to downshift all the way into first gear. Otherwise, the black smoke would begin to pour out, the transmission would lug, you might lose all your momentum and take forever getting up the grade. But Kris almost preferred it this way. *So much history, so much interesting narrative to pour into the climb up White Pass; anything prolonging the drive a bit is fine.*

"Deadhorse Gulch. The route favored by the more thrifty stampeders, who did not want to pay the entrepreneurial Native packers twelve cents a pound to haul a ton of gear over the Chilkoot. But they ran into a vastly more horrific scenario here.

"Below our present location, the trail was particularly steep and narrow. The spring melt and early summer rains made it into a nearly impassable mud bowl. But the sheer greed, the driven nature of some of the packers compelled them to force their horses into grossly inhumane, physically impossible conditions. Consequently, some three thousand horses perished on this stretch of trails during the height of the Stampede. A horse would sink to its knees from the weight of the load, drop in the middle of the trail, dead from exhaustion, and those behind would shove it aside and keep going, not even pausing to put the horse out of its misery. Or, worse still—I'm not kidding—they would carry on right **over** the horse, trampling it, creating a trail through the body of the horse until there was no midsection left, only bare ground."

Kris didn't like the gory detail very much, and he tried to temper his graphic description—but to him, it was one of the more vivid slices of Gold Rush history, crucial to understanding the worst aspects of the Stampeder psyche.

Lug, lug, groan, belch. C'mon old 602. At the end of the season I'll push you off the cliffs atop White Pass, watch you meet your appropriate demise. We will write an epic, Robert Service-style poem about you. "The Cremation of 602." But not yet.

Wispy patches of fog, right at the pass, socking in the view. It could snow any month of the year atop the pass. Even though it was only about 3,200 feet elevation, it looked and felt much higher.

The big patch of snow was still there, about four feet deep, right by the pullout. A number of small divots evidenced previous samplings—but for what nefarious purpose? "Snowballs in July? Who'd-a thunk it. But here it is, just like I promised. Snowball time. But remember: he who pegs the driver gets to walk back down the pass."

Nearly all of the passengers poured out, excited, childlike. Snow Belt citizens, who only four months before were sick to death of the stuff, scooped up dirty semi-slush in their hands. With varying levels of aim and velocity, they engaged in a brief skirmish. Kris good-naturedly allowed himself to be pegged in the back. Those remaining in the bus laughed at him, and Kris responded by splattering huge slushballs against their windows. Finally the frenzy was spent, and soggy senior citizens piled back inside the bus. The trip continued, over the summit, into Canada.

Out across Torment Valley, the jagged peaks were decorated by patches and strips of snow. They looked as if they could be some kind of alphabet (ala AB Mountain), or perhaps messages to extraterrestrials. This triggered Kris' anecdotal reflex once more:

"Did you know that the Eskimos of northern Alaska, the Inupiat, have more than **thirty** different words for snow? Snow is such a major part of their lives, omnipresent for nine months out of the year, and there are a vast number of distinctions they can make as to the snow types and what they mean: the appearance, the feel, the role it plays. One word for light, dusty, freshly-fallen snow. One word for hard-packed snow, the stuff that makes for good sledding. A word for the muddy slush that is the last to disappear come Springtime. Probably nowadays, there is a Native word for dirty urban sooty snow. An interesting example of linguistic priorities at work.

"As for the Native name for the type of snow on those mountains across the valley: I believe they call that 'Apache here, Apache there'."

The serious informational anecdote, followed by the inexcusable gag: a popular tour ploy. Kris always inwardly grimaced at each telling of this world-class, death-penalty level of pun—but Indian Snow always got a laugh.

At the next picture stop, on Lake Tutshi, Kris experienced a different reaction to the joke. A fiftyish woman approached him, smiling politely but clearly with something on her mind. "I'm one quarter Native. Not Apache, but Lakota Sioux. You're a pretty good guide, better than most—but I'm tired of all the stupid Indian jokes. I hear them everywhere, from all you tour people. Why?"

There wasn't much for Kris to say: he smiled, was professionally apologetic. The woman remained polite and, after a moment, turned away.

The rest of the trip to Carcross went smoothly. They had their stew and biscuits, saw the professionally corny Gay '90s show, and nearly everyone fell asleep on the way back to Skagway. At the trip's conclusion, back on the dock, the part-Native woman gave Kris a decent tip. All in all, he made out well for his day's work.

But, at what cost? Does the "perfect tour" necessarily exude a cynicism that makes light of, or insults, all the history and traditions? Is there a way to walk a fine line between lecturing and entertainment, without slipping into superficiality or condescension? How do I communicate the essence of this place, without coming across as a soap salesman? I've got a long way to go yet.

THE ONLY NIGHT OF SUMMER

She stood on a front
porch in the yukon
wearing her faded yellow
cotton dress,
barefoot gentle breeze billowing
the skirt around her lovely legs
how much like summer
it feels for the first
time all season she said
    i said yes it does, feeling the
    heat of the red-streaked
    midnight sky

Fun Fact #17

▼

Most of the cabins along the northern Lake Bennett waterfront date from Gold Rush days. Unlike other wooden cabins along the Stampede route, the Carcross relics are very well-preserved, due to the much drier weather on the leeward side of the Coast Range—not to mention the desiccating winds coming from the nearby "desert." Of particular interest to modern-day visitors is the tiny size of the cabins: since timber was harder to come by in the semi-arid terrain, most are scarcely larger than ten by twelve feet—about the size of Dyea Gary's sauna.

Sauna, Svim (Part II)

▼

Mia descended the rope down the riverbank like Sheena, Queen Of The Jungle. Her toes curled and her nipples sprang to attention as she bravely entered the frigid glacial water. Then, as she slid into Kris' arms, the silty river loofah-brushed her bravura away.

The cycle repeated itself, many times over: "Sauna, svim, sauna, svim" (the all-purpose Finnish mantra). Finally, all the impurities were sweated out; the river had scrubbed them clean. Kris and Mia went streaking back to the tiny cabin, successfully dodging the mosquitoes but getting small twigs stuck between their toes. Once inside, the stove was lit and straight hits of Yukon Jack were procured. Warmth cascaded down from their gullets to the soles of their feet.

They found a couple of Dyea Gary's flannel shirts and toweled each other off briskly, as if they were car-wash attendants bucking for a promotion. Mia's body was a '65 Mustang: sleek, shiny, full-featured and...no spot was neglected. A labor of love, followed by buff and polish.

They found some leftover sourdough biscuits and homemade blackberry jam, greedily feeding each other about a dozen in all. "**Man** howdy, do I have an appetite," said Mia. She sat upright, partially wrapped in rip-sleeved flannel shirts, licking jam off her fingers. A glob of blackberry hung precipitously on the underside of her left breast—as if on a cliff's edge, waiting for an intrepid, search-and-rescue tongue.

Then Dyea Gary entered, glacial droplets clinging to his chest and beard, and shook himself like a bear. The rescue was delayed, for a time—but Gary, after replenishing himself with Yukon Jack, shortly produced yet more Matanuska Thunder-Fuck. A pipe was lit up, and...

Eons later, Gary sat on the woven rug, Indian-style, still wearing nothing save for some ragged boxer shorts and his red suspenders with "COLDFOOT, ALASKA" printed down them. His balls rested comfortably on the floor like two tired, old dogs.

"You should go to **town** that way, sometime," mused Kris. "Like in the middle of winter."

"I will," said Gary. "I'm not kidding, man. No one will notice. We'll go to the Red Onion—**you**, of course, will go too. But we'll have to find you some suspenders."

Mia reached over to Gary, grasped a suspender, pulled it back and gently let go. Thwapp. Then, she did it again, slightly harder. Thwapp! Under the present conditions, this was highly fascinating.

"We'd make a fine duet of vikings..." murmured Kris.

a duet of vikings
a duet of vikings sat
inside a sad cafe and
ordered thunder and water
  their blond braids swayed and
  fingers snapped as they
  dug the norse mythology w/a
  jazz beat

At one point, they found a one-pound bag of peanut M&M's lurking in one of the cupboards. They spent a lengthy time throwing the *I Ching* with M&M's, by withdrawing three candies at once from the bag. "It's all in the colors," Mia explained. They read their fortunes and devoured them, until the entire bag was gone.

"I've got to **live** this way, someday," was Kris' last coherent thought of the night, before Mia, almondine eyes glowing, showed him the spark-plugs she had pulled from the van and placed on the kitchen shelf, next to the sourdough starter. They weren't going nowhere—except up to the loft, into a warm blizzard of blankets, pillows and ripped flannel shirts.

What Happened to Randy

▼

Did You Know: that the "sister cities" of Skagway and Haines, Alaska, although less than twenty miles apart as the raven flies, are more than 300 miles distant by road? Since no bridges span the Inside Passage—or are ever likely to—one must drive north from Skagway to Whitehorse, catch the Al-Can Highway, follow that route all the way to Haines Junction, Yukon, hang a left, cross back over the Coast Range and into Alaska again before completing a journey that takes about fifteen minutes on a puddle-jumper airplane. Skagway and Haines: typical neighboring Alaskan towns.

Kris and Peter had met Randy during the first summer in Ketchikan. Several of the Seattle office's up-and-coming junior executives were making a swing through the company's Alaskan outposts, and on a city tour Randy had asked to take the helm of the old manual-transmission bus. Randy himself was a former tour guide, having taken the typical route from a Seattle-area university to a couple of years doing time behind the wheel to a place amongst the company "elite." He met all the qualifications for such an ascent: fastidious, dutiful, another whole-milk-and-apples product of the Northwest.

Randy, wearing a nice suit, tie slightly loosened, had escaped from a narrow slot in the Totem Bight parking lot, without the aid of outside helpers or power steering. "**Damn**, I'm good!" he had said, to the amusement of his fellow junior executives. He hadn't lost his touch.

Up in Skagway, Kris and Peter heard through the company grapevine that Randy had been promoted once again—but, this time back to Alaska, for the managerial slot in Haines, just a stone's throw down the Lynn Canal. One day in late July, while the Southeast Alaska State Fair was going on in Haines, Kris and Peter decided to hop over on the ferry: to drop in on Randy, check out the fair, do whatever else came to mind.

"I figure," said Kris on the way over, "that if the fair is no good, maybe we can swipe a vehicle and head up the road a ways from Haines, towards the pass into Canada. Randy should be cool about it."

As they came into the ferry port, Kris and Peter saw that the setting of Haines was very similar to that of Skagway: same spectacular peaks dropping straight down to the ocean; same narrow strip of glacial river debris providing the town's foundation. The primary difference was to be found in the architectural style: since Haines had not experienced the brunt of the Klondike Gold Rush, its buildings were functional, solid, nothing fancy. In fact, Haines, if one could possibly ignore the mountains and water, was the least "Alaskan" looking town Kris and Peter had seen.

"Main Street, USA," said Kris, not without approval.

"A plain old, non-cutesy, working town," said Peter. "I **like** it."

They followed a line of cars, motorcycles and hitchhikers to the Southeast Alaska State Fair, located a little ways from downtown. The fair was decent: a logger's skill exhibition, cotton candy and corn dogs, a minor convention of the Alaskan biker gang, 'Humpies From Hell'. Nothing they hadn't seen before. After browsing through the Haines phone book, Kris and Peter started to walk across town, hoping to find Randy at the company office.

Over by the Halsingland Hotel, home of the famous Ft. William Henry Seward Howitzer,[5] there was a long, narrow shed-like building that still had a faded-paint advertisement for a machine shop on its side. Two antique wagon wheels hung from the eaves in front, and a company sign stood half-hidden in a window.

"Pretty rustic looking," said Peter, "but this must be the place."

Kris and Peter stepped inside, wiped the mud off their feet, and looked around. Business was not booming at the Haines company office; the only sign of life emanated from a coffee machine that someone had forgotten to turn off, scorching the brew. Brochures and lapel buttons lay scattered like leaves on a nearby table, as if Autumn had arrived early.

"Hello? Anyone home?" They paused, turned and were just about to leave when some sounds of activity came from behind a door. There was some bumping and rustling, some muffled words of male and female conversation—and through the door, buttoning up a flannel shirt, emerged Randy.

Something had changed. Was it the 3-week old beard, still filling in gaps in the boyish face? Was it the bemused, almost sleepy countenance? Or was it the low, almost bashful voice:

"Kris and Peter. Hello. Welcome."

They exchanged greetings, then there was a semi-awkward pause. Randy read their expressions, waited calmly for the inevitable question:

"So, uh, how many people do you have working here in Haines? Where are they all today?"

"I'm **it**," said Randy. "I'm the manager, chief salesperson, driver/guide, mechanic, bus-washer. I'm a division of one."

---

5. Kahlua, Bailey's Irish Cream and a dash of Grand Marnier, poured in that order into a four-ounce glass- slowly, so that the ingredients form distinct layers. One then "shoots" the entire beverage at once.

"Wow. Quite a change from the Seattle rat-race, eh?"

"You'd better believe it," said Randy, brightening. "No more suit and tie, no more bosses to please. No more 'fine young man.' Oh, Seattle does keep tabs: but so long as my numbers jibe, they don't bother me. Once in a blue moon they'll send someone through here. Hasn't happened for a while. I'm not holding my breath."

Randy pointed to a kitchen table, just inside his apartment. "I run the show from right there; Haines is a table-top operation. My 'flow sheets' from Seattle are more like a trickle, really. Any local business that might pop up: they just leave a message. Meanwhile, I'm out on tour in the van, or in that manual-transmission '63 GMC bus, the one that burns two quarts of oil an hour. Or, I'm out fishing."

Randy turned and stepped back through the door. "I'd better check my messages. Come on in." Kris and Peter followed him inside to listen. There was a brief clip of background music (sounded like Steely Dan), then Randy's half-bemused voice, explaining the significance of the beep, then a gruff fisherman-sounding voice: "Well, I don't like your music, but I might have some customers for ya…"

Kris and Peter looked over the former "fine young man," who was scratching his incoming beard and smiling faintly. As Randy made some notes on a pad, the boys caught some movement behind him. The next room over, through half-drawn curtains, they accidentally-on-purpose saw someone get up out of bed and reach for what looked like a uniform, hanging from a nail on the wall. Randy caught the drift of their glances. "My girlfriend," he explained, softly. "One of the City's Finest."

Kris vaguely remembered, from the previous year, wallet photos of a pretty, Lutheran-looking girl, still finishing up college: Randy's wife. Kris thought it prudent not to ask what had transpired since then.

Randy yielded his pickup truck with no struggle, no admonitions, just a smile and a wish to have the vehicle back safely by dark. This meant that they could have the truck until approximately September.

Kris and Peter cruised back by the fair, waving to the Humpies From Hell (they waved back), then set off up the Haines Highway, the route over the mountains into the Yukon. They passed by the Chilkat River, home to the highest concentration of bald eagles to be found anywhere. In a month or so, about three thousand would be nesting within a five square mile area; they were just beginning to arrive in real numbers. "Look at them all down there," said Peter. "They just hang out on the riverbank, waiting for the spawned-out salmon to drift by. It's like Domino's to them: fast, free delivery."

"The eagles would have no problem with the Haines to Skagway commute," said Kris. "A little water, a few mountains: piece of cake. People are the only ones truly isolated in this part of Alaska."

They left the Chilkat River and drove on in silence for a time. "Man, can you believe Randy?" Peter finally said. "Isolation can do funny things to people. Skagway's got new people constantly drifting in and out of town—that much hasn't changed since the Gold Rush. You don't really feel trapped, during the Summer at least; after a time, you don't think too much about that drive to Whitehorse. But from Haines, where do you go, unless you can afford to fly to Juneau on a regular basis? It's a situation that spawns hardcore bush-bunnies: if you're too broke to do more than just get by, you're basically stuck. You start 'going native,' like Randy."

"Well, maybe isolation isn't always such a bad thing," replied Kris. "Randy probably never really wanted to be a Yuppie. Maybe he was always straining at that power tie, always reluctant to pick up that razor in the morning."

"But did he figure on being such a backslider? We're talking, from pedigree Lutheranism to Sin City."

"Probably not. Maybe he'll soon level out between the two extremes. He just needs to find something, or someone, to tune him into focus. And, I figure, whatever it takes is okay. Policewoman nookie, the sound of the ice in the river, a view from the top of the eagle's nest, a long free-fall from high altitude. And speaking of free-falls—this road doesn't have a guard-rail, if you haven't noticed. Mind the fishtailing on this gravel, OK?" Kris grabbed the "Oh, Shit" handles on the truck's interior as they brodied around a bend.

Peter slowed down as they reached the pass marking the boundary into Canada. They pulled the truck off the highway and gazed at the snow-capped peaks back towards Skagway.

"I **do** feel like I'm in Alaska again, coming here today, " admitted Peter. "All of that Disneyland tourism stuff is out of my mind. We're all alone on this road, no one around for miles and miles. Over that next mountain there, I've got a six-pack of Chinook Amber and a freezerful of salmon waiting for me. It's **home**."

"What more could you want?" said Kris.

SOAPY'S WAKE

▼

August eighth: escaped clutches of
parisian drunkards, true believers,

riverboat captains and other ordinary
skagway citizens, somebody's lost chorus-

line, shuffling with a swagger to the far end of town
jumping the railroad gate, hard-of-sight from

the imaginary sun, seeking the cemetery on a
special night: no longer do you have to wait to

know me says disembodied trickster soul of
soapy from its home on the ridge

chattering, laughing, squinting
trying to read the illiterate poetry of

the tombstones, settling instead for the
pop of the champagne cork; one by one, sometimes

two by two or *en masse*, the scandalous
death and life of soapy is celebrated by golden showers;

to the uninitiated it's just pee on a rock

Ringers

▼

It was a quiet, ship-free mid-August afternoon in Skagway. The silence of the downtown streets was broken only by occasional equine sounds: the clip-clop of the horse-drawn trolley; the gargling roar of the muffler-impaired "Old Paint," being started and giddy-upped away from the Portland House, audible from blocks away; the clang of horseshoes, being tossed by Kris and Mark in front of the Eagles Hall.

More subdued sounds, noticed only by the horseshoe contestants, emanated from within the Eagles Hall theater: a matinee "Days of '98" show, playing to a half-full house. The stage door, rather than leading to somewhere in the building, actually opened up onto the street, so Kris and Mark were privy to all the comings and goings of the actors. By this time, they were familiar enough with the show to track the plot via the dramatic exits.

After a while, they heard the sounds of the climactic scene: loud murmuring, the stomping of heavy boots, shouting, then a single, muffled gunshot. BLAM!

"Well, there goes Soapy again," said Kris.

"'**Damn** you, Frank Reid'," commented Mark.

Jim Richards, the local man who played Soapy Smith, burst through the streetside stage door, caught his breath, said hello to Kris and Mark, and even had time to pitch a horseshoe or two before returning onstage for the grand finale: the singing of the "Alaska Flag Song."

"How does he do it?" wondered Kris. "Well over a hundred shows per season, year after year."

"I don't think he ever really leaves character, all summer long," said Mark. "Whenever the tourists see him walking down Broadway, they always say, 'Hi, Soapy.' I have to catch myself from doing the same. I think he was just born to play the role: you look at old pictures of Soapy, and you would swear they were the same person."

Unlike the "Days of '98" actors, the Portland House cast members were finding it easy to break from their tourism-based characters. The trips were going well; everyone had developed tour styles which, though widely varying, all more or less worked. Kris had maintained his enthusiasm for the peculiarities of the Klondike Gold Rush, and had found a happy medium between boring his guests with historical minutiae and devolving into "Indian Snow" jokes. The days were not particularly demanding: a morning Skagway city tour/ afternoon Dyea junket, or an all-day Carcross excursion, meant an eight to ten-hour work day at the most.

With such a relaxed work environment, it was easy to let go and enjoy the many diversions Skagway had to offer. Nearly everyone in the house had hiked to Lower and Upper Dewey Lakes, the latter of which featured a weather-beaten but cozy cabin for overnight stays. Several of the boys, plus Susan, had scaled AB Mountain, in part to scrutinize Kevin's theory that the snow patterns on the peak spelled messages from extraterrestrials ("I **know** they're stopping there—and that they must be trying to say more than just 'AB'," Kevin had insisted). Fishing off the town docks was a regular activity, whether for the standard bottom fish or to intercept some of the humpies now squeezing their way into Pullen Creek. And of course, rain or shine, the Red Onion was the most frequent diversion of all.

Kris had also occasionally filled in as a ringer first baseman for a City League softball team. He discovered that Alaskans took their summer ballgames seriously, playing on no matter what the weather. "We never get rained **out**," he had been told by another muddied combatant in a game that more resembled the Battle of Hastings than a genteel summer-lemonade sport. "Just rained **on**."

Kris and Mark's present diversion came to an end when Julia, their expediter friend (and occasional "Days of '98" dancer), emerged from the Eagles Hall in full can-can regalia and came over to them. "Let me show you boys how it's done," she said, reaching for a horseshoe. Kris stood back and watched in wonder as Julia hitched up her hoop skirt, wound up and hooked two shoes in a row on the metal stake, narrowly missing a third. "Now **this** is a true Skagway woman," Kris thought to himself as she walked over to the other side, kicking off her high-heel shoes in mid-stream, threw back in Kris and Mark's direction and made another ringer.

Julia straightened from picking up the horseshoes, caught Kris' wandering eye, smiled. "You just reminded me of something, Kris. René says that someone got off the southbound bus in Whitehorse earlier this afternoon: tall, good-looking guy, seemed to be about fifty or so. He was asking about you. And the funny thing is, he looked just like **you**."

"My Dad finally made it: **hot** damn!" Kris dropped the horseshoe he had been holding, grabbed his flip-flops and hot-footed it over to the company office, to see about swiping a vehicle for picking up his Dad in Whitehorse.

The company offered a hefty tour discount for the families of Driver/Guides: free bus travel, half-off on the hotels. Kris' father Bill, upon learning of this, had set aside two weeks for riding the entire bus route: from Anchorage up to Fairbanks, then all the way around to Skagway. Kris obtained permission from Norm to "personalize" the final leg of the tour from Whitehorse and, once he had ascertained his Dad's location, set off in a company van for the big city.

A couple hours later, Kris pulled up to the Fourth Avenue Residence, a tall cinder-block barrack where the long-haul drivers stayed while passing through Whitehorse. He called at the drivers' apartment, the door opened, and he was embraced by an older, nearly as tall, equally joyous version of himself.

"Look at you," said Bill Westerberg, finally holding Kris at arm's length. "Alaska's been good to you."

They loaded Bill's luggage into the van and, after loading up on High-Test (by special Portland House request), sped off back to Skagway. "This is definitely luxury travel, after what I've ridden through," said Bill. "Nothing wrong with the buses—a couple of them were pretty fancy, actually—but the roads are rough up North: all that permafrost damage. An 1,100-mile bus ride is tough going, no matter where you are…but do you know what? I wouldn't trade the experience for anything."

Kris was very curious about his Dad's adventures, and Bill filled him in on the highlights: Talkeetna, Denali National Park, the deep Alaskan interior, the St. Elias Mountains, various colorful watering-holes in between. "You've **got** to see it, Kris."

"Don't worry: I'm planning on it."

Kris had to work the next day: the standard AM city tour/PM Dyea. His Dad, figuring that he could pretty much do Skagway on foot—and needing a break from the buses—decided to roam the town with his camera for the morning. He made plans to link up with Kris for the trip out to Dyea Gary's place.

Bill photographed the sole cruise ship in port, looming huge against the buses and longshoremen on the dock, but looking tiny against the logo-painted cliffs. He photographed the driftwood-encrusted Arctic Brotherhood Hall, with its namesake, alien-alphabet mountain in the background. He got a big smile from Vicki the waitress as he photographed her coming off her early shift at the Bigger Hammer Café. Around eleven, he was drawn into the vortex of the Red Onion, and had the bartender pose in front of a risqué portrait of "Dirty-Neck Maxine," one of the more colorful Gold Rush "variety actresses."

Just before leaving with Kris for Dyea, Bill took a photo of the "unfinished" side of the Portland House: the side where one could readily observe the temporal phases of spontaneous construction. Kris posed by the clothesline, holding up a freshly washed bit of cotton-polyester Tour Guide gear. "I have to take this picture," said Bill, so amused he could barely hold the camera still, "so your mother will **believe** me when I tell her where you're living."

On the cruise ship dock, Bill took his place among the other tour passengers, anonymous until Kris made an announcement over the bus P.A. system. "This afternoon's trip is special, folks, because my **Dad** is here. He came here to check up on me: he didn't believe that I was actually being **paid** to come to Alaska and do this for a living. Rumor has it that he's after my job, even."

Thus unveiled, Bill was instantly the hit of the back of the bus. Some of the elderly women were compelled to ask him whether his son was really such a "fine young man" as he appeared to be. Bill obliged them: "Yep, I'm afraid it's all true." The ladies pressed him for more dirt, but he tactfully declined.

At a scenic overlook, Kris and his dad posed together for a photo: Kris in his obligatory white tour-guide shirt and tie, Bill in his favorite old red buffalo-plaid flannel—a shirt older than Kris. "You're right about me being after your job," Bill told Kris. "Your Uncle Stan and I were talking about this, just before I came up: how much we would like to kidnap you and make you trade careers with us. At least when you're wearing a tie, you're out **here**."

At length they pulled off the Dyea road, onto the familiar track to Gary's place. "Here is my future homestead," said Kris to his passengers. "I just need to do something about this crazy sourdough who's been squatting on the land. Oh, look: there he is."

Gary emerged from the underbrush, stepped into the bus stairwell and warmly welcomed his guests. As they disembarked, making their way towards the creekside gold pans, Bill was more formally introduced to Kris' bushy friend. "Damn, if you two aren't dead ringers for each other," said Gary. "But what I want to know, Mr. Westerberg, is whether you're as much of a **sauna** maniac as your son is."

Bill had heard only an abbreviated, somewhat edited version of the chief attractions at Gary's place. However, he gained a fuller appreciation as he strolled the homestead, checked out the sauna and its environs, tried a gold pan or two and helped Kris mix up some hooch by the campfire. Towards the end of the visit, he and Gary got to talking, and found that they had a fair amount in common: the fact that Alaska had been the fiftieth state seen by both ("Saving the best for last," Gary asserted); a deep love for the woods and the water; a vicarious interest in the doings between Kris and a certain woman of Finnish descent.

"Looks like old Kris will be bringing home an interesting guest to the Thanksgiving dinner table," winked Gary.

"If she's anything like you say she is," said Bill, "she's more than welcome."

Once the local touring was done, fishing rose to the top of the agenda. Because it was a special occasion—and because there were no tall, skinny baggage-boys to bribe with Snickers bars for boat usage—Kris and his dad decided to spring for a charter. The morning after Dyea, they caught the puddle-jumper over to Haines, found their captain on the docks, and ventured out into the deep halibut-holes of the Lynn Canal. The captain steered them to a spot off a broad, stony delta, where a river rushed directly from a hanging glacier's base to the sea.

"There's **nowhere** like this in Washington—or anywhere else in the lower 48," marveled Bill. "Yet, this is just one of about a dozen such places I've seen along the way."

"Probably a hundred like it on this coast," replied the captain, handing them some heavily-chummed bottom fishing gear.

The action was slow at the outset, with only a few love-taps from pesky rock cod disturbing their morning reverie. As the sun slowly shifted in position, it found new glaciers and snowfields to shine on, dappling the calm water, the gently-rocking boat and its nearly-snoozing occupants.

"Dang, this coffee isn't working too well on my **head**," commented Kris, "but it's working on other parts just **fine**." He rose from a deck chair, stretched and sauntered to the back of the boat. As he was peacefully hanging it off the stern, he suddenly heard a WHIRRR!!

"**SHIT!**" Kris arrested himself in mid-stream, abandoning any pretense of zipping up as he dashed back to his secured fishing pole, which was paying out line at an alarming rate.

Kris released the drag, began trying to reel in, and quickly found that this was nearly impossible. "Let it play," advised the captain. "Set the drag again, and let the fish wear itself out for a while."

For about fifteen minutes, the fish yo-yoed between the surface and the bottom, flashing its large tail above the water before plunging for the deep. When the pressure on his line began to feel more like a load of bricks than a piscine acrobat, Kris released the drag and began to crank in his rig.

Hovering above the gunwales, gaff in hand, the captain looked exactly like his professional counterparts, Ahab and/or Hook. When the exhausted barn-door finally broke the surface, the captain swung the gaff, catching the fish right behind the eyes and swinging it on board. Kris let out a whoop of exultation. His Dad stared, wide-eyed and impressed. The captain was nonchalant but respectful: "Looks just like a halibut—sure fought like one—but that's about the biggest **flounder** I've seen caught in these waters in some years."

About forty pounds of dinner wriggled on the deck, then lay still after a time. A signal seemed to have been sent to the other bottom-feeders, as for the next half-hour or so, about every other cast resulted in a fish: mostly pan-sized, ten-to-twenty pound halibut that the captain called "chicken of the sea: the best eating fish around."

Finally, Kris and Bill were content to put their poles aside and relax on the sunny deck. Kris grinned at his Dad: "Will we be the heroes of the Portland House, or what?"

"Will I ever be the hero back home," replied Bill. "I did what you said, and packed an empty cooler along. It will go back **full**." He paused, looking thoughtful. "And by the way—when that flounder first hit, and you came dashing back to your pole, trying to stuff yourself back together: that was about the funniest damn thing I've ever seen; I almost peed **myself** laughing. Now, there's a fishing story for the ages." Kris laughed along with his father, knowing well that he hadn't heard the last of that particular incident.

The captain turned the boat back towards Haines, smiling to himself in the cockpit: another perfect father-and-son bonding day.

Sometime the next afternoon, Peter came calling at Kris' chambers. "Where's your Dad?" he asked. "I haven't seen him all day."

"He's on his own today," said Kris. "He asked to borrow my fly-fishing gear this morning, and I pointed him towards the mouth of Pullen Creek. The humpies are **thick** in there right now."

"What's the matter: didn't you catch enough fish yesterday?"

"Strictly catch-and-release today. And besides, those salmon aren't much good to eat: remember those spawners you caught in Ketchikan last year? Dad's having a blast: who am I to stop him?"

Indeed, Bill spent the greater part of the day on the banks of the creek, tossing out barbless wet-flies and hooking into fish about four times the size the trout rig was designed to handle: tussling with them a while, losing most but landing a few. Those he landed, he gently unhooked, revived in the creek, and sent on their way. He was having the time of his life.

That evening, the final evening of his visit to Skagway, Bill picked up a case of Henry Weinhard's beer to go along with the freshly-caught halibut and flounder, and together he and Kris hosted an impromptu dinner for several of the Portland House gang. Bill and Karl entertained each other by comparing first-hand notes on American versus Australian-rules football, while Kris baked cornbread, then broiled the fish with butter, lemon, basil and fresh vegetables. Bill, Karl, Derek, Llary and Peter saluted Kris as he entered the dining room with a heaping platter of food.

"Where did you learn to cook like this?" asked Bill. "Certainly not from **me**."

*But I **did**: I practically grew up on fish that we caught together, and you cooked.* "It's hard to go wrong, with ingredients like this," said Kris.

Throughout the meal, and the conversation that followed, a smile tinged variously with pride, amusement and pleasure never left the face of Kris' dad. At times he would steal a glance at Kris, then look away, shaking his head. "If I were your age again," he finally said, "I'd get my ass up to Alaska, and **stay** there. I can't think of a better place to start out in life. You've got **everything** here."

ICE CREAM CONVERSATION: 8/20/87

▼

The old wooden bench on the sidewalk outside the Big Dipper ice cream shop was the best place to hang out in Skagway on a sunny day—especially if one had a honking double-dip cone in hand. "Sometimes," said Kris, slurping his Rocky Road and gazing up at the glacier hanging off Mt. Harding, "as much as I love Skagway, I wish I could trade places with you long-haul drivers. You have something different every day, tour-wise: no back-to-back city tours. You get to keep your groups for three days at a time, as opposed to our hello-and-goodbye encounters. Plus, from everything I've heard, your gratuities are pretty spectacular." Having reached base level of the ice cream, Kris began to munch, horse-like, on his sugar cone.

Kris was talking to Kenny and Don, two Fairbanks-based guides who were doing the famous Skagway Turnaround: start the day in Whitehorse, drop passengers off at the cruise ships, hang around town for a couple hours, pick up a fresh group and head back to the Yukon. "What you've said is true," said Don, moustache dripping with molten Butter Brickle. "But, from our long-haul perspective, what you've got here in Skagway looks very appealing. You get to stay put and meet people: the locals, your fellow drivers. You get to explore a place: we've barely seen any of the area around Fairbanks. When we're actually home, we do things like catch up on laundry and sleep. In general, you have much more time for 'real life' activities than we do."

"For example," said Kenny, "we would never get to hike the Chilkoot Trail, like you and Peter will be doing. I can't think of anybody in our division who has had three days off in a row this summer."

"Good point," said Kris. "I have no complaints at all about spending the summer here. But I'm ready to be a long-haul driver next year."

"Another thing about the highway is that you get to deal with Klaus on a regular basis," said Kenny. "Chief mechanic, safety manager, royal pain in the butt. He's been known to trail buses down the highway, in his white station-wagon, just to make sure everything is ship-shape. He won't hesitate to pull you off the highway in case things aren't exactly kosher. And, according to him, all of you down here aren't 'real' drivers: you're just a bunch of 'kids on a joyride'. His words, not mine," he quickly added.

"Speaking of safety," said Don, "I heard that Peter just lost his Safety Bonus, in kind of an odd way."

"It only happened two days ago," said Kris. "I guess the company gossip flies pretty fast. Yeah, he lost it, but it wasn't really his fault: it was just a strange set of circumstances. He was wrapping up a city tour, and a couple of his passengers asked to be let off right downtown, in front of an art gallery they wanted to visit. Pete, nice guy that he is, said no problem, and pulled up in front of the gallery. What he failed to realize, never having parked there before, was that the wooden store awning actually extended a bit over the street, no more than six inches. This, of course, was out of conformity with the rest of the downtown buildings—but what conforms to anything in Skagway, anyhow?

"So, as he swung in to get close to the curb, the top front corner of his bus hit the awning. He was only going about one mile per hour, but the force of the collision was enough to slightly jar the building—which was just enough to topple over an old brick chimney. I mean, there was probably no mortar left to hold those bricks together, so any mild tremor would have done the same thing. But the damage was done: the gallery owner came storming out and chewed Pete's ass; Pete felt like chewing his ass right back, for having such a cockeyed awning, but kept his mouth shut. Norm defused the situation by offering to pay for the chimney damage: maybe one hundred bucks, tops. But when company management caught wind of the incident, they yanked Peter's bonus. I don't think it's fair, but what can you do?"

The highway drivers shook their heads in sympathy. "Usually," said Kenny, "when one of us loses our Safety Bonus, it's for something a bit more spectacular, like smacking a moose or sliding off the road in an unpaved area. We get more 'bang' for our bonus dollars, I guess."

THE CONTINUING ADVENTURES
OF SKOOKUM JIM

▼

"I was almost there, at the top of the Stairs,
screamin' in the rain…"

—Neil Young

One morning towards the end of August, an old Ford Courier pickup truck pulled off the Dyea road, just short of the Taiya River bridge. Kris and Peter jumped out from the truck bed, grabbed fully-laden backpacks, and waved goodbye to Mark, the driver: "See you in three days." The truck sped off; road dust hung in the quiet air, the old log bridge blinked in the feline sunshine. Just above the whittled wood sign-post, the Chilkoot trailhead disappeared into shadowed ferns and alder, like a tunnel into a monastery. The time had finally come.

Norm, true to his word, had given Kris and Peter enough consecutive days off from work to hike the Chilkoot. Their trip would be much faster and lighter, of course, than the historic journey; there were no more Canadian Mounties at the summit, enforcing the 2,000 pounds of gear requirement. All told, they had to cover thirty-nine miles: two days over to Lake Lindeman, then a hike out along the old WP & YR railroad tracks to meet up with the White Pass highway. The morning was beautiful; the packs felt light.

"Let's **hit** it."

The trail pitched sharply upward at the get-go, over a surprisingly steep hump. The boys grumbled slightly—wasn't the hard stuff supposed to wait for the next morning?—but it was over within a quarter mile. Past the hump, the Chilkoot Trail became a stroll down a muddy country road. Grass and fireweed grew tall between the wagon ruts, still fairly deep after ninety years. Cottonwoods and birch whispered about the newcomers.

"God, this is pleasant," commented Peter. "I know what it'll get like later, but still…I can see how people were lulled into complacency. 'This ain't so bad,' they'd be saying to each other."

"True," said Kris. "But then, you've got to remember the hell-of tough time they had getting to this point. I figure the typical story ran something like this:

"Okay. You've just come ashore at Dyea—or, to put it more realistically, you've run aground on the mudflats out there. After a couple weeks on some utterly unseaworthy craft, you're eager as hell to touch dry land, kiss a hummock of grass, hug a tree—but one look at the muck under the bow, and you know it ain't gonna happen so easy. So you drop anchor—it disappears in the goo—and you wait for the tide to come up again.

"The horses on board are real nervous. Having considerably more common sense than the prospectors, they knew from moment one that they would have to swim for it. When the moment comes, they still balk as they are eased up to the gunwales, but over they go. Survival instincts kick in, and they make it to shore.

"Now, for all your stuff—you know, the 2,000 pounds worth. When you were packing it, you didn't figure it would have to swim, too. 'This is really stupid,' you think as they throw all your crap into the murky tidal effluent. Of course, half of it sinks, is swept away by the current, or just gets ruined. So finally you're sitting there on the shore, in your wet wool trousers and slimy boots, about ready to cry. Welcome to Dyea. The horse is still pissed-off about having to swim, and offers no commiseration.

"But then you hit the trail, get over that hump, and make it to this part here. Everything's OK again: you've dried out, you're trucking up the trail, thinking that the trek to the Klondike can't be too tough after what you've already been through. And then you spot...a riverside sauna and rope-swing?"

Indeed, the trail swung right past Gary's place, on the opposite bank of the river. No nekkid folks came dashing out to dip in the river, unfortunately—but there was the faint sound of chopping wood: the sound of good things to come.

Peter shook his head. "Those with any sense should have hung it up right about here, I think. Why not just pitch your tent along the trail, set up your cookstove, slap some rough planks together and call it a hotel, offer saunas and foot-massages?"

"Ah—but that's not why most of those people came here," Kris replied. "Most folks still could have made a decent buck back home, if that's all they were interested in: why drag your butt up here just to do that? But on the other hand, making it this far may have been adventure enough for many of them. I'm sure those who hung out in the camps ended up doing better, for the most part, than the prospectors.

"All kinds of entrepreneurs plied their trade on the trail. Even the local Chilkat Indians took crash courses in capitalism. They would hire themselves out to hump your gear over the Stairs, at around six cents per pound—a rather modest fee, actually. But what the greenhorns who hired them didn't know was that there was a kind of 'graduated' fee schedule: in other words, the further along you got, the higher the price. When they reached the Stairs, the Chilkat packers would throw down their loads and refuse to go any further unless the price was doubled."

"That sure would suck, wouldn't it?"

"Yeah, it would. But one of the sole, honorable exceptions to such trade practices was our friend Skookum Jim. What a career that guy had:

probable discoverer of the first major Klondike gold, all claims by George Carmacks notwithstanding; legendary Golden Stairs packer; founding citizen of the great burg of Carcross. I guess he was kind of your 'Renaissance Native'."

The pleasant country road gradually devolved into an odd trail—odd in that there was not just one way to go, but several: one for the straight-and-narrow; one for dogs to run off, sniffing for Gold Rush boojums; one each for almost any hiking preference. Kris was reminded of a braided river channel. Numerous, tiny log bridges crossed glacial rivulets, upper tributaries of the Taiya. Then, the valley widened, the river flattened, and the boys were on the Main Street of a ghost-town.

"Ah, Canyon City. Time for a scenic detour." They crashed off the trail, into a dense stand of deciduous forest and the first vivid slice of Chilkoot history.

"Canyon City," recited Kris: "population 5,000 or so, founded 1897, deceased about eighteen months later. 'Will the last one to leave for the Klondike please turn out the lights?' they must have said."

"But they didn't exactly pack up and go," said Peter, "they cleared out in a hurry—leaving quite a mess here, apparently. According to the guide book, a good deal of heavy-duty junk is lying here in the woods. And there's some right now."

The forest growth could not completely conceal the giant hulks lurking in the Canyon City grove: stoves, tram-cable spools (the kind Paul Bunyan's mother kept in her sewing-kit), steam engine boilers, and other items, losing the long battle with moss, rust and history.

Kris poked an oven door open with a stick: Sam McGee was long since thawed-out and gone. "All the guide books keep calling this 'The World's Longest Museum.' I think it's more like 'The World's Longest Striptease.' Here they came up the trail, loaded down all the crap sold to them by Seattle hucksters. About this point, reality would set in: mainly, the fact that your horses and wagons were no good once you reached the base of the Golden Stairs—and, presuming that you could haul maybe fifty pounds (of the two thousand) at a time, you'd need to make forty-plus trips up."

"Unless you were Skookum Jim, of course."

"Yeah, yeah. So maybe that cast-iron, 4-burner cookstove wasn't such a necessity. Maybe the 100 collapsible wood-and-canvas boats you planned to sell at Lake Bennett could be whittled down by 99 or so. Anything to get you on your way without breaking your back. Everything else was ditched here in the woods, left for anyone fool enough to try hefting it over the Stairs."

A few minutes was enough. "Spooky. Let's get going again."

By the time they were nearing Camp Pleasant, the boys were encountering a fair amount of fellow hikers. They were mostly overtaking them, with their long-legged gaits, rather than passing by in the opposite direction: not many hikers reversed history by coming down the Stairs from the Canadian side. As they strolled through the camp, Kris and Peter saw that most of the day's travelers were hanging it up at the ten-mile mark: bright nylon tents and cooking fires ringed the log cabin shelter.

"Seems pretty crowded to me," said Peter. "Let's mush on."

"Yeah, feels kinda like a city, after all the solitude. But just imagine what all the camps felt like during the Stampede. For all the ruggedness, the Chilkoot was hardly a backwoods getaway." And on they went.

The trail turned upwards a notch just out of Camp Pleasant. The remaining three miles to Sheep Camp were hiked mostly in silence. Kris focused on the tiring but steady footsteps of his friend, the rocks on the trail, the thinning trees, and let his mind wander.

every step we take brings us closer to
home: whether the night's camp, trail's end,
summer's conclusion or the next adventure

every step the stampeders took

brought them into unknown: a trackless gray ocean, a
vast snowfield unmarked by footfall
    there has always been a narrow path here: a few
    friendly stonecairns guiding the chilkat, the inland tutchone,
    other seekers;
    the raven always circled high overhead
    but then the flood, the gold rush: and the narrow path filled to
    overflowing, like a high fast muddy torrent

enough lives passed this way to stoke the mind of
a dozen chaucers, to burn down the canterbury cathedral
their footsteps still clatter in the glacial scree,
their voices are cacaphonous, echoing in the night:
northwest, southwest, farmer, millworker; chicago new york boston and
all points foreign; human and animal

the strangest passage: the circumstances that
sent a phalanx of reindeer, complete with
lapp herdsmen, up the trail: help the hungry citizens of
dawson said the peoples' friend, the u.s. congress
after two years of pointing and staring, of drowning, starvation
wolves and insanity, ten percent of the original herd remained
to arrive grandly in downtown dawson, long after the famine and
the gold rush had ended

    observers of the scene: earnest college-kids, seeking
    adventure, hiring out as packers for tuition money,
    students in a human-nature class
    unavailable back home, the teacher alternately
    patient and cruel;
    viewed with clear eyes

    contrast: the clouded eyes of delusion, not only
    those who stood to profit but those who should have

known better; senile old joaquin miller, the 'bard
of the high sierra,' waxing rhapsodic on spired peaks
and woodland glades; true enough in the best of times but
deadly-false as the first high snowfalls snared those fallen
prey to his words

and for every tortured step, a step taken in grace
more unlikely trekkers, the
so-called 'variety actresses': later immortalized in
lurid behind-the-bar rubensesque detail but then known by
more earthy sobriquets like 'dirty-neck maxine'
why not wrap like ivy around the spires of the stampede,
why not flee from sordid surroundings, to walk 500 miles
under the saloon of the sky, opening your eyes to more than
the cracks in the ceiling

why not join the ordinary people: the
diggers of earth, the snake-oil salesmen
the ones who form the unsung heart-and-soul of any
grand-scale adventure
nothing left behind to lose, an eventual return empty-handed
but for the stories they all could keep:
the stories that made each person unique

then as now,
what we want, above the gold, is
to be free

Sheep Camp turned out to be completely empty. Kris and Peter had
planned to camp out, but since nobody was using the shelter cabin, they
decided to save themselves some hassle and crash inside. They threw down
their packs, cooked supper, sipped some hot cocoa and brought their thir-
teen-mile hiking day to a close.

The next morning dawned cool and drizzly. Kris and Peter rose with the early light, assembled a perfunctory breakfast and, eager for the trail, set off. Only a hundred yards away from the Sheep Camp cabin, the Chilkoot abandoned all pretense of being a trail: a crooked arm of glacial scree pointed sharply upward. Over the first thirteen miles they had gained about 1,000 feet in elevation: they would scale the remaining 2,700 feet in the next three miles.

Around the first bend, at the top of the sky, stood the Golden Stairs, vivid and cruel in the gathering clouds.

"Well, there it is. Up we go."

Trail-marking runes, made of several flat stones piled atop one another, provided the only guidance up the scree. The boulders were as tall as their waists, then their shoulders, then became mini-mountains as they would scramble up to spot the next rune.

More antique trail debris now appeared along the way. It was considerably more desperate-looking than the mossy behemoths of Canyon City: a shattered cable, a heap of iron barrel hoops, the legendary abandoned footwear scattered in the rocks.

"This must the Scales: the place they weighed your gear for the 1898 bucket tram," said Kris. "They weren't kidding about the boots."

"There's no kidding about this place at all. Here you would likely do anything to make that 39th trip up the Stairs lighter. But shedding your boots? What did they do, hike up barefoot?"

"Nah, not likely. I think they just wore out a lot of pairs from all the repeated climbing. You'll notice that most of these boots are kind of cheap and crappy: good for maybe a dozen trips up. Remember, L.L. Bean and REI weren't even a glimmer in anyone's eye in 1898."

"Too bad that most of the serious Stampeders never got to use the tram. That's the way it was with the later 'conveniences,' like this and the White Pass railroad: they were a couple of years too late for the brunt of the Gold Rush. I guess they figured the bonanza would last forever."

As if on cue, the wind and rain picked up as they started their final ascent up the Golden Stairs. The summit disappeared behind the storm, and there were no more stone cairns; Kris and Peter, figuring that Up was the correct way to go, pushed blindly ahead. It was now too steep to stand upright, so they scrambled on hands and knees, clinging to the face of the slope.

"Man," exclaimed Peter, "this is tough enough with our good gear and wimpy thirty-pound backpacks. How would you like to try this with bare ropes digging into your shoulders, about double the weight, and those flimsy boots?"

"It would be grim as hell," replied Kris, with panting breath. "And you couldn't even stop. If you paused to catch your breath, the guy behind you would run into your ass, probably scream at you. If you were to step out of the way, you'd lose your place in line. They wouldn't even let you back in."

Both Kris and Peter thought about that famous winter picture of the Golden Stairs: the one with a continuous, thin black line, like a line of ants, marching up a massive field of white. The determination, and desperation, of the Stampeders was brought home in a way that it never had before.

The crawl seemed to take forever: three-quarters of a mile was a long ways, straight up. They paused for rest several times, were not booted off to the side. At last, some type of edge became apparent through the tempest. They pulled themselves up to it, looked ahead and saw a narrow, rocky gap through which clouds and water streaked. A few feet to the left, a weather-beaten stone monument told them that they had made it.

Kris and Peter, out of breath, threw down their backpacks, then thought better of it as the wind began to scoot the packs along the ledge. They stood on the summit, facing back down the Stairs, heads to the wind as their ponchos flapped madly behind. Rain and sleet plastered their faces. "Get that camera out," shouted Peter, "so someone will **believe** this."

They took Famous Explorer pictures of each other. "As Skookum As They Wanna Be!" yelled Kris, for future photo captions and posterity.

They crossed the narrow lip of the pass, re-kiltered their windblown packs, wiped the mud and slush off their faces. Patches of snow still lay about everywhere. They would not have been surprised to find the glaciated remains of a prospector's cache (or a prospector) wedged in a crevasse. Shaking their heads, and silently saluting the Customs agents who had had to stay there year-round, they came into the Canadian side of the Chilkoot. The terrain flattened out before them: the mountain saddle in which they stood broadened into alpine tundra, the start of a gradual ten-mile descent to Lake Lindeman.

Just ahead, above an ice-rimmed Crater Lake, stood the Stone House, a shelter built from the remains of a tramway anchor. As Kris and Peter approached, they saw someone standing before the shelter: none other than Frank the ranger, a Skagway local they had met at the Gold Rush museum. "Congrats, guys," said Frank, grinning. "You're the first hikers I've seen today. But when you were fooling around there with your cameras, I thought you were gonna do a Flying Nun in your ponchos, back down the Golden Stairs."

Inside the Stone House, Frank had set up a small backpacking stove, and had some hot water perking away. Kris and Peter paused for some much-appreciated hot tea, thawing out while shooting the breeze with Frank about the perils and rewards of Chilkoot rangering.

"Things look fairly quiet on the trail: more so than I expected," commented Kris. "We saw a fair amount of people back at Camp Pleasant, but no one at Sheep Camp. I would imagine your hands are full during the peak of the hiking season."

"That's more true than you could imagine," said Frank. "You saw how tough the Golden Stairs are—and you two are young, in good shape. We get some people out here who are totally unprepared: they start off on some nice sunny day, and don't figure that they need to bring much in the way of foul-weather gear. You know: 'Hypothermia in July? Hah!' But I've seen it more than once.

"During peak times, we'll place rangers every few miles along the trail, to keep tabs on folks, make sure they're OK. At the end of a day we'll sweep the trail, make sure there are no stragglers. This, of course, means that we get to hike the whole Chilkoot a dozen or so times every summer. Gets us in shape pretty fast."

"Seems like a good gig for you," said Peter. "It's got to beat being stuck indoors, showing Gold Rush movies to tourists."

"Without a doubt," said Frank. "We have to sign up for active trail duty in our Park Service office, so everybody gets a shot at it. If I had my 'druthers, I'd be up here all summer long."

As they left the Stone House, Kris and Peter were asked to keep their eyes open for an older English couple who were very slowly making their way down the trail. They said no problem, and set off into the tundra.

The terrain around the rims of Crater, Blue and Long Lakes was very similar to that of Torment Valley: rough boulders and glacial scree; lichens and gnarled shrubs; tiny, crystal pothole tarns, small enough to serve as personal mirrors. As they descended slightly in elevation, the clouds and mist remained above, forming a very low ceiling: socking in the view of the nearby mountains and giving the false impression that they were heading through flat country. Various Gold Rush relics were still visible along the route: wagon remains, a boat shell crushed by the weight of the snows. The surreal weather conditions, plus the fact that they were so alone, made it very easy for their minds to drift: Kris and Peter felt variously as if they were exploring not only the Klondike, but also the North Slope of the Brooks Range, Siberia, even Antarctica.

A series of sharp switchbacks brought them back down into the trees, and finally to the shore of Deep Lake, a gorgeous, dark blue knife-slit in the rocky terrain. They crossed a footbridge and came upon a small campsite, perched on a promontory into the water. Kris and Peter were very footsore, after having walked across so much stone, so they decided to pause for a foot-soaking rest break. Kris had put on some extra layers back at the Stone House, when he had been chilled, and now was warmed up enough to consider a full-body dip in the lake. The first dunk of his bare foot into the frigid waters quickly changed his mind.

"It's sure tempting just to **stay** here," mused Peter, sitting against a tree trunk, nibbling on some trail mix. "A pristine lake. Nobody else around. Plenty of provisions. To hell with the gold."

Shortly after they left Deep Lake, summer returned in full force. The sun was warming, then hot; mud and bare rocks gave way to standard Western trail dust; sleet-drenched shirts became sweaty. Kris and Peter, shedding nearly all their layers, legged their way down a long creek canyon, picking up the pace due more to gravity than willing acceleration. After the twenty-mile mark, they were more pack-mule than prospector, thoughts meandering towards food, campfire and rest.

Then a sliver of blue became apparent through the thinning pines. Kris and Peter found themselves atop a bluff, looking down at Lake Lindeman and, further to the north, Lake Bennett. In the distance, they thought they saw the ghosts of the great flotilla of May 1898: 7,124 homemade boats, sailing for Carcross and the Yukon River headwaters on the far shore.

FISHSTORM

▼

Did You Know: that putting together an improvised sawmill, for making planks used in boat construction, was the first task for most of the Stampeders arriving on the shores of lakes Lindeman and Bennett during the winter of 1897-98. The most common set-up was the "Armstrong Mill": scaffolding was built across four poles or tree trunks, cut off just above head level; whole logs were laid lengthwise across the scaffold; a two-man whipsaw was used to saw planks from the logs, with one man stationed above and one below.

Unfortunately, since the whipsaw could only cut on the downward stroke, the person stationed below wound up with a faceful of sawdust at every stroke. Disagreements about turns on the lower end of the Armstrong Mill thus became the leading reason for ruined partnerships on the trail. Under the overall stress of the circumstances, those who felt that they had been on the bottom too long became bitter, frustrated to tears, vengeful, even violent. In one particularly acrimonious Chilkoot split, the partners cut all their supplies in half, rather than sensibly dividing them: shovels, sacks of flour, even a boat were sawed in two before the men went on their separate ways.

Kris and Peter were too hot and tired to be particularly communicative when they finally arrived at Lake Lindeman. They scanned the lakeshore for a suitable campsite, and found two that looked good: Kris preferred one on the high part of a sandy beach, while Peter thought that a higher site in a grove of lodgepole pine would suit them better. Kris, wishing to defuse any disagreement, proposed a compromise: Peter could set up the tent at his preferred spot in the pines, and Kris would be responsible for dinner. "Not only cooking, but **catching** it. I can see the fish jumping in the lake from here." Peter nodded his approval, threw down his pack and began pulling out tent stakes, while Kris retrieved his collapsible pole and Mepps spoons and went down to the shore.

The tent set-up only took a few minutes, and Peter wandered off the explore the surroundings while Kris made long, arcing casts into the lake. About an hour later, Pete returned to camp, very hungry.

"I'm starving. What's for dinner?"

"Well…" Kris had a bit of a hang-dog look about him. "I was sure I'd be catching a mess of trout here—and, mighty fish-slayer that I am, I got skunked, of course. Kind of ironic, considering what we have in the freezer back home. So, I'm afraid the victuals are a bit low."

"You don't mean…"

"Yep: mac 'n cheese. Again."

"Tell me that you at least sprung for Kraft dinner."

"Sorry, they were fresh out, all over Skagpatch. Besides, I **like** the cheap stuff. Some people have their Spam; this is **my** soul-food. I got two boxes, one for each of us. Dig in, partner."

Unfortunately, Kris had neglected to remember that higher elevations make water boil at a cooler temperature—which tended to turn pasta into library paste. The resulting yellow, cheese-flavored glop quivered and gurgled as Kris scooped up a Sierra-cup full and gamely had at it. Peter poked at his portion with a fork, checking it for signs of intelligence. There were none.

Their camp neighbors, the older English couple that Frank the ranger had told them about, had been observing the scene with some amusement. And, with one timely action, they rescued Kris and Peter's Chilkoot partnership: "Do you boys have enough to eat? Come over and join us; there's plenty for all."

The boys were introduced to Mr. and Mrs. Simmons, of rural Somerset: two long-time teachers who had adopted anything but a sedentary lifestyle in their retirement. Mrs. Simmons had stirred up a delicious beef stew, complete with dumplings, and the boys gratefully dug in as the dinner party got to know one another. Kris and Peter, after going into some depth on their various Tour Guide adventures, inquired as to what had brought the Simmonses into such seemingly unlikely circumstances.

"Well, it's quite simple, actually," said Mr. Simmons. "Every year, right about this time, we get tired of knocking about the house. We fetch our rucksacks, and our tea-kettle, and off we go."

The Simmonses were holding hands, utterly comfortable with their rustic surroundings, and one another. It looked a lot like love, in Kris' estimation.

"It sounds like quite a lifestyle," said Kris. "I bet you've had all kinds of adventures. But tell me—have you ever been on a trip like this? Have you ever had a hiking or camping experience as wonderful and strange as this one?"

"Wonderful and strange...hmmm." Mr. Simmons thoughtfully puffed his pipe. "Well, I suppose the famous Fishstorm would have to qualify."

"Oh, do tell them!" Mrs. Simmons clapped her hands in delight.

Mr. Simmons leaned back against a log, harrumphed appropriately. "Well, it was like this:

"Several years back, we were off in the Wallowa Mountains, in eastern Oregon. A place where the Swiss Alps suddenly rise out of Hell's Canyon: utterly remote, pristine and unpopulated. Well, we hiked back to this splendid, crystalline lake, at about 7,000 feet elevation.

"We had thought that we would be all alone, but of course this was not the case: across the way was a fairly large group of young people, a dozen or so. And, they did not seem your run-of-the-mill weekend hikers, more like a colony of mountain men (and women): long hair, buckskin, tepees rather than tents. Sort of that Daniel Boone/ American Gothic thing. They'd been there a while, and looked to be staying until the millennium.

"Anyway, we were all compatible enough: the sun went down, we boiled our stew and sipped our tea, they built a bonfire and danced around it. That was that.

"But the following morning, something else was in the air: the dawn was dark and portentous. The sky seemed vastly unsettled: great billowing clouds moving about. Black curtains of rainshower skirted the nearby peaks, the high winds driving them into nearly horizontal streaks.

"Then, all became eerily still. We anxiously watched the sky. Our pioneer neighbors had halted their breakfast ritual and were gazing upward, almost expectantly. And then it happened:

"At first one, then several scattered droplets fell, spotting the still lakewater, pinging the tent. But then, as the precipitation increased, we noticed that it wasn't water that was falling: it was **fish**. Tiny trout fingerlings, by the score, then by the hundreds, rained down from the sky. The lucky ones landed in the water, were momentarily stunned, then swam off; the others splattered the shoreline, not quite so fortunate or three-dimensional.

"The fishstorm lasted about a minute. Our friends across the lake were as stunned as the fingerlings, at first. Then they fell to their knees, raised their arms to the sky, began to rejoice in loud, musical voices: 'It's a miracle from God!', 'Manna from heaven!', 'Jehovah be praised!' and the like.

"I looked at Mrs. Simmons. She looked at me. 'It's raining fish,' she said.

"'Hmmm…quite right.'

"'Well, that's **silly**, isn't it?'

"'Yes, it certainly is. Mind your head, dear.' "

Mr. Simmons calmly puffed his pipe, shrugged his shoulders. "And that was that. We could only surmise that some lake reseeding project had gone awry: the fingerlings dropped from a plane, caught in some updraft and finally deposited somewhere far from sight and sound of the plane. But it was wonderful and strange, nonetheless. Our young camping neighbors certainly thought so."

Ready For The Country, Part One

▼

The next day dawned sunny and dusty, soon to be hot. Kris and Peter roused themselves, scrunched the Rice Krispies out of their eyes, ignored protesting muscles and stuffed their gear hurriedly into their packs. They had grabbed some chow and were at a primitive level of readiness when Frank the ranger rounded a wild rose bush and popped into camp, maddeningly bright-eyed and bushy-tailed.

"Up and at 'em. Let's make like a baby and head out."

"Who asked **you**, pal?" This morning, Kris and Peter definitely preferred the pace of the Simmonses (who were still enjoying their morning cuppa, and waved gaily at the boys as they departed), but they had agreed the night before to hike out with Frank. Shortly, their legs regained glacial memory and settled back into a trail groove: it felt as if they had been walking like this for a very long time.

Frank redeemed himself somewhat by pointing out a cut-off for the railroad tracks that the boys otherwise would have missed, saving about three miles. The three hikers left the lakeshore, climbed a pine ridge, spotted the twin lines of the WP & YR and made their way down to them. Their boots settled into a clickety-clack that would carry them the remaining nine miles to the highway.

And, as it turned out, Kris and Peter became glad that they had joined Frank for those miles. Having traversed the Chilkoot all summer long, observing the seasonal changes, Frank was able to point out many things to the boys' relatively untutored eyes.

"See that muddy little access road, down to the side of the tracks?" asked Frank. "It's a perfect place for the local critters to walk: flat, free of tall brush, soft on the feet. At times, especially early in the mornings, it reads like a superhighway: innumerable comings and goings in the night. Let's go down there: I'll show you."

They abandoned their cross-tie walking for the moment, migrating down to the narrow road. Kris shortly spotted a set of round, very large animal tracks on the edge of a mud puddle.

"What would **that** have been? It's huge."

"Moose," Frank said quickly. "Cloven hoof, oval shape, almost the size of a frisbee: it's the only thing around here that could make something so large. But if you need another hint, look at the surrounding vegetation. It's clear that the moose was browsing: the green summer growth on the willows has been nibbled down to the nub. Go to a truly moose-infested area, and the shrubs will have been browsed so heavily that they resemble Japanese *bonsai*.

"Incidentally, caribou tracks look quite similar to moose: same basic shape, almost as large. But caribou hooves are rounder: they spread out like snowshoes, to give them better footing in the more severe winters they generally face up North. I've seen a few caribou tracks around here—so the herd that gave Carcross its name likely is still out here, somewhere."

A little farther along, in a slightly drier part of the road, lay an interesting sight: a series of scratched grooves in the dust, in which some animal droppings were half-buried. "Put your scatological skills to work," said Frank. "What do you think is the story behind this?"

Kris and Peter knelt down to inspect the site. "Well, it had to come from a carnivore," said Kris. "All that indigestible fur in the droppings, not to mention the teeth and bone fragments—but nothing else. That probably rules out a bear or another omnivore."

"Looks like some kind of rodent was the meal," commented Peter.

"A 'lowbush grizzly,' I bet," said Frank. When Kris and Peter looked puzzled, he smiled and said, "Arctic ground squirrels. That's just our park-ranger vernacular for them."

"But, what kind of carnivore chowed on this tasty little morsel?" continued Kris. "What all do they have around here? Wolves, coyotes, foxes, raptor birds...some kind of cat, maybe?"

"Yeah, that might be the ticket," said Peter. "This doesn't look much like a dog turd or a bird dropping. Plus, if you look at all those scratches in the dust, isn't that just what a cat does in a litter box? I'd guess that a lynx was here—or, if one somehow got this far north, a bobcat."

"Damn," said Frank. "You guys are pretty good. That's just what I would have guessed. I actually spotted a lynx not far from here, early in the summer: the first time I'd ever seen one on the wild. It looked like a big dog from the rear, but then it turned its head, and it had that distinctive kitty-face. The way it was walking, too, was a giveaway: no mistaking a cat's attitude."

Besides animal signage, Frank knew enough about the flora and fauna of the region to make the miles go by very quickly. "It would take several more Chilkoot hikes for me to pick this guy's brain," thought Kris. "And, that would be just fine with me." Curious, Kris pressed Frank as to the source of his knowledge and enthusiasm.

Frank thought for a moment. "It's kind of like this. Did you ever read the book 'Siddhartha'? Towards the end, the namesake character, after a long and very chaotic life, comes to rest beside a great river. For the first time, he learns to be still—and he learns that the river is constantly speaking to him: indeed, it had been doing so all along, through his comings and goings.

"Well, I feel the same way about this trail. The Chilkoot country says something new to me every time I come to it. Not to get too metaphysical here: but if one gets to know a river, or a trail, or any special place, making sure to listen carefully, to observe—one will hear it speaking." Frank paused, smiling. "And, like Siddhartha, once one realizes that the river has so much to say, one is free to grow old—senile, wrinkled and grinning— by the river of one's choice."

At length, the hikers became aware of some subtle differences: a different kind of dust hanging in the air, a strange rushing sound. They rounded a bend, and realized that these foreign sensations came from the White Pass highway, just a football field's length away. "Always kind of a shock to see and hear cars again, after three days in the Bush," commented Frank.

As they reached the parking lot, another shock presented itself: **people**, lots of them, or so it seemed. "Geez, what's with all the people? There must be at least, uh, at least twelve." Some fellow Chilkoot veterans were hanging out by the side of the road, knotted in small groups, plaintively attempting to flag down kind-hearted (and odor-resistant) drivers.

Kris and Peter looked at each other. "We always make fun of these guys when we fly by in the bus," said Peter. "Now we are them. They is us."

"Would you pick **me** up, looking like this?"

"Of course, man. That trail grit is a badge of honor. But I'd definitely stick you down in the luggage bay."

There was no sign of Park Service Green amongst the scattered vehicles in the Log Cabin parking lot. However, the boys didn't have to wait long before their ride pulled up. Mark grinned as he threw their gear into the Courier. "You made it. You're one of **them**: the few, the proud, the scruffy." They waved goodbye to Frank the ranger, who was slowly making a U-turn back towards Lake Lindeman, and fish-tailed out of the lot.

"Hey: a bunch of us came up for the afternoon, to try out some of those pothole lakes in Torment Valley, see if we can catch a few grayling."

"Sounds fine. Might be a good place to take a dip, clean up a bit."

"Well, get ready to freeze your ass off. Kevin's already been in: he hit the water, yelped and was right back out again. Looked just like a salmon going up some falls."

They drove a few miles back up the road towards Skagway, stopping just shy of the Fraser customs station. They parked the truck on the highway shoulder, walked over a rocky hummock and came upon signs of a Serious Fishing Expedition: empty beer bottles, the remains of a picnic feast, a boombox blasting the New Riders of the Purple Sage into the thin mountain air. But despite the hoopla, the grayling had not responded to the fishermen's exhortations, save for a couple of small, despondent specimens ("Natural Selection: ain't it a bitch," Llary had remarked). Kevin swore that he heard the fish laughing from the depths, in their high-pitched silvery voices.

Kris and Peter, upon their arrival, selected fishing rigs from the stock at hand, made a few casts for show, popped lake-chilled beers and then were content to watch their bobbers drift lazily across the water. The others seemed to be following suit, applying similar intensity to their fishing efforts as beer supplies continued to dwindle shockingly.

After a time, only Karl persisted in trying to uphold the family honor: "Goddamn, I know they're in there somewhere." Denying any further drink, his face and forehead grew red with exertion and sunburn, as he flailed the lake with Daredevil spoons and Fireball salmon eggs.

Finally, with a yell he let out a mighty cast. The lure flew out nearly halfway into the pothole lake. Unfortunately, the rest of Karl's rig flew out along with it, landing with a large splash and sinking immediately.

There was a moment of stunned silence. Karl just stood there, hands empty, simmering. Then, as everyone braced for a burst of expletives, Karl burst out laughing instead.

The tension released, everyone else completely lost it. Their laughter flew over Torment Valley like a flock of ravens. And Karl, wiping the tears from his eyes, began taking off his clothes, shoes, socks, t-shirt, jeans and skivvies, and dove into the icy lake.

For a scary second or two, Karl struggled under water, completely submerged. Then he shot up, bellowing like a bear, hair plastered to his balding head like a monk's haircut. "Cold! Cold! Aauughh! Fuck!" He paddled out to the approximate site of the pole's sinking, "Cold! Cold! Aauughh! Fuck," went diving down, was gone for another scary few seconds, shot up again, "Cold! Cold! Aauughh! Fuck," and swam back to shore as fast as a man can swim with a fishing rig in his hand.

It took a long time for everyone to wind down. "That," said Kevin, squinting knowingly, "was **classic**."

As soon as Karl had passed from the hypothermic danger zone, the gang began slowly to pack up for the return trip to town. Brian let the day's catch go, back into the clear depths: "Grow up, little guys."

Riding back down the mountain was a strange sensation for Kris and Peter. Even the slow S-curves seemed very fast; their legs were still fighting to maintain a pace. The outer fringe of Skagway seemed downright suburban; the Portland House seemed like an Upper West Side brownstone. Kris and Peter entered the front door, set down their packs, plopped themselves onto the one-armed sofa. Upstairs, a toilet flushed; water cascaded into the pail in the room next door.

"Home?"

"**Home**."

READY FOR THE COUNTRY, PART TWO

Several hours later, Kris sat up abruptly. A Kris-sized facial imprint slowly disappeared from the sleeping-bag portion of his backpack. There was commotion in the hallway outside his door.

Séan poked his head inside. "Beach Party. Red Onion. Get your Jimmy Buffett protective gear on."

Soon Kris and the others were amongst a rather unusual street crowd. Retro and neo-Parrotheads, streaming into downtown from all corners of the woods, jostled elbows with an invasion of young, Spandex-clad, very fit-looking people: the Klondike Road Relay, an annual 110-mile team running race from Skagway to Whitehorse, was underway. Those seeking beach sand and decadence were pointed in one direction; those seeking aerobic stress and shin-splints, in another.

"I guess Civilization has changed since I've been away," Kris remarked to Séan as they bucked the Spandex tide.

The Red Onion had been redecorated in a "Gidget Goes 1890's" motif. The main floor, even the barside spittoon gutters, had been covered in glistening white beach sand, specially imported from the local cement-mixer. Ersatz palm fronds concealed, in peek-a-boo fashion, the fleshy expanses of Dirty-Neck Maxine and her portrait colleagues. Sunglasses, costume earrings and a Panama hat adorned Myrtle (the Transvestite

Moose); party streamers dangled from his/her antlers. Lush Beach Boys harmonies filled the sultry saloon air.

Most of the people that Kris had come to know over the Summer made appearances at the Beach Party over the evening: the whole Portland House gang, Norm and René (and even baby Josey, wrapped in a tropical sarong), Dyea Gary and Vicki, several softball teammates, and many others. Wheatgerm served as the anarchic Master of Non-Ceremonies; his legendary bent trombone, lurking to the side of the platform stage, promised future histrionics. All in all, the festivities carried sentiments of closure: the feeling of wrapping up Summer with a bang; the feeling that Skagway's seasonal residents would soon pack up to go home; the strong possibility that this year's cast of characters would not be similarly united again.

Gazing over the *frou-frou* cocktail umbrella in his tropical smasher, Kris spied a familiar-looking crew entering the premises: the Whitehorse expies. Annabel, Kara and Yvette spotted Kris and Séan across the room, waved hello and signaled that they would come over to their table as soon as drinks were procured.

"I haven't seen that bunch in a while," mused Kris. "I haven't seen Mia in over a week. I wonder where she is tonight."

"She's gone." Séan looked over at Kris, somewhat guiltily. "Sorry, I was going to tell you."

Kris looked at Séan questioningly. "Something tells me that I don't want to know why she's gone. But tell me anyway."

"I don't really know that much about it," said Séan. "All I know is that some boyfriend showed up in Carcross a couple days ago: someone from back East. Tami says that he was an RCMP officer: an actual Mountie. Anyway, Mia's contract with the company was just about finished, so Norm cut her some slack, said she was done for the season, if she liked. She and the Mountie cleaned out that little cabin and, as far as I know, headed back towards Toronto together. I'm sorry, man."

Kris paused for a long moment, his mind echoing with visions of 'Sauna, Svim.' He let out his breath, slowly. Then he clinked drink glasses with Séan. "Good times. Some really good times. No regrets."

As the evening progressed, the Red Onion beach became as packed as Santa Monica on a sunny Saturday. Surfer dudes and dude-ettes pushed the action outside the door, extending the dance to the Boardwalk. Nighttime had returned to the North, but the temperature was still balmy; this was almost certainly the last night of Summer.

Towards midnight, Kris found himself on the street, Chinook Amber beer in hand, face-to-face with Julia, the gorgeous local girl. A Jan 'n Dean song pounded away in the background; a cacophony of loud tropical colors danced as if there were no tomorrow.

"What a day it's been: waking up beside Lake Lindeman, hiking out, the fishing expedition in Torment Valley, and now this." Kris shook his head. "You know, I keep thinking that a day in Skagway is really great: that things couldn't possibly be any nicer. And then another day, just like it or even better, comes along."

Julia smiled. "This is Skagway. Anything can happen."

And then something else happened. The musical din was broken by the low throb of a motorcycle, high cc's, Slow-Bicycle Racing down Broadway. The rider, clad in black denim jacket and chinos, large duffel bag bungee-corded onto the back of the cycle, pulled up in front of the Onion and killed the engine. He undid his helmet, shook the road-dust from his hair—his not-so Preppie hair—and became Dan Vanderwal.

"**Dan**…what the hell!!" Kris embraced his old Ketchikan roommate.

"Figured I might find you here," said Dan, nonchalantly. "Is Skagway **always** this festive?"

By this time Peter had witnessed the unveiled identity of the Slow Rider, and he flew from the door of the Onion into an incredulous, gleeful, highly improbable three-way reunion. "Old buddy: you look **great**. That cycle…I don't believe it."

There were far too many questions. "Let me make it easy for you," said Dan, proceeding to explain his circumstances. While working as a guide out of Anchorage, he had gotten to know some workers who were building a new machine shop at the bus yard. The head of the construction firm, upon learning of Dan's college credentials, had offered him some part-time accounting work. By the end of summer, the firm's workload had grown to such an extent that a permanent, full-time accountant/ controller was needed. Dan, upon being offered the position, had said "I'll take it: just give me three weeks." He purchased a used BMW motorcycle with his Tour Guide savings and, when his season was done, pointed the machine down the Al-Can: to pick up his car and winter gear in Seattle, put the bike on a trailer and move everything back to Anchorage. "Of course," said Dan, "even though it's a bit out of the way, a scenic detour to Skagway was a must."

Kris shook his head in disbelief. "Well, congratulations: you're the first person I know who has taken the plunge, and decided to stay in Alaska. You're also the last person I expected to do such a thing—especially after our experiences in Ketchikan."

"It's a big state," said Dan. "And it just keeps **growing** on you."

As the three friends continued to catch up, the Jimmy Buffett album that had been blaring out into the street was pulled, mid-song, from the turntable. A group of mildly-disreputable looking people had gathered on the boardwalk in front of the Onion, musical instruments in hand, and seemed to be trying to organize themselves into some kind of formation. Finally, Wheatgerm came to the forefront.

"The name of this band," announced Wheatgerm, "is **Tattoo**. We'd like to play a few tunes for you now, I reckon."

Tour Tidbits #184-87 (Autumnal Section)

▼

There are a variety of ways in which the change from Summer to Autumn becomes apparent in Alaska. True nightfall reappears: the brief late-night dusk evolves into an actual dose of darkness, gradually increasing in length until things completely even out at the equinox. This slows down the frenetic summer-long pace: midnight croquet, 24-hour road construction and other such games are no longer viable, and some people catch their first real breather since early May. Nighttime temperatures also begin to drop; mornings start to carry a certain crispness about them.

The changing sunlight and temperature trigger a nearly instantaneous barrage of fall colors, starting in the far north in early-to-mid August, then working its way southward. The colors are mostly yellows (aspen, birch, cottonwood), with a few interesting variations of red mixed in: flaming orange-red (willow), maroon (blueberry), and others. As the low foliage drops, berries that were missed in the first round of pickings are revealed: good for late-season treats, or to freeze-dry over the Winter, to become delicious wild "raisins" that keep well into the next summer. Low-bush cranberries, although very sour to the palate when fresh, make probably the best raisins.

One of the more interesting types of berry that emerges is that of the devil's club, *Oplopanax horridum*: a broad-leafed plant of the ginseng family, common to temperate coastal areas, with giant thorns and a height than can reach ten feet or above. Devil's club berries form a bright-red cluster at the end of high stalks, and actually are mildly poisonous to humans (although bears do not seem to have a problem with them). When the plant's leaves fall, some areas of coastal forest seem, at ground level, to be nothing but toxic red berries and wicked, barbed spikes.

The Natives of such regions had a very respectful name for the ominous devil's club. The exact name is unavailable to this author, but it translates as "Prickle-prickle Big-big."

THE TRAIL OF '42

▼

Rather than making its usual left-hand turn at the Alaska Highway junction out of downtown Whitehorse, the tour bus turned right, following the signs for Dawson, Beaver Creek, Fairbanks and other exotic points North. For most of the Skagway crew, this would be brand-new territory. Derek and his brother Karl were the only ones aboard who had been up the entire highway. They would be dueling tour guides for this training run: lecturing on the land, key logistical points, more vintage jokes, and other snippets of Coach Commander culture. They would, however, leave the driving to the others, so the rookies could see first-hand whether a 40-foot motorcoach actually could "catch air" on the finer frost-heaves.

It would be a quick trip: up to Tok, Alaska in one day, then all the way back down to Skagway the next day, as there was not enough time to get all the way to Fairbanks. Norm had found two days of slack schedule—not too hard, now that Labor Day weekend had passed—sufficient for sending up all but a skeleton crew. Most of the tour guides on board would be driving this route the following summer: hence, the official "Fam Trip" status. But, as everyone, including Norm, well knew, "Fam Trip" tended strongly to be a euphemism for "Party Bus."

And, it would be a well-stocked trip. Sacks of groceries occupied dual seats; a fine collection of cassette tapes, from Séan's Neil Young to Mark's

King Sunny Ade to Kris' Tattoo bootleg, were lined up for airtime. In the
rear of the coach, Kevin, holding court in his Gilligan hat, had the mix-
ings for Dyea Hooch. This would be dispensed to non-driving parties as
the need arose.

Kris brought his journal, for making some general observations
about the journey. The full detail could wait until next year's "serious"
training session.

*Heading North feels like another great unknown. The safety of the
Whitehorse "suburban fringe," cleared in just a few miles, then the famous
turnoff to Dawson—another road to explore, sometime soon—and on up the
highway. 410 miles to Tok, all on the Al-Can.*

I think just about everyone aboard will be doing this route next year,
except for Derek and Karl: Mark, Brian, Tami, Susan, Llary, Séan, Kevin.
Pete's gone already, but I'm sure we'll see him again. Funny, it seems kind
of a given that we'll all be back, regardless of what happens this Winter.

Kris looked over at Brian. His lean face was silhouetted against the
window in the autumn sunlight. He was relaxed, chewing a toothpick,
head bobbing to Neil Young's **Harvest**. It pretty much was harvest
time, all around: the faded-flannel weather, the fruits of summer mostly
stored away.

"Hey Brian: you'll be back next year, right?"

"Damn straight. I've salted away enough this season to finance a
whole winter of unsold art. It's too good a deal not to do it again. How
about yourself?"

"As far as I know, yeah. Figure I'll road-trip across the U.S. or Europe
this fall, maybe ski-bum again over the winter. That career stuff can wait."

In the front of the bus, Derek and Karl assumed tag-team lecture positions as Mark drove. *It's hard to believe they're brothers: the schoolteacher and
the rugby player.*

"How did this highway come to be?" posited Derek. "What is it doing
here? What are **you** doing here?"

"Being paid to sit on my ass and eat tortilla chips?" guessed Karl.

"Indeed," said Derek. "But most importantly, for our present purposes: the Alaska Highway—or 'Al-Can', as it is still popularly known—was created in one incredible year, 1942. Does anyone recall what was happening that particular year?"

"World War II, of course," said Séan. "That was the year that the Japanese campaign more or less reached its peak: the northern theatre of the war extended all the way to the Aleutian Islands."

"Right you are," said Derek. "Enemy forces had bombed Dutch Harbor and occupied Attu, Kiska and a couple of other places. Naturally, there was a strong concern that the Alaskan mainland would be attacked next. This generated a number of potential strategies. Coastal defense was obvious—witness the 25,000 troops sent to Kodiak—but the Allies really needed a land-based option, in case the coast became impassable."

"In short," said Karl, "they needed to be able to get men and supplies up there through the 'back door': overland, via northern Canada, a place so rugged that no one had ever punched a road through it."

"Enter the U.S. Army," said Derek. "They showed up in the Yukon in early 1942, along with Canadian troops and contractors, and split into two teams: one to work North, the other South. In an amazing nine months, they surveyed and built the first continuous overland route to Alaska: from Dawson Creek, British Columbia to Delta Junction, Alaska, about 1,422 miles."

"Of course," said Karl, "that road was pretty rough: nothing but Jeeps and other heavy-duty vehicles could make it. So, immediately after finishing the first go-round, the troops were put right back to work improving it: straightening the curves, regrading the hills, replacing the log 'corduroy' sections over the muskeg. The reconstruction process has never really stopped, as you'll learn for yourselves."

By the time they were thirty miles out of Whitehorse, the landscape had changed to semi-arid flatlands, with mountains in the distance: looking more like west Texas than northern Canada. Here and there, blackened tree trunks stood out from the dun-colored soil.

"As you may guess, there was a big forest fire through here," said Derek. "It burned across this entire valley. But it happened all the way back in 1958. The burnt trees have been preserved: essentially, freeze-dried in this climate."

"This is kind of a funny area," said Karl. "Being so dry, it looks like it would have been a breeze for road construction. But there are some real sneaky patches of swamp here and there, popping up where you would not expect them. During the spring thaw of 1942, the road crews had a bitch of a time working through the muskeg. It was fairly common for a big piece of road equipment to get hopelessly stuck in the thawing muck. Worse still, as a machine tried to work itself out, the engine heat often would cause more thawing—which of course would cause more sinking. Kind of a 'Catch 22' situation.

"Now, don't quote me on this—but there are stories that some of the equipment rigs became so stuck in the mud that they were abandoned: after they had sunken nearly out of sight, they were finally buried and **built** over. If this is true, just imagine going over the original Al-Can route with a powerful metal detector. You get to some muskeg patch, the detector goes berserk, you dig down into the roadbed and Bingo! You have yourself a vintage 1942 tractor or backhoe."

After the burn area, we entered a series of low, rolling ridges. Little surprises lay between the ridges, at the bottom of each narrow valley: tumbling rivers, a ghost town (Champagne), a Gold Rush-era log bridge, supposedly built by the legendary Sam McGee (Aishihik River). The St. Elias Mountains, the tallest in Canada, hove into view on the hilltops, growing closer and closer with each successive ridge.

We flew through Haines Junction without stopping. Essentially, it's a wide spot in the road (truck stops, burger joints), but there will not be a larger town until Tok. The eponymous "junction" is marked by a truly bizarre sculpture—Derek and Karl call it the "Wildlife Cupcake"—and we made a hard right turn there. If we had kept going straight, we would have eventually wound up back in good old Haines, Alaska.

Just a few miles outside of Haines Junction is Macintosh Lodge, our morning or afternoon coffee break, depending upon tour direction. A dim little bar with moose-racks and Molson on one side of the lodge, decent soup and sandwich lunch on the other. Scored some free pie (blueberry); these folks just love to see us come in, even without tourists.

Tami and Mark cracked the ceiling escape hatch and walked out on top of the bus, taking pictures of the mountains. You're so close to them here, they seem to leap out at you. The new snow was already halfway down the first ridge: all is golden up to the treeline, then white. Spectacular.

Kevin found a flock of turkeys around the corner of the lodge; I guess they belonged to the owners. He quickly made friends. He was down on his hands and knees, relating to them, taking close-up, character-laden photos. We dragged him away. "Look at the wattles on that one. Don Knotts? Buddy Ebsen? Ronald Reagan?"

South shore, Lake Kluane. A feast of colors here: the purple-and-white of the distant ranges to the east; the Slims River, draining the glacier fields, a creamy cafe au lait from the silt; the autumnal hues of the trees and shrubs, dotting the sparse flanks of the slopes facing the lake, looking like...

"Like a giant bowlful of Trix," said Brian, squinting artistically. "Lemon-yellow, raspberry-red and orange-orange, all the way up to the lip of the bowl. The optimal view is from up above, of course...but I can tell from here."

Tami was delighted. "A pre-sweetened Yukon breakfast. God probably looks down and says, 'Yum,' fetches His giant spoon and pitcher of milk. The Slims River is where some of the milk slops over."

*I can hear the thundering commandment of God: "Silly rabbit...Trix are for **kids**."*

Lake Kluane is bound to be the highlight of the second tour day: from Sheep Mountain to Burwash Landing, about thirty miles of gorgeous lakeshore driving. Just out of Burwash, however, is where the real fun begins.

"**Whoa** Nelly." Susan did not see the sudden dip in the road. For a second her airborne rear-end was horizontal to her hands, locked vise-like on the steering wheel. The driver's seat accordioned as she came back down, then settled into more-or-less equilibrium. "What was **that?**"

"Frost-heaves," said Derek, shaking his head. "We've just run into our first official patch of permafrost. Around here it's pretty sketchy: the yearly mean temperature is right around freezing, so your local microclimates with slightly cooler temperatures will have the stuff. Dig down into this low-lying muskeg about four feet or so, even this time of year, and it'll be frozen. Conversely, south-facing slopes likely will be free of permafrost.

"Anyway, the biggest problem with these roads up North is that the heat picked up by the asphalt in Summer will seep down into the permafrost. When they initially built the road, everything seemed perfectly stable—even when they'd get down to within inches of the permafrost. But when it melts, it becomes that same soupy muck that mired all the equipment down near Whitehorse. Consequently, the asphalt sags as the warmer weather sun hits and summer traffic passes over.

"Road builders haven't yet figured out a way to beat frost-heaves. I'd sure like to be the person who secures that patent."

"So why try to beat 'em?" countered Karl. "Why not accept 'em as part of the game? Anyhow, the best ones are usually marked by little flags on the roadside. After a while, you get to know where they are—and give names to your favorites. Most of my personal frost-heave names are unprintable in family publications.

"Some of us old-timers even developed a ratings scale for our favorite frost-heaves, based mostly upon passenger response. On a one-to-ten scale, for example, a three might elicit something like, 'Uff.' A four might be 'Uff **da**,' especially if there are any Midwesterners on board. On an eight, the passengers need not stand to reach the overhead luggage compartments. On a nine, they lose their upper dentures. Haven't run into a **ten**…but I know it's out there, somewhere."

The road from Burwash on gets pretty gnarly. The scenery abruptly shifts into something very different: the subarctic taiga forest, the last tree zone before tundra. Miles and miles of rolling taiga, brooded over by Canada's tallest mountains: Mt. Logan gets up over 19,000 feet. About the only tree hardy enough to survive—I wouldn't call it "thrive"—are those skinny little black spruce: the ones that Derek and Karl call "Alaska Pipecleaners." To me, they look more like the pathetic Christmas tree from the old Peanuts TV special: wizened, anemic, bending over double when one sticks a bulb on it. Imagine: a million acres of Charlie Brown Christmas trees.

The last seventy miles or so to Beaver Creek are wild and desolate, and toss you around pretty well: plenty of "seven" and "eight" frost-heaves. The passengers will be glad to see the town, I bet.

"Why, it's Beaver Creek!" said Derek excitedly, as they passed through a rather forlorn group of lodges and cabins. "The Most Westerly Community in Canada. The majority of southbound tours will stop here overnight, rather than Tok; northbound tours will have a coffee/ frost-heave break before continuing on. Regardless, you all will be spending a lot of happenin' times here."

"What is there to **do** here, for God's sake?"

"There's a killer horseshoes court, just like in Skagway. A miniature golf course, made from plywood and recycled Astro-Turf. Some serious drinking, certainly: the main lodge in town has a spacious Animal-Head Room, just like the one in Carcross."

"**Yikes**," said Tami.

"However," said Karl, "If you end up staying at that lodge, it's generally considered very bad form to get sloppy-drunk with your passengers. So, what I used to do is sneak off to Ida's, that little motel/ bar on the edge of town. Having a beer or two there will more properly introduce you to the 'local color', anyhow."

It's twenty miles from Beaver Creek to the border: the Alaskan interior, at last! This final stretch of Canadian highway is probably the roughest I've ever ridden, though: we're averaging no more than twenty-five or thirty. My handwriting is just about illegible, from all the dips, potholes and curves.

"Have you ever heard the story of how Canada got its name?" inquired Derek, bouncing off the ceiling from a lulu of a frost-heave. "Back when the hitherto unnamed land was about to become a country, the Founding Fathers decided that they wanted, above all, a snappy acronym: kind of like 'USA.' But, they didn't know quite how to go about this. After much discussion, they decided simply to draw three random letters out of a hat, get the acronym from that, and then come up with the country's name: kind of a backwards approach, but better than nothing.

"So, they tore up some paper, wrote a bunch of letters on the strips, placed them into a hat. After a dramatic pause, the head Founding Father reached in, pulled out a letter and said..." Derek turned to Karl:

"**C**, eh?" Karl's voice carried more than sufficient gravity.

"The next letter was pulled. The result..."

"**N**, eh?"

"And finally..."

"**D**, eh?"

"And of course, C-eh N-eh D-eh spells..."

"BOO! HISS!" The response from Derek and Karl's audience was unanimous.

As the bus bottomed out in a permafrost hollow, its occupants sensed that they were about to see something unusual. Sure enough, a break in the boreal forest became apparent: not a natural break, but a clear-cut, perfectly straight line, stretching to the horizon in both directions from the road.

"The international boundary," proclaimed Derek as the bus pulled into a turnout, precisely in the middle of the line. "The Alaska-Canada border has always been controversial: recall the 'gunboat diplomacy' that set the boundary in Southeast. Well, to avoid any ambiguities in this region, some years ago a team of surveyors cleared this swath: thirty feet wide, 800 **miles** long, stretching from the Arctic Ocean to Mt. St. Elias, just off the

Gulf of Alaska. Every so often, they have to reclear the entire swath—all 800 miles—so it doesn't become overgrown."

"Man, that's a **long** ways to carry a Weed-Whacker," commented Kevin.

"Some kind of festivity usually goes over well at the border," added Karl. "It can be something simple, like a dashboard flag-changing ceremony. Or, if you have an especially frisky group, you all can sing the 'Alaska Flag Song' for the U.S. Customs agents when they board your bus. Sometimes, they even smile."

The Portland House gang, as motley as they appeared, cleared Customs with no problem, and they re-entered Alaska. While the terrain did not change at all, the road immediately was much improved.

"The U.S. has always had a bit more money to maintain the Al-Can than Canada," said Derek. "They have been able to reconstruct twenty-mile sections of the highway in Alaska every year, for as long as I can remember. From here to Delta Junction is about two hundred miles, which means that the entire route is redone about once every ten years. As it turns out, that's just about the lifespan of a paved highway in these climate conditions.

"We're just about to enter a section that, for me, was always the toughest to drive: the Tok Hills. If you have a northbound tour from Whitehorse, this is what you have to face at the end of a 400-mile day: steep grades, hairpin curves, a highway narrow enough so there's no margin for error. Plus, if it's the right time of year, you get here around sunset, so the sun is right in your eyes as you're heading northwest to Tok."

"There's about ninety miles of this up-and-down-and-around," said Karl. "When you finally round a bend and see the Tok River valley spread out before you—flat as a pancake, highway straight as an arrow—you are deeply thankful."

The cumulative effect of curves, frost-heaves and Dyea Hooch indulgence put most of the crew in a sleepy mood as they approached Tok. Kris, leafing through Karl's collection of campy Alaskan postcards, found one that summed up this portion of the Al-Can quite well:

> "Winding in and winding out,
> the Alaska Highway gives serious doubt
> as to whether the lout
> who planned this route
> was going to hell, or coming out!"

ONE TOK OVER THE LINE

▼

"The road between Fairbanks and Tok, Alaska is situated in the scenic Tanana River Valley. To the south of the highway rise some of the more majestic peaks of the Alaska Range. Visitors may occasionally see wildlife—or, on rare instances, a weather-beaten Alaskan lying spent and discarded along this famous route."

The postcard text was accompanied by a grainy black-and-white photo of some guy in a chewed-up parka, lying supine on the gravel highway shoulder. Kris set down Karl's card collection and shook his head. "Everybody says the darndest things about Tok. What is so peculiar about it? Bomber-sized mosquitoes? Fifty-foot tall, flying husky-dogs? Psychedelic ice-fog?"

"Well, you have to see the town, and spend a few nights there, to understand," said Derek as they entered the Tok River valley. "It's a strange place, in that it hardly feels like a cohesive 'town' at all. It has all the amenities: gas stations, lodges and campgrounds, a grocery store, a post office, a school. But most of the buildings are incredibly spread out and tucked away from sight: hundreds of yards away from each other, hidden in the black spruce. There are the two main highways—the Al-Can, the Tok Cutoff—the one big corner, and not much else that's apparent to the eye.

"Outward appearances notwithstanding, hints as to the true nature of Tok may be divined from the story of its naming. As with so much North Country lore, there are at least four different explanations as to how Tok got its name."

"Here we go again," said Karl.

"Explanation number one. There is a word in the local Athabaskan dialect which sounds something like 'tok,' meaning 'peace.' This river valley, at the confluence of what are now known as the Tok and Tanana rivers, was a meeting place for local tribes. The modern name 'Tok' thus loosely translates as 'peace crossing.' "

"**Borrrr**ing," said Karl, rolling his eyes and yawning.

"Number two is sort of a variation on the first one. According to some, the Athabaskan name for the river sounded something like 'Tokyo' rather than simply 'Tok.' When the highly patriotic workers of the U.S. Army were punching the Al-Can through here, they came upon this place and were offended by its name; the word 'Tokyo' just wasn't very popular in 1942. They decided that the place name had best be shortened to 'Tok.' And so it was."

"Historically interesting," commented Mark, "but not very politically correct, these days."

"Explanation number three. A toque, pronounced 'tuke,' is a type of hat, historically popular in Canada. It's kind of silly looking, actually: sort of a tri-corner style, made of or lined with fur. Well, there used to be a lot of Canadian fur trappers around here; this was one of the regional gathering points for those of their profession. After a time, the settlement came to be known for the type of hat most popular hereabouts: the toque, later Anglicized to 'Tok.' "

"Are Doug and Bob MacKenzie aware of this?" pondered Séan.

"And, number four. Back when they were surveying the route for the Alaska Highway, the engineers were looking for a likely location to place the intersection of the Al-Can and the eventual highway to Anchorage. The engineers happened upon this valley, and one of the surveyors decided to go up in an airplane, to have a look around and select a promising location. The surveyor flew above here, liked what he saw, got out a map and put a large cross, or 'T,' where he thought the intersection should be. When he got back down on the ground, he went to his supervisor and showed him his selection. The supervisor looked at the map, saw the large 'T' on it and marked, 'OK' next to it—meaning that it was OK to plan the intersection there. The spot marked 'TOK' on the map became the town known as Tok."

"An additional, unofficial explanation," continued Karl, "is pretty obvious. Remember that old song, 'One toke over the line, sweet Jesus, one toke over the line...' It's like, THERE'S NOTHING ELSE TO DO HERE, MAN."

"'Tok Up In Smoke'," mused Kris. "Sounds like a bad Cheech and Chong movie. Although I do understand the town nearly burns down every summer."

"Yep," said Karl. "This river valley bakes in the constant midsummer daylight; it gets up to around ninety degrees here, believe it or not. The muskeg dries out, and those skinny little black spruce get like matchsticks. Late July rolls around, and the town is covered in a thick haze, filled with working smokejumpers, trying to save the darn place."

"From one extreme to another," said Derek. "It can get down to seventy below in the winter. Two hundred miles from anywhere at all—and even then, the 'anywhere' is just Fairbanks. It's a town of extremes. But it does make for interesting people, interesting stories. And apparently Tok is not without attractions for some."

"You talking about that guide's mom?" inquired Karl.

"I sure am," chuckled Derek. "The story goes something like this:

"One of our guides—I'll call him 'Dave'—was touring through here a couple years back, with his mother as a member of the group. This was fine: Dave incorporated her into his normal witty banter, and she told embarrassing childhood stories in the back of the bus. However, I believe that she was a tad **bored** on the trip: she was quite young, early

40's; still very pretty, apparently; just divorced, I believe, wanting to kick up her heels a little bit. There wasn't too much room for that, amongst all the oldsters.

"Well, the tour pulled into Tok for the night, and Dave pointed out all the local hot-spots, as he always did. Among these, of course, was Fast Eddy's—with the normal jokes and admonitions about it being extremely "local," and best avoided. Anyway, after they had made it to the hotel and disembarked everyone, Mom came up to Dave, with a little smile on her face. "Son," she said, "I think I'll just stroll down to Fast Eddy's, there: see what's happening."

"Dave was a little concerned: this was his **mother**, after all. "You sure, Mom? That place can get pretty rough."

"Mom straightened herself up, looked young Dave in the eye. "I'll be all right, son. See you tomorrow." And off she went, down the gravel high-way shoulder towards Fast Eddy's.

"Dave tried not to worry too hard when he indeed failed to see her until early the next morning. As everyone was lined up, ready to board the bus for the day, Mom walked right to the front door, all chipper and smil-ing—no carry-on luggage in hand.

"Good morning, Mom."

"Good morning, David. I'm staying here, in Tok."

"You're WHAT?"

"I'm **staying**." Mom proceeded to tell Dave about everything—well, maybe not **everything**—that had transpired at Fast Eddy's. She had met this **won**-derful gentleman: a Tok local, a bush pilot, single, very hand-some and dashing. He bought her a beer and a burger, and then employed his best line—which of course was to offer an aerial tour of the city in his vintage Piper Cub. She accepted, naturally: who could resist such a smoothie? Up they went, high over the muskeg, skirting the Alaska Range, into the eternal sun…into that ethereal dimension called Love At First Sight. By the time they got back down to the ground, they were already discussing future plans. He would fly, she would learn to fly, and in the meantime she'd cook for him and share his cabin with him and his dog, Big Dog. No matrimony, or anything complicated like that, just a happy co-habitation.

"Dave of course pleaded with his mother to come to her senses. This was Tok, for God's sake. Do you know what winters are like here? Are you out of your cotton-pickin' mind? But Mom's mind was made up. She had nothing to go back home to in Seattle, really. Bye, son: hope the rest of your tour goes well.

"Dave passed through Tok again about two weeks later, figuring that Mom had had enough, and was now ready to split town. No dice: she was happily, flamingly in love, and she wasn't going nowhere.

"That was about three years ago. Dave's mom and the bush pilot were still together, last time I looked. In fact, if you go down to the little store by the campground, you can probably find her working there and see for yourself. But don't tell her I sent you."

There was contemplative silence, as various mothers came to mind.

"There's another Tok story I love," said Karl. "This one's about huskies."

Derek groaned, and clapped a hand over Karl's mouth. But Karl spoke up, pushing the hand away. "They tell the story of yet another tourist, a lady about fifty-five or so. Well, the tour driver was going on about the husky puppies at the Burnt Paw, and this woman went berserk: just **had** to have one. Of course, the tour guide made some joking comment about no puppy-smuggling allowed in Tok, something dumb like that. The tourist lady dashed over to the Burnt Paw, fell in love with this little husky pup, and bought it right on the spot.

"But, what to do about the tour guide? The lady at the Burnt Paw, realizing the problem, assured the tourist that the pup was well-behaved: wouldn't yip, wouldn't piddle on the floor of the bus. Why not hide the husky pup inside her coat and smuggle him aboard that way?

"The tour guide didn't notice the squirming little lump under the lady's coat as she boarded. The lady went right to her seat in the rear of the bus, smiling to herself. They drove off, and she had her pup; she had beaten the system.

"But then, as the ride went on, the lady began to look a little uncomfortable. She began to fidget in her seat, and waves of mortification crossed her face. Other nearby passengers noticed this and became concerned; the lady looked awful. Finally, someone went to the front of the bus and told the driver that he'd better stop, some lady was sick in the back, almost looked as if she were having a heart attack or something. As the driver stopped and went back there to take a look, the little lump wriggled free, and the puppy landed on the floor, skittered off a few seats away and began to whimper.

"'Aha, I knew it,' said the driver accusingly. 'I knew it had to be a husky pup. But, what was the problem? Why were you so uncomfortable? What's the matter—wasn't it potty-trained?'

"'No, not that,' replied the miserable woman. 'This puppy's not **weaned** yet.' "

GENNA

▼

The Tok Tundra Lodge, just past the big turnoff to Anchorage, was the northerly limit of the Skagway crew's road trip. After checking in for the night, they would turn around and head back South the next morning—at least, those who did not meet their life's mates overnight in a local bar.

The motorcoach pulled up to the log-cabin motel office. In a moment, a young woman stepped out, clipboard and key packets in hand. The standard expie uniform in Tok, to Kris' eyes, apparently was a faded denim shirt, rolled up at the sleeves, untucked; blue jeans, wearing out in the right places; dirty white tennies, no socks; red bandanna fighting a losing battle with long, curly light-brown hair; very nice eyes: large and hazel, almost golden.

She stepped lightly up the bus stairwell. "Well, hi—I guess you're not the typical busload." A subtle, bemused smile. The name on the red plastic tag, above and to the left of the middle button on the denim shirt, below the golden eyes, was Genna. "What brings you to our fair city?" asked Genna.

Circumstances were explained, introductions were made: nice to meet you, welcome to Tok, did you have a decent drive? Yeah, good to be here. Just you and your mom running this place? Yep, that's what we do. Everyone disembarked, popped the luggage bays, hauled out road-gritty bags with well-practiced motions. Kris caught the room key as Genna tossed it to him, and with his eyes followed her sweetly-perfumed cloud of dust through the unpaved parking lot.

Great golden-eyed, long-legged wow. What in the world is someone like her doing in Tok, of all places?

A short time later, after people had thrown their gear onto beds and were just thinking about heading out on the town, Genna reappeared, in aquamarine t-shirt and tropical jams, volleyball in hand. "I've got the net set up, if you want to play. Actually, you'd **better**: not too often we get a group like you around here."

The exploratory mission to Fast Eddy's was nipped in the bud, to the relief of some. Genna led the crew around the back of the lodge, to a surprisingly nice sand court. She kicked off her shoes, wiggled her toes. "We put this in earlier this summer, but I haven't found hardly anyone to play on it. I hope that you guys will be more fun than **this** year's long-haul drivers. "

"Beach volleyball in Alaska: who'd-a thunk it." Karl was impressed.

"It's pretty much the national sport here, when it's above freezing. I learned how to play up in Fairbanks, where during the Spring thaw they have their annual Mud Bowl game at the University. They pick the filthi-est, gooey-est unpaved parking lot on campus—usually the one built up out of coal tailings—set up a net, hose the lot down for good measure, let people go at it. Cross-checking and tackling are acceptable. Great way to let off steam after that long winter."

The Skagway boys, Tami, Susan and Genna split into sides and posi-tioned themselves on either side of the net. Genna planted her bare feet squarely in the sand, like any good Malibu girl. "Now, if anybody says, 'Don't hit it to her, she can't play,' I'm taking down the net," she said.

Kris looked at Genna and saw that, despite her gentle tone, she wasn't joking. They made eye contact: she looked away briefly, and then returned his gaze. She tossed him the volleyball, smiled shyly, and the game began.

Part Three: How Heavy Is the Mountain

▼

"first there is a mountain,
then there is no mountain,
then there is…"
—donovan

Top Twenty All-Time Greatest Alaskan Tourist Questions

▼

"There is no such thing as a stupid question."

—Kris the Tour Guide

The key word in the list of vital Driver/Guide job qualifications was "politeness." This meant that guides were required to keep smiling, no matter what the circumstances: excessive "ground turbulence," undumped Blue Lagoon, non-English speaking smoker on board, invisible wildlife and mountain ranges. It also meant keeping a straight face whenever a completely inane question was asked (a fairly frequent occurrence)—as well as combining professional politeness with a gentle but firm straightening-out of the passenger in question.

The following is Kris' list of all-time favorite tourist questions, with his answers: selected for entertainment value and originality.

#1) Asked while disembarking from an ocean-going cruise ship at the port of Skagway.

Q: What's the elevation here, young man?

A: Would that be at high or low tide, sir?

#2) Asked while waiting for the 8 o'clock bus.

Q: What time does the 8 o'clock bus get here?

A: I beg your pardon?

#3) The all-time non-sequitir. Asked while driving through the beautiful snow-capped peaks of the Alaska Range: on a perfectly clear day when, against the odds, Denali is actually visible—all 20,320 feet.

Q: How heavy is the mountain?

A: Would that be with or without snow, ma'am?

Actually, here is the way, according to Kris, to weigh Denali: fetch an ordinary bathroom scale; first, weigh yourself with the mountain, then weigh yourself **without** the mountain—and simply subtract the difference.

#4) Asked at the Alyeska Pipeline Terminal, Valdez.

Tour Guide: This facility produces crude oil at the rate of 1.5 million barrels per day.

Tourist: What do they do with all the barrels?

Tour Guide: I beg your pardon?

Tourist: No, seriously—what do they do with all the barrels?

Tour Guide: Well, when they come to the end of the line, volunteers scrub up all those barrels; then they send them all back up to Prudhoe Bay by dogsled, to be used again.

Tourist: Thank you.

#5) Asked while counting the mileposts until the next coffee break, on an exciting stretch of the Glenn Highway between Glennallen and Eureka Summit.

Q: How far is it between those mileposts?

A: (no answer possible)

#6) Asked while on the outer suburban fringes of Chicken, Alaska: population "26 nice people, one old grouch."

Q: In the Alaskan North during the summertime, when there is no darkness, what do the local roosters do, to keep from going insane due to the lack of sunrises?

A: Why, they lose their cock-a-doodle-do's.

A variation on this theme scientifically explains the fact that Alaskan sunflowers, since their heads must follow the sun around a circular horizon rather than a straight path from sunrise to sunset, end up corkscrewing themselves into the ground. That's why you never see Alaskan sunflowers.

#7) Asked while enjoying a sun-drenched vista of Bridal Veil Falls, off the Richardson Highway—resplendent with prismatic rainbow effects, the turbulent grey of the glacial Lowe River, and great roaring wet noise.

Q: Is that waterfall there every year?

A: Well, it's been in that same spot for a number of years now; they used to move it every winter, put it into storage, but not any more.

Kris thought of Richard Brautigan's "waterfalls for sale" by the foot: stacked up in varying lengths like fenceposts, available at the friendly neighborhood hardware store. Trees, trout and wildlife available at a nominal fee; insects included *gratis*.

#8) Asked while enroute to Portage Lake, south of Anchorage: some five miles or so inland from the Turnagain Arm.

Q: Are we going to see any **whales**?

A: No—it's not their spawning season.

#9) Asked at Milepost 115 of the Dalton Highway, at 66 degrees, 33 minutes North latitude.

Q: How do they know where the Arctic Circle is? Does the Army Corps of Engineers decide?

A: No, it's really very easy: all you have to do is look for the dotted line across the landscape.

#10) Asked in Beaver Creek, Yukon, "The Most Westerly Community in Canada," population ninety or so: subject of the popular song, "Three Hundred And One Miles From Nowhere."

Q: "Do we have to go through Customs to call Alaska from here?"

#11, 12 & 13) Donated courtesy of Kris' friends on the cruise ships. Asked while at sea.

Q: Where does the crew stay every night? Are they on board our ship?

Q: Where does the ship get its electricity: from ashore somewhere?

Snide comments about separate dinghies for crew members, as well as 500-mile extension cords, are always tempting, but considered too tactless for public use.

Q: Are these islands connected?

A: Yes—except for the ones that are completely surrounded by water.

#14) Asked somewhere north of the Arctic Circle.

Q: Do they allow the Eskimos to cut Christmas trees?

A: (unspoken) Sure—if they don't mind walking five hundred miles or so to find a tree.

A: (spoken) I beg your pardon?

#15) Asked, unbelievably, by the same person.

Q: When do they turn on the Northern Lights?

A: Not until it gets dark.

#16) Asked while riffling through gold-bearing gravel just north of Fairbanks.

Q: What color is the gold supposed to be?

A: Uh, gold.

#17, 18, 19 & 20) Asked on the morning Wildlife Tour in Denali National Park. The 4:30 AM wake-up call may offer a partial explanation.

Q: What time do they let the animals out in the park?

Q: Where's the road to the summit (of Mt. McKinley)?

Q: How often do you mow the tundra?

Q: What time of the year do the moose turn into caribou?

#21) (bonus question) Asked while chatting with passengers at an unnamed picture stop—simply taking in the beauty of the unspoiled Alaskan landscape.

Q: Alaska? Are you from Alaska, young man?

Fairbanks Journal Entry: 5/15/88

▼

"Tomorrow I'm leaving for Alaska. I'm going to find an ice-cold creek near the Arctic where that strange beautiful moss grows, and spend a week with the grayling."

—Richard Brautigan, **Trout Fishing In America**

On May first, I was on a beach in Australia, wrapping up a four-month Pacific Rim excursion: diving off the Great Barrier Reef, living on tropical fruit, Greek salads and Foster's beer. Two weeks later, I found myself jetting over the Alaskan interior, gazing down at the slowly-greening landscape, wondering at the ice that still filled many of the rivers. I was heading Back To Work, after a winter and spring of travel and adventure—which basically exhausted the bankroll I'd built up over my summer in Skagway. Veteran Alaskan tour guides had warned me of this vicious cycle: work like a dog for several months up North; spend the other eight months playing, traveling, whatever; just as the funds are about to run dry, return to Alaska. Well, here I am again.

My arrival in Fairbanks was marked with minimal fanfare: a smooth touchdown in a flat, broad river valley; a quick grab of my backpack and guitar that, at this point, have been just about everywhere with me; a company bus, waiting amidst lingering snow heaps and freshly-planted flower pots in the airport lot.

"Welcome home, Kris," said Susan, my Victorian-madam housemate from last summer. "This isn't exactly Skagway, is it?"

I watched out the window as the bus drove through a cloverleaf interchange (the only one in the state) and entered the strip of fast-food Americana that lined Airport Way. "No, it isn't," I finally said.

Most of the Alaskan towns I've seen are profoundly affected by their physical settings: the ways in which they are oriented towards mountains, sea, forest or whatever leave a deep imprint on the town's collective psyche. Ketchikan was long and drawn-out, almost entirely fronting the Tongass Narrows: hence, its near-total obsession with the water and its finny denizens. Skagway was aimed, like an arrow, from the head of the Inside Passage to the Yukon interior: a portal, a gathering point for gumption and energy.

Fairbanks is sprawling and, in the city center, absolutely flat—but from the drive across town, and my recent aerial perspective, I was able to see how the place makes its own kind of sense. Flying up from the south, I was able to see scattered signs of civilization: highways, small communities, individual cabins. But looking north just before landing, I saw complete wilderness: trackless, rolling hills, all the way to the Yukon River and beyond. Once you get away from the roads that peter out within about 100 miles of town (the North Slope haul road excepted), it's probably still possible to walk from Fairbanks to the Arctic Ocean—about 500 miles— without encountering any signs of human habitation. From this, it's clear that Fairbanks is truly the edge of Modern Civilization: the capital of the northern Bush, the service hub for the hardy souls inhabiting that vast frontier. The place where the bush-bunnies come to file their mining claims, or have their wisdom teeth yanked, or load up on six months worth of macaroni and cheese at the Safeway store.

Fairbanks ain't much to look at, that's for sure. But it's not just a random, suburban drag-strip thrown into the middle of the muskeg. It has its purpose.

The drivers' apartments were at the far end of Airport Way, just south of downtown. They're in a huge development: the Anderson Apartments, the largest complex in Fairbanks. The Anderson Apartments remind me of the enlisted housing on an aging military base: boxy, drab, function-over-form. Not nearly as decrepit as the Portland House, but far inferior in character and funkiness. Oh well: we won't be there a hell of a lot, anyway.

When Susan and I pulled up to the complex, we saw some people hucking a football around on a large, ragged lawn, with a big barbecue cranking away off to the side. A familiar figure in a loud tropical shirt, drink in hand, greeted me at the bus door. "It's your official 'Welcome To Squarebanks' party, Skipper," said Kevin, arching an eyebrow in welcome, ceremonially handing over a cold one. Soon other, very familiar faces hove into view: Mark, Llary, Séan, Tami. Good to see the old Skagway gang again.

"Your buddy Peter snagged a spot in one of the apartments for you," said Mark. "That makes **five** of you in the place: you all get to fight over the single bed. But don't worry, all five will be together maybe once or twice the entire summer. In fact, Pete and Brian are already training on the Denali run. They'll be back in a couple of days."

In between the football tosses, grilled burgers and beverage, my colleagues gave me the lowdown on the work scenario. A dizzying array of tours emanating from Fairbanks: Denali/Anchorage, Skagway, Dawson and even Prudhoe Bay (the latter two being reserved for the most senior drivers). A pronounced distinction, both professionally and socially, between the veteran Coach Commanders and long-haul greenhorns such as ourselves. Kind of a hands-off boss (named Frank Graydon), who kept things on the straight-and-narrow, but didn't have the time to be as personable as Norm Devereaux or Roy Haverman. Klaus the ill-tempered mechanic within close proximity, but relatively low-profile so far: no real run-ins, just a presence.

"It's about what I expected," I said. "Bring on the highway."

"Actually, K, you should know that they'll likely start you off with a couple of Fairbanks city tours first: to show your stuff, and prove that you're **ready** for the highway. That's the phase most of us are just coming out of now." Séan's face revealed a particular lack of enthusiasm for the assignment. "But I'm guessing that you'll be on the long-haul—probably Highway Two, down to Skagpatch—in about two weeks."

"Okay: bring on the Chena Pump Road, then. Whatever."

"*Skøl*, buddy," said Llary, as he and the others offered a six-beer salute.

P.S. It's funny, but over the Winter I found myself frequently thinking about Genna Hodgson, that outrageously beautiful girl I met in Tok last September: the golden-eyed beach volleyball *aficionado*. I hope that I see her again, sometime soon.

DID YOU KNOW

▼

That Fairbanks may not be in its present location if not for a lost riverboat captain. The story of the city's founding—possibly, with a bit of poetic license added as the years have gone by—goes something like this:

Around the turn of the century, there was a minor gold rush in Circle, Alaska, located on the Yukon River. An entrepreneur named E.T. Barnette decided to relocate to Circle, in order to partake of its lucrative business opportunities: in particular, by opening a trading post there. In 1901, he chartered a riverboat, the **Lavelle Young**, to take him and the supplies for his store up the river to Circle.

The Yukon River, though it can accommodate shallow-draft boats for more than two thousand miles of its length, is nonetheless very tricky to navigate: sandbars, island-studded flats, multiple channels and deceptive tributaries are all too common. The captain hauling Mr. Barnette and his goods came to one such difficult spot, the confluence with the Tanana River, and lost his bearings: he inadvertently left the Yukon and began heading up the Tanana. Even worse, since he was now on an unfamiliar river (and probably didn't want to admit it to Barnette), he got sidetracked from the Tanana and wound up on an even smaller river: the Chena. Unfortunately, the Chena is navigable only for a small portion of its length—which the captain did not realize until the river got too narrow for turning around and too shallow for going any further forward. The boat became hopelessly stuck.

To top everything off, Winter was just around the corner. This river-boat was likely the last one of the season, so the prospects of any help arriving before Spring breakup were virtually nil. Mr. Barnette undoubt-edly was upset at the captain's navigational ineptitude—but, opportunist that he was, decided to make the best of the situation by unloading his store supplies and setting up a trading post right where the boat was stuck. A few prospectors occasionally trickled through the area, and Barnette likely figured that their meager business was better than no business at all. Once springtime came, and the riverboat was back on its proper course, Barnette could continue on to Circle, as originally planned.

This plan never came to pass. Felix Pedro, an Italian immigrant, had been prospecting for some time in the hills above the Chena, with minimal luck. One day in 1902, Mr. Pedro's luck changed: he made a major gold strike, just a few miles north of the stranded riverboat. Word of the discovery quickly spread, and within weeks, many of the region's gold-mining communities—including Circle—had virtually emptied as newcomers streamed towards the Chena River country. And of course, what should they find waiting for them but a fully-equipped trading post, ready and willing to sell them whatever they needed. E.T. Barnette thus realized the ultimate capitalist dream: the Gold Rush had come to him, rather than the other way around.

The new community flourished. However, this boomtown, unlike so many others, demonstrated some real staying power: a more stable popu-lation base spread itself along the river, survived enough extreme Alaskan weather to be considered somewhat permanent, and in 1903 incorporated itself as the town of Fairbanks.

Barnette and his business enterprises also continued to flourish—although several years later he was caught embezzling from a bank he had started, was forced to flee town, and was never heard from again. Similarly, it is unknown what became of the lost riverboat captain: the man who may have founded a city by accident.

BUSH POETRY

▼

"You've been in town for over a week now. It's about time you guys took the True Fairbanks city tour." Sandy, a short, wiry woman in her late thirties, dressed in boots and denim jacket, loaded Kris and Peter into a rusted-out Ford truck. "This is my Winter Wagon," she said. "It starts at forty or fifty below, thanks to that plug-in headbolt heater. That's why you see all the electric outlets in parking lots around town. I didn't try driving at all when it got down to sixty below a couple years back: my tires would probably have cracked from the cold."

Reluctantly, the truck arose from slumber and roared to life. "This one picked up some pretty bad Car Cancer during its Anchorage years: all that salt air. But I won't stop driving it until I can see the road going by through the floorboard."

The boys had been introduced to Sandy during one of the early-season company meetings. Unlike many of the veteran drivers, Sandy had gone out of her way to make the newcomers feel welcome and, in this case, familiarize them with the interesting nuances of Fairbanks that they otherwise could very well miss. "Ain't true that this town ain't got no heart," Sandy had quoted to Kris and Peter. "You just got to poke around."[6]

---

6. The Grateful Dead, Shakedown Street.

Sprawled across the wide bench seat, the truck's three occupants got a pockmarked, bug-splatted windshield view of Fairbanks as they poked their way across town. "So, what brought you here in the first place, Sandy?" asked Kris. "Must have been something pretty drastic."

"Two words," said Sandy: "Alaska Pipeline. Fairbanks, as the jump-off point for the whole northern half of pipeline construction, became a real boomtown in the '70s. Imagine all these multi-million dollar oil companies pouring into this half-frozen little backwater, throwing money around like it was going out of style. Who could resist such excitement? I couldn't."

Sandy grinned at the boys as she turned off Airport Way, onto University Avenue. "Of course, boomtowns are **the** history of Alaska. But what made '70s boomtowns different was that they attracted a fair amount of '60s flotsam and jetsam: people for whom the journey never ended. A surprising number of these folks wound up here in ol' Bearflanks. And, a lot of them—not to mention their kids—are still here: they're not to hard to find, if you know where to look. **That** is what gives this place its 'hidden' character."

The truck turned off the road onto a gravel parking lot, splashing through snowmelt mud puddles. "I give you True Fairbanks Hangout #1: the Hot Licks ice cream shop. Besides what I've just told you, there's another factor to consider: every college town **must** have its counter-culture contingent. Since the UAF campus is right up the hill, this is their major congregating spot." In the parking lot, a number of multicolored, casual young animals were gathered in a circle, doing the ubiquitous hackysack dance. Kris and Peter were nostalgically reminded of similar scenes on the docks of Skagway.

They paused in the doorway to read a colorful, hand-printed business flyer on the wall: "Happy Traveling—from Douglas Fir at Astral Travel!"

"I know that guy," said Sandy. "Doug is an old Humboldt County rabble-rouser: used to chain himself to redwood trees, stuff like that. Now he's mellowed out, gone legit, as you can see. But he still attracts an extra-crunchy clientele."

"Specializing in long, strange trips, no doubt," commented Peter.

Once inside, they contemplated the tall wooden flavor board as a smiling scooper waited. "The selections are a bit mind-bending as well," said Sandy to the boys. "It takes a creative talent to come up with ice cream flavors like Tiger—that's orange sherbet with licorice stripes—Oatmeal Raisin, Malted Grape-Nut and the like, and make them taste great. You just don't get that from Baskin-Robbins."

Pete opted for a mix of Salmonberry and Malted Grape-Nut, Kris chose a huge scoop of Prudhoe (extra high-viscosity chocolate), and Sandy grabbed a double-decker Oatmeal Raisin: "I skipped breakfast this morning."

They lingered for about fifteen minutes, slowly making their way through the ice cream and enjoying the parade of customers. "Did you know that Alaska leads the nation in per-capita ice cream consumption?" asked Sandy. "This place is hoppin' all year long, even in the dead of winter. It takes a frozen people to appreciate this kind of creativity."

Since they were right in the neighborhood, Sandy decided to drive the boys up to the University of Alaska campus next. "Thank God this campus is on such a big hill," she commented.

"Why would you be thankful for **that**?" asked Kris, listening to the old truck's lugging transmission. "This grade has got to be a bitch in the Winter."

"True enough. But when it gets really cold in Fairbanks—minus 40° or lower—the whole river valley can get socked in with ice fog. You see, the air is usually so still at such temperatures that **any** type of emission, whether from cars, the electric plant or people's breathing, just hangs there in ice crystals, without dissipating or evaporating. If the extreme cold sticks around for any length of time, it becomes damn near impossible to see or breathe outside. But here on this hill, we're above it all: from upper campus, you can look down at a sea of dirty-white ice fog. Some folks, myself included, come up here just to escape for a while."

"I bet the students hardly ever feel like leaving bed, much less the campus, when it gets nasty like that," said Peter. "But overall, don't they get a little stir-crazy during the winters here?"

"Yes, in fact: they do. It's absolutely unavoidable. But they have ways of dealing with it." As the truck reached the main part of the campus, Sandy pointed to a tall, copper-roofed building across a sunlit courtyard. "Which leads us to the next subject: the Wood Campus Center, our second True Fairbanks tour stop." She pulled into a muskeg-swamp of a parking lot: thick black coal-tailing mud, with electrical car plug-in posts sticking up at jaunty angles. "This has got to be the site of Genna's famous Spring Volleyball games," Kris thought to himself.

They got out and walked over to the Wood Center, entering on the main floor and stopping to gaze upward at the high, vaulted ceilings and huge skylights. "It's all one big, open space in here," said Peter. "From your comments, I get the feeling that this design is not accidental."

"Yep: this place is kind of the 'healing temple' for Cabin Fever. You get inside here on a clear Winter day—during those precious few hours of daylight—see the sun streaming through those skylights, shed several layers of outerwear…it's definitely good therapy.

"But it's **not** the entire solution: this space gets at the symptoms, but not the cause." Sandy turned from the atrium, gestured towards a set of glass-walled offices on the second floor. "That's the headquarters for the student newspaper: the Sun-Star. I got involved with them a few years back, when I was taking some classes here. Anyhow, one of my best friends on the staff, during the height of an especially hellacious cold snap, addressed his illness in a rather unique way: he borrowed a video camera, bundled up like Admiral Peary, and set out to make a documentary. A Nature documentary, starring God's creature the raven. He marched around outside in fifty-below for a few days, filming everything, seeing how ravens were dealing with it all. Towards the end, he initiated conversation with the birds, attempted diplomacy, tried all kinds of weird things. But once we dragged him back inside, we saw what he had shot and helped him edit it into an interesting, fairly presentable video. He called it 'Scream Obscenities To The Ravens'."

Sandy shook her head. "Of course, most people aren't nearly so creative with their Cabin Fever cures. As you might guess, this is definitely a 'party' campus, especially in the high rise dormitories. There's probably way too much drinking, in fact. But at least the cold comes in handy: if you pick up a lukewarm sixer at the store and hang it outside your window at forty below, you've got some frosty brew-ha's in about five minutes. Just don't forget about 'em out there for too long. And watch out for fishing lines from up above: some folks have been known to angle for free beer.

"Another popular dorm pastime is, if you live on one of the top floors, to try and nail the lower windows with some thick liquid stuff: something that'll freeze hard and look interesting. Something impossible to scrape off, to be stared at until Spring. Campbell's Soup concentrate is popular: extra-chunky minestrone, cream of mushroom. Don't ask me why."

Leaving the Wood Center, Kris and Peter followed Sandy back towards the truck. "Students will be students," commented Kris. "But of course, **we** never pulled any stunts like that when we lived in the dorms, did we, Pete?"

"Of course not," said Peter, flashing his finest expression of innocence for Sandy. "We was **angels**, everyone said."

Sandy rolled her eyes, shrugged and started up the old truck. "Whatever. Anyhow, I'd now like to take you out a little ways north of town, on a road called the Farmer's Loop. The deep woods off the Loop are the stomping grounds of the 'suburban bush bunny': a species particular to this area. That's why, as opposed to Airport Way, I consider this to be the true 'Main Street' of Fairbanks.

They turned left from the campus intersection, onto a strip of asphalt road made rolling by chronic permafrost. Sandy pointed off in the general direction of the tall birch trees. "It's hard to tell from here," she said, "but back there are a whole bunch of little cabins—you can rent 'em for maybe two or three hundred bucks a month—and they figure that a third of 'em have no modern conveniences whatsoever. Who would want to live like this? Well, students are **always** looking for cheap digs. Others are looking for that rural Alaskan experience, without getting too far from civilization. On the Farmer's Loop, people can have it both ways."

"Back to the basics, eh?"

"Damn straight: who needs plumbing and electricity, anyway? Those dark, frosty Winter visits to the outdoor john build character. And of course, if folks get to feelin' **too** bushy, why, they can take a bus back to campus, go into the Wood Center and stare at some higher ceilings."

Sandy jerked her head towards a narrow dirt road, choked by budding willow and freshly emergent fireweed. "My friend Dusty lives up that way; he's been back in the boondocks for about two years now. Has a cabin so small, you have to step outside to change your mind—but it's built so tight that you can fire up the woodstove with a couple spruce logs, and quickly get the place so warm you can walk around barefoot. Only thing is, you just can't forget to keep the stove stoked. Once, he did. His pot of soup was froze solid by morning. He doesn't forget anymore.

"But Dusty has gone mechanical now. Rebuilt a diesel generator, which gives him about enough juice to run his Macintosh, a boom box, and a couple lightbulbs."

Looking at the rolling hills, Kris tried to imagine all the tiny, wood-stove-heated cabins, inhabited by high-tech Daniel Boones. "Do you know what?" he asked Sandy. "I still don't understand the name of this area: 'Farmer's Loop'. I don't see a hell of a lot of farms around here."

"You're right," said Sandy. "There aren't many farms anymore. But back in the 1930's, there was a major effort to make Fairbanks more self-sufficient in food production: people were worried that the Great Depression would threaten their thin lifeline to the Outside. This particular area was chosen because of its south-facing slopes: better drainage, less permafrost.

"For a time, there were some going farm concerns: raising dairy cattle, producing hay and grain. But then World War II came along, and after that big shot of infrastructure came to this country—not to mention all the men and supplies—local farming no longer paid, at least as far as staple foods were concerned. There's still a fair amount of summer produce grown around here: you should **see** some of the gardens. But that's about it."

A large clearing had come into view, spanning both sides of the road. "This used to be one of the farms," said Sandy. "Guess what it is now? The nation's northernmost **golf course:** complete with Astro-Turf putting greens. Only a one-stroke penalty for hitting moose on the fairway."

She pointed out beyond the end of the furthest fairway. "My place is out that-away: a little further off the beaten path than most local cabins. I'd love to have you all over soon: I'm thinking of having a get-together on the Summer Solstice, for whomever is in town. I'd take you there now, but I'm afraid we'd have to test my new batch of homebrew—bottled it two weeks ago—and we'd be **sure** to piss away the whole afternoon."

"God forbid," said Kris.

After a few more miles of trees, hills and cabins, and one Permafrost Nightmare house (a '70s suburban abode, built without adequate ground insulation, that gave new meaning to the term "split-level"), the truck turned north, up the Old Steese Highway. "Just up ahead is Goldstream Valley," said Sandy, "which is really outside of city limits, but still help defines Fairbanks. I've already shown you some of the best: in my opinion, here's some of the worst."

The landscape was decidedly different in the valley. Rather than the ubiquitous spruce bog/birch hillock mix, there were randomly dispersed ridges of gravel and rock, covered by a thin sketch of scrub alder and weeds.

"At one time or another," said Sandy, "this land—**all** of it—has been chewed up and spit out by machines: the gold dredges. There were about a dozen dredges, each one the size of a big riverboat. They sat in their own ponds, scooping up rocks, gravel and dirt in the front ends, sifting out the gold, then dumping everything else out the back side: slowly working their way forward. They moved miles that way, up and down the valley. Some 80 years later, the land still hasn't fully recovered."

"And of course, the big mining companies didn't have to restore **any** of this." Kris shook his head in wonder. "I can hardly believe it."

"Well, this was the 'Last Frontier', after all. Still is, to a considerable degree." Sandy gestured expansively towards the horizon. "At least nowadays, where there are still placer operations in the Interior, they're more strict about keeping the water clean, grading and replanting the tailings, and all that. But it's still not enough."

She excused herself: "Sorry, I tend to get on a soapbox sometimes. The reason I came out this way wasn't to preach at you, but to show you another True Fairbanks spot: a place where the old and the new ways of raping the land—whoops, I mean 'harvesting natural resources'—are side by side. Gold Dredge #8, and the Alaska Pipeline."

They stopped and got out. Atop a long, low hill of tailings sat several dilapidated buildings, behind which a boat's cabin tower was barely visible. "Sorry, we can't really go back there anymore," said Sandy. "Some guy just bought this whole property, if you can believe it: he plans to develop it as a sort of goldpanning/ theme-park thing. He even wants to raise the old dredge; the whole lower deck is below water. It'll be interesting to see if he can pull it off."

After a moment or two, Sandy pointed them away from the dredge site and began walking them into the tall brush. "Just up here is one of the few places where they'll still let you walk right up to the pipeline. Whether you like the idea of the thing or not, it's still an impressive sight to see."

A sense of motion, felt rather than seen, was apparent as the Alaska Pipeline unfolded before them. They perceived something almost organic: seemingly alive, like an artery.

"Four feet in diameter, exactly 800 miles long, a flow of 1.5 million barrels per day," recited Sandy. "But that doesn't even begin to tell the story of what the Alaska Pipeline means.

"What is the name of that 'landscape artist'—Christo?—who does things like gift-wrap buildings, or build long fences around nothing? Well, I don't think he could've topped **this** if he'd tried. See how it bobs and weaves, not only from side to side, but above and below the ground's surface? See those finned cross-bar supports for the above-ground sections, looking like some '50s Cadillac designer's idea for football goalposts? Don't you get a sense of infinity from the way the pipeline snakes across the hills, both north and south, over both horizons?"

Kris and Peter, not expecting such verbiage, were mildly nonplused. Sandy sensed this, somewhat sheepishly cleared her throat and continued:

"Ahem. Of course, there are technical explanations for all those features. The presence of permafrost in a given area determines whether the pipeline is buried or above ground. The radiator fins on those 'goalposts' prevent the oil's heat from seeping into the supports, melting the frozen ground and causing the whole line to sag. All those jointed curves provide flexion: if a big earthquake comes, the pipeline is designed to straighten, rather than bend and break."

"So, how do you **feel** about all this?" wondered Peter.

"Well, I'm violently ambivalent, as usual. I don't like the idea of this bold gash across the entire state: this piece of human technology that, if it ever failed, would ruin some huge areas of wilderness. But there's no doubt that it pays for just about everything worthwhile that the state government does. The Alaska Pipeline affects me on a gut level, as I've already demonstrated to you. And, I'm by no means the only one: people have reacted to its presence in any number of, uh, 'primal' ways."

Kris pondered this. "Well, isn't that just what the artist strives for: that type of visceral response?"

Sandy laughed. "Yep: those folks at Alyeska are a bunch of artists, but don't know it. Anyhow, the best-known 'primal response' took place right around here. You see, the majority of bushers, to no one's real surprise, didn't take too kindly to having the pipeline in their back yard. One local gent, kind of a gold prospector/explosives freak, felt sufficiently moved by the pipeline's presence to conclude that the thing **had to go**, in one swell foop. And, what better way to accomplish this than to borrow liberally from his stash of ordnance, steal out to the line in the middle of the night and set 'er off? Put the fear of God in them damn oil companies: take your dirty work elsewhere, thank you very much.

"Well, he actually carried out his plan: pulled his truck up to an above-ground section of pipe, unloaded a fair amount of fireworks underneath, lit the fuse and ran. Apparently, the explosion just about blew his truck off the road as he was high-tailing it out of there. But all that happened to the pipeline, they say, was that it jumped up about a foot in the air, settled back down on the supports—granted, a tad off-kilter—and was pretty much undamaged, save for some shredded pipe insulation.

"To soothe the jangled nerves from his commando operation, the sourdough explosives-freak retired to the Howling Dog, a very dubious watering-hole not far from here. Flushed with his success, he could not resist buying a few pitchers and, as his lips loosened, entertaining his bushy colleagues with the tale of what he had just done. Well, you know the rest of the story: little pitchers have big ears, as they say, and shortly the Feds had their vice-like hands on our friend. They threw the book at him for sabotage, terrorism, endangering national security interests, you name it, locked him up and pretty much threw away the key—and he didn't even get the satisfaction of putting more than a dent in the Alaska Pipeline."

After a few contemplative minutes, Kris became insatiably curious. "So, how **about** that dubious watering hole? Hadn't we better go and get a first-hand look, for history's sake?"

Sandy laughed. "My thoughts exactly. To the Howling Dog: the ulti-mate True Fairbanks spot."

They drove for another couple of miles, into the tiny hamlet of Fox. Perched on the main intersection was a sprawling, rough-hewn log struc-ture, infused with the memory of many an out-of-control evening. "I can tell, just by looking, what this place must be like at times," commented Kris as they entered the door, sat down and ordered a big-eared pitcher with homefries.

"You can't imagine," said Sandy. "For example, look at what you're sitting on: the heavy-duty barstools. They're solid **logs**. Makes it a bit harder for folks to pick 'em up and fling 'em around. It doesn't stop some.

"But it's not usually a **violent** kind of rowdy." She gestured towards the outdoor beer garden. "When the summer begins to heat up, and we start getting the midnight sun, you'll see some great volleyball games out there. Bands will come, people will dance all night; the bar will kick' em out between 4 and 6 am, only because of the state law. It's a grand time of year at the Dog.

"Just one drawback: the place is quite a bit more crowded, and less abnormal, than it used to be, since the townies have discovered it. These days, you need to go out to Chatanika Lodge, about 30 miles up the Steese Highway, to find the old-time busher crowd anymore. That neck of the woods is even more spirited than the Farmer's Loop: per capita, the hills north of town are full of as many characters as any Appalachian holler."

"Kind of an 'Alaska Hillbilly' thing, huh?"

"Actually, **no**. The local color is very colorful, but they're not a bunch of inbred yahoos. There are poets, artists, non-conformists of all stripes. If you were to gather up all my rowdy bush-bunny friends in one place— which you just might see, at my solstice party—you'd be surprised at all the advanced degrees, all the intelligence and humor. And all the beer they can put away in one sitting.

"Anyhow, the Chatanika Lodge is where these folks go when they need to hear the sound of their own names." Sandy got a nostalgic look on her face. "Saw an amazing band out there once: called Buck Nekkid and the Tattoos. They had a guy who could do some surprising things with a trombone. The crowd was wild for 'em: folks were ripping off their long-johns and throwing 'em onstage."

"You know, I think I've heard of an Alaskan band like that." Kris turned to Peter, raising his eyebrows; Pete nodded. He understood.

NOTE ON FRIDGE: 5/27/88

▼

Dear roomies (whomever you may be):

I'm off to Skagpatch (finally)! Training on the downhill run with Don; making the quick turnaround, then doing my first solo tour northbound. Wish me luck!

Pete—have fun in Denali. Wish I could hang with you in the Park; we'll do some hiking there sometime. Maybe I'll get to train to Anchorage soon, and you'll learn the Highway Two trip. I'll have a Hot Red Onion for you.

Y'all help yourself to any of my stuff in the fridge; it'd just go bad anyhow. With one exception: I know that you wouldn't be so heinous as to drink my last beer.

Later on—Kris

Buffalo In The Barley Patch

▼

Fun Fact #395: the Delta Junction area, about one hundred miles southeast of Fairbanks, is home to a herd of free-range buffalo. Back in 1928, twenty-three buffalo were imported from the National Bison Range in Montana and released near Delta, in the hope that they would thrive in the relatively open spaces and ultimately provide another local food resource. The buffalo succeeded beyond most realistic expectations: as of the late 1980's, the herd had grown in number to nearly three hundred head.

During this same time span, fledgling agricultural enterprises also took hold in the Delta region: acres of muskeg were cleared, drained and planted in short grains, primarily barley. This endeavor has survived for the most part—but success has been marred by a large buffalo herd that marauds through the planted fields on an increasingly frequent basis.

"We're just about to cross the Tanana River, folks," said Don the tour guide, a boyish-faced fifty year old. "If you'll look to your left as we drive across the bridge, you will see a dramatic view of…San Francisco?"

Strangely enough, a twin-peaked suspension bridge, similar in shape and design to the Golden Gate (albeit considerably smaller) came into view. However, instead of Bay Area traffic, this bridge bore a single pay-load: the Alaska Pipeline.

"Of the hundreds of river and stream crossings along the pipeline route," said Don, "this one is the longest, spanning nearly a quarter-mile." He then turned to Kris, who was up front in the bus stairwell, serving as the Ed McMahon-style sidekick. "And what **next** do we have for our guests, Kris?"

"Well, we're almost in Delta Junction, the present significance of which can be summed up in one word: **lunch**. But not just **any** lunch: we will be dining at Rika's Roadhouse, an historic stopover point along this route. The site has been.. let's see…" Kris riffled through his memory banks for the recently-acquired information: "an Athabaskan fishing camp on the Tanana, since time immemorial. A territorial military outpost. A stopover on the Valdez-Fairbanks trail, then the Richardson Highway. Built in 1910, since restored as an historical park—and site of the best old-style lunch this side of the Klondike."

"Not bad, for a rookie," said Don, winking in the rear-view mirror. After another moment or two, he pulled the bus off the highway, into a large birch grove. He and Kris disembarked their guests and led them up a gravel footpath. They came to the riverbank, turned to the left, and beheld a large, grassy expanse, dotted with old log buildings. The nearest building emanated chimney smoke and various smells of good cooking.

"Lunch is right over there, in the old cookhouse," said Don. "First things first. But then, just after we eat, one of the people who lives and works here will give us a little walking tour. I think you'll really enjoy Rika's. I know I always do: I've been dreaming of blueberry **pie** for the last fifty miles."

There was a mild stampede towards the door at Don's mention of the "P" word. Inside the cookhouse, a long table was heaped with a variety of mouthwatering home-cooked goodies: hot beef sandwiches with gravy, fresh sourdough loaves, three kinds of soup, blueberry and strawberry-rhubarb pies that were still bubbling from the oven. Don and Kris took their places in line, behind the guests, and loaded up. They took their lunch trays to an outdoor picnic table that overlooked the fast-flowing river and dug in.

After silently tending to business for a time, Kris wiped his mouth with a napkin and spoke to Don. "This reminds me just a little bit of being back in college: you know, loading up on dinner at the cafeteria. Unlimited quantities, heavy-ballast food—even though this stuff, obviously, is ten times better than dormitory food ever was."

Don looked thoughtful. "You're closer in your analogy than you think. Remember the 'Freshman Fifteen', the standard consequence of such dorm-food hedonism? Well, if they don't watch it, rookie highway drivers are apt to experience the same thing: rapid, shocking weight gains from all the free chow down the road. All that meat and potatoes, all that sitting behind the wheel. You have to learn to cut back after a time—easier said than done, at places like this—unless you **really** want to start looking like a bus driver."

"I'm not particularly worried about the 'Freshman Fifteen'," commented Kris. "I swear, I must have the metabolism of a hummingbird: I can hardly gain weight if I try. What I do worry about, though, is getting **sleepy** after these big lunches."

"The old behind-the-wheel nods." Don shook his head. "Not very reassuring to your passengers. Know what I used to do, for long, isolated afternoon stretches of driving? Load up on a gallon or so of Mountain Dew, or iced tea, or some other effective diuretic. If you have to race like a pisshorse for a hundred miles, you will **not** become sleepy, trust me."

Kris laughed. "My God, you really **are** a pro at this, Don. But, what keeps you going? What is left for you, after so many years of touring?"

Don ruminated over this question as he chewed the last of his pie crust. "Well, first of all, you've got to realize that I'm a bit of an exception, in terms of longevity. I just never found myself susceptible to the burn-out that hits so many drivers around their third or fourth years: I was always able to let the stress slide off me. If you react by bitching and moaning, making fun of the tourists behind their backs and all that, negativity starts sneaking into your tours, until it become painfully obvious to all: I've seen it happen, every season. When you stop **liking** people, it's time to get out of the business. This is year number seven for me, and I intend to keep on going for as long as I can.

"But it's still a grind at times—especially towards the end of the season. Consequently, I rely on a lot of little things to keep me going. The stops we make along the way are a major bonus: not just for the free chow, but for getting to know the **locals** a bit more than we have to. Sometimes I feel as if we just barge into these little Alaskan communities as if we were bulls in a china shop. Or buffalo in the barley patch, as it were. Sure, they want the business—they **need** it, to get through the Winter—but we needn't disrupt their lives so much with our daily invasions. It makes me feel better to do the little things that make our hosts smile. If they're in a good mood, their hospitality will be that much more appreciated by our guests. It all comes around, you know?"

Kris nodded in agreement, commenting that the people at Rika's seemed extremely warm and friendly towards Don—and making a mental note to cultivate the same type of relationship wherever he stopped along the road.

"Something else I live for," Don continued, "are the 'drive-by relationships' you develop with your fellow drivers. You've already noticed that you hardly ever see your so-called 'roommates' at home. But out on the road, you all kind of follow each other around: by running tours together, sharing overnight accommodations, or simply by flashing past one another on the highway. On the first day out of Fairbanks, Dot Lake is where we usually wave at our colleagues, ask them why they're giving the tour backwards; the following day, we usually meet up around Lake Kluane. It's amazing how much one can look forward to those extremely brief encounters.

"But, most of all, my primary enjoyment comes from my passengers. Some of the stuff you see and hear over the years is mighty fine entertainment. One time, a man lost his upper dentures in the Blue Lagoon—and he actually asked me to **watch** for them when I dumped the tank that evening. Thankfully, I did not see them. Another time, in the frost-heaves, some poor guy lost his **pants** while reaching for some overhead luggage: FWOOMP! Down to his ankles. If he had been wearing polka-dot boxers shorts, I would have totally lost it. Those kind of tourist stories have a way of sneaking into one's personal folklore, which is worth the price of admission in itself.

"The other side of the coin is what I can give **back** to my guests. I love to watch those rapt expressions in the rearview mirror, when they spot some wildlife, or see something they've never seen before, or learn something about Alaska that strikes some kind of chord deep within them. It's the best kind of 'rush' a good driver/guide can hope to have.

"Sometimes, all scenery aside, the guide himself can create that kind of memorable experience. As you've undoubtedly learned by now, all those facts and figures you spout off don't really stick in the minds of your tourists. For the most part, what they'll remember are general impressions: was the guide a fine young man or woman? Did he or she seem knowledgeable, responsible, forthright? Or, was the guide total squirrel-bait: a nut-ball who did things to make them laugh until their sides hurt? Or, some combination of the two?"

Don smiled mischievously. "Me, I like to find the perfect balance. Up until now, you've seen me in my 'serious' mode. But here at Rika's, in fact, is one small opportunity for a memorable Tour Guide antic. And, since I don't want to spoil the impact for you, I'm not gonna tell you what it is. Excuse me, I've gotta go: see you back at the bus." He returned his tray to the cookhouse and walked away briskly.

Having no idea what to expect, Kris waited until the tourists had finished lunch, and moseyed over towards the main lodge once the Rika's guide, a Little House On The Prairie-looking guy with a diamond-willow walking stick, had gathered everyone. As they strolled across the grounds, Kris admired the well-crafted log out-buildings and the flower and vegetable gardens that were roaring to life. About a baseball field's width away was the historic Roadhouse, a solid wooden structure that looked as if it would last well into the next century. They paused on the porch.

"And now," said the walking-stick guy, "I'd like to show you how your predecessors—the original highway travelers—lived when they stayed at Rika's Roadhouse. We've set up a display of old-time lodge rooms, furnished with the household accoutrements one would have found in the Teens or Twenties." He held open the heavy-beam door and beckoned everyone inside.

Just inside the door was a small, cordoned-off living room, equipped with heavy oak furniture, a Victrola, thick rugs and an upright player piano. The tourists oohed and ahhed over the antique furnishings—some, fondly recalling the very same pieces from their parents' or grandparents' living rooms. "These were pretty rough times in Alaska, in the early days of the territory," said the guide. "That's why the comforts of home were so roundly appreciated by travelers. That's why it was worthwhile to haul furniture and a piano over Thompson Pass and up the trail."

After letting them linger a moment longer, the guide gestured the group towards another cordoned room. "Right next door is the kitchen and parlor. You'll no doubt recognize many of the furnishings here as well."

Kris stepped next door along with everyone else, and saw a very similar display: an old cast-iron cooking range, gingham curtains, shelves lined with crockery, spices and canning jars. Seated at the kitchen table, behind an incongruously dainty tea service, was a mannequin dressed as an old sourdough. His heavy furs hung near the door, but his buckskin jerkin and breeches continued to warm him; a battered but trusty wool toque perched on his head like some kind of weird bird. His frozen gaze was directed towards the window, as if contemplating distant trap lines over his steaming Earl Grey.

The tourists were very impressed by this tableau, noting the familiar dishes and furnishings, commenting on the uncannily realistic appearance of the sourdough mannequin. Indeed, its eyes seemed a little **too** lifelike: a little too humor-creased and sparkling, an little too Don-like as finally he was unable to hold a straight face for any longer. They let out gasps of recognition: many laughed, a few applauded, nearly all took pictures. As a mischievously grinning Don shed the remainder of his sourdough gear to rejoin his group, Kris knew that this was the memory the tourists would carry from this day, above all others.

THE BACK STEPS

▼

The portland house sways as i lay down my
burden on the back steps; the right harmonics, an old
drinking song maybe, and
all would tumble down

    there is no entrance or egress from the
    portland house this sunny backlot weed-growing
    skagway morning, in fact the whole place is boarded up, city
    fathers having decreed it too decrepit, even by local standards
    dust on the floor, spillwater in the buckets, probably hints of leftover
    stew in the slob kitchen, growing daily in scientific significance
    my own memories tacked on woodbeam walls like
    last year's peeling wallpaper, lawn chairs abandoned on asphalt
    shingles;
    no rooftop party this year

but the train whistle still blows, the streets are full, and the
portland house waits, in inimitable christmas-fruitcake fashion;
there surely is life in the
old place yet

Things To Remember: Northbound Skagway-Fairbanks Tour

▼

1) Load passenger baggage onto bus at cruise ship dock; make sure it's all there.

2) Pickup at Fraser railroad depot (the WP & YR lives!): 2:00 p.m.

3) Check off passengers against manifest; make sure everyone is there. Advise any foreign guests regarding Canadian customs (as if they would even mildly hassle anyone). Meet 'n greet; smile!! Maybe some semi-corny "introductions" game (e.g., "Two Truths and a Lie").

4) Hit the road, Jack. Explain the "big picture" re tour itinerary.

5) Brief coffee break/ pit stop in Carcross. Try not to lose anyone to the Caribou Hotel/ Animal Head Room.

6) Continue tour to Whitehorse; advise re places to go/ things to see in town. Turn 'em over to expies; see you in the morning! Wash and dump the bus. Go have a beer somewhere.

7) Up and at 'em: 6 am. Quick breakfast and coffee; load luggage (count those bags, carefully); meet 'n greet once again. Put on that smiley morning face. Hit the road.

8) Brief explanation of day's itinerary: coffee breaks, lunch, other pit stops. Caution about long (albeit very scenic) day: 410 miles, all the way to Tok. Crank up the Tour Guide charm.

9) Coffee stop: Haines Junction/ Macintosh. Lunch: Destruction Bay, Lake Kluane. Afternoon coffee: Beaver Creek. Definite picture stops: Champagne, Aishihik River bridge, Sheep Mountain, St. Elias Range overlook, Donjek River bridge. Other picture stops as the occasion warrants.

10) Finally land in Tok, between 7 and 8 p.m. Unload bags, wash and dump bus. Try to spot elusive but very cute motel proprietress.

More Uses For The 55-Gallon Oil Drum

Tour Tidbit #25: large metal fuel-oil containers, popularly known as 55-gallon oil drums, are the ubiquitous construction/craft material throughout rural Alaska. Their handy cylindrical shape and indestructible nature—and sheer numbers, in yards and trash-heaps—have made them the choice for a mind-boggling array of homemade applications. Oil drums are commonly used at Bush airstrips, as weights for tying down the planes and otherwise grounding them in reality. Dyea Gary and many others have built sturdy wood-burning stoves from them; Sandy uses them for backyard flower planters; a Dawson buddy of Norm and René built an oil drum pontoon raft, which has floated him up and down the Yukon River for a number of years. According to Derek's brother Karl, a bar owner during the 70's Pipeline boom made an impromptu stage using oil drums, wooden shipping pallets and plywood sheets—and thus created a portable, fly-by-night strip joint.

To this day, Alaskans of an enterprising stripe (as nearly all the bushers are) can hardly pass by a rust-free but inexplicably abandoned oil drum without clucking "What a waste," and either throwing it into the back of their old slant-six International, or letting a friend know about the unclaimed treasure.

For the first time all season, the Tok River valley carried a hint of the Everglades about it: thunderheads, hatching mosquitoes, humidity hanging like a shower curtain in the soft June evening. Maybe there were even some 'gators lurking in the dense muskeg swamp: it was hard to tell for sure.

Sweat staining his uniform shirt, Kris rolled up to the Tundra Lodge. Upon arrival, he had put his passengers in the care of Glenda, Genna's mom, who closely matched her daughter in terms of welcome and good cheer. However, he had seen no sign of Genna; indeed, he had caught only a fleeting glimpse when he had stopped with Don for coffee the last time through. Where was she? Did she even remember who he was? Kris had pondered the mystery as he finished unloading luggage, took the bus to the washing yard, scrubbed calcified insects off the windshield and dumped the Blue Lagoon. Thoughts of Genna had merged with reflections on his first solo tour as he munched a double-cheeseburger at the Tok Tastee-Freez.

I'm definitely winging it this trip: pretty much the "all-charm" tour. Typical first-time struggles. But the facts and logistics will straighten themselves out soon enough. The tourists seem to like me just fine. I'm just tired, mostly: glad it's only a short drive to Fairbanks tomorrow.

Guess I'll hang it up early tonight; maybe I'll get a chance to see Genna in the morning.

Now, work and dinner done, Kris parked his bus for the night, briefly visited the drivers' Airstream trailer (their Tok accommodations), grabbed a towel from his gear bag and strolled to the campground shower: the lodge had a back lot for RV's and tent campers. Bugs hurled themselves insensibly against the window as Kris turned on the water, lathered up and scrubbed off his own road grit.

He returned to the trailer, and had just changed into shorts and a clean t-shirt when suddenly an unruly head of curly light-brown hair popped into view through the door screen. Kris drew in his breath, the door opened, and Genna slipped into the Airstream. "Hey, Kris. Long time."

She smiled her bemused, full-mouthed smile. "Sorry I missed you before: things are a little nutty around here right now, with just me and Mom running the show."

The face and voice—and the **eyes**—that had trailed Kris through his exotic Winter travels were finally before him. For a long moment, he was at a loss for words. As Genna continued calmly to look at him, still smiling, Kris regained rudimentary speech functions. "Um, yeah. I only caught a glimpse of you last time through: you seemed pretty busy. Uh, how are you, Genna? How was your Winter?"

"**Butt** cold: what do you think, silly boy?" Genna laughed at him, picked up a stray magazine and fanned herself with it. "Nothing like it is now: you wouldn't believe how quickly the seasons change here. Come on, what do you say we get out of this metal sausage, go chat somewhere else?"

Genna's snowmelt laugh had a tonic effect on Kris: he relaxed, nodded his agreement, was able to return her smile. Together they stepped out into the evening. There was no sign of an imminent sunset, even though it was pushing ten o'clock.

"I'd suggest a walk on the town," said Genna, "but the skeeters are at their absolute peak right now. We'd be sucked dry before we made it to the Burnt Paw. Know any bug-free places?"

"How about the bus?" offered Kris. "It's all swept out and clean. There are even **tunes** in there: I actually got a decent tape deck this time."

"Old-people music, or something hipper?"

"Oh, **nothing** but hipness, of course. Some Guy Lombardo, some Mantovani Strings. The very latest sing-alongs from Mitch Miller."

Genna gave him a sidelong, golden-eyed smile as Kris opened up the bus. She stepped up the stairwell, peered into Kris' cassette case, lingered approvingly for a moment before selecting Crosby, Stills, Nash and Young's "Deja Vu" and popping it into the sound system. "I grew up with all this Sixties music," explained Genna. "I'm glad that somebody else my own age has such good taste."

"What do you mean, 'my own age'? Don't you realize what a **geezer** I am?"

Genna looked conciliatory. "Yes, Kris: you had me fooled for the longest time. I've finally figured out that, in actuality, you're forty-five years old. With a wife, 2.5 kids, and a home in the suburbs. And a crew-cut." She sprawled into a cushy bus seat, wrapped her long legs around the seat in front. "Besides, I'll be twenty-one next January. Plenty old enough to hang with you grown-up tour guide types."

"I don't know: us Coach Commanders can be pretty wild. Do your Mom and Dad know you're out here with me?"

"My Mom had **you** sized up as a 'fine young man' from the moment she laid eyes on you, Bucko. As for my Dad: well, he's in no real position to pass judgment on you one way or the other, because, unfortunately, he's dead."

Kris was taken aback: not only from his own *faux pas*, but also from Genna's seemingly cavalier attitude. "Gosh, I'm **sorry**, Genna: I had no idea."

"It's all right: really. It's been a long time." Genna looked directly at Kris. "I was just a little girl. I don't mind talking about him: in fact, I enjoy it, because he was such a cool person. And because it helps keep his memory alive for me."

Kris looked at Genna with a measure of wonder and surprise. "Please tell me all about him. But let me secure some refreshment first." He rummaged in his ditty bag, came up with a pint flask of Yukon Jack that had somehow wandered away from Dyea Gary's stash. "Need any lubrication for the vocal cords?"

Genna smiled goldenly up at him. "It never hurts." She took a sour-dough-sized hit of Jack (surprising Kris again), wiped her mouth with the imaginary ripped-flannel sleeve, and began to speak.

"My Dad was an Alaskan bush pilot. The real thing. He learned to fly float planes on the lakes of Michigan as a teenager. Then, times being what they were, he became a hippie: bought a Volkswagen bus, hit the road, met my mother at a Rainbow gathering, the whole trip. Anyway, once he and Mom finally landed in Alaska, he took up flying again, and shortly found that his skills were greatly in demand. It was a real boom time in Alaska: Pipeline construction was gearing up; surveyors, construction moguls and hucksters of all stripes were swarming the state. Dad took 'em wherever they wanted to go: float pontoons in the Summer, skis for Winter landings.

"He made a very good living for a time, supporting his wife and new-born daughter in style. In between flying adventures, he was able to build for them a nice cabin, on the outskirts of this tiny, God-forsaken hamlet called Tok—the place where they had first landed in Alaska, in fact. Sometimes, mother and/or daughter were even able to join him.

"I can still remember flying with my Dad." Genna's eyes glowed as the memory took shape in her mind. "I don't remember all that much—'cause I was so young—but what's left is pretty vivid. I remember villagers gathering around the plane as he would land in some remote Bush community, regarding him as if he were Santa Claus: he had the mail, the groceries, the L.L. Bean orders. I remember the splash of the floats as we would land on some broad, diamond-flecked river: he could set the plane down as softly as if he were placing a toy birch-bark canoe onto a pond. I remember, more than once, my Dad making quick emergency pit-stops, so I could get out and pee behind a bush or a rock. I remember what it was like when, after a long flight to some far-flung corner of Alaska, he would finally make it back home: he would tiptoe into my room, I would pretend to be asleep—I had stayed awake, waiting for him—and he would give me a little kiss."

Genna paused for a moment, reached for Kris' bottle, then changed her mind and abstained. "And then, one day, he didn't come home. It was March of '77; I had just turned nine. The Iditarod dogsled race was being run; it had just been revived after a number of years. It was a small affair compared to now, but they still had a substantial support crew, including bush-pilot 'spotters': to track the progress of the race, render assistance as needed, report any problems they couldn't handle themselves. Well, the '77 race was rife with difficulties: teams and equipment breaking down, mushers getting off track, generally shitty weather. Towards the end of the race, a big storm began to brew, out over the Bering Sea, and there was much concern for the safety of the teams. It was decided that one plane should go out, despite the weather, to keep close tabs on everyone over that final stretch. My Dad volunteered: he had flown in plenty worse, and could always duck down and sit out the storm if things got really bad.

"What he, and everyone else, failed adequately to consider was the terrible swiftness of the storm. No sooner had he gotten off the ground than things began to sock in: soon there was snow and freezing rain, with near zero visibility. The people on the ground advised Dad to get his butt back down; he rogered that, and then was silent. They presumed that he had landed somewhere, with no problems—otherwise, they surely would have heard about it—and he was simply behind some mountains that were keeping him out of radio contact. He had been through such 'typical' Alaskan flying conditions plenty of times before and, given his abilities, most everyone figured he was OK.

"They didn't worry too much about him, until the storm finally passed through, the weather cleared, and everyone had checked in. Except for him." Genna looked up at Kris. "They searched and searched. They never did find my father, or his plane. Later, people speculated that, during the storm, his wings iced up almost instantaneously: too quickly for him to do anything about it. But nobody really knows what happened."

Kris was stunned into silence by Genna's forthrightness, her matter-of-fact telling of the story—but she gently waved off Kris' expression of concern. "Like I said, it was a long time ago. I still wonder about the how and why of it all—and I still miss my Dad—but it's water under the bridge. Really."

She cleared her throat, and continued to speak. "Anyhow, after Dad was gone, Mom kind of drifted: spent some time in Anchorage and Valdez, got into EST and other strange 70's stuff for a while. I was more or less a bystander through it all. But then, she got this offer to come back to Tok, to manage a motel and campground for some old friends. After a couple years, the owners were ready to move on, and Mom was ready not only to buy them out, but also for some long-term stability: she was herself again by then. The rest is history: Tok Elementary, Tok Junior High, and Tok High School for me—all in the same building, of course— two semesters at UAF before I realized I wasn't the college type, then back here. A few trips Outside: mainly to the Seattle Nordstrom's (before I realized I wasn't the Nordstrom's type), one trip to Southern Cal, to realize my dream of playing honest-to-God beach volleyball. That's just about it."

"Essentially, then," said Kris, "you've spent your whole life in Tok. After a night or so here, **I'm** generally ready to blow out of town—present company notwithstanding. I'm not sure I understand what keeps you here."

"I don't know, it's hard to explain the attractions of Tok. I'm the first to admit that it's not much to look at: there isn't hardly **anything** to look at, in fact. But, on the other hand, it's a pretty hopping place in the summer: it's the crossroads of Alaska. A lot of interesting people end up spending at least a night in little ol' Tok."

"So, the world comes to **you**: I kinda like that. And who knows: maybe some dashing young man will come down the highway, sweep you off your feet and remove you from this place, forever."

"Don't think they haven't tried," said Genna, rolling her eyes. "But what about the **opposite**: some charming local Tok-head snags the way-faring stranger, causes him to take up permanent residence. You know: the 'Fast Eddy's syndrome'."

Kris, recalling Derek and Karl's story of the hapless tour guide and his mother, had a good laugh over this. "Yeah: as much as everybody gripes about being 'stuck' here, I think that most of the drivers actually look forward to Tok. I have no doubt that your being here has something to do with it."

Did she blush just a tiny bit? "It's true: drivers have always had a pretty good time here. I essentially grew up with this stream of wacky tour-guide types parading through here in the summer. And, every summer has its different adventures and rewards."

Genna gestured towards the woods. "One of the legacies from last summer, in fact, is out back by the campground: a homemade barbecue. Some of the drivers made it from an old 55-gallon oil drum: they sawed the thing in half lengthwise, stuck some wire mesh over the top, and created just about enough cooking space to grill a whole moose." Genna smiled, envisioning the upcoming midnight-sun evenings. "We tend to congregate back there: the smoke from the grill keeps most of the bugs away. Besides, that's where the volleyball court is."

"But of course: I fully intend to pack my v-ball gear along on all my highway runs. And who knows: maybe I'll get lucky and smack a moose with my bus, for some good **barbecuin'**."

"You do that, and I'll smack **you**," said Genna, whacking Kris with a conveniently-placed tour brochure. Kris stoically took his punishment.

Their conversation, and corresponding Yukon Jack sipping, continued on until a surprisingly late hour. When the beverage finally reached its last dregs, Kris stretched, noted the time, and made as if to go. Genna followed suit, but then stopped as Kris held a silence longer than he expected. As she gave him a somewhat quizzical glance, he finally spoke again:

"Um, I wanted to ask you about something, Genna. You know Sandy, right? Long-time tour guide? Well, she's planning to have a little social gathering out at her place, on the Summer Solstice. It's a tradition of hers, apparently: homebrews, live music, general rowdiness. Would you like to be my date for her party? I know it's a ways off—and you don't even know me that well, yet—but I thought I'd ask you, just the same."

Genna definitely blushed this time. "Well, I don't know. It's pretty hard for me to get out of Tok during the height of the season. Fairbanks is almost four hours off, even the way **I** drive. But on the other hand, I do know Sandy pretty well: she's been coming through here for years. And I know she would throw a damn good party." She paused, looking askance at Kris. "What do **you** think: do I dare go off to some wild Bush party with a strange young man like you?"

"I don't know: I don't usually go to parties with strange young men. But please think about it, OK?"

"OK, I will." Genna smiled again, more softly: making Kris dream briefly but vividly of backyard oildrum barbecues, the midnight sun and many more good things to come.

Midnight Gardening

▼

"White nights"—the term used in subarctic Russia to describe high Summer: the lack of true darkness, even in the wee hours; the sunsets that barely occur, far to the north-northwest, followed in mere minutes by the north-northeast sunrise; the nonstop photosynthetic opportunities that kick plant metabolisms into hyperdrive. The pent-up moods and energies, finally liberated, that shed the urge to sleep like a heavy fur coat. Scandinavia and Alaska are also extremely susceptible to this seasonal phenomenon.

The snowpiles that had greeted Kris upon his arrival in Fairbanks were long gone, without a trace; gardens and other local vegetation were sprinting towards the midnight sun at a breakneck pace; the Anderson Apartments and their environs buzzed with activity, illicit and otherwise, at all hours. The white nights were upon Alaska.

Kris, highway-trip laundry completed, bored with his windowside surveillance of the apartment block's comings and goings and with nothing better to do, had joined Peter on the evening Fairbanks tour. He had the rear of the bus all to himself; it was mighty pleasant to watch the city slip by in air-conditioned comfort. Kris smiled at Peter's low-key tour rap. An hour's break, at the University of Alaska Museum, was forthcoming: time to take a walk with his old friend, whom he very seldom saw these days, and try to catch up on things.

When the break came, Kris and Peter strolled the fields of the university's Experimental Agriculture Station. Bursting out of the ground were long rows of what would soon be freakishly large fruits, flowers and vegetables. Grenade-sized strawberries, lying in wait amidst jungle foliage. Exploding-snowball bunches of honey-scented alyssum. Towering, tough-stalked sunflowers, glowering like Wilt Chamberlain. Carrots, beets and other root veggies that likely would require a backhoe to extricate. Canoe-like zucchini: suitable for hollowing out, and either stuffing and baking, for feeding to one's church youth group—or, for grabbing a paddle and floating off down the Tanana.

The cabbage, in particular, would be astounding. "They tell me," said Kris, "that the Alaska State Fair is the greatest freak show of them all. The major highlight, of course, is the Giant Cabbage Contest. People treat it like one of those giant pumpkin contests, like they have back in the Midwest—or, like a tractor pull. It's almost a macho sort of thing. According to Sandy, the winner last year was some guy who fertilized his cabbage with the **placenta** from the birth of his daughter. That sucker grew to eighty pounds by fairtime."

"What, the kid?"

"No, the cabbage, you knucklehead. That's a lot of coleslaw, eh? People would walk by the display, and couldn't believe it; Sandy says young children would burst into tears, looking at that big old cabbage. It was a **monster**."

"All this daylight affects everything, and everyone, rather strangely," said Peter. "Look: it's pushing nine o'clock, and it may as well be high noon. They could pretty much run 24-hour tours this time of year."

"Why not?" said Kris. "Just like the highway construction crews on the Al-Can: endless rotating shifts. I doubt the tourists would really mind: if it weren't for the extra-thick motel curtains, I think they'd lose track of time altogether."

"That's the way I'm feeling," said Peter. "I'm kind of messed up these days. All the comings and goings: Fairbanks to Denali to Fairbanks to Anchorage to Denali. Wondering where home is: it sure isn't the Anderson Apartments. The goofy sleep patterns, or lack thereof, generated by this constant daylight: it's much more drastic here than Skagway ever was. I see people doing stuff at the weirdest hours: graveyard-shift Jiffy Lubes; extra-inning softball, stretching well into the following morning; gardening at midnight. I'm not sure that I'm in Alaska so much as inside some kind of space-and-time distortion."

"But you **are** in Alaska, my friend," said Kris. "Right in the heart of it. And most everyone feels the same way you do, from what I can tell."

Peter clapped his friend on the shoulder and allowed that, all things considered, he still felt fine. "Heck—the white nights are so good for the plants and vegetables. They must be good for me, too, somehow."

Reaching the end of the long rows, Kris and Peter turned around and slowly began to make their way back towards the museum. Their continuing conversation changed channels fairly frequently: touring tidbits, company gossip, comparative notes on cute expies and motel proprietresses. Somehow, they wound up on the latest hot rumor to sweep the Fairbanks area: namely, that the great tendrils of media publicity had finally permeated Alaskan agriculture, and none other than David Letterman apparently was scheduling after-prime-time, in-depth interviews with some very large produce (and their growers), sometime around the August harvest.

Given the typical, condescending media treatment of Alaska, not to mention Letterman's often sarcastic interview style, Kris and Peter wondered whether things might degenerate into vegetative violence in the studio—whether such post-modern sensibilities might be lost on the veggies, who would then feel compelled to stick up for themselves and Alaska. Lumpy, elephantine taters and turnips, transcending their humble upbringings to assert proletarian dignity. Medicine-ball cabbages, rolling over and squashing the ineffectual Paul Schaeffer. Letterman being repeatedly creamed by quarter-pound strawberries. The whole ugly affair spilling out into the streets: pulpy, vitamin-laden splats adding to the general din of Manhattan.

*   *   *

"Let's get this show rolling," barked Genna. She had spent the earlier part of the evening scouring the campground, the driver's trailer, seemingly everywhere in Tok (save, perhaps, Fast Eddy's), scrounging up a crew to partake of an utterly perfect volleyball night. The contingent had been gathered, but was milling about in lackadaisical fashion on the sand court while Genna tossed the ball from one hand to the other, impatient as a puppy with a juicy stick and a stinky summer pond to dive into. Finally she simply sky-balled a towering serve into the social milieu, and the volleyball more or less began in earnest.

Shortly, Genna and Kris found themselves standing opposite one another in the front lines of their respective sides, pawing and snorting like the bulls of Pamplona.

"In yo' **face**," Genna promised Kris.

When the inevitable confrontation came, Genna bravely stood her ground, preparing to reject whatever came her way. But when the set came to Kris, he faked a hard spike and, as Genna went up for the block, gently tipped the volleyball over her outstretched arms. The ball dropped harmlessly to the sand, like a stunned seagull.

"Point, our side," said Kris, with a gee-whiz newsboy grin.

Several games were played, each featuring its quota of brilliant serves, flubbed serves, gritty digs, knuckleballs, screaming spikes and face-plants in the warm Malibu-esque sand. Genna got Kris back for his fakery, and then some. However, the volleyball finally began to degenerate under the pressure of the relentless sunshine. Point totals see-sawed back and forth, going largely unrecorded; players shamelessly defected from side to side, openly schmoozing, showing no team loyalty whatsoever. Ultimately, the majority of players found cold beer and nicely-stoked oildrum barbecue a more attractive option, and retired to courtside.

"Why do our games **always** end like this?" queried Don the tour guide, winking at Genna as he took a well-worn seat on a log that had been adzed to make the top side flat and smooth. He popped a Pabst Blue Ribbon, placed the bottle cap next to him onto the log, found a hand-sized rock and hammered the cap in. "The 'seat of honor'," explained Don to Kris' curious gaze, "the place where good beers go to die." There were probably over a hundred glittering bottle caps hammered into the log.

"Or, not-so-good beers, as the case may be," said Mark, studying his PBR with a critically-raised eyebrow.

"As the case formerly **was**," rejoined Kevin, pointing to the empty half-rack beside them.

Beef smokies and vegetable shish-kebabs sizzled on the handcrafted oildrum barbie; cheap beer vanished in thirsty gulps; a sense of timelessness took over. Kris idly picked up a guitar that someone had left behind at the campground (and now lived in a hollow log by the barbecue), and began strumming. The strumming metamorphosed into songs; the songs begat singing, which continued until no one could remember the lyrics, and strumming took over again until another song came to mind.

"Can you play 'Me and Bobby McGee'?" urged Genna. "I like the '**Na** na na, **Na** na na' part best."

"Can't forget **those** lyrics," admitted Kris as he complied.

In the middle of about the fourth round of "**Na** na na, **Na** na na, hey hey, Bobby McGee," the oildrum revelers were startled by a heavy crashing sound. Some stood up with a start, upsetting their beers, but Genna made frantic shushing sounds, motioning everyone to keep still. "If this is who I think it is," she whispered, "there's no need for alarm. Keep still: here she comes."

Not more than fifty feet away, a gigantic cow moose came crashing out of the underbrush. "That's 'Mabel'," whispered Genna. "She's lived in the woods behind the campground for several years now; she often comes out this time of night. And look who she has with her. Oh my God, it's…"

A few feet behind Mabel, making smaller but equally clumsy-sounding crashes, was a moose calf: all long, gangly legs and brown eyes. She dutifully followed her mother out of the woods and stood in the clearing just behind the volleyball court, sniffing the air. "This is the first time I've seen the baby up close. She was just born this Spring. Look, this is all new to her."

The mother moose nonchalantly munched on some nearby willow, keeping one eye on the youngster. The calf seemed to be dazed by a sense of wonder at her surroundings, oversized moosey head wobbling to and fro. The spectators could almost feel her curiosity in the twilight. Then, with tentative steps, she began edging towards the volleyball court.

"Will you look at this!"

"Do you suppose she can spike?"

Mabel raised her head and began to move towards her offspring, but did not stop her as she gingerly stepped onto the court, testing the footing. The baby moose seemed surprised at the sandy surface: it was soft and yielding, yet did not tangle up her awkward feet. She seemed to give a little skip, found that this was agreeable, cantered forward about five feet and stopped. She looked back at her mother, who seemed to nod her approval as she sidled up next to her on the court. Mabel stared down at her own ponderous feet, gave a snort. Suddenly, the baby moose put it all together, realized she was on a play surface, and actually began to skip around in a circle, kicking up sand with her hooves, enjoying the new sensation. Her mother followed as she circled across to the other side of the court—thankfully, dodging the net. There were a good two minutes of supervised playtime, until finally Mabel edged her child off the court with her nose, and the two moose shambled off back into the woods.

The partygoers sat in stunned silence for a time, contemplating the once-in-a-lifetime exhibition they had just seen. Genna shook her head; this was just as new to her as to anyone. Finally, however, Kevin's gaze shifted down to the PBR cans that had been upset in the hubbub: laying on their sides, lifeblood drained onto the spongy soil. "Beer Tragedy," he said, gesturing sadly.

This broke everyone up, and the conversation resumed into the night, albeit a little quieter. Kris plucked a few random notes on the guitar, finally stopped playing and put the instrument to rest inside the tree trunk. The coals of the barbecue dwindled with the sunlight, some people began to stretch and yawn, and somebody finally noticed that the time was pushing one o'clock in the morning. It was still light enough to clearly make out the faces of everyone.

The crowd began to thin. Kris found himself seated next to Genna on the log. "What a night it's been," he said. "All this light. All this energy. You know what? I just don't feel like going to sleep at **all**." Ever so subtly, he edged closer, letting his hand brush casually against her blue-jeaned thigh.

Genna arched an eyebrow at him, picked up a broken alder switch, stood and pretended to Zorro-mark his chest before poking the coals. "Remember," she said to him, "you've got a tour starting in about six or seven hours now. **You're** the one who has to be chipper and perky in the morning. I'm just waitressing: I can look tired and harassed."

She tossed the stick aside, stretched goldenly, like a lady puma, and began walking down the footpath towards home. "Besides," she said over her shoulder, "there's a solstice party coming up, if I'm not mistaken. Best to save our late-late night for that occasion." She turned her back and padded off through the forest.

The white night filled the Airstream trailer window as Kris lay awake in bed, his head swimming with visions of the times to come. The early daylight merged with his dreams as he finally drifted off to sleep.

The Dandelion Side Of The Mountain, Part One

▼

"The old man was not magic. He was not a three-legged crow on the dandelion side of the mountain."

—Richard Brautigan

The sight of Derek's skinny rear-end sticking up out of the hood of a '62 Bluebird school bus was about as amusing as anything could be at 5:30 AM. The temptation of a gentle shove, bootheel-to-tush, crossed Peter's mind fleetingly—but, good guy that he was, he refrained from acting on his impulse. He sidled up to the venerable Bluebird, poked his head inside the cavernous engine compartment, and said good morning.

"Just shoring up some of these loose connections," said Derek, by way of greeting. He pulled out of the bus innards, wiped his hand on his jeans and shook Peter's hand. "Checking the lubricants. Waking up those ground squirrels—the ones that make the engine go, I mean."

Peter had chosen to rise at an ungodly hour on his day off, in order to ride the Denali National Park tour with his old Skagway housemate (and tour guide extraordinaire), Derek. Peter was on a layover from the Fairbanks-Anchorage run, while Derek was staying put in one place all summer long—a drastic change from past touring years, but a welcome one.

The bus yard sat behind the park station hotel, in a dusty grove of aspen and skinny spruce, and (unsurprisingly) was nothing fancy at all: a tool shed, a gas pump, a hose, bucket and brush for bus-washing. Derek and Peter were surrounded by a covey of aging, dignified vehicles. "Reminds me a little of the old Ketchikan fleet," mused Peter.

"These old buses just keep on going forever," commented Derek. "It's amazing: years of abuse at the hands of schoolkids—then, for your 'retirement,' you get shipped off to the back roads of Denali. Some **re**-ward."

"Guess you'd know about such abuse first-hand by now, eh?"

Over the past year, Derek had been teaching school up in Healy, a coal-mining community just north of the park. Derek's teaching time had been about equally divided between the "3 R's," stoking the old schoolhouse furnace against the minus-fifty winter temperatures, "with coal—what else," and "disciplining those tough miner's kids. Just **you** try it sometime."

"I suppose it would have helped if you'd been your brother Karl's size, eh?"

"Nah, he's just an ol' **softy**. The kids'd be able to see right through him; they're pretty good at that sort of thing."

Peter filled in Derek on his summer thus far: for the most part, bombing up and down the Parks Highway between Fairbanks and Anchorage, with stops in Denali and Talkeetna as the tours warranted; waving to other company drivers as they whizzed by him on that same highway; a few fun nights out in Los Anchorage, with some of those sophisticated big-city expies; the odd laundry stop/ night at home back at the Anderson Apartments—where sometimes one or more roommates, including Kris, were around, but never all five.

Derek allowed that, early mornings and cranky old buses aside, there was truly something to be said for the stability of staying put in Denali all summer long. "You get on a first-name basis with all the people in the park—even some of the critters. Speaking of which, it's almost tour time. Let's go round up the troops."

The pick-up point more resembled a dusty Old West railway stop than a standard, sanitized tourist facility. The park station hotel was comprised primarily of vintage Alaska Railroad coach cars, parked parallel and joined by walkways. The cars leaned slightly into one another, suggesting a rocking motion, but the wheels were rusty in the tall grass, and wildflowers grew in the tracks. A boot-worn plank gangway led down from the hotel portal.

Instead of desperadoes, however, the gathering crowd consisted of the usual, genial middle-aged to elderly windbreakered collection. Derek (and Peter, who could never disguise that distinctive Tour Guide look) meeted 'n greeted as the bus filled up. Soon the 44 adventurers were packed into the sixth-grader sized seats, buzzing in anticipation despite the hour, balancing cameras and tote bags on their knees. The tour was off.

1. Special Touring Instructions

"Just to preempt the most frequently asked question at the start of a tour," began Derek: "**yes**, there will be animals, and plenty of 'em. I can give you as close to a guarantee as you can find in this business. Generally, on our tours we expect to bag the 'big four': moose bear, caribou and Dall sheep. Occasionally we might get lucky and see mountain goats, wolves, or even a lynx. Not to mention multitudes of the infamous 'lowbush grizzly'. More on those later. The high success rate is thanks in large part to that horrendous 4:30 AM wake-up call—so that particular hardship wasn't for nothin'.

"One caveat, though, concerning all you shutterbugs out there: we'll be seeing a lot of the critters at a considerable distance, especially once we get out onto the open tundra. Plus, there's a very good chance that they'll be running **away** from us shortly after we come upon them. So, unless you have a serious telephoto lens, and are very quick on the draw, you might not get those professional-quality wildlife shots that you might have expected. I say this not to discourage you, but merely to

advise you: to not get too hung up on capturing everything on film, but simply to enjoy the moment.

"It took me a while to learn this. Early on in my guiding career, I developed a very distinctive photo collection. I now call it 'Derrieres of Denali': it's nothing but fleeing wildlife and tiny specks in the distance. Now, I just take it all in visually, and store the image in my mind— unless a bear sticks his head in my window, asking for M&M's, or something unusual like that.

"Another thing: we do have a special system for wildlife spotting. In order to avoid total chaos whenever there is a sighting, we use the 'clock system'. Remember those old World War II movies—or maybe the real deal, for some of you folks—in which you'd hear fighter-pilot expressions like 'twelve o' clock high,' or 'enemy plane at 9:00,' or something similar? Well, here I would like the first person to spot an animal to say, for example, 'moose at 3:00'—meaning that the moose is straight to our right. That way, everyone will know where it is right away, instead of people putting their necks out of joint trying to look every which way. Similarly, straight ahead is 12:00, dead left is 9:00, and straight behind is 6:00.

"Simple enough, eh? But you know, there always seems to be at least one person who doesn't quite **get** it. Last week someone got all excited and said 'Bear at 6:30!!—but while everyone was craning to look over their left shoulders, she was looking at her **watch**. Five minutes later, she said, 'Bear at 6:35!!' You folks look like a **way** more intelligent group than to do something like that."

2. Into the Park

The park road began a gradual, rolling ascent through a series of forests: primarily the standard white spruce/ black spruce, "Alaska Pipecleaner" variety. Occasional stands of birch and aspen broke the ubiquity.

"Drunken, Igloo, Porcupine, Big Timber," Derek chanted like a mantra: "four forests to pass through, before we hit the high tundra. Five major rivers to cross: Savage, Sanctuary, Teklanika, East Fork, Toklat. Obviously, there's a ton of terrain to cover today."

> **Fun Fact #471:** Denali National Park was established on February 26, 1917, by signature of President Woodrow Wilson. The park expanded to its present size in 1980, and now encompasses some 6 million acres—slightly larger than Massachusetts.

"Imagine," said Derek, "that all of Massachusetts was designated as a **park**. Not a theme-park, like Euro-Disney or Kennedy World, but a wilderness-type park. You'd resettle everyone, Kennedys and all, except a small cadre of workers and hangers-on: say, the concessionaires from Fenway, maybe the scoreboard guy, too. Then, take out all the buildings, roads, billboards and other man-made detritus, save for a hundred-mile stretch of the Mass Turnpike, plus a few tollbooths and HoJo's at the east end. Remove the pavement from the road, all but a fifteen-mile stretch. Then, spring the locks on all the cages at the Boston Zoo, as well as other places where various critters may be incarcerated. Finally, stick a 20,320 foot mountain right about where Worcester should be. Do all of that, and you have the rough equivalent of Denali National Park—in terms of size, population and infrastructure, if not necessarily ambience.

"Part of what I'm trying to get at, folks, is that this is a very grand and special place—and very **different** from anything you likely have back home. No Kennedys whatsoever to be found hereabouts: only moose, bear and the odd tour guide or two."

"Emphasis on 'odd'," added Pete.

"Ahem," rejoined Derek. "Anyhow, another very special characteristic of Denali is that it is a wholly intact ecosystem: one of the very few you're ever likely to see. No species whatsoever have had to be reintroduced: all the plants and critters you'll see got here by their own means. As opposed to the overwhelming majority of places in the West—not to mention Massachusetts—the conservationists got here first, before the developers."

3. Among the Wildflowers

> **Fun Fact #79:** the Savage River campground (Milepost 12) is not only the gateway to the heart of Denali National Park, but also the historic site of the construction camp for the workers that built the park road. Between 1922 and 1938, the road was hacked out of the muskeg, tundra and mountainsides: from the McKinley railroad station to Wonder Lake, a distance of 85 miles. The workers, clad at times in head-to-toe mosquito netting, resided in canvas tents staked out by the river, sleeping on wooden cots—a type of accommodation typifying the early days of Denali.

Just past the Savage River, the bus left the last of the spruce forest behind, entering a treeless but vibrant landscape. Green hummocks galloped off in every direction: liberated from the winter, seeming to sprint towards the sky. The wildflowers were everywhere, splayed jazzily across the tundra and over the boulders: lupine, Queen Anne's lace, daisies, Arctic poppy, wild geraniums, Labrador tea…and a certain, ubiquitous mustard-yellow bloom that lined the roadside up the mountain pass, as far as the eye could see.

"**Dandelions**," declared Derek. "Plain ol' dandelions. Nothin' special. And yet, have you ever seen anything so beautiful?"

"Looks like they're just as at home here as they are in my lawn," commented one older gentleman. "I can't get **rid** of them."

"Wildflowers or weeds?" rejoined Derek. "It's all subjective, isn't it? Anyway, we'll **take** 'em. Think I'll pull over here for a second, let y'all take in the dandelion side of the mountain."

As the cameras clicked away, Derek gestured expansively over the landscape. "Really something, isn't it? Anyhow, something else notable about our entry into this wide-open topography—this taiga-to-tundra crossing—is that here we'll begin to see the wildlife."

"Is it because they've got nowhere to hide?" came a query from the back.

"Nowhere to run...got nowhere to hide," sang Derek. "Martha Reeves I ain't...but never mind that. The lack of cover is just part of the story; rather, something called 'edge ecology' is also at work. You see, each topographic zone in the wilds has its own distinctive population, plants and animals alike: i.e., moose generally prefer the wooded areas, while caribou like the tundra better, just to cite two of the larger examples. But at the border of each zone—or 'ecotone,' in the parlance of the biologists—you have a lot of criss-crossing and overlapping, a lot of border-hopping: maybe a patch of fireweed establishes itself in a forest clearing, or a moose comes out of the woods to check out some tundra cuisine. Consequently, there's a lot of a lot of species movement, and a lot of hybrid vigor—leading to very rich growth. Of course, the predators love all this abundance and diversity as well: if things aren't happening for a fox in one zone, he can readily try another.

"What I'm getting at is this, folks: what we're now entering, and the vast majority of what we'll be driving through today, is this type of ecotone. Hence, the near certainty that there will be plenty of critters to watch."

As if to drive this point home, there came a shout from the right-hand side of the bus: "Caribou at...at three o'clock!" Sure enough, a medium-sized band of caribou grazed away, about 100 yards in the distance; then, at some indiscernible cue, they bounded off. On the bus, the cameras clicked away.

"Derrieres of Denali!" exclaimed Derek. "Here we go."

4. The Spiny Bears of Teklanika

The wildflower zone yielded back to forest as they dropped down into the Sanctuary River valley (Milepost 22). The valley was home to one of the first substantial patches of permafrost encountered along the park road, and the black spruce leaned every which way. Derek related the explanations (long familiar to Peter) regarding discontinuous permafrost, solifluction, and their deleterious effects on the vertical capacities of the trees.

Since the herd of fleeing caribou derrieres, there had been a mildly surprising dearth of wildlife sightings. *Do the guides ever get 'skunked,' despite all the expectations and buildup? How do they deal with it?* But shortly thereafter, just as they were about to drive onto the Teklanika River bridge (Milepost 31), the safari call came again from the rear: "Bear!! At nine o'clock!" Derek pulled the bus over for a look-see.

Sure enough, below the bridge, a stout figure ambled at the river's edge. He shuffled along like Boxcar Willie, snuffling at the low shrubs, nibbling on this and that, occasionally pausing as if to ruminate on his existence (perhaps with a small harmonica solo). After a time, he turned to the river's edge, hesitated, then stepped off the sandy bank, into the braided river channel. He made as if to swim, then discerned that the water was shallow enough for wading, so gamely began to trudge across. Upon reaching the other side, he looked up and realized that there were about ninety-nine more braided channels to cross. He shrugged his round shoulders—causing his oddly long, spiny fur to rise—and shuffled into the next channel.

A look of sudden realization crossed Derek's face. "Holy smokey: that ain't no **bear**," he told the group. "That, my friends, is a **porcupine**. We're fairly high above the river here, and there are no trees to lend any sense of perspective: hence, it's hard to tell how big, or small, things are sometimes. Obviously, I've, uh, misjudged a bit here." Derek shook his head, sheepishly. "But I swear: thet thar porky-pine has been studying some home videos of his friend the grizzly. What's next: a moose who thinks he's a beaver? A marmot who thinks he's Judy Garland?"

5. Glamour Profession

Fun Fact #112: Igloo Mountain (Milepost 33), a prime habitat for Dall sheep, brings to mind the original *raison d'etre* for the formation of Mt. McKinley National Park. Charles Sheldon, a turn-of-the-century naturalist/ adventurer, spent a good deal of time in the Denali region, including a winter along the Toklat River—and subsequently lobbied, along with various influential friends (including Judge James Wickersham, Alaska's first territorial delegate to Congress) for the creation of the park. Shelton's primary argument for preserving the lands: to maintain a habitat for Dall sheep, in order to support their numbers for hunting purposes.

"Not necessarily to preserve the pristine areas around the mountain," remarked Derek, "not necessarily because the land had intrinsic value. Conservation efforts in those days typically had a utilitarian aspect to them: it wasn't enough to protect the land for its own sake. But give Mr. Sheldon credit: we can see the results of his efforts today, regardless of his original rationale."

Just past Igloo Mountain (upon which, sure enough, a sheep herd could be seen, as distant white specks), the road began a sharp ascent to Sable Pass. The increasing barrenness of the terrain made every detail of the land much more apparent than before: the hummocks; the sandhills; the glacial "accidentals," large, randomly scattered boulders left behind by retreating iceflows. In particular, Peter was able to pick out a number of winding, well-worn trails—one of which crossed the road before them. "Dall sheep crossing?" he inquired of Derek.

"Created by the sheep, but used by just about everyone in the neighborhood, I reckon: foxes, caribou, even bears. In fact, Sable Pass is such a critical bear habitat that it's actually been closed to all human access. Anywhere else along this road, one is entitled to get off a bus and start trekking off into the tules. Lots of people—rather brave people, in my opinion—do this, all summer long. But along this five-mile stretch, the park biologists want to take extra care that none of the pristine habitat is disturbed."

After Sable Pass (Milepost 39) had been summited, the road dropped down once again, to the valley of the East Fork of the Toklat River. "Speaking of brave people trekking off into oblivion," continued Derek:

"this is the valley where another famous early naturalist, Adolf Murie, undertook his famous study of wolves. Murie did as much as anyone to dispel the mythologies about wolves: namely, he was one of the first field biologists to conclude that, rather than decimating the herds of caribou and other prey, wolves were actually beneficial to such populations in the long term. He concluded that the wolves helped keep animal numbers within sustainable limits, commensurate with what the land could support—and, rather than preying on healthy breeding stock, they primarily took older, sick or wounded animals. The poisoning, shooting and other means of eliminating wolves, hitherto widely accepted, were not only ill-considered, but actually harmful to the herd animals the bounty hunters supposedly were protecting.

"Thus, the 'conventional wisdom' regarding wolves was turned on its head—thanks in large part to the efforts of Adolf Murie and his colleagues. But lest you think that they were engaged in a 'glamour profession', consider what their work-a-day lives were like. Up before dawn, rain, shine or snow; tracking critters for miles and miles across rugged terrain; remaining motionless for hours on end, in some freezing observation point; collecting copious amounts of wolf scat, and analyzing it to help determine diets. And, more than once, staring down the gray-green barrels of a wolf's gaze, far closer than comfort afforded."

> "The wolf takes your stare and
> turns it back on you."
>
> —Barry Lopez

6. The Road to Polychrome

Upon leaving the East Fork river valley, the road narrowed drastically, and pitched upward more sharply than before, towards Polychrome Pass. The washboard road surface attested to many sets of aging, chattering bus brakes, piloted down the hill by prayerful tour guides.

"Note," said Derek, resolutely, "the tremendously panoramic view to our left. You look; I'll drive. Trust me, I **know** it's there."

Meanwhile, Peter was doing some figuring. As a professional driver, he gauged the width of the road, noted the absence of guardrails, and wondered exactly how much room there was for another bus to pass in the opposite direction. He got his answer when he saw a dusty, terrified Bluebird edging down the grade towards them—and Derek, ever alert to such a possibility, pulled over and hugged the hillside with his vehicle. Peter was able to read the whites of the opposing passengers' wide eyes as they crept by, with mere inches to spare.

As the dust settled from the passing, a bushy red-headed figure emerged from the underbrush, crossed the road without looking, and scrambled atop the uphill bank. The fox trotted briskly up the steep hill, as if on his way to an important business meeting. In his jaws he carried, like a lunchbox, his noontime repast: a plump "lowbush grizzly," or, in the non-vernacular, an Arctic ground squirrel.

> **Fun Fact #303:** The Arctic ground squirrel, Citellus columbianus, thrives in conditions that many creatures of its size and stature could not tolerate. It burrows in the sandy hillsides of the Alaskan interior, where temperatures may reach minus sixty degrees or colder in the Winter—emerging in the Spring to greet the first Denali tour buses with its ubiquitous, perky—CHIRP!—
>
> Unfortunately (for the squirrel), its ubiquity is also well-known to a wide variety of carnivores: from raptor birds to foxes and coyotes to grizzly bears. In fact, bears find them such a tasty, Twinkie-sized treat that they have been known to root through entire hillside burrows to get at them—surely expending more calories in the effort than they would derive from the terrified (but delicious) rodents.

"Life in the food chain…" sang Derek, improvising on an old Eagles riff: "surely make you lose your…lunch?"

Peter groaned. "**Dang**, man…you have a song for every occasion."

Derek, utterly unremorseful, simply grinned like a fox in the rear-view mirror as he pulled back into the road, to resume the uphill grind.

Finally, they reached the top of Polychrome Pass (Milepost 46). A turnout had been hacked from the side of the mountain, affording shutterbugs and onlookers a safe place to stand without tumbling down to the base of the Alaska Range. A small footpath led up to a rocky outcropping, and Derek beckoned those fit enough to follow him to do so.

"Welcome to the high country," said Derek. "We're at about 3,600 feet elevation here—which, if you were to compare to terrain you'd find in, say, the mountains of Colorado, you'd find at about eleven or twelve thousand feet. Needless to say, winters are very harsh here: I've heard of it getting down to sixty-five below on this pass. Of course, summers are **very** short.

"This helps to explain some of the landscape features we see below us." Derek gestured out over the broad, dun-colored steppe. "See all the crisscross markings below us: the ones that look as if some giants had been playing tic-tac-toe? Those are river channels, both old and new, gouged out by the ice during Spring break-up, but never really given a chance to heal, due to the short summers. Since you never know which direction the break-up will take you—an interesting philosophical point to consider, by the way—you never know which channel, existing or new, the river will take from year to year. It's like a couch-potato husband with a TV remote: endless channel-surfing.

"Contrast that with the landscaping action of the glaciers, also apparent in this valley. You have the glacial erratics, of course: some of which are bigger than a house. You have the 'kettle ponds': places where very large chunks of ice broke off from the retreating glaciers, formed deep depressions in the tundra, and eventually filled with meltwater. You have alluvial terraces: representing the boundaries of reservoirs that formed behind ice dams, then were left high and dry when the dams finally broke. All of these phenomena are visible before us."

Turning his attention away from the valley, Derek gestured at the slope around him. "Repairing all the bulldozing is too big a task even for Ma Nature—but she does try to compensate in the summers. We get an eye-popping array of wildflowers up at Polychrome: still lots of dandelions, as you can see, but the local champ seems to be the shrubby cinquefoil. See those yellow blooms that look a bit like wild roses? Well, that's pretty much what they are: another one of those surprisingly hardy *rosaceas* that do so well all over Alaska. Think about that, next time you're gazing at those 'delicate' garden blooms back home: they're way tougher than they look.

"Plus, there are plenty of other residents of the garden. I suggest you take a good, close look at the tundra while we're up here: I think you'll be quite surprised."

Right about then, a ground squirrel stepped chirpily from behind a rock, as if to acknowledge its fine gardening job. "That reminds me," said Derek, "there are snacks in the rear of the bus. Hot drinks, cookies and doughnuts, cheese and crackers. No Twinkies, though."

I followed Derek's suggestion, and took a good, close, hands-and-knees look at the tundra. I was amazed at the diversity of plants: lowbush cranberry, blueberry, dwarf willow, crowberry, bearberry, moss and lichens, others I couldn't name. I felt as if I were a mountain-sized giant, looking down at a complex, beautiful forest canopy.

7. The Toklat Grizz

As they finally descended the dizzying heights of Polychrome, Derek—keeping both hands on the wheel—began his Road Rap once more:

"We're now entering the Toklat River drainage: an area that is perhaps best known for its large and distinctive population of grizzly bears. As you may have discerned by now, all bears are not alike: witness the so-called 'black' bear, which in reality can range anywhere from cinnamon to pitch-dark. Similarly, your grizzly bear can range from a sunny California blonde to coal-miner's daughter.

"Here in the Toklat valley, the grizzlies tend to be a very lovely chocolate brown, tipped by a sandy beige—almost as if some very brave hair stylist had been out wandering the bush, adding highlights. Even though they're about one-third smaller than their close relative, the coastal brown bear, they generally run a little larger than other bears in the park: more food in this valley than up on the high tundra. Finally, they tend to reproduce in threes, rather than the usual two cubs per den. More often than not, when you see a mama bear, there will be three identical little bears trailing after her—sans Goldilocks, presumably."

The Toklat River (Milepost 53) had the look of serious bear country: broad gravel banks atop probable fish-laden river channels; plenty of high brush, mostly willow and alder; ripening blueberry patches, stretching as far as the eye could see; lots of elbow room. And sure enough, around a bend in the road, Derek spotted a phalanx of vehicles pulled off the side of the road, long camera lenses protruding from the windows like antennae—the universal signal for a serious wildlife sighting.

Derek cut the bus engine, so as to make as little noise as possible, and coasted up to the turnout. At first, Peter could see nothing but green and brown vegetation. "The bears are probably wearing hunter's camouflage," he reckoned to himself. But then, he remembered a wildlife-spotting approach taught to him by, of all people, Derek's brother Karl:

"Look without looking," Karl had advised: "you know, the old Zen approach. Seriously: rather than fine-scanning a broad slope, trying to pinpoint one solitary critter, it's much easier to relax your vision, to take in the whole area—and let your peripheral vision spot some movement. Ever flash on something out of the corner of your eye, when you weren't even looking for it? You do it all the time. Exact same principle here."

Thus employing the "Zen approach," Peter defocused his eyesight. After a time, he caught some movement, and his vision lit on an enormous Toklat grizzly sow, less than 100 feet up the slope. Then, playing within safe range of their mother, ducking in and out of the alder, he spotted one, two, three cubs. Peter whistled to himself: "Unbelievable."

"Just another day in the Park," replied Derek, quietly: "for them, and for us." He spoke no more, and the entire busload turned its attention towards the bears.

The cubs looked to be several months old—the rough equivalent of mid-teenage years—and were engaged in behavior appropriate to that stage of development. Galumphing down the hill, tumbling and rolling; flipping over good-sized boulders, looking for tasty grubs, or just for the hell of it; snuffling, clouting and chewing on one another—in general, acting as if they were taking the scenic route home from junior varsity football practice, and were fixing to bust into the kitchen: to demand milk and cookies, chips, Arctic ground squirrels and other snacks from Ma.

However, the grizzly sow was having none of it: she regally, serenely sat above it all, looking for all the world like Big Mama Thornton, and conveying the same sense of authority. She looked as if she'd seen it all, twice, and was still not impressed: yawning, stretching, and finally, sticking a gargantuan rear paw behind an ear for a good scratching.

"And another defining characteristic of the Toklat grizz," said Derek, starting up the bus again, breaking the reverie: "sometimes they think they're **dogs**. Although probably not lap dogs, I'd venture."

8. The Ordinary Course of Caribou Business

Shortly after they were underway again, an unanswerable question came from the back: "With all of this wide-open terrain—a place the size of Massachusetts, like you say—why is it that we're seeing the wildlife along this tiny stretch of road? What are the odds that they would choose to hang out here, of all the possible places?"

"Beats me," admitted Derek. "Bags of Purina Bear Chow left by the side of the road? All I can do is speculate. But my educated guess would be that this road runs through some of the more accessible terrain in the park: more or less following the river valleys and mountain passes. In most instances, the road cut is the easiest way through a given area.

"Plus, out here on the tundra, our view goes on for miles and miles: it's not as if those white specks on the mountainside were within a stone's throw. Plus—in the case of the bears, particularly—maybe there's some curiosity going on. Maybe our big, huffing buses break up the monotony of their day. Who really knows?"

"But you're a tour guide," rejoined Peter: "you're supposed to know everything. What's the matter with you?" *But why even ask this question, much less try to answer it? There seems to be the notion sometimes that, somehow, this can't be real, or there is some neat, concise explanation for it all: 'They must feed the bears', and other such nonsense. But to be fair, this is such an amazing place—and so foreign, to most of these people—that I can see how some might think that way.*

On their way out of the Toklat drainage, they ran into a traffic jam: a band of caribou was jaywalking across the roadway. Their lack of haste connoted generations of indifference to pedestrian signals and traffic cops, in an almost New Yorkish way. "Whaddya think: you own the **road** or something?" chided Derek, in mock exasperation.

The delay afforded everyone a good look at the band. They numbered about fifty in all—well short of the entire herd, but a pretty decent gathering nonetheless—and nearly everyone was represented: young bucks, old uncles, moms-with-kids, middle-aged Rotarians. What they all had in common were antlers, on both males and females old enough to bear them,[7] and a certain defining, yet surprising trait:

---

7. The only members of the deer family with this characteristic.

"They do seem somewhat of a **scruffy** lot, don't they?"

"Yeah," replied Derek: "they're kind of like deer from the wrong side of the tracks. But if **you** had to put up with their living conditions, you might look that way, too. Consider: for them, as for the other denizens of the Denali biota, the entire summer is simply a sprint towards the next winter. Thus, their bodies are in a continual state of transition: once the weather finally warms up enough to shed some of that thick winter coat, WHOOPS! Here comes the first frost. Rather than neatly brushing out, their fur tends to fall out in big clumps this time of year. Hence, the appearance of someone having forgotten to buy mothballs.

"The thrift-store appearance of their antlers is explained similarly. When the antlers start growing in the spring, they are covered by a fine-haired, living tissue, known as 'velvet'. When this velvet starts dying in mid-summer, it begins gradually to rub off, in the ordinary course of caribou business: grazing in rocky tundra, pushing their way through alder hell. Plus, the males, especially the young bucks—like young bucks every-where—tend to educate each other in the school of hard knocks. Through all the alder-stripping and head-banging, the velvet begins to dangle in these unsightly strips, which are seldom completely gone until it's almost time for the antlers to fall off in the autumn. Kind of a bummer, after all that hard work growing them and burnishing them, finally, to a socially acceptable appearance.

"Finally—and here is where I feel most for these critters, seriously—insect repellent is largely unavailable to caribou. Plus, they can't bat away the bugs with a forepaw, or a swishing tail, or any other defense mecha-nism. Consequently, they are plagued all summer long by biting flies and great swarms of mosquitoes. If you were to look closely at the faces of these animals, you likely would see masses of bites and welts—not to men-tion somewhat of a crazed expression. It's said that mosquitoes can drain a quart of blood per week from a wounded or dying caribou.

"Thus, the first frost, and the harsh winter that follows, are actually preferable to these balmy summer days—because all the bugs are finally gone. No, the caribou of Denali will not win any beauty contests. But they are some **tough** hombres."

9. The Great One

In the shadow of the Mountain, sensed more than seen: an increasing feeling of heading into the Far Pavilions, or Shangri-La. The air is becoming more rarified: clear and cold. Around the next bend, we might expect to see Machu Picchu, or a Tibetan monastery, or...

"Denali, the Great One," declared Derek: "now only 37 miles away." The gray overcast that had increasingly cloaked the mountain since the start of their journey had grudgingly parted, for God-only-knows how long—revealing the entire north peak, clear up to the summit. Derek pulled into the Stony Hill overlook (Milepost 62), a place that lived up to its name, for an extended picture stop. *Compulsory, on an occasion like this. I wonder if these folks realize what a treat this is: about a one-in-three occurrence.*

From the overlook, about 3,900 feet in elevation, there arose a vertical relief of over 16,000 feet: one of the world's great massifs. At a distance of only 37 miles, the view of the mountain was terrifying, beautiful, snowy, rocky, windblown: truly awe-inspiring, dominating the consciousness as well as the entire field of vision. Many in the tour group, Peter among them, forsook the usual multimedia response to simply stand in silence, trying to record in their minds the most defining characteristic of all: the sheer size; the outlandish scale; the way that the mountain dwarfed the nearby, otherwise substantial peaks in comparison. *How does one possibly record that on film?*

After everyone had absorbed the spectacle in their own way, they filed back onto the bus, and Derek resumed the westward journey, ever closer to the mountain.

A seventy-ish woman, with a retired Park Ranger look about her, spoke first: "I don't know how words can possibly describe what we've just seen.

Even naming the mountain seems silly, in a way. Along those lines, there's one thing I've never quite understood: why the seemingly interchangeable names? Why do I hear 'Mt. McKinley' here, 'Denali' there, for no apparent, logical reason?"

"Uh oh, soapbox time again for me," replied Derek. "Just for the record, the official names in the books are 'Mt. McKinley' and 'Denali National Park and Preserve'. But many Alaskans, myself included, very strongly prefer the latter, Athabaskan-derived name—which means, simply, 'The Great One'. So no, I didn't just pull that nickname from thin air, or cop it from Jackie Gleason. That is literally how the word 'Denali' translates. If you're going to try and name the mountain, that's about the most aptly descriptive name there is, in my book.

"Further, a quick look at U.S. history will reveal how arbitrary the 'Mt. McKinley' naming really was. Not only arbitrary, but political. To wit: recall what was happening in Alaska back in the 1890's. What, back then, was the sole attractant to 'Seward's Icebox'? In a word: **gold**. The state was crawling with prospectors—relatively speaking, given the size of the territory—and a variety of gold strikes, substantial and inconsequential, were made: Cook Inlet, Dawson, Nome and Fairbanks, to name just a few.

"Well, one of the gold strikes occurred in Kantishna, about fifty miles northwest of where we are now, and one of the miners through the area was a gent by the name of William Dickey. It seems that Mr. Dickey was a good deal more literate than many of his counterparts in the field, as upon his return to civilization he actually published a descriptive report of his adventures in the New York Sun, in January of 1897. One of the items in his article was a glowing account of a majestic peak, just south of the Kantishna goldfields—a peak which he called 'Mt. McKinley'.

"As you may or may not know, Senator William McKinley of Ohio—at the time, the Republican nominee for President—was a strong advocate of the gold standard for backing the dollar. Naturally, as a miner, Dickey had a vested interest in the success of Senator McKinley: so, to publicize his favorite candidate, he 'named' a 20,320 foot mountain after him. The strategy seems to have worked: McKinley was elected, and the gold standard shortly ensued.

"And, to Dickey's everlasting credit, his name stuck: the U.S. government adopted the McKinley naming in its mapping, not knowing that the mountain already had been called something different by the locals for centuries. Something far less ephemeral than a President who had come and gone within four years—albeit, under unfortunate circumstances—and is not remembered for too terribly much else.

"So, in these modern times—given our present understanding of the peoples who preceded us here, by a long shot—I ask you: is the name 'Mt. McKinley' really appropriate? I think you can guess my feelings on the subject, but decide for yourselves. Write your Congressperson."

After a thoughtful moment or two, another query came from the back: "Why is Denali so much higher than the other peaks? Everything else around it is dwarfed in comparison. Is it a volcano?"

"That's an astute question," complimented Derek. "Everyone: the reason why Denali is so much higher than the surrounding peaks of the Alaska Range? No, the mountain is not volcanic: it was formed tectonically. In most places, the Alaska Range was formed by the collision of two tectonic plates. Denali—composed mostly of erosion-resistant granite—also might be a place where **three** such plates come together, all pushing upward. The mountain continues to rise, to this day. It's a miracle of uplifting: kind of like the Miracle Bra, I suppose."

Derek's glance into the rearview mirror noted a mostly amused reaction to his mildly risqué undergarments analogy. "Actually, there's **much** more to this mountain formation story. Check it out:

THE STRAWBERRY CHEESECAKE
THEORY OF THE UNIVERSE

▼

"I have another illustration of plate tectonics for you, one which more or less explains the geologic formation of all Alaska—and is very visual, besides. I call it the 'Strawberry Cheesecake Theory Of The Universe,' and it goes something like this:

"For those of you at all familiar with the theory of tectonics, you may know that the west coast of the U.S. resides at the intersection of two major segments of the earth's crust: the North American continental and Pacific plates. That's the reason, of course, for all the seismic activity in that area: the Pacific plate is continually bumping and grinding against the continent, trying to move northward and—whenever there is a substantial earthquake—succeeding, in tiny but measurable increments.

"However, the Pacific plate finds a large, immovable object at the end of its northerly journey: Alaska. Imagine the plate as a conveyor belt—upon which there rides a cheesecake. A very large, strawberry cheesecake. And imagine that Alaska, waiting at the other end, is also a gigantic strawberry cheesecake."

"Colliding cheesecakes?" interjected Peter. "**Yecch**—sounds like a big mess. And why **strawberry**? Why not raspberry, or chocolate?"

"Hold on just a minute, young feller: I'm **getting** to that." Derek's eyes twinkled mischievously. "As you know, the Pacific plate is not entirely devoid of land formations. For example, everything in California west of the San Andreas Fault is on the plate. Most significantly, ruptures in the plate have caused magma to well up and form mid-ocean volcanic land masses, such as Hawaii. So, imagine the big island of Hawaii—which **is**, in fact, shaped a little bit like a strawberry—surfing ever northward on the Pacific plate."

"**Cowabunga**," thought Peter, but he did not interrupt again.

"Now, here's the kicker: the oceanic plate, being denser than dry land, subducts under the continental plate when they collide. However, the lighter land formations riding atop the Pacific plate—the "strawberries"— do not subduct, but attach themselves to the continent. Meaning that, as eons go by, the Alaskan cheesecake collects more and more strawberries. This, essentially, is how the majority of the state was formed.

"Thus, the further north you go in the state, the older the land is. Any number of scientists have made careers of trying to figure out the geologic crazy-quilt—or smushed-together cheesecake—that is Alaska.

"And finally, consider again that this is an ongoing process. Meaning that, in 50 million years or so, Los Angeles and Anchorage will be **neighbors**."

The Dandelion Side Of The Mountain, Part Two

▼

Fun Fact #51: In a good year, about half of those who attempt to climb Denali actually make it to the summit. Those who do not are stymied not so much by the technical nature of the climb (which is, in fact, a near walk-up—albeit a very long one) as by such factors as weather, altitude, endurance, and any number of small, yet crucial things that can go wrong. Further, the consequences of ill-considered climbing decisions are more potentially dire at Denali than on comparable peaks elsewhere: about one percent of all climbers, generally several per season, perish on the mountain.

The modern way to tackle Denali is to be flown up, usually from Talkeetna, to the Kahiltna Glacier, at approximately 7,000 feet elevation. After establishing a base camp on the glacier, climbers typically proceed up the west ridge of the south peak: allowing a considerable amount of time for the summiting, as conditions and supplies warrant. It is not unusual for a summiting to take two weeks or more—much of which may be spent huddled in one's tent and sleeping bag, waiting for the weather to clear.

However, the first persons successfully to climb Denali did not have it nearly so cushy. In 1910, a group of weather-hardened sourdoughs set out from Fairbanks by dogsled, established a camp at 11,000 feet—and, unbelievably, summited the north peak in a single day. Their primary supplies for the final push: thermoses of hot chocolate and a sack of doughnuts for lunch, plus a long spruce pole, which they planted on the peak as proof of their success.

"Every time I come out here," said Derek, "I fix myself a cup of hot cocoa, grab a doughnut, and give a toast in the direction of the mountain." The bus had arrived at the Eielson Visitor's Center (Milepost 66), the tour's turnaround point, and Derek had once again cracked the rear emergency exit to reveal his cache of goodies and hot drinks. Most everyone in the group had partaken, and were either already inside the interpretive center, or were meandering in that direction.

The Visitor's Center seemed to be carved out of the stone mountain-side, perched on a barren slope. Below the building, a steep precipice dropped down to a rocky ravine. Yet, clinging to the side of the slope was a single caribou, as nonchalant as a Swiss mountaineer: grazing away as if the entire world pitched at a 45-degree angle.

"Odd place for wildlife," mused Peter.

"Well, it's a south-facing slope: more light and vegetation. Maybe the Visitor's Center gives off just a smidgen of extra heat, allowing for more plant growth. Plus, not many predators around—except the ones toting cameras, of course."

Indeed, tourists from Derek's and other groups had lined up all along the guardrail, immortalizing on film the indifferent ruminant. *Seems like overkill to me—but this is probably the closest most of these folks will ever get to a wild animal of this size. Plus, the caribou doesn't seem to mind.*

Derek and Peter entered the visitor's center, said their hellos to the rangers, and immediately proceeded to the observation room, which offered a commanding, panoramic view of Denali. Through the plate-glass windows, the mountain was now playing 1920's flapper/ peek-a-boo, clouds parting like a slit-skirt to reveal a flank here, a false summit there. For about ninety seconds, the entire cloud curtain gave way, in Wizard of Oz fashion, to reveal the entire, terrible beauty of the Wickersham Wall—a 14,000 foot sheer rise. Then the curtain quickly closed, seemingly tighter than before.

"Now, the day you get tired of **that** view," remarked Derek, "it's truly time to hang up your tour-guide wings."

Peter shook his head. "I feel as if I've seen a different mountain every time I've been lucky enough to see it. The view is seldom the same, in my experience."

"You've got it," replied Derek. "The 'ephemeral' nature of the mountain is its central paradox. Who can imagine anything more steady and immovable than a 20,320 foot mountain? Yet, in just these few minutes here, we've seen several distinctive pictures of Denali: pictures which, like the blind men examining the elephant, could lead one to entirely different conclusions as to its nature. And of course, as I've already explained, the mountain itself is constantly moving and growing.

"This point has hit home with the park rangers stationed here, in a big way. Here, let me show you the daily chart of mountain sightings that they keep. It's just a bit beyond the ken of the average tourist."

Derek led Peter into the rangers' office, just off the observation room. It also had a fine vantage of the mountain, through a large window on the far wall. Amongst the clutter of Park Service documents and memorabilia, Peter spied some charts, covering the wall immediately perpendicular to the window. One set of charts appeared to be official weather readings, recording numerical data on temperature, precipitation and the like. The other set, considerably less official-looking, consisted of pictorial, day-to-day observations of Denali's many moods—rendered in sketch pencil, crayon, Magic Marker and other handy media. Each month was represented on a large sheet of butcher paper, blocked off into days and filled with colorful, almost psychedelic illustrations of the mountain.

"Lighting, cloud cover, wind, moisture," remarked Derek: "the mixtures of variables are endless. Observed at any time of the day, high noon or twilight, as inspiration warrants. To those who wonder whether a season spent exclusively at the mountain could ever be dull or monotonous: I would point them to **this**."

Peter was silent, staring transfixed at the charts. *Here a windstorm, with lenticular clouds; there an indigo/ orange/ cinnabar midnight sunset; there a monochrome cloudbank, with corners of Denali peeking out. No, I don't see how such intimate knowledge of this place—and of Alaska, for that matter—could ever get boring.*

1. double rainbow

> heliotropic trellis trailing over
> stony shoulderpeak, a
> red-to-violet robe;
> > orion's arrow-in-the-
> > sky, piercing twilight

2. alpenglow

> > minorkey mellotron-organ sunset slips
> > into mezzopiano then bursts fountain
> > fortechord on highest peakflank:
> > > glowing snowpyramid,
> > > gone seconds later

3. nightfall

> circles in the jetstream, cloudmass
> questions, greyspinning to nothingness
> but then
> > denali peeks from under the covers, winks and
> > pulls them up again

SANDY'S SOLSTICE PARTY

▼

among the wildflowers, blue lupine and golden-eyed daisies
winking in the twilight, fireweed high as the proverbial

elephant's eye; kris, genna and various extra-crunchy
friends wind along farmer's loop footpath, bearing gifts and wine

quite the chaperone entourage for our first date says
genna, in cotton-print sundress and sandals, smiling; at their approach

little eric, sandy's towheaded son-flower says
mommy, the vegetable people are here

sandy gives genna aproned biscuit-dust hug, says
my don't you clean up nice, genna blushes like the

latenight sun that is only now dipping into
avocado-dawn hills; see here says the notorious douglas fir, on the

north porch we catch both ends of the solar feature, sunrise
sunset, sunrise sunset, just like the old movie-song

grinning, douglas fir does cheshire-cat fade into
dwarf spruceforest, where he knows the wild homebrews live

kris and genna follow, guess its not the secret stash anymore says
kris as he reaches into coldspring, pulls out two lovingly

handcrafted bottles, thank god they're the grolsch stopper-tops says
genna, otherwise we'd have to use our teeth like the sourdoughs do

talking, laughing, murmuring calypso nonsense, kris and genna wander
the woods, find party-denizens under tree, bush and vine; soon their

hands entwine as they make the rounds and sandy gazes
approvingly from hostess duties and eric-to-bed-i-don't-wanna

obligations; endless possibilities she says, the party is young and the night is
light as she declares a moment of silence for the stroke of midnight;

the sun takes a bow and partygoers applaud; it comes up for curtain-
call minutes later in very much the same spot, seeming to signal the

real beginning of festivities as the most bushy brigands of all arise from
the undergrowth and take up instruments, declaring we are the 'dead reds,'

we reunite solely for the summer solstice; some kind of frontman gives a
signal and the early-early morning is a lemon-colored blur as the dead reds

work salmonesque magic upon a variety of chestnut/grey rock-n-
roll standards: mmm, just like mother used to make says douglas fir,

grinning ubiquitously; somehow kris finds himself with one arm
draped around
genna, the other around timeworn vintage guitar that looks as if it
should be

pedal-powered, but in fact drives like the '57 buick roadmaster it is; he
rises to
trade fresh chords with the dead reds through the wee hours as a new
kind of

sunrise reveals itself in
genna's goldenhazel eyes

THE BALLAD OF MUSKEG MARY

▼

HOME BY DARK

Still riding the social high from Sandy's solstice party—and the start of something new and exciting—Kris cruised the frost-heaves from Fairbanks to Skagway and back in smooth, easy Cadillac fashion. The road spread itself before him like a well-read map as the month of June closed out; his head was filled with the hues of the midnight sunset. Thinking often of Genna, he could not wipe the grin off his face. His passengers commented on his eternally cheery nature. His fellow tour guides laughed at him.

The first weekend of July found Kris running southbound with a four-bus caravan. Due to a scheduling quirk, he did not have to do a same-day turnaround with the other drivers, but got to lay over a full day in Skagway. Consequently, he caught the Backwards Parade, the Slow Bicycle Race and all the other Skagway 4th of July hoopla for the second consecutive year. He even placed a respectable second in the Watermelon Seed-Spitting competition, being obliterated in the Finals by an old local pro. Due to the safety code-imposed vacancy of the Portland House, there was no Rooftop Party, alas. However, he did find enough diversions in town to keep him out until the wee hours, and was still a little woozy when he went to pick up his motorcoach the following morning.

"Eight-hour 'bottle-to-throttle,' buddy," cautioned an equally-bleary Norm.

"Not to worry," replied Kris as he slowly completed his pre-trip inspection, "mere sleep deprivation here. Mostly. You know, I'm actually kind of glad we don't do pick-ups in town anymore. I'm not feeling too impressive right about now."

Norm smiled forgivingly. "The drive up to Fraser should clear your head in time; you'll be OK. Anyhow, this is your big solo gig: exciting stuff. You'll have the whole northbound tour to yourself, all the way to Fairbanks." He turned away from the bus stairwell, loaded himself into the tattered bucket seat of the idling Old Paint (still running strong, amazingly) and waved at Kris through the open window. "Have a great trip."

As he left Skagway and chugged up White Pass, Kris' mental fog began to lift. He began to go over the logistics of the trip in his mind. The manifest said forty passengers: nearly a full load. He would be stopping in Beaver Creek, rather than Tok, on the second night out. On one hand, this meant that he could save the Tok Hills for the third morning, rather than doing four hundred miles from Whitehorse in one exhausting shot. On the other hand, this meant only a coffee-stop visit with Genna, rather than an overnight at the Tok Tundra Lodge. And indeed, he was the only northbound bus: all of his other tours had been caravans of three or four.

A note of slight nervousness crept into his planning. This trip would mark the fifth time that Kris had led a multi-day tour. He was just getting to the point where all the pieces were falling into place: the history, the people management skills, the corny jokes. Inexperience and unfamiliarity were no longer excuses. The tour would say much about his evolution into a true Coach Commander: by now, he would either have it, or he would not.

Kris pulled into the gravel loading area, shut down the bus engine, cracked open his door and stepped outside into the sun. Summer was taking care of the final patches of snow at Fraser, the end of the line for the Wait Patiently & You'll Arrive Railroad. The tiny alpine lakes were pure and still, reflecting the jagged basalt spires of Torment Valley. *There's the place where Kevin dove in last summer, chasing grayling.* A day almost too gorgeous to be true: a great talisman for beginning a tour.

He waited in the stillness, caught between eager anticipation and an urge to rip off his uniform, jump nekkid into Fraser Lake and swim away with the fish. For a long while, there was nothing; the few birds were almost eerie in the way they disrupted the silence. But then a thin plume of steam appeared from behind the peaks, and a train whistle echoed across the valley. *Here they come. They'll be in a good mood from this beautiful crossing. Hope they like me.*

The antique train cars rattled into the tiny Fraser station. Kris saw his old, huge friend Karl standing on the caboose, dwarfing the back porch. Karl saw him, and saluted smartly. *He sure fits the part, anyhow: that moustache and uniform make him look like an old-time railroad man. Or Sergeant Preston of the Mounties.* When the train came to a halt, the ever-gentlemanly Karl opened the passenger doors, set down a wooden step and assisted the disembarking tourists. Kris swung open his motorcoach door, stood up tall and straightened his tie.

The positive mood was palpable as Kris meeted 'n greeted, checked his passenger lists, threw in some last-minute luggage and hit the road. He adjusted his sunglasses and rearview mirror, smiled at his guests and began to speak.

"Good afternoon, everybody. My name is Kris Westerberg, your guide for the next three days, and first of all I want to say 'Welcome.' Welcome aboard, welcome to the tour. Welcome to Canada—and to the burgeoning metropolis of Fraser, BC. But most of all, welcome to Summer.

"Summer around here is fleeting: just a few weeks ago, this particular place was covered in snow, and the first frosts are maybe a month away.

But Summer is definitely here now, so **enjoy**. In fact, some people are surprised to learn that we do have the four seasons here in the North Country. I was surprised at this myself, until I learned that the four seasons have slightly different names in these parts: June, July, August and Winter."

"I thought," piped up someone from the back, "there were supposed to be only two seasons here: Winter and Road Construction."

"Aha: I see **someone** has done their homework. Yes, that's a valid interpretation, too. Which brings me to my next point: for nearly every North Country phenomenon you encounter, you're bound to hear at least a couple of different stories explaining it. It's all a degree of poetic license, I suppose."

Where did that come from? Talk about laying the cards on the table. Kris' passengers were oblivious to his bold disclaimer as the next question came from the middle of the bus: "Are we going to see the midnight sun?"

Kris glanced knowingly at his guests in the rearview passenger mirror. "Well, to make a short answer long—a chronic Tour Guide affliction— we're at that special time of year when it's not really going to get dark at all. If you're up chasing around in Whitehorse in the wee hours tonight, you'll see dusk close to midnight; stay in that pub just a couple hours longer, and you can greet the sunrise. It's quite disorienting: your normal urges to hit the hay at a reasonable hour get all messed up, and you may not want to go to bed at all."

"Is that a problem for the people who live here?" wondered an elderly woman, in what sounded like an English accent. "Especially for young children: do they struggle against an early bedtime?"

"Absolutely. You'll notice that most of the windows up here, including those in your hotel rooms, have extra-thick curtains: it's the only way to get any semblance of darkness. But that's not enough: you have to get peo- ple **indoors** first. It's hard to control children, when they get all wound-up from chasing around in the midnight sun." Kris shrugged innocuously. "It's an even bigger problem if the parents have made the mistake of telling their kids to 'be home by dark.' If they do that, they may not see them again until August."

As he crested the big hill above Lake Tutshi, Kris decided that it was time to cut back on his verbiage and let his guests have their say: namely, it was time for Passenger Introductions. Introductions were key to getting a tour off on the right foot. By the end of three days and 750 hard miles, people either would have bonded, or would be surly and isolated; the former was infinitely preferable. It was a smart move for a driver-guide to get an early sense of group dynamics and foster a positive vibe from the outset. *What is this group like? What will work for them? Hmmm…*

There were a number of tricks a guide could utilize to break the ice—most of which involved minor embarrassment. On Kris' tours, the commonality to such endeavors was a hand-held microphone with a very long cord—long enough to reach even the most recalcitrant back-seat passengers. If the mood was just right, and especially when a single group was traveling together, Kris' favorite introductory game was "Two Truths and a Lie": each guest was called upon to make three autobiographical statements, two true and one false, and the other passengers were called upon to ferret out the falsity. The trick was to couch one's truths in as fantastical terms as possible, in order to disguise the lie. Some very interesting revelations arose this way—and Kris always amazed himself at his own fictional capacities—but the game could be a bit much if the passengers felt too inhibited. Within the first few minutes of a tour, Kris could generally gauge the crowd and determine the appropriate level of embarrassment and humiliation for getting things off on the right foot.

For the present tour, Kris decided to stick with a simple, tested-and-true introductory round. At the Tutshi overlook, while his guests were outside taking pictures, he fetched the microphone, unwound the long cord and made it ready for circulation.

"There are four things," intoned Kris, "that I want to know about you—**each** of you—before we can proceed any further: your name, where you're from, your present or past occupation, if retired, and what brought you to Alaska. I need to know what kind of motley crew I'll be stuck with here in the boondocks. And who knows: you might find some real commonalities with your fellow travelers."

Kris noted the demographic spread as the microphone was passed from seat to seat—something that always interested him. *The Midwest: Wisconsin, Minnesota, Iowa. A couple of Chicagoites. 4 Californians. New Jersey. More Midwesterners: downstate Illinois. Always seem to be plenty of people from the heartland, but very few from the Northwest: I've hardly seen a Washingtonian all Summer. Maybe it's because we're all **working** up here, rather than vacationing.*

Retirement, as always, is the main occupation. Retired merchants, retired professionals, retired professors and teachers. Lots of teachers take these trips: must be hard to leave that lifelong learning mode. I like having them on tour: plenty of good questions. The crowds are surprisingly middle-class: as if this is something they saved up for, and have been looking forward to, for a long time. I suppose the really 'upscale' tourists are back on the cruise ship, indifferently sipping cocktails on the mezzanine deck, or are paying a helicopter pilot a few thou to fly out somewhere and land on a glacier, or shoot a bear. No thanks: you can have 'em.

"Why did you come to Alaska?" My favorite part of the Introductions game. Clearly, Alaska has been on everyone's mind for quite some time. But what started it all? A Jack London story or Robert Service poem? A friend or relative who came here once upon a time, and returned home bursting with stories? A surprising amount of the older men were sent to Alaska during World War II—like Roy Haverman, back in Ketchikan—and are returning for the first time since then. Everyone has their well-considered reasons; you don't just pick up and go to Alaska on a whim. You don't just casually hop into the family wagon and head up the Al-Can.

The microphone reached an elderly woman with an English accent: the one who had inquired earlier about children's Summer bedtimes. She identified herself as Mary Thomas, eighty-one years old, from Sussex, in the south of England. She and her husband, who was gone now, God bless his soul, had been professional horticulturists. Mary herself, in fact, was still certified as an expert gardener. And, she had come to Alaska "to walk the muskeg. I understand it's this wonderful, marshy, springy trampoline ride. Now, in our peat bogs at home, why, one does nothing but sink to the top of one's Wellies. I'm hoping that this fine young gentleman here can show us some true muskeg."

"Absolutely, you betcha. There is no shortage of quality muskeg up here. I promise you that, before this trip is through, we will find the perfect place for you to take your Muskeg Walk."

Mary handed off the microphone to the next person, executed a polite little bow and sat down, beaming. *'Muskeg Mary'. Hmmm, has a nice ring to it. Looks like we've found your nickname for this trip, ma'am.*

Right about the time that Introductions wrapped up, the bus pulled into Carcross, for a quick pit stop and ice cream break. While the venue was not quite as exotic as Hot Licks, back in Fairbanks (and no one quite like Douglas Fir was lurking about), the Carcross general store served an amazing Peanut Butter ice cream. Kris' highly impressionable guests (it was no mistake that Driver/Guides got free goodies along the way), seeing him order a humongous double-dip cone, with thick ribbons of peanut butter hanging precipitously off the edge, followed suit, and more or less decimated the city's frozen-dessert supply.

Kris strolled the main street for about thirty minutes (competing traffic was mostly of the stationary, sleeping-dog variety), slurping his ice cream, chatting with his passengers, getting to know them. *What a luxury this is: actually talking to my guests on more than a superficial, see-ya-later basis, without the prospect of saying goodbye in an hour or so. This kind of conversation never happened last year in Carcross. But then, there were plenty of diversions here: a blonde-haired Finnish one in particular. Water under the bridge.*

Carcross Desert: Affectionately known as "the smallest desert in the world," this area was originally covered by a large glacial lake. As the glaciers retreated, causing lower water levels, sandy lake bottom material was left behind. Strong prevailing winds from Lake Bennett have constantly worked this sand, making it difficult for vegetation to become established. Species of plants that have survived include lodgepole pine and kinnikinnick.

"What's 'kinnikinnick'?" inquired a passenger.

"Athabaskan for 'scrawny little shrub," replied Kris. "Probably. They say it makes a useful medicinal tea. That's about all I know."

Muskeg Mary, with some difficulty, knelt next to a small bush. She plucked some leaves, rubbed them between forefinger and thumb, and smelled them. She smiled. "Actually, young man, the word 'kinnikinnick' comes from the Algonquian jargon for tobacco and other smokable mixtures. Your tea would likely taste something like a brew made from tobacco leaves."

Kris shook his head, smiling to himself as everyone reboarded the bus. *Once again, a passenger has educated me. It never stops.*

Once past Emerald Lake, a spectacular desert jewel colored by water-soluble minerals, the remaining highway from Carcross to Whitehorse was more or less a dragstrip. For the most part Kris was silent, letting his guests do the chit-chat thing. *More important for them to get to know one another than for me to talk about nothing.*

As they made the big left turn onto the Al-Can, entering the Whitehorse suburban fringe, Kris cued up the boom mike once more. He began with a brief overview of the highway: its length (1422 miles total, about 500 remaining miles to Delta Junction), and the fact that they would be on it for most of the next two days; the circumstances of its construction; the ongoing process of re-construction, to which they would undoubtedly be first-hand witnesses. He briefly alluded to Karl's famous story about the buried backhoes, saving the full telling for the next day.

They turned off the highway and began a descent down a long hill, into Whitehorse proper. Far below, the city huddled before the long, green, serpentine curves of the Yukon River. Kris rattled off the vital stats (population 17,000, about half the people in the Yukon, territorial seat of government, etc.) then delivered his "picks and pans" for evening entertainment choices: a service he greatly enjoyed providing.

"What is there to do in Whitehorse, you might ask? **Plenty**—especially since tomorrow's destination, Beaver Creek, will be a **lot** smaller. Therefore, I strongly recommend that you take at least some advantage of the local amenities.

"First, if you're in the mood for live entertainment, there's the Frantic Follies: fun, old-timey song-and-dance in a Klondike vein; Robert Service poetry, delivered slapstick-style; musical saws and other hoopla; corniness level mostly within human tolerances. However, my favorite thing to do here is simply to stretch my legs and walk around town, taking in the sights. There's the S.S. Klondike riverboat, down in the waterfront park; the old church that was home to 'The Bishop Who Ate His Boots'; the Log Skyscraper, which must be seen to be believed. There are plenty of restaurants and watering holes along Main Street, not to mention the ever-popular gift and souvenir shopping." Kris glanced knowingly at his passengers, sensing that at least a few cruise-ship canvas tote bags were due to be filled with gift items. "So have a fun time here in Whitehorse," he concluded as he pulled up to the hotel and turned things over to the local expie. "And of course, be sure to be home by dark."

COMBAT SHOPPING

▼

Unit #1002 of the Yukon Combat Shopping Squadron pauses tensely in the motorcoach doorway, waiting for the signal to invade. Eyes narrowed, credit cards revving up, shopping bags at the ready.

"…We hope you will enjoy your stay in Whitehorse. Your hotel rooms are…" The expie's words are smothered in the surge of forward movement. They're off.

Combat objectives: 1) scout out all available bargains, bargains, bargains (Hurry! The stores close at 9 p.m.!); 2) test weight, volume and torque capacities of top-secret X-20 Canvas Shopping Bag; 3) successfully divest of all remaining "funny money" before departing Canada; 4) successfully inflict hernia damage to Driver/Guide as he picks up top-secret X-20 Canvas Shopping Bag in the morning.

It's a tough job, but someone's gotta do it. The economy of the Yukon Territory hinges upon their success.

The ever-creative Kevin had left behind a bunch of self-designed, self-penned "travel brochures" on the kitchen table at the drivers' apartment. The Combat Shopping quip was one of the items listed under "Things to Do in Whitehorse While Alive." Kris could only guess that the brochure was intended to augment, and perhaps help interpret, Kevin's tours (which, although highly entertaining, bordered on the incomprehensible at times). Just for the hell of it, he helped himself to a short stack of brochures, for his own crowd's perusal.

Kris contemplated the dismal array of dehydrated soups and canned Chef Boy-Ar-Dee in the apartment kitchen, stared at the prison-like cinder block walls, and decided it was time to hit the town on foot. He beat a hasty retreat from the Fourth Avenue Residence, stepped out into the dusty but balmy evening, and began walking towards downtown.

The "historical district" of Whitehorse was long and narrow, parallel to the Yukon River and sandwiched between two dusty-pickup dragstrips: 4th Avenue and 2nd Avenue. In between the Canadian government's well-meaning but generic attempts at urban renewal were scattered vestiges of the Yukon past. Among these were several old churches, some funky dwellings, and one remarkable structure people had dubbed the Log Skyscraper: four stories worth of log cabins had been set atop one another, each slightly smaller than the previous one until the top story, presumably the sleeping loft, was about the size of a woodshed. The whole ramshackle structure was linked by a series of metal ladders, which looked as if they had been welded together from concrete reinforcement bars. Kris shook his head, wondering what it must be like to shimmy down three sets of rebar ladders to take a midnight leak.

He reached the main drag, looking right and left. No secret X-20 canvas shopping bags were in sight; not that Kris minded socializing with his guests, but a little personal space was greatly appreciated in the evenings while on tour. Ordinarily he would have made a beeline for the little Greek restaurant near 2nd and Main, which served by far the best pizza in the whole Territory. However, since he was solo this evening—and solo pizza was no fun whatsoever—he instead turned towards the No-Pop sandwich shop, the only self-admitted health-food eatery in all the Yukon. His exciting evening would likely consist of hunkering down over a whole-wheat hoagie and fruit juice, maybe a High-Test somewhere for dessert, followed by a relaxing stroll along the river on the way back to the barracks, and an early bedtime, around ten o'clock—to rest up for the big touring day ahead.

MOSQUITO RIVER

▼

Kevin's mock "travel brochure" also contained the following useful information about a leading species of Northwoods critter:

"We can guarantee that you will sight at least one form of wildlife on your trip: the mosquito. There are twenty-seven varieties of mosquito found in the North, ranging from the tiny, invisible, painful "no-see-um" to the large but maneuverable B-1 (Stealth) mosquito. There is, of course, that one Alaskan species particularly irksome to visiting tourists: Bitus swatem itchem (and its Canadian counterpart, Bitus swatem itchem-eh?). These noxious beasts have a disturbing tendency to swarm and carry off forty-foot motorcoaches. Be on the lookout: carry your portable mosquito netting, anti-aircraft missilery and Skin-So-Soft[8] at all times."

---

8. Oddly enough, the most effective mosquito repellent around, this side of 100% Deet. Keeps the bugs away and makes your skin soft and pretty. Heartily endorsed by the most grizzled of bushers.

On the next morning of the tour, while heading north out of Whitehorse, there was indeed widespread buzzing as the passengers puzzled over Kevin's elliptical prose. Mosquitoes? Oh my. Nah, they don't seem so bad to me. Haven't seen hardly any yet, anyway.

Kris decided to further fuel the discussion, since he was conveniently passing over the Takhini River. Convenient, for the word "Takhini" translated to…

"**Mosquito** River. That's what the Tutchone people called this place. Apparently, it was a much deserved name: it's hard to tell from this view, the way the channel cuts through the high, dry banks here, but upriver there are some big, broad flats, substantial wetlands: major mosquito country. So, mosquitoes figured very prominently around here: not just in everyday life, but also in legend. The Tutchone believed that the origin of the mosquito people was right around here, a very long time ago. The story runs something like this:

"A very long time ago, a terrible giant walked these woods. He was mean and ugly: hairy, snaggle-toothed, hump-shouldered, and a cyclops to boot. Worst of all, though, he was a man-eater. He would stalk young hunters after they left the safety of the local village: follow them all day, steal upon them in the dead of night, stare them down with that one big yellow eyeball, laugh wickedly, gobble them up. Very few persons had survived to tell of such encounters, but they were universal in their depiction of utter terror: the heavy footfall and severe halitosis of the giant pursued them through their dreams.

"Finally, the village decided they'd had enough. Too many young men were vanishing out in the woods, leaving no trace but their shiny, picked-clean bones. A party was gathered to hunt down the giant and bring him to justice. They were sent out into the woods, and after some time located the giant: this wasn't too hard, what with his deep footprints and lingering, odoriferous trail. Shaking with fear, the party fell upon the giant with spears and stones, administering a beating that would have brought any ordinary being to its knees. But the giant was too strong for them: "Ha ha ha, you will never kill me," he taunted, swatting away his attackers. The hunters, seeing their failure, cut and ran, but not before several of their party were knocked out and gobbled up by the ravenous behemoth.

"It took some time before the villagers gathered up enough courage to send out another hunting party after the giant. Finally, they did so, but unfortunately the results were the same: a fruitless attack, the taunts of the giant: "Ha ha ha, you will never kill me." The same bone-crunching death for a hapless few.

"This happened twice more before the villagers (who were now starting to seriously dwindle in number) hit upon an alternate strategy. One midnight in July, when the sky was still light and the woods were tinder-dry, they tracked the giant to his sleeping grounds. Rather than directly attacking, they quietly surrounded the giant, took out their flints, sparked piles of brush into flame, and stoked an inferno that completely enclosed the giant within a fiery wall. And, luck was with them: the giant awoke to see himself trapped, no chance of escape.

"But the giant was still defiant. "Ha ha ha, you will never kill me," he swore, even as the flames engulfed and began to consume him. His burning flesh filled the sky with a horrible smudge, and his laughter was a most terrifying sound. "You will never kill me," he chanted until the very end, as he disappeared from view and ashes began to drift up from the center of the flames…Small, black specks of ash that grew in number, and swirled upwards in a cloud of their own. A hologram of tiny ashes, seeming to take on a life of their own. "You will never kill me." The flames died down, the giant was gone—but the vast cloud of black ashes lingered, swirling faster and faster, growing tiny wings…swarming down to attack the howling war party, going for blood: too minuscule and numerous ever to defeat.

"Those, ladies and gentlemen, were the world's very first mosquitoes. The spirit of the evil giant lives on in the Northern forests and swamps…and it will never be killed."

CHAMPAGNE, YUKON

▼

ancient crossroads ghost-town, vibrant in dream-memory:
inland tutchone toting furs to the
coast, seashore tlingit packing salmon over the
snowy pass, super-imposed by 1890s stampede;
    silvery birches winking at passing prospectors

here in champagne they stayed a while
wrestled some logs around, stuck some sod
on the roof and called it home
later the mud washed out of the cracks in the
cabins but wildflowers still grew in the eaves;
    freeze-dried sod clinging like quasimodo's toupee

the best places in town are the cemetery spirit-houses:
tidy 4x4 abodes in chipped borealis hues, tables and
place-settings, like tea-parties for the departed
the tutchone believed that if the spirits had a
nice place to come home to, they wouldn't
    have to wander around so much anymore

in another dimension, the champagne elders raise their
teacups and toast the dust-clouds from departing tour-buses

CINNAMON GIRL

▼

The solitary motorcoach bisected the scrub mining country at the base of the St. Elias Mountains. Shallow, fast creeks and low mounds of silver tailings bounded off in all directions, like a field of grasshoppers. In the middle of the 301 Miles To Nowhere lay the blue glacial jewel of the central Yukon, Lake Kluane. To the side of the road, just before the big descent to the lake, stood the Cinnamon Girl. Tall and tanned, freckles covering her bare arms, shock of flaming hair rendering pointless the orange Highway Department vest. More than a little sexy as she told Kris, in the thickest of oot-and-aboot accents, how to call for moose without using one's voice.

"You take a big gallon jar, eh." She brushed the firestorm from her eyes. "Big pickle or mayo jar works best. Fill 'er up with some warm water and vinegar. Cut a slot in the lid—just wide enough to slide a chunk of rubber through. Get the rubber good and wet with the vinegar, and scrape it through that slot. Play it low and mournful, but **loud**. You're playin' on that old bull moose's libido like you was sawin' on a cello."

The construction delay ended; the lovely Cinnamon Girl, a dreamer of pictures, fantasy date of Neil Young, waved Kris' bus on through, ready to share her moose-calling secrets with the next line of stopped traffic.

Those passengers within earshot of the conversation rummaged through their carry-ons for gallon pickle or mayonnaise jars—to no avail.

THE DONJEK RIVER JIG

▼

The downhill stretch from Boutillier Summit to the south shore of Lake Kluane was more of a soar than a drive. The dusty-green flanks of the central Yukon spread in hawks-eye fashion before the front windows of the motorcoach. The lake was blue-eyed and calm, far below.

"This is the most loaded section of the tour," said Kris, excitedly. "Concentrated within the next fifty miles is probably the most spectacular scenery we will see on our entire journey. We'll skirt the foot of the St. Elias range, then pick up the Kluane lakeshore, following that for a time, winding in and winding out…"

Kris' snakelike hand motions, used to graphically illustrate the curving road ahead, were arrested in mid-air as, without warning, another motorcoach hove into immediate view. He quickly flipped on the CB radio and strained his eyes to make out his fellow driver in the opposite lane. As the two buses hurtled towards one another at 60-plus mph, Kris soon spotted the telltale frizzy blonde hair and diminutive stature of the person in the driver's seat: his old Skagway cohort, Tami.

"WNCB-569, 810 to 179. Tambourine, how are you doin'?"

Tami gave Kris a way-cool Driver-Guide wave (2 fingers lifted slightly off the steering wheel, in a quick salute) and a broad smile as she whizzed by. "Just hunky-dory there, Special K. Got 'em eating out of my hand. All the old men wanted to know how such a little girl could drive such a big bus. Guess I've convinced 'em by now."

"Well, knock 'em dead, Tami. Whoops, better not do that. Just have a good trip, and see you down the road. WNCB-569, 810 out."

They finally reached the bottom of the Boutillier grade, making a sweeping curve to the left, and the front ridge of the mountains hove into close range. The highway picked up an escarpment overlooking a glacial river valley, and Kris cued up the microphone once more:

"This particular range of the St. Elias Mountains offers some of the finest hiking in all the North Country. Right here is the only trailhead leading into this entire region—providing the sole means, short of helicopters, of human access to Kluane National Park.

"Unfortunately, some other critters are highly aware of this human presence: namely, bears. And, their primary objective is **food**: not so much you, though, as what you might be carrying. Just like Yogi, they worship that great Picnic Basket in the sky. So you must exercise some common-sense measures when setting up camp in bear country: mainly, do not bring smelly food. Avoid opening cans of tuna fish; do not fry up a batch of bacon for breakfast. Do not walk around with a salmon draped over your shoulder. And, your food cache should preferably be up a nearby tree: do **not** keep food in your tent, ever. Backpacker-grade nylon is like gift-wrapping to a grizzly breakfast guest.

"Another thing you do not want to do is **surprise** a bear..." And here Kris went into the well-rehearsed Dyea Gary lecture on the importance of the human voice and the futility of "dinner bells"—with one final elaboration, based on personal experience:

"My favorite method for alerting bears to my presence? Bring a harmonica along on hikes. When rounding the bend near a stand of blueberries or something, out comes the trusty harmonica, and music fills the air. I've found that my harmonica playing scares away about **every** living thing in a given area, so I feel completely assured of safety.

"Just one more thing. If one of you should happen to be chased by a bear while on tour, I will not, unfortunately, be able to help you. Why? Well, company policy strictly prohibits me from letting anyone on this bus with a bear behind."

[BOO! HISS! much laughter]

Kris simply shrugged. "Canadian law restricts me to one bad pun per day. I guess I've used up today's quota, eh?"

They came down off the escarpment, onto a flat, muddy plain. To their left, the mountains stood shoulder-to-shoulder like a rugby scrum, daring anyone, whether clouds or ocean, to pass. A chocolate-milk colored river trickled at their feet, narrowly escaping detection. To the right of the motorcoach, the terrible truth was revealed: the single, innocuous river was not-so-slowly (by geologic standards) washing away the giant mountains and filling in the south end of Lake Kluane.

"Another several millennia," commented Kris, "and the lake will be just a big valley. Provided, of course, that another glacier doesn't march down the mountainside and dig things out again. It's pretty obvious that glaciers are the dominating moving force around here, as far as surface topography is concerned: Nature's Bulldozers."

They came to the bridge over the river, the only pronounced feature on the glacial flats. "This is called the Slims River: named for, believe it or not, a prospector's **horse**, who got stuck in the glacial silt and, unfortunately, perished here. Poor ol' Slim. This silt is treacherous stuff, but it has some very interesting properties. More on that later."

On the other side of the valley was a barren, rocky south-facing slope. Random groupings of white specks were visible, far up the mountainside. "This, of course, is Sheep Mountain: the summertime grazing range for a herd of Dall sheep, a relative of the Rocky Mountain bighorn. We will be taking a little break here."

The Canadian park service had set up an interpretive center at Sheep Mountain, complete with telescopes, sample horns (which Kris liked to mount on his head, feigning charges at his guests), and a local Tutchone woman who knew just about everything there was to know about the local flora and fauna. Kris gladly steered his passengers, and himself, towards her expertise; he had learned a great deal from this woman, and was learning more every time he stopped here.

They lingered at Sheep Mountain for about twenty minutes, until Kris, looking at his engineer's pocketwatch, gently herded his flock back to the bus. As they departed the parking lot, an important piece of information, lodged in his head by Don the tour guide, dislodged itself like a piece of shale:

Q: Why did the Dall sheep ram fall off the mountain?

A: Because he didn't see the ewe-turn.

Having used up his Bad Joke Quota for the day (sadly), he was unable to relate the information to his guests—this time.

Major Highlights of the Lake Kluane Shoreline Drive:

1) Soldiers Summit: the place where the northbound and southbound crews constructing the original Al-Can highway hooked up, in November 1942—an astounding eight months after they began. Road repairs began immediately thereafter, and have never really stopped.

2) Destruction Bay: about halfway up the western shore of Lake Kluane, this tiny community is named for a 1943 windstorm that leveled the wartime tent city. The present town is situated on a barren talus slope just above the lake, and still looks awfully vulnerable.

3) Burwash Landing: located at the northwest corner of the lake; jumping-off point for a very minor gold rush (long since deceased) and modern-day expeditions for lunker lake trout (very much alive). The highway sign for the local hospitality entrepreneur boasts "Rooms, Grub & Booze."

"What more do you need from life?" commented Kris. "All the basics are here."

The Donjek River bridge was visible for miles: bright steel-girder triangles spanning nearly a half-mile of braided channel. The water was fast, cold and silty, carrying away tons of pulverized St. Elias Mountains per second. The range, still ignorant of its rapid depletion, stood cold-shouldered and impassive to the south, a scant thirty miles away.

"The mighty Donjek: named for a local type of ryegrass, used for weaving by the Tutchone. One of your classic Yukon glacial rivers: 'a mile wide and an inch deep,' just like the Platte in Nebraska. This was one of the trickiest bridges to construct on the entire Alaska Highway—for reasons that will soon become apparent."

After crossing the bridge, Kris swung the motorcoach down a gravel lane to the river's edge. Everyone disembarked, and Kris led them to the gray water.

"Folks, I'm about to demonstrate one of the natural phenomena of the North. But it also involves some culture: I would like to perform for you a famous dance, known as the Donjek River Jig. It's fast and furious, it's highly visual, it's educational, it's **entertainment**."

Kris nimbly stepped down to an innocuous-looking sandbar and began to shuffle off to Buffalo, talking as he jigged. "You see, the dancing surface is what matters most, all nifty steps aside." Kris did a leaping 360, and gently came down, just like Mr. Bojangles. "This is no ordinary beach sand. This is not the stuff you find at Malibu: no sand-castle material here. This, of course, is glacial **silt**, washed away from the mountains and deposited downstream in places like this. Until now, no one had disturbed this little beach, offended its dignity with shameless high-stepping." Kris put on the Ritz, looking just like Gary Cooper. "But this silt is so fine, of such a tiny particulate size—when dry, it's just like flour—that this relative stability is highly misleading. Shake it up, do some energetic jigging for a minute or so, and the fragile suspension of particles and water becomes…completely **unreliable**." Cha cha cha, hey hey, boppity-bop shoo-bop.

"This beach…is about to become…cha-cha-chocolate **pudding**."

Just then the sandbar began to wobble, the ground displayed disturbing Jell-O tendencies, and with a final flourish Kris finished his jig—right as he started to sink. His driving shoes pulled out of the pudding with a loud SLURP as he leaped to safety.

The passengers stood by, too flabbergasted to applaud the dance performance. Kris, wiping the goo from his bootheels, spoke once again: "Glacial silt: worse than quicksand, much more misleading and potentially deadly. It got poor old Slim the horse, back there at Lake Kluane; it gets someone off the Turnagain Arm near Anchorage every few years; it's darn near gotten my shoes a couple times."

The long, flat stretches of nothingness following the Donjek River provided an opportune time for Kris to slow things down a little, let the tour catch its breath. *And anyway, how do I top that last act? Enough is enough. But there's just one more highlight to go, before that final push to Beaver Creek.*

The White River bridge was considerably shorter than the Donjek, but perhaps even more dramatic: steel girders bold against a high, sandy bluff; the place on the erector-set diorama where one would have poised one's plastic soldiers for an attack on the unsuspecting GI Joes far below.

"We are now crossing the White River, another of the series of glacial torrents emanating from the northern St. Elias range. Here is one of your best close-up views of such a river. Note, especially, the color of the water—or rather, its lack of clarity, its near opaqueness. The White River is even siltier than the Donjek. Additionally, this one comes from a range where the rocks are lighter in color—lots of limestone, probably. Hence, the light-brown, milky appearance.

"They have a pretty good idea who named the White River: a party of Englishmen, passing through sometime in the mid-1800s. However, they are not sure why it was named as such: no one in the party, or in the records of the time, was named White. The only explanation I've heard—and I think it's a pretty good one—is that this party of Englishmen, possibly lost, probably hungry and mosquito-bitten, certainly a long way from home, came upon this river...and were reminded of tea. Tea with plenty of milk, the way the English like it: what they call "white" tea. Hence, they christened the river after their great national love affair: ritual, civilization, nostalgia, bone china and sticky wickets. The White River, named for the torrents of whitened English tea flowing by. May the cups of all explorers, erstwhile and present, never run dry."

Kris paused, spent by his verbosity, and then suddenly realized something. "And, by an amazing coincidence, I look at my watch, and it's..."

"4 o'clock! On the nose! Teatime!" Mary was enthralled. "High Tea in the Yukon. Who would have believed it?"

Kris shook his head and smiled, spoke in genteel Knightsbridge tones. "I **say**—I never noticed this before, but every time we cross the White River, northbound, it is right around four. Most peculiar, what? Next tour, I'd jolly well better have some cups, saucers and fresh crumpets ready."

MUSH

▼

as gunshots echo across the windswept reaches of the
   wild northwest, quaker puffed wheat and quaker
      puffed rice (**kapow! kapow!**), the breakfast cereal shot from guns,
        present
        the **challenge of the yukon!**
(**woof! woof!**) it's yukon king,
   swift as the strongest lead dog of the northwest, blazing the
      trail for sergeant preston of the northwest mounted police, in his
   relentless pursuit of lawbreakers!!!

"**Mush,** you huskies!" commanded Sergeant Preston, in ringing stentorian tones.

"**Hush,** you muskies," responded Kris, with a slightly lesser degree of resonance.

I'm A Beaver, You're A Beaver

▼

Did You Know: that the boreal forest is a topography common to subarctic latitudes the world over. In Russian Siberia, the spindly larch forests are called "taiga," which translates loosely as "land of little sticks." In the Yukon and Alaskan interiors, where black spruce dominates the soggy muskeg, a favorite moniker for the land is "drunken forest": the trees' root systems are so shallow, due to permafrost, that heavy snowfall or a good wind will tip individual trees into crazy, haphazard angles. Odd stretches of "drunken forest" permeate the landscape for much of the northern Al-Can.

"Oh, what do ye do with a drunken forest,
Earlie in the mornin'?"
—Old sailors' chantey, noticeably skewed (thank you, Kevin)

One of the few drawbacks about the northbound tour was that the road kept getting worse instead of better. Conditions improved once the Alaskan border had been recrossed (eternal road construction aside), but the final stretch of Canadian highway was truly dismal. The road narrowed, snaking through endless peat bogs and drunken forests; the frost-heaves became like the open sea; highway maintenance seemed to consist of occasional shovelfuls of gravel, in a vain attempt to keep the whole thing from sloughing off a hill.

At first, the frostheaves had been an exciting experience. The passengers felt like they were finally getting into the boondocks, the wild, rugged North: the place where God did not intend Man to build paved roads. Kris' Sergeant Preston tape, which he played just after the White River crossing, contributed to this mood. But even the hardiest among them dreamed of dry land, or at least Dramamine, by the late afternoon, as signs for Beaver Creek began to rise from the blacktop.

Kris and the other drivers didn't like this stretch of road much better than the tourists, but at least they knew it was coming. And, some even managed to have fun with it. Playing "Sergeant Preston of the Yukon" tapes helped eat up the miles in vicariously adventuresome fashion. It was also amusing to take advantage of the natural anxiety about Beaver Creek itself, generated by the primitive highway conditions—which certain unscrupulous tour guides easily whipped up into a nightmare scenario.

"In keeping with our desire to give you as authentic an experience as possible," Kris began, "we would like to bring you back to the days of the Al-Can Highway construction. Yes, Beaver Creek is a full restoration of a 1942 Army camp—**no** detail is spared."

There were mutterings of surprise and confusion: **this** wasn't in the tour brochure. Kris resumed, in historical documentary tones. "Your accommodations will be perhaps more primitive than what you are used to, but they are appropriate and fully functional. Upon arrival, you will be issued cots, bedrolls and mosquito netting, and will be assigned to one of the large tents on the grounds. They're dry and comfortable, and should sleep thirty or so apiece. Latrines are out back; they were just recently dug, so they should still be quite sanitary and pleasant."

Now about half of the passengers were chuckling—most from amusement, a few from nervousness. Kris' tone switched to that of a benevolent drill sergeant. "For your dining pleasure, historic Army cuisine has also been preserved. Tonight they will be serving chipped beef on toast—'S.O.S.,'[9] for those of you familiar with the fond military vernacular." There were audible groans. "Indeed, that is what they serve **every** night here. For breakfast, expect more of the same, with some delicious Sanka or Kool-Aid to help it down.

"For the evening's entertainment, you're on your own—sorry, you just missed Bob Hope. Maybe you can build a nice campfire. Lights out at dark, of course—whenever that might be. The mosquitoes should hum you right to sleep. Finally, remember tomorrow morning's schedule: reveille at 0600 hours, followed by 10 kilometer 'fun run.' Be sure to wear your Army boots."

"I think your **mother** wears Army boots," came a loud call from the back of the bus. And, as they entered Beaver Creek, saw no tents or outdoor latrines, the last of the true believers finally relaxed and laughed with the rest.

As they rolled into the hotel compound (which did, in fact, have a disturbingly martial look to it), a group of young people, who had been lounging around on the sunbaked steps, sprang into action, attacking the luggage bays, yanking suitcases and heaving them into waiting carts.

"As you can see," said Kris, "they **love** visitors. They're grateful for human contact, with people from the Outside. They're 301 Miles From Nowhere, all summer long."

An expie materialized, hotel keys in hand, and gave a quick rundown of the basics. Kris had an addendum or two: "Prime rib. Steak 'n spuds. Maybe a Molson to wash it down. The food here is superlative. But you **will** need to walk it off, lest you fall asleep in your dessert plate. I would

---

9. "S**t on a Shingle," of course

suggest a stroll around town: going up and down the main drag takes about an hour, as it's all kind of spread out. However, this area also boasts some of the finest, most accessible honest-to-God **muskeg** you're likely to see—for the Muskeg Walkers amongst you." At this, he shot a glance at Mary, who seemed ready to bolt out of her seat like an octogenarian rocket. "So have a good time around town tonight. And of course, ask any hotel employee to sing the Beaver Creek Song[10] for you. I'm sure they will be delighted to do so." The expie shot Kris a mildly despairing glance.

Heh heh heh. Kris and the others delighted in tormenting the local staff this way.

After his passengers were safely ensconced, Kris booked himself for a standard Beaver Creek evening: drive his bus around back, wash it and dump the Blue Lagoon; find his motel room, rip off the polyester, grab a shower; head down to Ida's Roadhouse, buy a burger and a High-Test, converse with some local color. The muskeg walk would be an optional activity for the return journey, depending upon mood, ambience and number of High-Tests consumed.

---

10. The Beaver Creek Song: "Oh, I'm a beaver, you're a beaver, we are beavers all; and when we get together, we give the Beaver Call: (munch munch munch munch...)." Repeat, endlessly, all summer long.

PERMANENT WAVES

▼

"You have to watch every step you take,
  walking on the moon;
  I hope my legs don't break,
  walking on the moon..."

—Sting

The following morning, Kris opened the motorcoach door to see Mary first in line, eagerly clutching her cruise-ship tote bag, chipper as always— a tad unusual for 7 am in Beaver Creek. "I took my Muskeg Walk last night!" she cried as she bounded aboard. "Oh, it was delightful. I put on my tennies, packed a little snack and off I went. Off through your 'Charlie Brown Christmas' trees; sinking into the moss, springing back up again. Bouncy bouncy!" Mary clapped her hands in delight.

The story was repeated for just about everyone who cared to listen (e.g., everyone who subsequently boarded): the lilting "Bouncy bouncy!" concluding each telling. Mary was better than coffee.

It was another pleasant morning. Nobody on the road, Alaska only twenty miles away, the horrendous frost-heaves once again novel and amusing. And, of course, the rabbits were out.

"Oh, I do fear for those cute bunnies," commented Mary. "Hopping about in the sun, oblivious to the nasty lorries and motorcars. The poor dears that don't make it: left on the tarmac to become furry little Canadian flapjacks. Hors d'oeuvres for roving bands of ferrets. Raven smorgasbords. Eagle elevensies."

Ahem. Thanks for sharing, Mary. But then Kris had a flash of inspiration. This was the perfect segue to…The Rabbit Story.

"You know," began Kris, "these early drives can be really inspiring: the sun, the morning dew, nature in full force. All these **rabbits**. But I've always worried about them: some are old, some are bold, and some ain't too swift to behold.[11] Maybe it's just nature's plan, Darwinian natural selection and all that—but I've always thought, 'Boy, I'd sure hate to smunch one of those little bunnies with my motorcoach.'

"Well, about a year ago, on a morning much like this, with a group much like yourselves, my worst fears came to pass. The rabbits were everywhere: hopping about unconcernedly, blissfully ignorant of such problems as Detroit Diesel and Firestone. And up around a bend, right in the middle of the highway, was this poor, doomed rabbit. I had just a millisecond to look into its sad, hare-brained eyes before…well…there was a very discreet —BUMP!—

"I knew immediately what I'd done, but was hoping that no one had noticed. However, this English lady in the front seat—someone very much like our Mary, in fact—saw everything, felt that little—BUMP!— She rose from her seat, came up front, tapped me on the shoulder. "Please, young man," she said, close to tears, "you must go back and check on that

---

11. Frank Zappa, Po-Jama People, genetically altered.

poor, dear rabbit you smunched. Isn't there something, **anything** you can do to help it?"

"I sighed. I love wildlife, I'm a sensitive '80s guy and all, but this truly seemed like a lost cause. Besides, people come here to see **live**, not dead wildlife—roadkills tend to put a real damper on a tour. But this lady was insistent, so I stopped the motorcoach, backed up, and stepped outside.

"Sure enough, I had creamed it: not to be too graphic, but in Mary's words it was indeed a furry little flapjack. A lapidary *lefse*, for you Norwegians. Most deceased, seemingly: an ex-rabbit. But then I remembered something:

"I ran back to the bus, fetched the first aid kit, found a certain aerosol can. I stepped back outside with it, trotted up to the two-dimensional rabbit, shook the can—shicka, shicka—and gave the bunny a little dousing. But nothing happened. I tried again: shake, shake, schpritz. Still nothing. I sighed, turned away, shrugged my shoulders. I had done all I could.

But then, I heard an odd little sound: like ripping Velcro, or rabbit fur disengaging from asphalt. I wheeled about, and watched in disbelief as one little paw...S-L-O-W-L-Y rose. I dashed back and gave the bunny another, frantic spraying. In a few seconds, a second paw slowly came back to life. I then gave the rabbit all I had, emptying the entire aerosol can on the flat body. And, within a minute, the rabbit had become round, whole, **alive** again.

At first the bunny just sat there, blinking, licking its paws, sniffling a little bit. Then it hopped away a short distance, turned around, looked right at me...and **waved**. Just a sort of "Thank you...bye-bye!" wave. Then it hopped away another ten feet or so, turned and waved again: "Bye-bye!" And again and again—hop hop, wave wave—for as far as I could see, until the bunny vanished from view.

"Of course, all my passengers had been gaping in awe throughout this whole spectacle. The lady in front was ecstatic, nearly in tears. Nonchalantly I reboarded, placed the spray can back into the first aid kit. But I wasn't about to get off the hook.

"What did you do? How did you save that little rabbit's life? **What** was in that spray can, young man?"

"So I showed them the spray can. The label said, simply,

HARE RESTORER

Permanent Wave."

A Long Ways To Carry A Weed-Whacker

▼

Conditions for the crossing back into Alaska are optimal. The highway is absolutely still and quiet this time of day. The air is clear and bright, carrying the first hints of the day's summer warmth; the U.S. border guards are probably snoozing in their sunlit booths. The thirty-foot border clearing is straight as an arrow, stretching over the north and south horizons. Hope the man on the interminable weed-whacker patrol is enjoying his morning, wherever he may be.

My tourists look like schoolkids on recess. There's a cluster of four, having their pictures taken in front of the "International Friendship" plaque. There's the youthful 60-year old couple (who would have imagined I'd ever make such a characterization?), dressed in their matching sweatsuits, making a brisk circumnavigation of the lot. There's Mary, the eternal gardener, kneeling down to identify yet another species of subarctic wildflower.

How did this scene come to be, in such a short period of time? Is it a conceit for me to think I'm responsible for it, somehow? Well, yes and no: I think some of the shared experiences have been facilitated by wacky tour-guide antics, but the rest is a function of time (the third day together), space (96 inches across, 11 feet high, forty feet long) distance (750 miles, 55 to 60 mph) and simple group dynamics. If the tour were going badly—regardless of whomever would be at fault, if anyone—there's probably little I could do to fix it at this point. If a tour is going well—as this one certainly is—it takes on a life of its own, and all I need to do is to keep it pointed in the same general direction.

I think I understand how these long-distance tours work now: how they carry on because of—or in spite of—all the heart and soul that a Driver-Guide pours into it.

Top Ten Things To Do In Tok

▼

1. Take a walk. It's good for your legs, the air is refreshing.

2. Go to Mukluk Land. Experience the unparalleled excitement of viewing the World's Largest Mukluk. Many interesting genres of Alaskan footwear (and feet) are represented there.

3. Wash a bus! Scrape and chisel off the fine entymological collection. Get eaten by vengeful mosquitoes. Cure yourself of saying "You missed a spot" to your driver.

4. Take a walk. It's good for your legs, the air is refreshing.

5. Go to Fast Eddy's, meet somebody special. Be home by dark.

6. Go to the Burnt Paw, take a husky puppy home. Ensure that is it fully weaned.

7. Take a walk. It's good for your legs, the air is refreshing.

8. Go jogging, cycling or roller-blading, on the famous Path To Nowhere, paralleling the Al-Can. 24 miles to Tanacross and back. You are not likely to encounter much traffic or competition.

9. Go shopping at the Alaskan Gifts Factory Outlet, conveniently located right downtown. Bargains, bargains, bargains. Stock up on those moose-nugget souvenirs for the kids.

10. Take a walk. It's good for your legs, the air is refreshing.

"Welcome to Tok," said Genna to Kris' passengers, "the town **so** small that, instead of outskirts, it has **mini**-skirts." Genna had only one hour this time, instead of the usual overnight stay, to work her charms upon her guests (and hence, time was very limited for Kevin's Tok Top Ten activities). However, Kris' busload was quickly under her spell as they followed her trustingly towards mid-morning pie and coffee.

Once everyone was ensconced indoors, at rustic Tundra Lodge wooden tables, Genna switched into waitress mode and began taking orders. Kris, helpful young man that he was, grabbed a coffee pot and trailed close behind, filling up the waiting cups.

"You're looking a little short-handed today," commented Kris, when they had a stray moment together in the kitchen. "Where's your Mom?"

"I'm experimenting with Responsibility," said Genna. "Mom's not here; she's off in Fairbanks. I'm all by my lonesome."

"Lack of parental supervision: **hmmm**. Very interesting."

"Lest you get any ideas, Bucko: I'm a working girl today. You're a working boy. **But**...I **don't** think anyone's looking." Suddenly she pinned him against a refrigerator and gave him a silky, lingering kiss that tasted like blueberry pie and ice cream. Smiling goldenly, mischievously at him, she picked up some plates and disappeared through the swinging door, leaving him momentarily stunned against the refrigerator door.

Genna waved goodbye to Kris' bus as it departed her lodge and her town, saving a special wave and smile for the still-woozy driver.

VINCENT VAN MOOSE

▼

There were about one hundred miles of low, swampy areas and willow shrubs between Tok and Dot Lake. To liven up this stretch of road, Kris' narrative would take on an air of mysterioso:

"Folks, ordinarily I do not presume to guarantee wildlife. But today I feel something in the air: I can almost **smell** the moose out there. So, would you like to **see** a moose?"

[well of course; heck yes; you betcha; generally affirmative sounds]

"There are two generally-accepted ways to call the moose from the woods. One is the straightforward method, whereby I simply get one of you to yell out the door, 'Here, moosie moosie.' *[titters, guffaws]* But that's too easy. The second, preferred moose-attracting method relies on an old technique known as 'sympathetic magic':

"Prior to an important hunt, the Athabaskan people would prevail upon their friendly local shaman to invoke sympathetic magic, by drawing upon some buckskin an illustration of the animal sought. By producing this image, the shaman would be calling forth the moose, or bear, or woolly mammoth, so that the hunting would be good. Such artistic imitation was perceived by the spirit of the animal as a form of **flattery**—a traditionally potent attractant.

"Folks, we are now about to practice our own form of sympathetic magic. Shortly, I will be distributing artistic materials to you—and I would like each of you to draw a moose for me, to lure them out of the bush. If you have any inspirational hunting songs or poems you would like to add to your illustration, please feel free to do so."

At the next picture stop, Kris made a quick visit back to the Blue Lagoon, and grabbed a large stack of clean paper towels. As soon as everyone was back on board, he began distributing the towels from the front rows to the rear. "Our artistic medium: nothing but the finest sketch paper. I recommend pencils, crayons, charcoal, the fine pens you have swiped from your hotel rooms. No watercolors or oil-based paints, please." He finished, went back to the driver's seat, sat down and then remembered something: "Oh yes: I nearly forgot. Just to offer you some incentive, I wanted to show you what exactly we're shooting for, prize-wise." He reached into a paper bag and pulled out a choice trinket he had picked up (cheap) at the Tok Tundra Lodge gift shop. "A genuine product of Alaska: moose-nugget swizzle sticks. Add zest to any cocktail party. You didn't think it could be done, but here it is, folks. So let's hit the road, and **start drawing**."

The group settled down like a kindergarten class on assignment, exploring the artistic possibilities of Scott towels and ballpoint pens on clipboards, hardcover books, even their seatmates' backs. Whenever they started looking too serious about their work, Kris would aim the bus for a medium-sized frostheave, or swerve slightly to generate yaw and wobble in artistic lines. By the time he reached Dot Lake (where he had drive-by encounters with both Llary and Don, going the opposite direction), most of his passengers had completed their artistry, but a few were still bent to the task, brows furrowed in contemplation—a sure sign of moose-drawing masterpieces to come.

CHURCH ON THE LAKE

▼

the town is easy to miss, the lake even easier: literally one of
a million footprints in the spongy central-alaskan muskeg

but the church is one-of-a-kind: sturdy, boxlike, built to withstand russian-
epic storms and cold; squatting on the lakeshore like a dostoyevsky peasant

the steeple, stubby and timeworn like the finger of a farmer-
saint, pointing to the sky above reed-circled shoreline

> but it's so small, said my passengers as they
> piled out to visit the dot lake church; same

> idea as little-red-schoolhouse i said, home-
> on-the-range, function over form;

> not many people, not much space needed; the church is
> simply another feature of the prairie

ducking to enter, filling the belltower alcove, then
spilling over into pews, my group easily fills the dot lake

church; we've about doubled the congregation today
watching from above is the belltower's resident, not

quasimodo, not a family of deaf mice but a very patient
bronze bell, survivor of long buckboard journey from god—

knows where, surviving to be rung again but only for
starting the service or congregating the community i say,

    disregard that rapunzel bellrope
    tickling your necks

ETHEL'S FUR BIKINI

▼

Delta Junction was the major milestone on the map for the third day: this was where the Alaska Highway officially ended, although it was still another 110 miles to Fairbanks on the Richardson Highway. The road itself did not reflect any sense of ceremony, winding down with an utterly nondescript 30-mile shot through jungle-like muskeg. There were plenty of bumps, but no curves whatsoever; Kris felt like locking the steering wheel into position and taking a stroll down the bus aisle. "Hang in there, folks," he exhorted, "only a little further, and the Al-Can is history."

Finally, fields opened up on either side of the road, homes appeared, with actual lawns—the first since Whitehorse—and there was even a John Deere dealership. "Welcome to Delta Junction: Alaska's Breadbasket," said a sign on a tractor. And the number "1422," which had for days hovered in the collective psyche, appeared on a roadside stone obelisk: this number, of course, represented the mileage from Dawson Creek, British Columbia to this ultimate point.

The first order of business was to obtain proof of their road adventure. To this end, the Delta Visitor's Center provided official certificates, bearing the legend, "I Survived the Alaska Highway." The staff was also experienced in dealing with rattled kidneys, wobbly sea-legs and other telltale afflictions. But, as Kris told his group, "Just because you've made it this far doesn't mean the roads get any better from here. If anything, the highway conditions we've experienced are the rule statewide, not the exception. What these certificates mean is that you are now frost-heave veterans: you've shown that you have what it takes. Be **proud**." Certificates of survivorship were solemnly handed to all.

Next was a more informal introduction to the Alaskan Interior's true character: some local entrepreneurs, and one very special sales representative. "My girlfriend works across the way there," Kris casually mentioned. "Would you like to meet her?"

Oh my, oh yes. Gossip and speculation as to the love lives of Tour Guides were always rampant among passengers; wallet photos of unattached, eligible children and grandchildren had a way of popping out at opportune moments. Kris' passengers watched as he sauntered across the gravel parking lot, rounded a vendor's-booth corner and stood in adoration before…the lovely Ethel. A smile was fixed on her face as she stood with outstretched arms, resplendent in a stunning, hand-crafted fox-fur bikini. No goose-bumps whatsoever were apparent on her trim torso, although she seemed to shiver a bit when Kris put his arm around her. "She's glad to see me.. can't you tell?" said Kris, as he posed for corny pictures with the curvaceous mannequin.

The guy who ran the booth both trapped the furs and created the fashion statements: hats, coats and earmuffs in addition to Arctic swimwear. "Thanks for plugging those fur bikinis for me," he said to Kris in an aside. "I've sold several this summer already."

"Don't mention it," said Kris. "I'd do anything for Ethel."

The vendor called out to a sixtyish woman studying the skimpy but well-insulated bikini. "Hey—you buy it, you get to model it for us, OK?" The woman blushed prettily, like a teenager.

There was no such sale that day—but Ethel was easy, either way. She was just glad to be out in that fur-warming Alaskan summer sun.

From the modern conveniences of downtown Delta Junction (Tastee-Freez, the Motel Seven), it was a short drive, but a world away, to the day's lunch site at Rika's. The old roadhouse was by far Kris' favorite stop on the final stretch into Fairbanks: the log lodges, the simple but spectacular camp cuisine, the best guided history chat since Skagway. It was, in fact, run by a group of people who tried to live the old life as closely as possible: clothing of the period, traditional means of sustenance (winter trapping, huge summer gardens), friendly in the unique rural Alaskan fashion. Just far enough off the beaten path, the soft sound of wind in the birches prevailing over the rattle and clunk of RV's on the Richardson Highway.

The walking-stick guy (whom Kris now knew was named Luke), was waiting for them at the trailhead to the cookhouse, looking like a man of the times—old times—in his river-driver's shirt, suspenders and jeans. Luke introduced himself, gave a quick rundown of the Rika's itinerary and, without further ado, led his flock to lunch.

Dominating the foreground of the cookhouse was the Tanana River, high and dark and fast like a predawn freight train. Sitting at an outdoor table with his soup, sourdough bread and rhubarb pie, Kris felt as if he were waiting at an interminable railroad crossing. But he had to eat fast, lest some of his passengers finish ahead of him and slip away to the lodge. This would frustrate his little surprise, his own secret journey back into time. Kris took a final slug of cowboy coffee, left his tray by the door and trotted down the gravel path towards the old main building.

Elsa was waiting by the museum door. "Don was just through here, southbound; he told me you were coming." She smiled mischievously, helped Kris out of his blazer and stashed it behind the counter, held up a heavy buckskin and fox-fur winter coat. "This one's a **serious** parky. Go on, zip it up; it's like a bear-hug. This is just what you would have needed around here way back when."

"I feel like an old trapper. Or a grizzly. A very warm, furry one." The sensation was not altogether unpleasant—although a little toasty for late June.

"Try this to top it off." Elsa produced a fine beaver-pelt toque, undid the ear-flaps and tied the thongs under Kris' chin. She stood back and cocked her head approvingly. "**Now** you're ready for exhibit. Grab one of those diamond willow sticks, and meet me in the old kitchen."

The museum had laid out a rustic, authentic parlour: all gingham, crockery and cast-iron. An ancient Victrola was cranked up, and tinkling ragtime piano drove out the wild Northwoods boojums. Kris perched at the kitchen table, getting into character, feeling muffled inside the coat and hat. Elsa poked her head around the corner. "They're on their way. Let's see a pose." Kris froze, in contemplative, stoic pioneer motif. "Nah— we need something a little more rugged-looking. More profile: stick out your chin. Don't let that smile sneak out." Kris adjusted, Elsa nodded. "**Now** you're ready.

The footsteps of Kris' tour group sounded on the front porch. Elsa snuck away to greet them, giggling. And Kris was suddenly a museum piece: a 1920's sourdough mannequin, Ethel's crusty old grampaw.

The tourists slowly drifted towards the kitchen tableau.

"What an adorable kitchen!"

"I remember: we used to have dishes like that in my mother's house."

"How much do you suppose they'd want for that old wooden rocker?"

"How much do they want for that **mannequin**? What a handsome outdoorsman."

"That's no mannequin, that's…"

After Kris' wooden pose had given away to a telltale grin, after his group had oohed and aahed, and taken pictures, an elderly woman quietly came up to him:

"You know, young man, when you were sitting at that table, you looked just like my son, Champ. He was a tall, strong boy, just like you: a traveler, a mountain climber. He's been gone for some time now—but I swear, just for a moment…"

Sympathetic Magic, Part Two

Kris found himself wondering about "Champ" as they left Rika's and crossed back into modern Alaska, pausing briefly by the pipeline river crossing. *Conjuring up the spirit of an old sourdough is one thing: a woman's long-lost son is another. How many more "Champs" are out there?*

On the Fairbanks side of the Tanana River bridge was an open, marshy area the drivers called the "Moose Meadows": a place where, more often than not, moose could be spotted. Rather than approaching the area safari-style (as he usually did southbound), Kris decided to play things low-key, letting his passengers make the 'surprise' discovery.

Sure enough, about one-third of the way into the Moose Meadows, a cow moose munched lackadaisically on some aquatic plants, a scant fifty feet from the roadside. The cry came from somewhere in the back: "**MOOSE!**" Kris obligingly pulled the bus off the narrow highway, for a lengthy gander at the grazing ungulate. "Remember the 'sympathetic magic'?" he asked his guests. "See, it **works**." The moose twitched her banana-leaf ears, as if to acknowledge the flattery, but did not miss a moment of mealtime.

Two other moose, both females, were spotted on the far side of the meadows, for a total of three sightings. Not bad, but considerably off the all-time record of eight. Kris, noticing that his guests had snapped resoundingly out of their post-lunch torpor and irrevocably had moose on the brain, decided that now would be as good a time as any for the Moose Drawing awards. He'd only had about five minutes at lunch to go through the drawings, but his art-savvy eye had quickly managed to separate the classics from the riffraff. At the next available picture stop, Kris organized the winners, limbered up his pseudo-art critic's vocabulary, and made ready the Bag o' Prizes.

"Well, you made this very hard for me: you're such a talented, cultured bunch. There could have been any number of winners; indeed, consider yourself **all** winners. But someone has to get those prized swizzle-sticks. After much hand-wringing and angst, I've narrowed it down to two runners-up…and one Grand Prize Winner.

"The envelopes, please…"

Second Runner-Up

"Our second runner-up derives its exalted status from its lush, ethereal artistic rendering. Its title is, simply, 'Madeleine Moose.' This fine work is unaccompanied by explanatory prose, but the art truly speaks for itself, standing on its own. Note how the voluptuous curves of Madeleine express a Rubenseque sensuality, yet the lines are so light and graceful as to convey a Renoir-like lyricism. Truly a successful melding of classical styles.

"Your prize: a wonderful moose-nugget swizzle. Here you are."

First Runner-Up

"Incidentally, the prize for the first runner-up is a free, all-expenses paid, one-long vacation in Beaver Creek. For the second runner-up: **two** weeks in Beaver Creek.

"Next we have a rendering of the 'Moose-quito': a creature of a Northwoods nightmare, so horrendous as to make the Takhini mosquito myth pale in comparison. The artwork employs a sort of Dali-esque surrealism—note how the figures bend and curve, as if someone had been drawing while riding on a bumpy road—but the imagery is straight from Hieronymous Bosch, leavened by just a touch of Warner Brothers wit.

"The accompanying verse tells the whole terrifying story, I believe."

Mistress Mary Moose-quito

Mistress Mary Moose-quito, could not fill her need-o
for fresh tourist blood every night;
So she danced on the stage, to become quite the rage,
with the best can-can in sight.
Then after each production, she flew 'round in stinging seduction,
till her belly was full and tight.

But one evening after dancing, the flying moose a-prancing,
gave her audience quite a fright:
She waved her moose-ears, and her eyes filled with tears
As she gave herself a big bite.
Mistress Mary Moose-quito at last filled her need-o
By drinking her own blood that night.

The Winner

Kris' horde of pseudo-artistic lingo was just about spent. Nonetheless, he had one more extemporaneous critique in him:

"And at long last, our Grand Prize Winner. Your prize, in addition to the fine swizzles, will be widespread fame and recognition, not only amongst the artistic community, but amongst us bus drivers as well: a place in the vinyl-bound pantheon of all-time greatest Moose Drawings. Ahem."

Kris, studying the large-headed stick figure before him, tried to sound as significant as possible. "Note how the artist employs a sort of post-modern, post-Picasso minimalism. There is a use of contrapuntal perspective that is startling to the eye: the ascetic body, made lean by suffering, overwhelmed by the macrocephalous head, crammed with God-only knows what kinds of mysterious and wonderful ideas.

"But what is the artist **truly** trying to say? Let's find out."

The Thirsty Moose
Twenty years ago or more
in the town of Tok,
A moose came to a grocery store
and bought a can of coke.
The storekeeper, he shook his head:
"Coke is not made for deer."
The moose replied, "That's right, you bet:
I'd better drink some beer."

Home In The Snow

▼

By the time the lucky moose-nugget swizzle stick recipients had circulated their prizes amongst their fellow passengers, about half the bus wanted a set. Kris, somewhat incredulously, promised to circulate a sheet for names and addresses, so that people in Peoria, St. Cloud, Thousand Oaks could receive mildly pungent packages from Alaska in a couple weeks, and be the first ones on their block to own scatological swizzles.

Suburban hints of Fairbanks began to appear as far away as the Salcha River area, about fifty miles out of town. By the time they reached North Pole, and the slightly-cheesy but extremely tourist-friendly Santa Claus House (with its towering 50-foot plastic Santa), signs of the tour's end were imminent.

*I think, for about the first time ever, that I want to hold on to a group: why not just keep touring with these folks, all summer long? Well, maybe not to **that** extreme—but I can't believe the extent to which we've gotten friendly and comfortable with one another, within a very short time. Before, when I've said goodbye, I've wished them well, but I've felt no particular pang at parting. But this time...*

"As you can see, the end is near: soon you'll be back in America, back to Big Macs, traffic jams and air-conditioned hotel rooms. But before we end this journey, I'd like to leave you with something more: something to take with you from Alaska, even if your top-secret X-20 shopping bags are long-since full. It's a little song, taught to me by an old sourdough buddy of mine (Derek, in fact, had been the teacher). It contains a few simple truths about this place, and it's very easy to learn.

"I'll go through it once, repeat the lyrics slowly, then we'll sing it together. The song goes something like this:

*I wouldn't have guessed I'd **ever** be singing to my tourists. But here we are. And here we go.*

Home in the Snow

Oh give me a home, between Fairbanks and Nome
Where the moose and the caribou play;
Where nothing will grow, cause it's covered with snow
From June till the following May...

Home, home in the snow
Where it's mild when its forty below;
It's the tundra for me, to the great Bering Sea,
And the life of an old Sourdough.

Note on Fridge: 7/7/88

▼

Hey Kris,

"Missed ya by **that** much," as Maxwell Smart used to say. Heard you were coming back in; had barely enough time to replenish the beer supply before being sent out again myself. Down to the Park, then a couple days in Los Anchorage before heading back up here next Thursday.

Me and Kim (hotel expie from ANC; think I told you about her) had a wild time in Talkeetna over the Fourth: almost **too** wild, in fact. Hopefully I'll catch up with you soon in person, tell you all about it.

—Pete

TALKEETNA BOTTLE-ROCKET
MASSACREE

▼

Act I

*[**Opening scene:** from a blurred gauze of hazy sunshine, the camera eye slowly focuses on a hanging wooden sign, welcoming visitors to downtown Talkeetna, the de-facto capital of the south-central Alaskan bush. The sign, put up by hopeful merchants a couple of years back, is already riddled with chippings, whittlings and even a touch of buckshot. The sign hangs heavily in the sun; there is no breeze, or any suggestion of motion whatsoever.]*

[The camera then pans ever-so-slowly from left to right, sweeping over the Talkeetna main drag. We see the log-cabin ice cream stand, with the moose rack over the flavor list; the old general store and hotel; the gas station; the potholed street that terminates at the river's edge. There is a palpable aura of heat and dust, conveyed by the lemony lighting and the

shimmering of the street. Fourth of July bunting hangs limply from second-story railings.]

[The camera lights momentarily on each occasional, slow-moving passerby, before seeming to blink and lose interest. Some of the passersby, however, respond to the camera eye, smiling, waving a little hello, even saying "Howdy" or "How you doin', boy." Finally, the camera locks onto a target moving slowly up the main street; the figure moves closer and closer, the camera eye languidly widens, and the figure, a bearded man in a denim shirt and paint-splotched carpenter's pants, arrives, grins and reaches out a petting hand.]

Painter Man: Hey, big fella. Thanks for waitin'. I'll be back out in just a while. You keep on stayin' **put**, now.

[The camera angle changes, to reveal the target of the man's attentions: Big Dog, who is sprawled comfortably across the vinyl seat of a three-wheeled ATV. His fur is thick and dusty, his tongue lolls perspiringly out of his gaping but gentle mouth, and his expression bears the patience that passeth all understanding.]

[The camera follows the Painter Man as, leaving Big Dog, he enters the Fairview Inn, a boxy antique building anchoring the south end of downtown. The lighting dims abruptly; then, as the eyes adjust, we see a variety of interesting features inside the Fairview. Against the far wall is an upright player piano; the ghost of the Jag-Time Kid lurks in the antique scrolls, waiting to hit another tune. Next to the piano, in much the same spirit, a 1970's-era hi-fi is blaring out Bob Dylan's "Subterranean Homesick Blues." Various railroad bric-a-brac (the Alaska Railroad runs right through town) lines the walls and windowsills, including shot-up crossing signs, rusty iron spikes, a miniature

replica of a cow-catcher (or "moose-gooser," as the locals call them), even
some pennies flattened on the rail by the passing trains.]

[Most prominent of all is a sort of shrine to the most ballyhooed event in
the town's history: the visit of President Warren G. Harding in 1921.
There are flags, grainy black-and-white photos, even a presidential shot-
glass; a stack of flyers tells the story. At the table nearest the shrine sits
Peter Helgeson, tour-guide extraordinaire, sipping a cold one and
intently studying the Harding-related propaganda.]

Peter [*voiceover*]: Warren G. Harding…almost certainly the most
unqualified, inept President of this century; remembered only for
Teapot Dome and other instances of the flat-out corruption of his
administration. Except in Alaska, that is. You see, he was the first sitting
U.S. President to visit the Territory. Every jerkwater community in
which President Harding stopped to take a meal, blow his nose or whatever laid claim to a piece of the historical hoopla, and continues to do so
to this day. However, Talkeetna's role in the story is unique: it holds itself
out as the town that actually **killed** the President. More specifically, the
Fairview Inn itself—this standard, albeit classic, Bush-wah saloon—
played the determinative role.

Bob Dylan [*singing*]: Look out kid, you're gonna get hit…

Peter [*continued voiceover*]: You see, in those pre-restaurant code days,
the bill of fare could be mighty dubious at these out-of-the way eateries.
Moose pemmican, a slab of bacon packed in by Skookum Jim…you get
the idea. Anyhow, President Harding, on his whistle-stop tour through T-
town, dined at the Fairview. You can say this about the man, there is no
complaint on record regarding the surely humble-at-best fare—but
shortly after his repast, he fell ill. By the time he reached the Lower 48

again, he was clearly on his last legs, and he ended up passing away in San Francisco before ever making it back to the seat of governance.

Bob Dylan: By losers, cheaters, six-time users...

Peter [*continued voiceover*]: Talkeetna then was much the same as it now: kind of an, ahem, **irreverent** place. The President was none too popular hereabouts, and so news of his demise—traceable to a certain meal—became the pride of the town. As nothing of such grand significance has occurred since then, at the Fairview or elsewhere in Talkeetna, it still is.

> [*Through the last part of Peter's voiceover, the camera has been scanning the modern-day denizens of Talkeetna, as if to juxtapose them with the heroes of the past. We see smiles, laugh lines, crow's feet, frostbite scars; twill coveralls and boots, paisley and Birkenstocks, even some bare feet (no terse, unfriendly "No Shirt, No Shoes" etc. signs are to be found for hundreds of miles around); all manner of beards, great and small. Kate, the bartender: friendly, bemused, tough as nails. Everyone seems to be extremely local, except for a small group of German climbers, knotted teutonically at a rough-hewn table, plotting their forthcoming conquest of Denali. Other than the slight international flavor, not much has changed since the old days.*]

> [*Through the din, Dylan's "Bringing It All Back Home" has continued to blare away. Dylan at the peak of his powers, spinning off absurd/profound personae and scenarios as fast as his caffeine-addled imagination and tireless pen could create them. A couple of vintage sourdoughs listen appreciatively, seeming to realize that the songs could very well be describing their own environs.*]

Bob Dylan: He hands you a nickel, he hands you a dime, he asks you with a grin if you're having a good time...

Sourdough #1: "Bob...he was the **champ**."

Sourdough #2: No doubt about it. He coulda beat Cassius Clay, **any** day.

Sourdough #1: [*leans back in creaking chair, folds hands across flanneled belly*] I remember for a time, way back when, people throwin' these Bob Dylan theme parties. I might of even been to one or two: my recollection of that whole time ain't too clear [*pauses, smiling wistfully*]. The deal was to dress up like your favorite character from a Dylan song. You'd see Einstein disguised as Robin Hood, the teen preacher with 20 pounds of headlines stapled to his chest, the whole shebang. Wouldn't it be a hoot to do something like that now? [*pauses again*] Of course, no one would know what the fuck you were up to anymore. But they'd come anyhow, if there was beer. [*grins*]

Sourdough #2: So who would **you** have come as?

Sourdough #1: Me, I'd hafta be the Grandpa who builds a fire on Main Street and shoots it full of holes. What a hoot. How 'bout **you**?

Sourdough #2: I dunno. I kinda always wanted to be Maggie's Brother. The power trip and all.

> [*He fishes deep in his bluejeaned pocket, retrieves some linty change. His eyes dart about the room, and come to rest on Peter. He strolls over to Peter's table and slaps the change down.*]

Sourdough #2: Are you havin' a good **time**?
Peter: Huh?

> [*The other sourdough comes over, attempts to explain circumstances. Bob Dylan, unfazed, sings on. A round of handshakes ensues, another pitcher is ordered. Sourdough #1 introduces himself as Ed, originally from Wadena, Minnesota, but a long-time denizen of the woods around Greater Talkeetna. The other sourdough introduces himself as:*]

Sourdough #2: Hey, I'm Pete, too. Pete Two? Guess that'd make me Re-Pete.

Peter [*voiceover, as the camera again surveys the late-afternoon barroom scene*]: And so we talked and drank. Drank and talked. Drank some more. What the heck. The two sourdoughs attempted to explain Talkeetna to me.

Bob Dylan: They asked me for some collateral, and I pulled down my pants...

Re-Pete [*holding beer glass up to light, inspecting for impurities*]: It's kinda like what Dylan here talks about: these characters—**crazy**-ass characters—drifting in and out of some play. Crashing in and out of view.

Ed from Wadena: Big Dog out there [*arching thumb towards door*], he's got the best seat in town. Everything comes to him. He don't bat an eye. **Nothin**' ruffles his fur.

Peter [*resumed voiceover*]: I tried to explain to ol' Ed and Re-Pete why I was in Talkeetna for the Fourth. Part of it was just luck of the draw—being stuck here between tours—but part of it was seeking out another one of those Alaskan experiences. Preferring a colorful, Skagway-type spectacle over a more sanitized Squarebanks or Anchorage event. Celebrating Alaska's belated entry into this great nation of ours by blowing stuff up. They more or less affirmed that I'd come to the right place, on all counts.

> [*The camera lens narrows conspiratorially on Ed as he winks and scoots a beat-up paper bag from under the table.*]

Ed from Wadena: Made a run down to the Big Gorilla[12] for some pyrotechnics. Check **this** out.

[*He beckons Pete and Re-Pete over for a look-see. Pete can't believe the extent of the brightly-colored arsenal; Re-Pete has seen it all before, but is still impressed.*]

---

12. A locally famous fireworks stand, just north of Wasilla on the Parks Highway-the closest such stand to Talkeetna- identifiable primarily by its giant, inflated gorilla.

Re-Pete: See now, the idea is to go for **noise** rather than visuals, since it don't get dark enough these days to see nothin', anyhow.

Ed from Wadena [*visibly proud of his stash*]: Plenty of bang for the buck, as they say. [*He reaches down into the bag, pulls out a sparkler, and procures a wooden match, seemingly out of thin air*] Don't try this at home now, kids. [*He lights the match off a chipped front tooth, holds the flame to the sparkler. Kate the bartender looks up, seems sorely tempted to reach for a fire extinguisher and empty it on Ed, possibly on the sparkler as well; finally just shrugs. Ed, fascinated by the sputtering flame, holds the sparkler up between his eyes like a saber sword, as if to parody the famous Marine pose; the sparks are nearly close enough to singe his salt-and-pepper beard*]

> [*The camera is fascinated with the sparkler flame, as well, leaning way in, then gradually fuzzing out into red and blue light.*]

Act II

> [*As the camera slowly refocuses, we see that the sparkler flame has morphed into a lit candle. The Fairview Inn barroom hoves back into view, and we see that time has passed—but it is difficult to tell exactly how much. The sunlight through the age-rippled windows is a little redder; outside, the dust cloud in the street, from an increased amount of traffic and passersby, is more discernible. Big Dog is long gone; knob-tired ATV tracks meander off in a woodsy direction.*]

> [*The camera cuts back towards the candle once again, and on the other side of the flame we are surprised to see a female face: Kim, the expie from Anchorage, Pete's new-found friend and, hopefully, soon-to-be main squeeze. Kim is Asian-Alaskan (her family came up from the Philippines), petite and very pretty; she laughs a lot, white teeth flashing, as Peter recounts his two-pitcher conversation with the local Bushwahsie, Ed and Re-Pete.*]

Kim: So tell me more about this Talkeetna "Bachelors' Club" I've been hearing about. Sounds like sort of a questionable enterprise.

Peter: I don't know how much question there is to it, really: I think I know **exactly** what they're up to. Just a bunch of Bush desperadoes trying to **get** some. [*Kim raises her eyebrows at Peter's directness, amusedly*] Basically, the Club schedules social mixers all winter long: homebrew samplings, World War II sing-alongs, and the like. There's even an annual contest called the Frontier Wives Competition, in which women are timed in a decathlon of pioneer-type skills, such as bucking cordwood, running wet laundry through an old-fashioned wringer, gutting salmon— all with a good-sized surrogate "baby" strapped to their backs.

Kim: Not quite **my** idea of Alaskan matrimony, I'm afraid.

Peter: I think that's the point: they totally camp it up. However, the event attracts some pretty serious competitors—not to mention plenty of longing gawkers and onlookers. Hankering for one o' them strapping young brides, you can bet. [*Gestures to a bookshelf in the rear of the barroom*] All of the action is recorded in the "Bachelor's Book," that weighty volume in the corner over there. My favorite part of the book is the "Personals" section: impromptu scribblings designed to bring the authors to the attention of any potential spouses passing through. From what I've seen in there, poetic license is definitely enhanced after a late evening of imbibing. [*shakes his head*] Desperation will make men do funny things, I guess.

Kim: It's nothing terribly new. I've run across any number of such guys: especially some of the fish-heads at the canneries, when I used to work the camps with my folks. [*pauses, cocking her head like a blue-jay*] Anyhow, I guess you've got to hand it to them for creativity. If you want to hand them **anything**, that is. Making sure to wash your hands afterwards. [*smiles again*]

> [*Suddenly, we hear a loud, booming report from the street: ka-**BLAM**! Peter's knees bump the table from underneath, though not so hard as to cause a Beer Tragedy. He quickly reasons in his mind: **had** to have been a back-firing truck. **Must've** been. Or not...*]

Bartender Kate [*angling her head towards the noise, looking suddenly a lot like Miss Kitty on "Gunsmoke"*]: It's **beginning**.

Peter [*recovering somewhat*]: That had to be one **honking** firecracker. Either that, or someone ripped off the railroad's snoose-and-dynamite.

Kim [*smiling, perhaps a little too bravely*]: That was **Alaska**-sized.

[*Secondary explosions are now heard: like distant jungle grapeshot, or the first few popping kernels in the Jiffy-Pop pan. Following the gazes of Peter and Kim, the camera switches to an omniscient overhead view of the main street. Then, from a side street, the first roving fireworks death squad emerges: sauntering warily past the corner, then breaking into hot pursuit as it spots a rival gang. Shortly we hear the whistling explosions and cries of triumph—and the annual skirmishes are on in earnest.*]

[*Conditions quickly become both tribal and Bacchanalian, as the camera switches to a hand-held, ground-level view. Jiggling in terror, it zooms in on the packs of revelers that now fill the street. The gangs generally feature four to seven members: some are grim-faced, some are giddy with blood-lust, all are well-armed. The prevalent weapons of choice are bottle rockets, carried in impromptu Robin Hood quivers: ready for lighting and loading into long-neck beer bottles, then aiming with varying accuracy at anything moving. Some bear long strips of firecrackers across their chests like old-time bandoleers; they randomly tear the strips away, lighting and tossing them up to RATTA-TATTA-TATT! in the streets-of-Laredo air. There is even a guy running around with a lit Roman candle in his hand, shooting multi-colored fountains at those hapless opponents foolishly coming into range. Through the battle noise, we hear just a hint of a bluegrass-breakdown, Doolin' Dalton soundtrack, contributing to the artistic ambience.*]

[*The camera angle switches again, this time emanating from the rear of the Fairview, so that we see Peter and Kim sipping their drinks, calmly but with expressions of moderate trepidation as the howling packs skirmish in the background, like the Keystone Kops on amphetamines and cough syrup—visible through the windows and open door.*]

Peter: Well, looks like we're stuck in Lodi, as the song goes. Care for another beer?

Kim: Sure, why not. It's got to be safer in here than out **there**.

[Just then, Billy the Kid bursts through the door. His river-driver's shirt and camouflage pants are blackened and torn; his brows and lashes are burnt, and his eyes are crazed as he pulls out a six-shooter, screams something unintelligible, takes aim at the pay telephone up against a far wall and pulls the trigger. There is a loud report, the loudest yet, as the telephone shatters into a million pieces; nickels and dimes spin crazily onto the barroom floor as everyone hits the deck. Billy vanishes, leaving only a puff of smoke in the door frame. Everyone slowly rises from prone position.]

Bartender Kate [*dryly but slowly*]: That's a new one on **me**.

[Conversation gradually resumes. Peter and Kim slide back upwards into their seats, look at each other, decide against another beer, after all. Peter gestures with his head towards the rear exit, near where the now-deceased telephone resided. Rising, they pick their way across the shards of plastic and coinage. On his way past the bar, Peter, without knowing quite how or why, reaches into his pocket, finds a couple bucks and stuffs them into Kate's tip jar.]

Peter: Thanks, we'll be **going**, now.

[They duck out the back door, and slide along the side of building towards the main drag. The chaos and anarchy continue unabated; Peter and Kim pause, seeming to fear that, were they to peek their heads around the corner, a host of airborne ordnance would surely follow. Peter shakes his head in disbelief, then suddenly smiles to himself.]

Peter [*voiceover*]: It's a funny thing: the events of the afternoon and the day had really made me feel like I was in Alaska—in a wild and woolly corner of the place, to be sure, but a comfortable one. Now, especially

after the shattering telephone incident, it was clear that I was lost somewhere in the Wild West. But it was one and the same. The whole scene
had gotten so ridiculous, so out-of-control that I just had to laugh—and
suddenly, I was OK with everything. I felt like I had reached some kind of
turning point: if I was destined to die from a barrage of hand-held Roman
candles, I would die with my boots on.

Nonetheless, it was time to get the hell out of Dodge. It was time to
consider our next problem, which was to get back to Kim's car, wherever it
may be.

Kim [*undaintily*]: Oh, **shit**.

Peter: What is it?

Kim: I just remembered: I parked the car up there. On the north side
of town. Meaning, we have to somehow get through all **that**.

> [*Kim gestures towards the full-tilt melee swirling over Main Street. A
> nifty camera trick produces a slight swirling effect, as if walking down
> the street would be something less than linear, more like descending into
> a nautilus shell. Meanwhile, drunken genius Lowell George and undi-
> luted bluesman Howlin' Wolf duel from competing open doorways, disso-
> nantly. A stray bottle rocket whistles overhead, smashing like an atom
> into a hubcap nailed to a balcony post. There is a loud gonging sound.*]

Peter: Well, let's get out of **this** first, then figure out what to do.

[*They dash down the street, in the opposite direction from the fracas.
Panting, they duck into the safety of the closed ice-cream stand. The giant
moose rack offers pretty good aerial protection.*]

Peter: Damn, it's **war** out there.

Kim: No lie, banana. I think we're doomed.

Re-Pete [*materializing from nowhere, faced smudged with gunpowder*]:
What do you mean "we," white man? [*He gives them a lopsided grin, then is
instantly serious*] You gotta fight fire with **fire**, y'all. Here, take a few of
these. You'll need them. [*procures some bottle rockets from an invisible stash,
hands them over, along with a cheap Bic lighter*] Good luck. [*vanishes back
into the fray*]

[Peter and Kim look at each other. Pete stares at the lighter in his hand for a moment. Finally, he flicks the Bic, and in gentlemanly fashion lights two bottle rockets, handing one to Kim. They take a deep breath, and leap out into the dusty high-noon street, weapons a-blazing; they lunge, screaming, towards the camera as they are locked into an attacking-raven freeze-frame—virtually identical to the final movie shot of Butch Cassidy and the Sundance Kid facing down the entire Bolivian Army.]

[After a sufficiently dramatic pause, the smoky freeze-frame gradually gives way to a pastoral riverside scene. Sunlight glints off the broad Susitna as birds sing cheerful, perky songs. The camera spies a tent in the woods, tiptoes up to it, peeks inside. Peter and Kim are sprawled out across their sleeping bags, still in most of their clothes, looking pretty much like death-on-toast. Finally Peter stirs, stretches his arms, scowls at the singing birds. He winces, reaching around to his backside.]

Peter [*voiceover*]: Woke up by the river, much later; had a "mystery bruise" the size of a walnut, in the small of my back. Probably from a close-range bottle rocket. Didn't feel a thing, at the time.

[The camera finally leaves Peter alone to inspect his injuries, panning away into the gauzy yellow sunlight streaming through the tent-flaps; fade-out.]

THE THREE F'S

▼

"*Will I be married, first girl I see*
comin' down the road?"

—The Jayhawks

After the Muskeg Mary tour, which ended in hugs, promises to write and mass gratuities, Kris had exactly 36 hours in Fairbanks. He read his mail, unpacked, did his laundry, packed again, slept, picked up 42 new tourists and was back across the Canadian border by evening.

Once all his passengers had been stoked with Beaver Creek steak and spuds, placated with cocktails in the hotel bar and safely tucked away for the night, Kris felt justified in sneaking off for his burger and beer. He stepped out from the hotel compound and began to make his way down to Ida's. The dun flanks of the roadside were lined by tiny Canadian government cabins: off-white Mountie sheets and pillow-cases, red Mountie shirts and various Mountie unmentionables hung limply, dustily from clotheslines.

In the distance he spied a fellow Driver/Guide with similar intentions: Sandy, who was doing a northbound tour. Kris helloed to her, caught up, and together they entered the mildly disreputable roadhouse. They sat at a greasy red-checkerboard table, shook off their road grit. The local color, shooting pool ("Toasted Cheeseheads," Kevin called them), scoped them out momentarily before returning to their business. The Canadian long-haul truckers, knowing how it feels, barely gave Kris and Sandy a glance.

> weathervane waitress, faded
> prairieflower, grabs brown—
> skinned coffeepot, thinks better and
>   fetches hi-test instead

"So, who were your 'drive-bys' today?" Kris asked Sandy.

"You know, it's hard to keep track. I can hardly remember who I saw on what day; they're all a blur anymore. But I do remember Llary. And Kevin: he's a hard one to miss. Plus, I think Klaus is making the inspection rounds again: I could've sworn I saw that white station wagon pass me by."

"I saw Tami again: second tour in a row like this. I think our schedules are such that we're doomed to cross paths about every tour, but we won't actually meet in person again until the summer's done."

"Get used to it: this may be all you'll see of your friends for quite a while."

For a time they sat in silence, slowly sipping their perspiring O'Keefe's, taking in the 301-Miles-From-Nowhere ambience. "I sure feel like I'm in West Podunk whenever I'm here," commented Kris.

"You **are** in West Podunk, my friend: you can check out any time you like, but you can never leave." Sandy cackled mischievously. "However— this place ain't as Podunk as some. Consider that, in Alaska, only about twenty-five percent of the communities are accessible by road. Situated as we are here, along the main drag, we're uptown compared to most places."

"Now, didn't you live in one of those remote Bush communities for a short time?"

"Yep. Spent a Winter teaching school in an Athabaskan village, out on the Yukon River delta. And, I should correct myself: it's a mistake to characterize those places as North Bumfuck. The locals have been living their lives out there since time immemorial; to them, I was the hick who didn't get it, the Cheechako who didn't have a clue. And that was OK; I pretty much knew what I was getting into."

"Well, thanks for straightening me out."

"Well, yeah. You're not the only one. It can be really tough out there, and it's easy to get cynical. Hell, a little cynicism is good for you, keeps you honest. But you've got to have a sense of humor along with it, in order to do OK. I guess that applies to about anything."

The waitress came by again, bearing Yukon-sized cheeseburgers and baskets of fries with vinegar and salt. Kris and Sandy decided to make her life a little easier by simply ordering the remainder of the O'Keefe's six-pack, sparing her a couple of return trips.

"Some veterans," Sandy continued, popping another Hi-Test, "talk about the 'Three F's' of teaching in rural Alaska. At first, it's Fascinating. There can be some real culture shock: for many teachers, it's their first time hanging out in the Bush for any extended duration, much less for a whole Winter. The Native culture swirls around them; time stands still; it's all very interesting and different.

"Then, some aspects get Funny. Your carefully-nurtured sense of Cultural Relativism goes by the wayside as the follies of village life—the gossip, the silly arguments, nothing ever getting done—not only become apparent, but repeat themselves over and over. Then, as the cumulative effect sneaks into school life—and finally dominates it—teaching becomes Frustrating. This is especially true, and disheartening, once you figure out the realities giving rise to the 'funny' behavior: disorientation, hopelessness, depression, drugs and alcoholism. You realize that you're essentially powerless to budge the status quo during your short time there; what do you do when you learn that your favorite seventh-grade student is a hard-core drunk on weekends?

"This final realization gave rise to my biggest problem with living and teaching in the Bush: simple **loneliness**. The community leaders are reluctant to accept you, figuring that it's only a matter of time before you get frustrated and take off. Why should they commit themselves emotionally?

This can set the tone for your relations with the students, the parents, the rest of the community: they may be friendly enough, but seldom will they embrace you as one of their own."

Sandy smiled. "Unless you're like my boyfriend. He was a hunting/fishing/bullshitting fool from Day One, and the boys in town took right to him. They'd go out on their snowmachine expeditions, chop holes in the river ice, dunk a line or two, drink half-racks of Hamm's. They spent the whole Winter visiting like that. Of course, I made sure that Mike had his own kashim,[13] to keep all the riffraff out of my hair." Sandy laughed at the memory.

"But, it wasn't for me. The Bush teaching scene wasn't worth the emotional cost, even though the money was so good. Without Mike, I wouldn't have made it at all. The loneliness is part of the tradeoff for living in such beautiful, but remote, areas over a Winter. The lesson is that you've got to have a hell of a support community: family and/or friends. At the very least, hunker down with someone special. Else you'll be screamin' obscenities at the ravens by Spring breakup."

This last idea—the hunkering down, not the raven part—triggered something deep in my mind. "You know...I've been thinking about spending this coming Winter up here, Sandy. I've been looking around for a cabin to rent or house-sit: maybe outside of Fairbanks, maybe around Skagway somewhere. Do you think I..."

"**Hell**, yes," exclaimed Sandy. "And you should take your sweet young friend with you. What woman could resist shacking up with the likes of you, in some cozy Alaskan cabin?"

---

13. "Kashim": essentially, an Eskimo version of the All-Boys Club; a separate shack adjacent to a dwelling; exclusive province of the male species, with full female blessings.

Kris hadn't realized that he could still blush. "Uh, you mean Genna? Isn't it a little premature in our relationship to be considering that sort of thing?"

"Get to the point, Bubba," said Sandy. "Are you **sleeping** with her?"

"Well, yes and no," replied Kris. "These days, when I pull into Tok, things are extremely friendly. The last couple nights, in fact, she's even stayed over. But, there seem to be some mixed signals: some kind of tension. We're sleeping together, but…pretty much all we're doing is **sleeping**."

"Interesting," commented Sandy. "Things seemed pretty cozy between you two when you showed up at my solstice party. Holding hands and everything: kinda damn **mushy**, if you ask me." She chuckled. "But at the same time, it seemed as if she was holding something back. Maybe she has a hard time getting close to people."

"Well, she's beautiful. *(her golden eyes! her long legs! her bare feet. damn.)* All my guests love her, she's as charming as can be; I'm about as whupped over her as is humanly possible. How do I get through to her?"

News Item #23

▼

TOK, Alaska—For the sixth day in a row, central Alaska found itself under siege. The lightning-generated wildfires that have consumed over a million acres in the Yukon-Charley wilderness thus far continued to spread into the Tanana River valley, aided by persistent dry weather and tinder-like forest conditions. Meanwhile, fire-fighters launched a counter-offensive from the perimeter of Tok, lighting a line of controlled fires which, if successful, will stop the blaze from spreading into town.

Highway 2, as well as the Tok Cutoff, will be closed on both sides of Tok until further notice.

FIRES OF JULY

▼

The cycles of the Alaskan summer are no less intense than those of winter. The Interior bakes in the constant sun; heat and vapor rise up from the muskeg bogs; thunderclouds form, piling up higher than the surrounding mountains. Finally, all hell lets loose: lightning strikes the tinder-dry boreal forest and sets it aflame. The fire leaps from tree to stunted tree while smoldering slowly through the muskeg peat—which makes it almost impossible to extinguish quickly.

In the valleys of the Tanana, the Tok, the Fortymile and many other Interior rivers, the sky is opaque during the summer fires; the air is stifled with smoke, trapped by thermal inversions. In areas where winter weather can dip below minus seventy, the temperatures can rise to ninety above and higher: a 160-degree differential. The burning forests make the heat seem even more oppressive. But ultimately, the fires generate their own weather: more thunderclouds are created from the heat, and the cooling rain comes, clearing the air, putting out the flames. Maybe, another valley over, lightning from the new storm strikes, starting another forest fire. Alaskans of the Interior thus tend to view July with smoke in their eyes.

It was the last weekend of a hellaciously hot July. The highway into Tok had finally reopened, after the flames had, literally, come within fifty feet of town. Persistent spot fires remained throughout the valley—but, for the most part, the danger was over.

Smoke hung like ghost laundry over the Tundra Lodge lot as Kris pulled up in his bus. He saw that the hotel was still there, contrary to the rumors down the road, and smiled to himself as Genna emerged from the office. *Damn, I'm glad to see her. I hope she holding up OK, under all this tension from the fires.*

Without any particular fanfare, Genna stepped into the stairwell, smiled wanly at Kris, and welcomed the passengers to Tok. She ran through the logistics of the overnight stay, checked her guests in, and automatically began to help Kris pull bags from the luggage bay.

Very few words were spoken during the ritual. Finally he turned to her:

"Hey—I just came in from the highway. I haven't seen you for eight days." As soon as the words were out of his mouth, Kris realized how selfish they sounded.

However, Genna did not respond to this gaffe. "I'm glad to see you, Kris. Really." She tugged two huge bags from the bay, tumbled them onto the dusty ground.

Kris stopped pulling bags. "What is it? What's the matter?"

"Nothing. Nothing at all." She wiped her forehead with a blue bandanna, stuffed it in her jeans pocket.

"Like hell. What's wrong around here? I know that the fires have got everyone on edge, but there's something else. Talk to me—**please**."

Genna finally turned to Kris, and there was an expression he had not seen before: shock, sadness, the verge of tears. "Okay. Okay. Let's get the hell out of here. Leave these for the baggage boys."

Genna's cabin was hot inside, even though all the windows were open and the electric fan was whirring at high speed. The mosquitoes that ordinarily would be hurling their skulls against the window screens were strangely absent, cowed into submission by the acrid smoke. Even inside, there was no complete escape from the smell of the burning muskeg. Genna sat down on the edge of the wicker loveseat, put her chin in her hands.

"How do I begin to tell you what happened? I don't know how, Kris, it's so awful."

"You start from the beginning, I guess. Talk to me." Genna lifted her head, began to speak: calmly, but staring across the room at nothing.

"For days, I'd been watching for a storm. I could feel it building. I knew one was coming. But you never know exactly when, or where, or how it's going to strike.

"Then last night, the thunderheads came, the big black ones. At first, the flashes randomly lit up the valley, far away. Then a few came closer. I could hear some of them strike: a sharp crack you can tell from any distance. I remember the last real bad forest fire, the one that came right to the edge of town, starting the same way. Dangerous as hell to be outdoors about then, especially in the trees. I thought I'd better see if people were still in the campground, tell them to get their sweet asses indoors.

"Still no rain. A smell of dust and wood cinders in the air, but no wind: eerie and dark, absolutely still. I walked, then ran towards the grove of tall spruce: the place where a church youth group from Oregon was staying. The only campers of the night, and probably the only people in the whole town still outside somewhere.

"A premonition: a raising of the hair on my neck. Then a flash. The trees were illuminated, very briefly; for a split second a halo played about their tops. Then there was a loud noise, something like a snap or crack, but more static: I don't want to say 'sizzle,' God I don't want to think it. Then a sudden sharp smell." Genna paused, could not speak for a minute.

She continued once again, quietly. "I was stunned for a second, it was so close. Then I saw where it had hit: right in the campground. I ran over.

"The church kids were huddled in a small circle. I saw what was in the middle: I didn't want to see it."

She looked up, into Kris' eyes. "The lightning got them. Two of the kids had been hit. One of them was dead, I could tell right away. I held the other one on my arms. I once held a baby horse, a colt, while it had pneumonia or something: the shakes. It was just like that until she died—the eyes, everything. It didn't take long. The rest of the kids just stood around, crying: their world had fallen apart, no warning."

Her calm broke. Genna was agitated as she stepped into the bathroom and partially closed the door. There was the sound of water running in the shower. "I'm sorry—I've got to be alone now, Kris. God, I can't get rid of that damn smoke smell." She closed the bathroom door.

Kris didn't go away. He started after Genna, then waited, his thoughts tangled, emotion building inside him. He paced the cabin floor. As he was about to step outside, the sound of the running water stopped. The bathroom door opened, just a crack. "Hand me a towel? There's one in that basket." Kris fetched the towel, gave it to the outstretched hand, saw the brief unbroken glint of body before the door closed again.

In another moment, Genna stepped out, wrapped in the towel. She padded softly into the bedroom next door. He heard her sit down on the bed and sigh. "Please come in here, Kris. Talk to me. I need to hear your voice."

Kris came in, perched on the edge of a chair, searching for words. Genna made a pretense of gathering her clothes, then abruptly stopped. She caught his eye, read his thoughts. "That's my mom's bed. Antique brass. She hauled it up here from Michigan. It was her mom's before that." She paused, smiled softly. "It feels funny, having you here. But it feels right, too."

Kris moved to meet her. "Please hold me," said Genna. "Don't wait any longer." The towel slipped to the floor, and together they sank into the comforter. He took her into his arms, and finally her tears cleared the smoke from her eyes.

and then...
a meeting, a mirroring of souls
a tentative embrace of frontiers
        and a call: come to me, to the
        river of sound: whisper to me your
        secret name
and then
        a red bluff, a deep-blue canyon, a valley of smoke
        flames and heat giving way to rain
        the sunrise thru a parting of clouds;
        the silver warmth of morning
and then
a wish: a promise never to
fly away without you
without you, within
inside the things that
never arrived until now, a shadow
of all that you knew
        and then
                waterfalls, currents, eddies
                maelstroms, whirlwinds:
                a feather in a tempest that
                swirls and climbs and then
                gently lands.

They made love, far into the night. Afterwards, Genna lay in Kris'
arms, breathing a soft incandescence as she slept. Kris held her in wonder,
listening to the cooling rain of the thundershower on the cabin roof.

THE DAWSON GANG

▼

"Tell yer ma not to worry:
they're just my friends…"

—Bob Dylan

Outside, it was one of those home-of-the-north-wind days that the local Tlingit knew so well (and, some say, gave rise to their distinctive, hunkered-down walk). Inside the Red Onion, it was as warm, dim and smoky as ever. Norm, appreciatively, held his drink up to the light, bathing his face in a faint red glow.

"I love these sneak-preview days: the first hint of what it's going to be like here all Fall, more or less. And, it's finally cool enough again to fully appreciate a Hot Red Onion."

"Any time of year is good enough for me, I reckon," said Kris, raising his own warmed beverage in a toast. "Besides, I have time off down here so seldom anymore that I've got to take advantage." Kris had bypassed the standard Skagway Turnaround for the first time in many weeks, since the Fourth of July. It had been even longer since he'd had a chance to sit down and catch up with Norm—not since the end of the previous summer, in fact, when Norm had presided over all the Portland House hubbub. Now, in early August, with some mutual slack time, they had grabbed the opportunity to slow-bicycle-race down Broadway to the Onion, for catching-up, storytelling and general blarney.

Kris asked Norm about the Skagway locals (just about everyone was still around), the quality of the reindeer sausage/ sourdough hotcake breakfasts at the Bigger Hammer Café (still outstanding), and whether Dyea Gary wished to deed over his rustic cabin any time soon ("Why don't you ask him yourself: go ahead and take Old Paint out to Dyea tonight"). Norm asked about conditions in Fairbanks ("How should I know: I'm never there"), the doings of various friends, including Peter ("Well, we communicate primarily by refrigerator notes these days, but he seems to be doing fine"), and the veracity of rumors regarding a certain up-the-highway romance ("Man howdy: news sure travels fast down the road"). Norm allowed that having a fine girlfriend on one port or another did help the miles roll by—and beat hell out of scrubbing buses on a fine summer evening. "And in drastic situations," winked Norm, "it can even lead to matrimony. Look at me."

"I am lookin' at you. And it ain't a pretty picture. Unlike Dirty-Neck Maxine, up there on the wall." *Actually, a man could do a lot worse than winding up with someone like René. Hmmm.*

About mid-afternoon, the discussion shifted to the good old, primitive days of Alaska/Yukon touring—when Norm had been in his Driver/Guide heyday.

"You think you fellers have it rough..." began Norm, in mock decrepitude.

"I know, I know: you had to walk ten miles in the snow, barefoot, to the bus yard, and had to start the buses by rubbing two sticks together."

"Very funny, whippersnapper." Norm's glare cut through the murky Red Onion air like a pioneer's scythe, then dissolved into laughter. "But seriously: most of the problems that you guys face on the road are considerably different from what kept us awake at night. Your concerns are primarily people management: keeping a tour on schedule, staggering the distances between buses on multiple runs, so you don't overwhelm the lunch stop proprietors or the cruise ship expediters.

"Our problems were a lot more basic: longer distances between service facilities—and no particular certainty as to what you would find once you got there. Primitive road conditions, and the many ways in which they would take their toll on a bus. The simple fact that it was just you, and forty tourists, out there in the bush, for better or for worse."

"And it all 'built character', right?"

"Well, you had to be a character in the first place to attempt some of those trips. But yes, the old touring days gave rise to an interesting, 'all for one' camaraderie. My primary gig was the Fairbanks to Dawson run: up the Taylor Highway from Tok, then either to Eagle, and an upriver cruise to the Klondike, or overland all the way, across the Top Of The World Highway. Those of us who drove that route called ourselves the 'Dawson Gang': we were emergency mechanics, general crisis managers and world-class entertainers, all rolled into one."

Kris, sensing a long story coming on, signaled to the bartender for another round of Hot Red Onions, and settled back comfortably into his chair. "Do tell."

*   *   *

Stupid Driver Trick #1

[The setting: the Taylor Highway dives off the edge of the Al-Can in the Tok Hills, about twelve miles east of Tok. Pavement is dispensed with at the outset, as the road plunges into a canyon and begins crawling its way through dense muskeg and gravel-strewn mining claims—eventually finding the tiny, muddy community of Chicken, Alaska (population: "26 nice people, and one old grouch"). Beyond Chicken, the highway

leaps into the surrounding "hills" (which are, in fact, higher than most Appalachian peaks), past the turnoff for the aptly-named Top Of The World Highway, and through an endless series of bold vistas, blind corners and heart-stopping hairpin turns before, mercifully, terminating at the Yukon River's edge, in the town of Eagle. Standard highway conditions: mud and/or dust, and plenty of it.]

[Opening shot: from some unnamed wide spot in the road (a rarity), we hear distant engine noise: then, the noise abruptly cuts out. Several seconds later, we hear the sound again: this time closer, but stopping abruptly once more. As we scan the hills, we see a tour bus is edging along the far ridge, occasionally popping into view, but then disappearing as it cuts back into the steep drainages. Its serpentine path is generally a forward one.]

Norm [*voiceover*]: Customarily, it's best not to terrify one's bus passengers. Further, it is considered bad form to let your guests catch a glimpse of your own well-founded terror. For these and other reasons—including the simple desire to break up a long drive—us Dawson drivers would pick certain spots on the Taylor Highway to perform what we fondly called "Stupid Driver Tricks." These were little gags or vignettes that we dreamed up in our idle time together: frequently, very late at night, under lopsided conditions. These tricks were quite creative, actually—and more than a little dumb at times—but, if done with the proper timing and panache, were generally crowd-pleasing.

[The camera shot switches directly to Norm, who is speaking into the boom mike: both hands firmly on the wheel.]

Norm: Isn't this gorgeous country, folks? A little on the rugged side, road-wise: but that's why you came to Alaska, isn't it? These undulating, misty hills, stretching as far as the eye can see...

Passengers [*those who are not intently contemplating their brown-paper mal de l'air bags*]: Oh yes, mmm hmm...[*general sounds of assent*]

Norm: ...No one, I mean no one, for miles upon miles. So silent and still that there seems to be a ringing in the wilderness. [*pauses, cocking head, listening intently*] A ringing? I do believe I can even hear it. Wait just a minute, folks.

> [*Norm pulls off to the side of the road, by a stretch of dense taiga. He puts the bus into park, sets the air brake, pops open the door and steps out, to the mystification of his passengers. He plants himself on the soggy soil, looking this way and that, and finally strolls over to a nearby black spruce. He ducks behind the tree, and emerges holding a large, old-fashioned black telephone. He picks up the receiver.*]

Norm: Hello?

> [*As his passengers continue to stare, Norm mimes a brief but animated conversation. He then replaces the receiver, walks back behind the tree, sets down the phone and strolls casually back to the bus, hands in pockets, whistling.*]

Norm [*deadpan*]: Sorry, wrong number. [*He shrugs, releases the air brake, and resumes the journey.*]

Stupid Driver Trick #2

> [*The setting: deep in the hill country of the Fortymile River headwaters, just past the junction for the Top Of The World Highway, which traverses high ridges all the way over to Dawson. Similarly, the grades on the Taylor Highway become not only long and precipitous, but seemingly endless in their repetition.*]

> [*Opening shot: from the camera's vista at the top of a steep, nameless summit, we see two buses crawling up the grade. Thick black diesel smoke trails each struggling vehicle; the engine noises are low-pitched and uneven, sounding like moaning and sometimes, oddly, loud snoring.*]

Norm [*voiceover*]: In those pre-turbo days, it was a wonder that we made it up some of those hills when carrying a full tour. Worse still, the passengers were acutely aware of the difficulties: you'd have your old farmers and mechanics who'd wince every time you ground a gear, and occasionally you'd hear a "Giddy-up there, old hoss" from somewhere in the peanut gallery. Sometimes I'd try to distract them by saying something dumb like asking them to turn on their overhead lights, so we'd have a "lighter" load. Such witty banter would also help keep me from acting on my impulse to start jettisoning luggage, and/or the most stridently complaining passengers—or at least having them step out and help push.

But no matter what I did, the bus would be needing a break by the time we crested several of those big grades: the temperature gauge would be red-lining, and it'd look like I had the Homestead steel mill in my rear engine compartment. By that point, I could've used a time-out, too—which, unfortunately, I really couldn't justify if I was running solo. However, for tandem tours, us Dawson drivers devised a unique way to engineer an impromptu rest stop:

Incoming voice on CB radio: Breaker one-nine, WNCB-569, Ridgetop here; how's it goin' up there, Stormin'?

Norm [*into radio handset*]: Hey, backatcha Ridgetop; we're just keepin' on keepin' on, as the song goes.

Radio voice: Likewise here; just keepin' on truckin', good buddy. Looks to me, though, that thangs aren't too hunky-dory with ol' 602, there; she's really laboring up the big hill.

Norm: Laboring? You don't mean…?

Radio voice: Yep: I'm thinkin' we should pull you over at the next turnout up top. Looks like it's about time.

Norm: Will do, Ridgetop. WNCB-569 out. [*hangs up handset; glances into rear-view passenger mirror*] Not to worry, folks: we're about due for something like this. A bit overdue, in fact, but it's nothing we can't handle. If you would kindly stay on board: I'll be back in just a sec.

[Norm finds the turnout, pulls over, sets the brake and pops the door, grabbing a small canvas tool kit on the way out. The bus engine's idle is strong but uneven, feeling almost like heavy breathing to the passengers inside. Norm meets his fellow driver, Don, by the side of the bus; they confer briefly, then retreat to the rear engine compartment, passing out of camera view.]

[The camera then switches to a down-the aisle perspective, capturing the various expressions of uncertainty, concern, mild trepidation, continuing slumber for a few. A sixtyish, competent-looking man wearing coveralls rises, as if to render assistance to the drivers, but his wife pulls him back down to his seat.]

[After a few minutes, the engine idle seems to even out, to a calm, smooth hum. Norm and Don come back into the camera's view; Don is carrying a small, wrapped bundle in his arms. They step up into the bus stairwell, and Norm grabs the hand-held mike:]

Norm [*proudly*]: Ladies and gentlemen. We have just witnessed a very special moment, something we have been waiting for: the birth of a baby **bus**. Here it is, at long last: show them, Don.

[Don unwraps his bundle to reveal a gleaming, perfect, 18-inch replica of a motorcoach (uncannily similar, in fact, to the ones for sale at the company gift shop in Anchorage). He holds the baby bus high in the air, to the approval of the flummoxed, yet cheering passengers; Norm, reaching into his driver's bag, procures a box of cheap cigars and begins to distribute them down the aisle. There is even a bottle of Andre champagne, which Don pops as the camera fades out, fixated on the foam running down his oil-stained hands.]

Stupid Driver Trick #3

[The setting: a lowdown, boggy stretch of the Taylor Highway, fairly early in the going. It's a sultry, hazy-yellow morning, conjuring the feeling of bayou

much more than tundra. One can sense an impending onslaught: muggy heat; creeping vines; possibly small, winged critters, crawling, flying, oozing...]

> *[Opening shot: gauzy, unfocused, dominated by droning engine noise; gradual focus to the bus, then to Norm, behind the wheel—and in particular, his mirrored sunglasses, which contribute to an overall "Cool Hand Luke" ambience.]*

Norm [*jovial, yet portentous*]: Okay: who wants to play "Bug Bingo"?
Passengers [*more or less in unison*]: Huh?
Norm: Bug Bingo: a simple, yet disgusting game of chance; a game that takes advantage of, ahem, a certain natural abundance in this part of Alaska. How it works is like this: I have here in my trusty driver's kit a roll of extra-wide Scotch tape. I will be selling one-inch strips of this tape for a quarter apiece—you can buy as many inches as you want—and you will have the chance to place your tape on the inside windshield, with your identifying initials on it. Very simply, the person whose piece of tape collects the most bugs between here and Eagle wins the whole pot of quarters.

> *[For visual demonstration purposes, Norm pulls off to the side of the road, procures his roll of tape, and peels off a two-inch hunk. He turns towards the windshield and, after a moment of contemplation, slaps the tape onto a likely spot. With a ballpoint pen he scratches his initials onto a corner of the tape, then reaches into his pocket for a couple of quarters, plopping them into a spare styrofoam coffee cup.]*

Norm [*dramatically*]: The gaming table is now open. Any takers?
[*The crowd surges forward, rapidly filling the cup with quarters as Norm busily dispenses tape.*]
Norm [*voiceover*]: Any tour group will have its share of bettin' fools: you can guaran-damn-tee it. In fact, there's hardly a quicker way to get a busload all riled up than to raise the prospect of sure-fire gambling winnings: you know, something for nothing. So, Bug Bingo, revolting game

that it was, had the surefire effect of making folks forget all about the travails of the Taylor Highway—as well as bringing out those competitive juices.

[Shortly, the inside windshield—the outside is too high to reach, and too vile, besides—is covered with Bug Bingo gameboards, some up to six inches long. Norm sets off down the road once again, keeping an eye peeled for telltale, prize-winning swarms. And, not to worry: due to the season (very early summer, about two weeks past final snowmelt), Bug Bingo conditions are at their peak. Here a black thundercloud of mosquitoes (including delegates from all twenty-seven species); there an ill-guided cluster of black beetles; even a short-lived hatching of some fluorescent-green, gooshy mayfly-type bug that, en masse, sound like raindrops splattering the windshield.]

Norm [*shaking his head, in amazement and disrelish*]: Looks like I'll have to use my wipers here, pretty soon.
Passengers [*competitively*]: No!

[Cut to several hours later, as the bus arrives in Eagle, Alaska (population 150, give or take): the first territorial capital of Alaska, and the biggest town for nearly 100 miles around. We see a collection of funky, vintage cabins, yards overgrown with fireweed, wild grasses, Queen Anne's lace, oildrums, disemboweled snow-machines and other flora; half-dog, half-wolf things (one of which, remarkably, has green-tipped fur) are tied up in front of nearly every rustic dwelling, serving as the town criers for all important arrivals. Above all else, there is the mighty Yukon River, hissing by siltily. Just downriver from town are high, craggy bluffs, to rival the Columbia Gorge; upstream is the heart of the historic gold country, and ultimately Dawson, the tour's terminus. A riverboat waits patiently for Norm's group at quayside—but the tourists are all focused on another matter:]

Norm [*somewhat frazzled*]: Looks like we had a record-setting Bug Bingo game today, folks. Who will the lucky winner be?

Passengers: [*more general sounds of excitement/ competition*]

> [*The camera zooms in to examine, in full gory detail, the arriving bus. Even in the best of times, the Eagle-bound motorcoach looks like hell-on-wheels when coming off the Taylor: the sides are coated with mud or dust, no in-between, frequently thick enough to obscure the company logo—and, if the Driver-Guide has failed to pack his trusty long-handled squeegee in the luggage bay, passenger window visibility will be virtually non-existent. Similarly, the front of the bus is never pretty by the time the Taylor gets done with it. On this touring day, the marquee, windshield and grille are particularly interesting: covered with hundreds (if not thousands) of tiny, Hieronymous Bosch parodies of the Winged Victory of Samothrace. The gooshy-green mayfly hatch, in particular, makes a major contribution to the overall aesthetic.*]

> [*Norm, having paraded his prize collection through the heart of town, eases the bus up to the waiting riverboat. The captain's crew steps up to meet 'n greet the guests—but then, gathering the circumstances, pulls back.*]

Norm [*busily counting bugs, as competitors crowd around*]:…Thirteen, fourteen, fifteen…not counting bits and pieces. Who knew that one tiny rectangle of Scotch tape could be so, uh, vivid? Here's the winner: my heartiest congratulations. [*he hands the winner the styro cup o'quarters*] And folks, on your way out the door, kindly remove your bingo gameboards— so the local bus-washers don't scalp me next time I'm in town.

> [*Still buzzing with excitement, the passengers board the riverboat, are treated to sodas and snacks while Norm and other helpers heft luggage onto the vessel. At length, everything is aboard, and the riverboat shoves off from shore. As they depart, the bus-washers, a couple of Native kids*]

from the village just upriver, take one look at Norm's bus, turn to each other, shrug and fetch the high-pressure hose.]

*   *   *

"Of course, there were other, more normal tricks we had for passing time on the Taylor Highway," continued Norm: "little things like playing Alaska Trivia, or reciting Robert Service poetry—things you could easily weave into the fabric of your tour."

Kris nodded in agreement. "I do the trivia and poetry on a fairly regular basis: usually around Beaver Creek or Tok. But I like the idea of the elaborate gags. Maybe I'll start cruising the thrift stores for old telephones to stash in the woods, or baby buses: hell, maybe even a moose suit or something."

"You have my full blessing: just so long as you give credit where credit is due." Norm winked at Kris. "However, there's one Stupid Driver Trick I hope you never have occasion to try: rebuilding a starter by telephone."

"Say what?"

"I'm not kidding. One time, when I was doing a turnaround tour out of Dawson, I found waiting for me in Eagle one of the funkier buses of the fleet: one which, quite honestly, should have been put out to pasture long before. This one's leading personality trait was a quirky starter: sometimes it'd work, sometime it wouldn't, and you never knew what was going to happen when you turned the ignition key. Upon inheriting this fine piece of machinery, I tried to start it, and of course it didn't turn over—so I had to use the old 'screwdriver trick' just to get the trip rolling."

"The 'screwdriver trick'?"

"Yeah: it's an old-fashioned emergency way to bypass defective starters. Actually, I'm surprised they don't teach you that in training anymore: I'll

have to have a word with Klaus about that." Norm arched an eyebrow at
Kris. "Basically, when you stick a screwdriver in the right place in the
engine, the metal shaft completes the circuit between the battery and
sparkplugs when you turn the key, leaving the starter out of the picture.
It's a neat trick—and creates some pretty spectacular blue sparks on the
screwdriver shaft, besides—but you can only do it so many times before
potentially screwing up the engine, not to mention electrocuting yourself.

"Additionally, this bus had a real propensity to stall on some of the
steeper grades. Thus, the screwdriver was applied several times on the way
down the Taylor, and my hair was beginning to stand on end: clearly, this
couldn't continue. By the time we pulled into Chicken, and the bus had
stalled one more time, I'd had enough: the only thing to do was to call
Fairbanks, 250 miles away, to see if we could swap out buses, or even send
a mechanic down the road. I was told by Klaus that, since this was the
peak of the season, no spare vehicles or mechanics were available; however,
he generously informed me that he had a few extra minutes, so he could
talk me through the starter repair process, over the telephone: 'You have
all the tools, yes?' Thank God I actually did."

"Wow: I could've had all the tools in Alaska, never mind Chicken, and
still couldn't try something like that."

"Oh, you might be surprised at what you can do in that type of
situation. Klaus was actually pretty patient with me: never heard him raise
his voice, although I did hear some deep sighs. The biggest problem was
running back and forth between the phone—which, or course, was the
only phone in town, located behind the bar at the Chicken Creek
Saloon—and the bus, which was sitting in about forty acres of mud, by
way of a parking lot. While I was outside yanking on the starter, I'm sure
that Klaus got quite an earful of interesting background commentary from
Chicken's finest. However, once I had the thing pulled, I was able to bring
it inside, spread some newspapers on a table and go from there—of
course, with everybody in town, tourists and locals, looking on, giving
helpful instructions."

Norm sighed, shaking his head. "I mean, it wasn't exactly brain surgery: I actually managed to take apart that starter, put it back together again, slap it back into the bus and limp on into Tok. Yes, gratuities were spectacular for that tour. Still, I decided right then that this was a trick I'd just as soon avoid in the future."

"Hey: I'm still trying to keep my streak alive of never having had to change a bus tire while on the road. But if it does happen, I guess I won't feel too bad now: even if it's an inside dual."

Norm, smiling at the memory, leaned back in his chair, glanced at his empty glass (no spare engine parts cluttered the tabletop), and ordered another round. "But lest you think that it was all hardship on the Dawson run: the tough part was more or less over by the time we'd pull into Eagle and board the riverboat. I could kick back with a mug of coffee, put my feet up on the railing, and simply watch everything go by. And, I saw some pretty amazing things on that river..."

Squaw Candy

▼

like the mississippi, the amazon, the congo, all rivers of the imagination,
the yukon has its own distinctive cast of fellow-travelers: the steam-driven
paddlewheelers, chanting "wood, wood, wood" as they growled upriver
a modern-day variation, fueled by the endless ingenuity of the alaskan busher:
an old jeep straddling a raft, paddles appended to tires, hop in and
drive downcurrent; canoes, skiffs, logjams
 and every other watercraft imaginable

 in the winters, the frozen river is a highway for dogsleds, snowmachines,
bushplanes-on-skis, pickups with studded tires; even antique bicycle, pedaled all the way downriver from dawson by someone escaping the klondike gold rush, bound for the beaches of nome: pausing in eagle for lifewarming cup-ofjoe then thanks, i'll be leaving
now and off he went, pedaling frozen balloon
 tires over clear pack-ice and hardcrusted snowdrifts

springtime sees the railroad-car ice floes, creaking and groaning in switch-
yards until bursting in downriver runaway-stampede: for this rare time,
they have the river surface to themselves but below the chaos lurk the most
noble fellow-travelers: the salmon
kings and reds, pinks, coho and chum, arriving first by ones and twos then
filling every channel and backwater in heroic numbers, a silent city to the
    scattered souls on the shore who set their calendars by the arrival

    just upriver from eagle, we see the first wooden fishwheel: perched
    on the riverbank, driven by current, perpetually in motion: a zen fer-
    ris-wheel we watch as a silvery form is scooped from the current, is
    lifted to the apex of the carnival then delivered sliding and thrashing
    to the gathering basket: to be dried, cached, grilled over campfire coals;
    to become thick salmon-steak on dinnerplate, midwinter dogteam fuel
        or even squaw-candy

the athabaskans and other people of the river make a special salmon-jerky:
sliced long and thin, salted down, sweetened and slowly smoked; the aroma
of the smoker makes the bears dream in technicolor and the end-result
is squaw—candy: tough, sweet, chewy, essential; to be enjoyed while splitting the wood, walking the trapline, feeding the dogs, watching the
    big river go by between raised porchrail feet

    the natives who still run the riverside fishcamps always have plenty of
    squaw-candy to offer: some come in canoes, some in guttural-voiced
    motorboats to meet us mid-current; they tie up alongside like
    benevolent
    pirate-skiffs, long bandoleers of salmon-jerky draped over shoulders:
        only a buck a rope
the people of the river circulate among my guests, offering rough handshakes
and ready smiles; they quickly dispense their produce and are off again,

pointing their bows down the sunflecked current
and my guests, tasting the squaw-candy, are tasting the rich
    lifeblood of the interior country

    savoring my own strip, legs on the boat railing, i watch a moose
    swim across the yukon, not too far downriver: massive head and shoul-
    ders well above the waterline; just off the stern, a tangle of driftwood,
    torn by breakup-ice from some unnamed tributary, speeds by: bound
    for the bering seashore, to become fuelwood for the coastal yupik;
        a gift from a forest they can scarcely imagine

Sour Toe

▼

"A taste born of hoary nights,
when lonely men struggled to
keep their fires lit and cabins warm."

—The descriptive, even poetic Yukon Jack label (the "Black Sheep of Canadian Liquors")

"I always loved pulling into Dawson," said Norm. He drained the last of his Hot Red Onion and ordered another round for himself and Kris. "We'd round the bend in the river, see the familiar 'moose-hide' scar on the mountain, the old Gold Rush buildings leaning this way and that— and I knew we'd made it once again. We wouldn't have to hike out from somewhere, equipped only with salmon jerky and our bare hands."

"Like coming back into Civilization: I know the feeling," commiserated Kris. "Only, from my understanding, Dawson isn't exactly what you'd call 'civilized'."

"That's very true," replied Norm. "It was even **less** so back when I was hanging around there."

*   *   *

Norm disembarked from the Yukon Queen, refraining from his desire to fling himself upon the riverbank and kiss the ground. Several decrepit watercraft, tied against the dock, tilted their poopdecks in greeting—partly from the strong river current, partly from basic unseaworthiness. On the shore, a half husky-dog, half Swamp-Thing tilted at a wooden signpost, marking his territory. Down the street, two vintage clapboard buildings, foundations sagging in the permafrost, tilted up against one another, like two old drunks staggering arm-in-arm out of the Malamute Saloon.

"A city," Norm commented, underneath his breath, "designed by Don Quixote."

"Huh?" George the baggage guy, a Dawson native, peered out of the boat hold, long, wet mop of red hair clinging to his head like Ronald McDonald caught in a cloudburst.

"Never mind."

*   *   *

"So," continued Norm, "I would pull into town, drop off the passengers at the hotel; George and I would wrestle luggage for a while, we'd finish; I would lug my own stuff up the hill, to the drivers' house, clean up a bit, and begin to mosey my way towards Diamond-Tooth Gertie's, to lose more 'play money' at René's blackjack table. The hours would slide by in the midnight sun, and before I knew it, it was morning: time for the famous Dawson City Tour."

"I bet it was a lot like the Skagway tour," speculated Kris. "A little short on substance, as far as the actual miles covered, but long on the history, colorful characters and general Tour Guide B.S."

"You got it," said Norm. "First of all, most of us Dawson guides would get into the role of our favorite Gold Rush characters for the tour: Big

Alex McDonald, Tom Lippy, Gussie Lamore, what have you. Me, I'd typically choose Swiftwater Bill Gates. [14] We'd drive around town, I'd point out all the spots where I'd done this and that in 1897 or 1898: got into a saloon brawl, won a poke of gold dust in a poker game, *et cetera.*

"Then, we'd head out of town: past the confluence of the Yukon and Klondike rivers. I'd explain about the origin of the word 'Klondike': *Thron-diuck*, or 'hammer water,' referring to the way the Natives would hammer their fishing weirs into the riverbed at the confluence. This, of course, would provide a neat segue to the Discovery Story: how the locals regarded the few foolhardy gold prospectors who occasionally straggled through those parts; how they hardly took notice when George Washington Carmack—popularly known throughout the territory as 'Lying George'—went upriver in Summer 1896 with his wife Kate and two other Native companions: Tagish Charley and our old friend Skookum Jim."

"Skookum Jim, **again**," commented Kris. "Man, he was everywhere."

"Yeah: he was a remarkable man. At various times I thought about adopting his character for my Dawson tours, to tell the Gold Rush story from his perspective—especially since I sort of **look** the part. I didn't think I could truly do him justice, though.

"Anyhow, by the time I'd wrapped up the story, we'd be nearing the actual spot at Bonanza Creek where the first strike was made. I'd let the folks out to wander around for a bit, get the feel of the place—then, I'd have a little surprise for them."

---

14. Ironically, the richest of all the Klondike Kings. No relation to the modern-day version- and perhaps, a bit more colorful.

*   *   *

Norm removed his shoes, rolled up the cuffs of his chinos, and waded out into the middle of the creek. In true Swiftwater Gates style, he planted his broad feet on a sandbar and hitched a thumb through his suspenders, banging a tin pan against his thigh with his other hand.

"What y'all need to remember," he began, shouting above the sound of the rushing water, "is that gold is **heavy**. Much heavier than all the other rocks and gravel in this here stream. About 18 times heavier than the water itself.

"What does this mean? It means that the key to gold-panning is **washing**. And washing. And washing. You shake the gravel in the pan long enough, you run enough water through it, and sooner or later—usually later—the heaviest stuff will have sunk down to the bottom. That would be your gold, my friends."

Norm hunkered down by the creek, just downstream from a big boulder, and scooped up a panful of gravel and water. Slowly, he began to swirl the bigger and lighter stones from the pan, letting them drop over the edge. After he had done so, he would tip the pan's edge into the current, to let it fill with water again. He did this about a dozen times. "Lather, rinse, repeat. The key is to be **patient**. Don't throw the baby out with the bathwater. Just keep on washin', like your poor old pioneer Ma with a bucketload of clothes, 'till there's nothing left but the gold."

Finally, Norm washed away the final bits of rock and heavy sand, and peered into the bottom edge of the pan. Sure enough, two gold flakes, minuscule but unmistakable, winked back at him.

"Eureka!" exclaimed Norm. "At this rate, I'll be able to buy the Palace Saloon after, oh, about another 10,000 panfuls. But at least it's **something**. There's still gold in thet thar creek."

"Seems like gold-panning is much harder work than a 'real' job," observed one of the tourists.

"You don't know how right you are," agreed Norm. "Imagine holing up in a shotgun shack through one of the winters around here, with nothing to do but thaw permafrost and dig out the molten muck, all the way down to bedrock. Then, when Spring finally came, you got to pan out all your accumulated barrels of muck, to see whether your claim—and indeed, your year's work—turned out to be worth a damn."

Norm straightened up in the stream, chilly water swirling around his ankles. "But you are about to gain a personal understanding, folks—albeit, not such a drastic one. I've managed to get some of my sourdough acquaintances to donate their old gold pans—the ones they flung away in disgust, just before fleeing back to the Lower 48, stone broke—and I've stashed them under that big cottonwood over there. My advice to you: grab a pan, hunker down by the creek, and have at it. Show 'em how it's **really** done."

Nearly everyone in the tour group took up Norm on his offer of sure-fire fortune. With varying degrees of grace and agility, they knelt or squatted by the promising-looking gravel beds, loaded up their pans, and began gamely to slosh away. Norm circulated amongst the group, offering instruction, advice and encouraging but pointless homespun homilies, per his style.

What the group did not know was that Norm's finding of color in his first pan was somewhat of a fluke. That area of Discovery Creek, like all the others around it, already had been gone over with a fine-toothed comb for the better part of a century. While it was highly improbable that all the gold would ever be gotten, short of dredging and sluicing the surrounding mountains to the nub, the modern-day search was more akin to needle-in-the-haystack than instant glory.

However, Norm, considerate Driver-Guide that he was, never wanted his tour groups to go away disappointed. After debating the ethics, sometimes rather hotly, with his fellow guides, Norm picked up a small poke of gold flakes from a local who mined commercially, with a backhoe and large-scale sluice. It only set him back a couple hundred bucks, and Norm considered it a good investment, in the following way:

Prior to the day's tour, Norm had taken the poke and emptied a few flakes into a pants pocket, no more than fifteen or twenty. He had avoided disturbing the pocket throughout the morning, but now, by the stream-side, as he circulated amongst his tourists, Norm would occasionally wet a finger, dip it into the pocket, stroll up to someone and make sure that he or she was washing the gravel properly: reaching his hand into the pan and swirling the contents around once or twice. He would then walk away to assist others, and five minutes or so later he would listen for the excited cry of someone who had found two or three gold flakes—if that person hadn't inadvertently sloshed everything away.

Norm would carefully select his targets—his favorites being sweet, elderly women with overbearing husbands—and he would limit the lucky finders to four or five per trip. This avoided any suspicions of machination, but provided enough thrills, first-hand and vicarious, to make the morning tour. And, throughout his long touring career, no one ever caught on to Norm's trick.

*   *   *

"Salting the gold pans," tsk-tsked Kris, shaking his head. "Norm, you're a fine ethical example to Tour Guides everywhere."

"Ethics, shmethics," dismissed Norm. "It made people happy. Besides, Dawson ain't that kind of a town. Any way to make a buck, short of out-and-out robbery, has always been kosher. Like Skagway—only about tenfold—it was heaven to hucksters and charlatans of all stripe. Still is.

"For example, consider the way a certain Dawsonian of my acquaintance, name of 'Captain Dick,' made his living. And still does, to my knowledge."

*   *   *

"The 'Sour **Toe**' cocktail? I thought Captain Dick was joking."

"No joke," said George the baggage guy, his ordinarily bland visage brightening. "Real cocktail. Real toe. Not a live one, of course."

George sat down on a packing trunk. "It all started when Dick bought this old prospector's cabin, way out in the bush. The guy'd left all his stuff behind—no one to claim it—including his big **toe**, which his brother'd had to chop off after he froze it in a snowed-over creek, years ago."

"Chop **off?**"

"Yep—the brothers didn't hold truck with no city doctors. Just liquored him up, had him bite a bullet and **whack!**" George made a chopping motion with his hand. "Anyhow, the toe was just sittin' there on the mantel when Dick bought the place: in an old pickle jar, all dried-out and petrified. He didn't know right what to do with it then, but he hung onto it anyhow. You never know.

"Well, late one winter's night back in Dawson, Captain Dick and a buddy were hanging out in a bar, about three sheets to the wind, according to usual custom. The subject of Robert Service had come up, as it did sometimes—over one of these winters, about **everything** comes up, sooner or later—and they got to talking about his 'Iceworm Cocktail' story: you know, the one where some guy has to prove his sourdough manhood by downing a drink with an iceworm in it. Well, Dick and his buddy got to speculatin' about a sort of modern-day version—what you might have to drink nowadays to show your mettle—and Dick flashed on this old prospector's toe that he still had. 'What if,' he told his buddy, 'you dropped this thing in a drink, called it, I don't know, the Sour Toe Cocktail?' And so the idea was born.

"By the end of that evening, Captain Dick and his buddy had laid down the ground rules. The barkeep would take a beer glass, fill it with champagne, and drop the toe in. The customer'd have to drink the drink all the way to the bottom, tipping back the glass until the toe rolled up and touched the lips. After you'd done this, you were a true Yukon sourdough, deserving of membership in the Sour Toe Club—a very worthy brotherhood."

"How long did it take until someone actually had the guts to try one?" Norm wanted to know.

"Actually, it was a smash hit, right off the bat. Dick brought that old dried-out toe into the bar the very next night, and just about everyone in the place tried a Sour Toe cocktail. People were always looking for some kind of crazy diversion—or another excuse to drink—and soon Captain Dick, and the toe, were the toast of the town. In fact, it was so popular through the rest of that winter, and right on into the summer months, that Dick figured he could start charging folks for the privilege of doing the Sour Toe. At five bucks a pop, he began to make a pretty decent living from it, and even began to tour it around the Territory: Whitehorse, Watson Lake and beyond.

"But then, disaster struck. A big old placer miner from around here, name of Garry Younger, was going for the world's record one night, downing some twelve Sour Toe cocktails in a row—and putting the toe into his mouth each time, for extra bonus points. On the thirteenth cocktail, with the toe in his mouth once again, Garry keeled over backwards from his barstool. As he smacked the floor, **GULP**! The toe was gone."

"I s'pose Captain Dick must have tried the ol' Heimlich maneuver, then? Or grabbed a rusty saw from the wall, for an impromptu Toe-ectomy?"

"No deal. Would've been bad for business, probably. But once word got out that the Toe was gone, you wouldn't believe the offers that came in. Seems that a lot of folks had old toes lying around, for whatever reason. Finally, Dick accepted an offer from some lady up in Fort Saskatchewan, who'd some 13 years prior had her second toe amputated, due to an inoperable corn. That was Toe #2.

"Over time, other toes kept getting lost, or stolen, or swallowed: whatever. But Captain Dick never had a problem finding replacements. Last time I looked, he was up to Toe #7. Each one different, and in some ways gnarlier, than the other.

"And by the way," concluded George with a faint grin (thereby exceeding both his word and smile quotas for the next six months), "I already told your group all aboot it. They'll all be there tonight, to see **you** do the Sour Toe, tonight." George stood up from the packing trunk, hitched up his blue jeans, hefted a heavy duffel bag with a "Hup!" and was gone.

*   *   *

"Sure enough, my whole tour group was there that night," recalled Norm, rolling his eyes. "The little old ladies in cruise windbreakers, and their husbands with the zoom-lens cameras, rubbing shoulders with characters straight from a Robert Service story, or a really awful parody thereof. Seemed like the whole town was there. No pressure at all, of course."

*   *   *

Captain Dick grinned/ leered from under his filthy sailor's cap, reached by memory to a special place behind the bar. In his callused hand was a tiny metal coffin. With a small but perceptible CREEEAK! the coffin opened—and there, residing as peacefully as Tutankhamen's midget twin, was Toe #7. It lay in a bed of white salt, which Dick faithfully changed every year or so, or as needed. Dick reached in, gently picked up the toe, turned it over in his hands, tapped it with a fingernail (still plenty hard: no rot or mildew). Then, he quickly plopped the toe into Norm's beer.

The beer magnified the special qualities of the Sour Toe. This version still had most of its nail, but time and tide had darkened the keratin to a rather unhealthy shade. All the meat was still on the bone; thanks to the salt, it had desiccated to a point where nothing short of a chisel would remove it. It looked huge in the glass —and decidedly brown, thanks to the stoutness of the beverage—but was probably only a third or fourth digit: luckily, not one of the Big Toe monstrosities of past editions.

"Remember," admonished Captain Dick, "the toe must touch the lips."

"The lips that touch the Toe surely will **not** touch mine," muttered René, in the background.

Well, here goes nothing: Norm ever-so-slowly tipped his beer, seeking not to disturb the Toe's resting place at the bottom of his mug. *Worse things have gone into beer. Possibly.* He took a tentative sip, discovered that no off-flavors had been imparted thus far. As the bar patrons chanted "Go, go, go" (or maybe it was "Toe, toe, toe"), and Captain Dick grinned knowingly, Norm tilted back the mug a little further, gulping down a steadier stream of the beverage.

The chant of the crowd seemed to grow higher in pitch as the first hangnail was exposed from its sudsy resting place, then—as Norm, continuing to drink but watching cross-eyed in horror—the toe began to creep slowly up the side of the mug. Like some troll's hellish idea of a log-rolling contest, the petrified toe tumbled forward and, with the last of the beer, gave Norm a little kiss on the lips.

With a loud exhalation of "HAHHH!" Norm slammed down the mug, wiped his mouth with his sleeve, looked around for a Listerine or Lysol chaser. The bar applauded; René, thoroughly grossed-out but still impressed, joined in the accolades. Captain Dick offered his congratulations, along with a commemorative certificate and honorary Sour Toe Club membership card; then, with a special pair of tweezers, he carefully retrieved the Toe from the bottom of the mug, rinsed it with a little seltzer water, patted it dry and replaced it in its salty coffin home.

*   *   *

"After doing the Toe," Norm confided to Kris, inspecting his drink for foreign objects, "everything else—busted starter, grounded riverboat, bad-luck streak at the blackjack table—was a piece of cake."

BIRDS

▼

"When you see me fly away without you,
shadow on the things you've known;
feathers fall around you
and show you the way to go…"

—Neil Young

Tok had been spared from the fires of July. By the time the month had ended, the roads in the area had been fully reopened, the last few smolderings in the muskeg had been extinguished, and the air had cleared. Life at the Tundra Lodge more or less returned to normal after the lightning incidents, and the Driver-Guides resumed their here-today, gone-tomorrow sojourns through town.

One guide, in particular, began living for those time-stands-still interludes in Tok. The last shreds of pretense had fallen between Kris and Genna, and each revisitation was more of the same, only better. Kris' time behind the wheel was given more and more to reverie and anticipation, less to being the Ultimate Tour Guide.

One complicating factor in the routine was that Kris, having done his job well, had been tapped to train on other highway runs—to fill in for late-season attrition as needed and, presumably, as a head start to next year's touring. Consequently, he had several opportunities in early August to ride shotgun on various tours, keep his ears open, experience and compare a variety of other Driver-Guide styles, appropriate some quality (and not-so quality) road rap—and relate the events to an eager, ear-nuzzling audience back in Tok.

*   *   *

"On your left is the Potter Marsh," began the Anchorage driver. The bus had just cleared the outskirts of the city, on its way down to Portage Glacier. "The marsh was unintentionally formed back in 1916, when the new railroad bed blocked off most of the creek outflow—creating a small estuary. The Potter Wildlife Sanctuary is the summertime home of a wide assortment of migratory birds: several varieties of ducks, the Canada Goose, and a bird known as the Arctic Tern. The Arctic Tern, which resembles a small seagull, holds the distinction of being the bird with the world's longest migratory pattern. After spending its summer months in Alaska, the tern commutes to Antarctica for the winter (which is, of course, that region's summer)—a round-trip distance of more than twenty thousand miles."

But that's just the canned speech, for the turistas. I'd have to personalize my lecture about the phenomenon of the Arctic Tern—probably something like this:

"What can you say about this amazing little bird, but: **how** in hell do they do it? High-energy arcs of blood and feathers, true to some inexorable fate: the **drive** to get there—fleeing between lands of extremities above an inhospitable global ocean. Nature's F-16's (although Man has not yet, and never will, come close to approximating such a technology).

They make the frenetic heartbeat of the hummingbird, those ruby-throated sugar cubes, seem aimless and chaotic.

"Even as they build their nests and rear their young in the relative calm of the Alaskan summer, the intensity of the Arctic Tern does not slacken. I remember once riding a bicycle in Skagway, out near the ore terminal, a large landfill area covered with gravel. Someone had told me that this was a nesting area for the terns, a place where they dug shallow holes in the ground to protect their eggs. I quickly found this to be true as, upon approaching the terminal grounds, a fierce little tern came screaming out of the sky at me, determined in kamikaze fashion to keep unwanted intruders away from its offspring. Its sharp little beak was aimed right for my head, diving in a blur of speed, until it veered off at the last possible instant. The wind from its passing made a neat part in my hair. The fearless, diving attacks continued until I got the hell out of there."

*   *   *

Such coastal areas, as Kris well knew, also played host to the largest, fiercest-looking bird of all: the bald eagle. The eagles, however, did not display the fanaticism of the Arctic Tern (if they did, local dogs, cats, otters etc. could never rest easy). Rather, they preferred a more effete life: to feast upon dying, spawned-out salmon, like glorified seagulls, and to strike stunning, patriotic poses in the tops of tall, dead spruce snags.

One such snag on the outskirts of Valdez featured the nest of a particularly aristocratic eagle. He liked to sit stiffly upon his perch, as if waiting to be emblazoned upon a coin, while buses full of gaping faces would come to a screeching halt by the roadside. While riding the Valdez tour for the first time, Kris had watched as the driver pulled off the highway in front of the eagle's home. As the tourists gibbered in excitement, the guide turned to them and leered,

"Hey folks, watch this. Let's see if we can get a **rise** out of him."

The tour driver leaned on his air horn. The blast shattered the silence along the glacial river, causing three ground squirrels to run for cover, an incognito black bear to grumble and a raven to caw back, angrily. The eagle, looking offended (in a regal sort of way), slowly spread his wings, ran a brief preflight check, and took off from the snag.

*   *   *

Back in Tok, Genna did not take kindly to the actions of the tour driver. "Well," she said, "how would **you** like it if a bunch of eagles came over to your house and stood outside, gawking at you, flapping their wings and screeching, trying to get you to leave?"

Kris supposed that he wouldn't like it at all. He and Genna lay side by side in the infrequently-mowed front yard of her mother's home—quite possibly, the only grass lawn (sans 55-gallon oil drums) in that part of Alaska. Colored glass mobiles and braided straw wind sculptures, made by her mom, dangled and swayed above the porch in a distant cousin of a Midwestern farm breeze: balmy and just strong enough to keep the mosquitoes and no-see-ums away. Genna reckoned that, next time she was down Valdez way, she would have to have a word or two with that bird-harassing driver.

Just then, as if in juxtaposition, a willow ptarmigan stumbled by, fat and top-heavy with summer—with "Butterball" written all over him for some lucky fox or coyote. "Our State Bird," mused Kris. "Is that really an appropriate choice? I mean, they're so **dumb**. They're just chunky, broiler-ready pigeons, lobotomized game-hens. Can't we do better than that? Hell, nobody can even **spell** it." In grand Driver-Guide style, he recounted for Genna the famous tale (possibly true—and in any event, she had already heard it plenty, but did not let on) about the Alaskan

community that had wanted to name itself after the state bird—but
nobody there could remember how to spell "ptarmigan," so they ended up
calling the place "Chicken" instead.

"You know, despite my sympathy for such challenged creatures, I'd
have to agree that they're a poor mascot," said Genna. "And, I nominate
the **raven** as a replacement. They seem to capture the local spirit more
than any other bird. You know: wary, clever, scavenging, opinionated—a
definite 'Up Yours' attitude. A **survivor**."

Genna warmed to her topic. "And you know, they're one of the very
few birds that doesn't wimp out during the winter: they stick around here
all year long. You should see them in January: when it's real cold, they fluff
up their feathers to retain body heat better; they look they're on steroids.
Makes 'em more intimidating when they try to scare away schoolkids
from their sack lunches. No danger of them getting eaten, too—even
though some folks around Fairbanks call them 'Soul Chickens'."

Genna paused thoughtfully, squiggling her long toes in the summer
grass. "Or, how about the screech owl? A friend of mine was hiking in the
woods around Denali once, wearing one of those South American ski
caps—you know, the alpaca wool ones with the earflaps and braids hanging down. Well, all of a sudden he saw this lightning blur of feathers and
talons coming at him, and he felt something tear at his scalp. It was one of
those damn owls that live in the woods out there: apparently it had
thought that my friend's cap was some kind of weird rodent, and it was
trying to make a kill.

"Or, how about some combination thereof? I nominate all of the above."

"Might make for an odd bird," said Kris. "But then, your true Alaskan
is kind of an odd bird, as far as they go."

Genna took offense at this, and descended, raptor-like, on Kris. They
rolled together in the tall grass, as Kris thought briefly about birds, migra-
tion and nesting, before moving on to other matters.

DECONSTRUCTION

▼

The highways of Alaska are tough enough without Road Construction. However, every Spring, come rain or shine or mud (plenty of mud), the road crews emerge from hibernation, polish the rust off their earth-moving behemoths, and choose a whole new section of Al-Can, or Richardson, or Steese to chew up and spit out: round-the-clock, including midnight-sun shifts, all summer long.

For the Driver/Guides, this means a continuously shifting and changing obstacle course. Depending on the phase of construction, they can expect any of the following: open excavated pits and giant mud bowls; parallel rows of berms (ridges of plowed-up earth, often containing hidden rocks) which can last for miles on end, trapping a bus; fresh, gooey asphalt, slick with oil, and any variety of other hazards. Further, the construction crews, a proud and surprisingly powerful lot, tend to keep a close eye on the buses as they negotiate the zones, and are quick to report any "unsafe" driving or other perceived anomalies to tour company management. Thus, the construction areas represent probably the greatest hazard to veteran drivers, irrespective of their skill: not only to safety bonuses, but also to professional reputations and, correspondingly, livelihoods.

"Did you see our brother?He was here the other day, But he only came to say thatHe was leaving…"

—Jackson Browne

*   *   *

Kris, toting his travel bag, stepped over the threshold of Anderson Apartment Building B, dodging a plastic Big Wheel and a discarded pair of roller skates. He ascended the close, unventilated stairwell to the second floor, found his apartment door unlocked, and stepped inside. On the living room floor, he encountered scattered heaps of Driver/Guide paraphernalia: briefcases, tour manuals and books, shirts, sweaters, flammable polyester blazers. Kris quickly added his bag to the collection, loosened his tie and migrated to the refrigerator, where he discovered that a couple of his Hi-Tests had somehow survived his absence.

Hearing sounds from the back bedroom, Kris pulled his head out from the fridge and called out in greeting. Beers in hand, he strolled to the other room, to discern the identity of his accidental roommate. To his pleasant surprise, it was Peter, who was busily rooting through a closet, pulling out odds and ends and creating a large heap on the bed.

"Hey, Bro: looks like a major trip this time. Where are you off to now?"

"Well, to be honest, I'm not exactly sure." Peter emerged from the closet, took a clump of clothing from the bed heap and stuffed it into a backpack. "You see, this isn't exactly a company trip I'm taking. I mean, I'm out of here."

"What do you **mean**, you're out of here? You've got to be kidding."

"Long story. But the bottom line is, my touring career is over."

Kris was stunned. He sat down on the edge of the bed as Peter continued to cram his worldly possessions into his pack. "What the hell happened? Talk to me."

"Well, it has mostly to do with Safety Bonuses, or the lack thereof." Peter broke off from his packing, helped himself to one of Kris' beers and sat down cross-legged on the floor. He looked up at Kris with an odd expression on his face—equal parts grim, sheepish and amused—took a slug of Hi-Test, and paused for a moment.

"In a nutshell, the construction got me. And, ironically enough, it happened just as I'd made it back into town." He shook his head. "You know how they've been tearing up that stretch of Airport Way, out near the interchange? Well, I hit that stuff not too long after they'd repaved it, a little over a week ago: fresh asphalt, lots of oil still on the surface. Anyway, I was cruising along at a normal speed—I mean, I was back in town, home free, right?—and as I approached the first stoplight, I tapped on the brakes, to begin slowing down...but there was nothing. I tapped again: still nothing. Then, as the traffic that was stopped at the light grew closer, in a hurry, I slammed on the brakes, and this time I felt something: a skid. I slowed down a bit, but not enough, and I slammed into the car that was ahead of me at the light."

Kris whistled. "**Man**: was everybody OK? Were you OK?"

"Yeah: everyone was fine, amazingly enough. I figure that I was only going ten or fifteen miles an hour when I hit that car: fast enough to do a pretty good number on the rear end, but not enough to do too much more than shake up the other driver. My passengers were pretty scared as well, but there were no injuries to speak of.

"So, after this all went down, I called the accident in to headquarters. They dispatched another bus to the scene, to pick up my passengers, and pretty soon it arrived, along with Frank, our manager, in his van. Meanwhile, the police showed up, and almost immediately a cop was in my face: telling me that I had to have been tailgating the other car, speeding, et cetera. In response to this, I pulled out the tach card[15] from the bus, just to show the cop that I'd actually been doing about thirty-five: **below** the speed limit for that part of Airport Way. Well, then the cop went ballistic on me: figured I was trying to show him up, be a smart-ass, or whatever. All the while, my passengers, Frank and a large collection of gawkers and onlookers were viewing the whole spectacle."

"Nothing like a little free publicity—especially in front of the boss. Then what?"

"Well, the scene was more or less cleaned up: photos were taken, police reports were given, the tow trucks came. Frank gave me a ride back to the company office, and explained to me that, while an investigation was pending, they were going to pull me off the road. I told him that this was fair enough, given the circumstances, but tried to explain to him my side of the story. I told him about the excessive oil on the road, the skid marks, and the tach card showing that I was well within the law. Frank seemed understanding enough, seemed willing at least to listen, but still wasn't ready to cut me the benefit of the doubt. However, he did tell me that I was free to do some information-gathering on my own: to collect whatever evidence I could that might exonerate me."

"Sounds like 'guilty until proven innocent' to me. But, I'm not particularly surprised, for some reason."

"Yeah: obviously the company has its own sense of justice." Peter's voice carried a touch of uncharacteristic bitterness. "But I didn't fight that

---

15. Most buses have a tachometer card located under the speedometer, which records the speed of a bus over the course of an entire trip, for the viewing pleasure of management- unless, of course, a driver accidentally loses or mutilates the card.

particular call. Instead, I set out to do just what Frank had suggested: to gather my own evidence.

"My first stop was at the highway department. I actually managed to get some time with the head of the Fairbanks construction project. Interestingly enough, when I brought up my suspicions regarding the paving mix, he was inclined to agree with me: he affirmed the possibility of excess oil in the mix, and that they had been having some problems maintaining consistency among the road crews in this regard."

"Wow: that's a pretty bold admission. I'm surprised he would actually say something like that to you."

"I was surprised, too: I had no reason to expect such candor. I think he was even a little sympathetic. But, there was a definite condition to his disclosure: there was no way, no how that I could officially 'quote' him on this. He made it clear at the outset that everything was strictly off the record. Privately, he was able to confirm my suspicions, more or less. Publicly, he would not, or could not, make a statement that I could use."

"What about if you were to call him into court: wouldn't he have to testify then?"

"Yeah: I could try get a subpoena, or some such thing. But, I'm sure that wouldn't have endeared me to this individual if I'd mentioned it at the time. Which brings me to my next step: actually visiting a **lawyer**."

"Can't say that's something I'd care to do, under any circumstances. But, it sounds like you were a man on a mission. What did the lawyer have to say?"

"Well, he basically shot down all of my grand designs for defending myself. I had planned to get a bunch of letters from people—other drivers, mostly, but anyone I could have found—testifying to the condition of the road, my overall experience and ability, anything that could've helped show that I'd been operating the bus in a reasonably safe manner. However, the lawyer told me that such letters likely would be inadmissible in court, for a whole bunch of reasons I didn't particularly understand: hearsay, lack of relevance, lack of notarization, blah blah blah."

"It almost makes you want to go to law school, or something," commented Kris: "just to learn precisely **how** you're being screwed over."

"That thought actually crossed my mind—for about an instant. Anyway, he then went on to talk about the costs involved in putting together a case, properly obtaining evidence, subpoenas and the like, and that's about when I politely said 'No, thanks' and headed for the door."

Peter picked up a tour manual, idly flipped through the pages and tossed the book aside. "So, then I was sitting on my hands for a day or two, grounded from touring—and **all** driving, except for transfers—while the company completed its own investigation. Finally, Frank called me into his office, where of course Klaus and a couple of company bigwigs were sitting. They informed me that, on the one hand, conditions on that stretch of road had been unusually hazardous on that day—but on the other hand, I should have been able to perceive the danger, given my years of driving experience, and act accordingly."

"Boy, there's nothing like a little hindsight and second-guessing. It sounds to me as if you did all you **could** have done."

"I'd have to agree. But that's not all: they actually brought up my 'chimney' incident from last year. You know, the one where I hit that overhanging awning in Skagway at about one mile per hour, and toppled a century-old stack of bricks? I was informed that, because of these two occasions, there was an ongoing safety issue with my driving, and that the company's reputation may be suffering as a consequence."

"Suffering, my ass," retorted Kris. "Everybody who was there at the time just laughed about that old chimney. However," he conceded, "reputation **is** the name of the game, from everything I've seen. In fact, I'd say it's the company's most valuable asset: they've got to pitch a product—in this case, a motorcoach tour—that is absolutely beyond reproach, from a safety standpoint. However, it's the **perception** of that safety that controls—regardless of reality, or fairness, or individual circumstances. It's the way they **have** to be, if they're to survive in this business."

"I'm willing to give them that," replied Peter. "It's just lousy to be on the wrong side of the perception."

He stood up, set the beer bottle aside and resumed his packing. "But the meeting wasn't **all** about 'bad' news. Frank very generously offered me the chance to complete the remainder of my contract—but as a city tour guide only. I considered this option for about one second before respectfully declining."

"I don't blame you at all," commiserated Kris. "After all you've seen and done, all the highway miles…I just don't see how endless repetitions of the Farmer's Loop could possibly cut it. But, what a way for a touring career to end. I'm genuinely sorry for you, man."

"**Don't** be," replied Peter, in a surprisingly resolute voice. "It's not as if this is the end of my time in Alaska."

Kris was somewhat taken aback. "What do you mean?"

"Yeah, I've got some plans. As soon as I can sort out my worldly possessions here—cram what I can into my pack, and ditch the rest—I'm off to the 'Banana Belt': down to the Kenai."[16] He contemplated a salmon-slimed sweatshirt, gave it a cursory sniff, shrugged and tossed it in. "I'll stop in Anchorage first, to pick up Kim—she's about ready to hang up the expie thing, as well—and then we'll head south, probably to Seward or Homer: she's got a bunch of relatives down there, and plenty of places to crash."

"Hey, I hear Homer's a great town: just about as liberal as Talkeetna, but not quite so bushy."

---

16. The Kenai Peninsula, at the southern end of the Alaskan mainland, enjoys this fond moniker courtesy of interior Alaskans: primarily for its relatively balmy, mud-and-slush winters.

"Thanks, I've had enough Talkeetna-style 'bushy' for a while—on major holidays, at least." Peter smiled: his mood had shifted appreciably, with no remaining trace of cynicism or irony. "Anyway, the thing about Homer is that it's a real fishing capital: a lot of the major halibut fleets go out from there. It's even better fishing than Ketchikan, apparently. So, I'm guessing that I'll be able to find some fisheries work down there: in one of the packing plants, or on a boat, even. Who knows, maybe I'll even get to go out to Kodiak, or the Aleutians, or somewhere."

As Peter continued to dream out loud about his future prospects, Kris smiled to himself. *Most people I know would have looked upon this as some kind of disaster, or at least highly acute circumstances. At the very best, a burned-out Driver-Guide could have considered this a good excuse to hang up the touring shoes, and head home a bit early. But, I think it's a sign of how long we've actually been in Alaska now that Pete's instinct is to view this as an opportunity. At this point, being set free to roam the Kenai and beyond is like "going home" to him.*

I guess it'll probably be a while before we hear from him, communication being what it is around here. But, it'll be fun to think of him out there, somewhere in the elements, on the water, living rough, but free— *while the rest of us are stuck behind the wheel of an air-conditioned bus, dodging the road construction...*

Peter informed Kris that he would be hitching a ride on the Alaska Railroad down to Anchorage early in the morning. "However, there **are** a few places in Fairbanks that deserve a farewell or two."

"Hot Licks? Chatanika? The Howlin' Dog? All of the above? What'll it be, friend? This night on the town is on me."

Peter set down his full backpack and, clapping Kris on the shoulder, followed him out the door, into the soft night.

Helpful Hint #79 (Whole Earth Catalog, circa 1974)

▼

Anybody living at all rough in Alaska (or elsewhere) can use the invaluable publications from the University of Alaska extension service. Well-handled subjects like "Canning Moose and Caribou", "Sourdough", "Fruit Trees In Your Yard", "Greenhouses in Alaska", "Fur Parka", "General Pelt Care", "Game Is Good Food", "Wild Berry Recipes".

Write to: Cooperative Extension Service
University of Alaska
Fairbanks, Alaska 99701.

Free to Alaskans, $.25 per copy on all publications mailed outside the state. Wild Berry Recipes an additional $.50.

FATHER CHRISTMAS

▼

By late August, Kris and his fellow guides had slipped into survival mode. They were well-accustomed to the Coach Commander schtick: the road rap, long relegated to rote memory; the tourists' perception that the young people tooling them down the road were certified, card-carrying geniuses of the muskeg. However, for the geniuses themselves, the thrill was pretty much gone. 80 to 90-hour work weeks, fueled by late-season tour discounts and employee attrition, were the norm; the primary motivation was to hang in there for another few weeks, to collect those longevity and safety bonuses.

In Kris' case, the hard work didn't detract too much from his conviction that, all things considered, this still was a pretty good way to make a living, particularly from a financial standpoint—plus, the drudgery was broken up by those extremely pleasant interludes in Tok. Even so, the long hours were taking their toll. Further, the departure of Peter from the touring scene had left him troubled: the whole adventure felt somewhat hollow without his old friend. He had no idea where Peter had gone, on the Kenai, or elsewhere in Alaska—or whether he had in fact departed for points Outside.

Nonetheless, the company remained sufficiently impressed with Kris' performance to tap him for another training run: this time, he (and Séan, as co-captain) would instruct a rookie Driver/Guide crew on the nuances of the Highway Two trip. They were to lead tours of their own down to Skagway, then pick up the newcomers for the return to Fairbanks. Kris was looking forward to this trip as a welcome break from the pressures of a solo tour—plus, he greatly enjoyed the teaching aspect. If he could do for these drivers what people like Derek and Karl had done for him, well, that'd be justice served.

*   *   *

The second day out from Skagway, towards the end of lunch break, Kris and Séan were standing outside the Macintosh Lodge: catching some fresh air, comparing notes on the progress of the training, reminiscing about Kevin's famous interview with the resident turkeys. However, as they turned to head back towards the bus, they saw that someone had been watching them.

An old man stood on the edge of the gravel. At first, Kris thought that he was one of the tour passengers. Then, he saw that the man's appearance was considerably more "local": blue jeans, suspenders, flannel shirt older than most of the tour guides. No beard, but several days of salt-and-pepper stubble, like the muzzle of a retired black Labrador. Dirty feedcap, bill warped like old floorboards. But, something was still different: something was wrong. The man's eyes were confused; he stared down the highway, then back at Kris and Séan, and his mouth worked without words. They came to his side.

"How can we help you, Mister..."

"North Pole, it's right down the road, I know it. I know I'm almost there..."

Kris and Séan looked at each other. North Pole was just outside Fairbanks, still a good five hundred miles away—and the opposite direction from that in which the man had been gazing. Kris was about to point out the obvious, before deciding that the obvious would do no good.

"Just a minute, Mister…"

"Martin. My family's expecting me. I…I could've sworn I was almost there, but I don't know this place at all."

"Tell you what," said Séan, softly. "Why don't we sit down here for a minute, relax a bit, and we'll try to find out what's going on: get some directions, maybe." Séan eased the man over to a log bench, sat him down, and gestured for Kris to go inside the lodge: to get some help, or at least to try and figure things out.

Walking past his trainees and the tour group, Kris entered the lodge and took the proprietor aside. "Do you know anything about this gentleman out front? How long has he been here?"

"He came in a couple hours ago. Bought a cup of coffee, had a cigarette, didn't eat anything; didn't say much. Looked in pretty rough shape, to be honest. He did mention that he was on his way to North Pole, had some family up there—but I could have sworn that he drove in from the **north**."

"He said his name was Martin. You heard of anyone by that name in North Pole?"

"Martin…huh, you don't suppose. You know that big Christmas shop up there, where all the tour buses stop on their way into Fairbanks? Isn't the family that runs that place named Martin?"

Something in Kris' vast store of touring minutiae clicked. "You know, the guy who founded that place was named Cord Martin. This couldn't be him, could it? I had no idea that he was still around: he'd have to be in his eighties, at least."

"Tell you what: why don't you go ahead and use my phone, call up to North Pole and see if they're looking for someone."

The call to Alaska confirmed their suspicions. They got Mr. Martin's daughter on the line, who told them that, yes, her father had driven Outside, to visit some old friends in Montana, despite their objections:

"He's done that trip a thousand times—but he's eighty-five now. We told him that it wasn't a good idea, to just take a plane instead, but of course we couldn't tell him anything." She informed Kris that he had been due back to North Pole several days ago, and that they had heard nothing from him: while she wouldn't have been too concerned about this a few years back, she and her family were now starting to go out of their minds with worry. After expressing her gratitude and relief, she asked Kris to make sure that her father somehow made it to Beaver Creek, where she could meet them and take Cord home.

Kris mulled over the options as he walked back outside, where Séan and Mr. Martin were still sitting. Séan excused himself, and Kris filled him in on the situation.

"The Al-Can, solo, at age eighty-five," whistled Séan. "This highway is tough enough, even in the best of times."

"Apparently it was pretty small potatoes to him, way back when—especially after they actually **paved** the road. But, obviously, he's in no shape to go on now: God only knows how long it's been since he's rested. What do you think?"

"Hmmm…well, we could just point him in the right direction, and kind of follow him up the highway. Or, we could let him ride with us on the bus to Beaver Creek—but then his car would still be here. He probably wouldn't be too keen on that idea."

"How about if we ask him to let one of us drive him there in his car? It'd be familiar surroundings, and he wouldn't be letting go of things entirely." Kris paused, looking back at Mr. Martin. "I bet he could use some company, anyhow. What do you think: can you handle the rest of the training run by yourself?"

"I reckon so," said Séan. "Good luck, and see you this evening."

*   *   *

"Wait, I was just up this way. I told you already: North Pole's the other way." Mr. Martin was edgy, adamant.

"You'll just have to **trust** me." Kris wasn't quite sure what else to say. It had already taken a fair amount of convincing to get Cord to agree to be a passenger, rather than a driver. Reason probably was too much to ask for; therefore, Kris decided on a different tack.

"North Pole? Isn't that where all the Santa letters go?"

"Yep," said Mr. Martin, automatically. "That's the place. That's my place."

"No kidding? You're the guy who started it all?"

"Back in the Forties."

"You know, I've always wondered about that: how it all got started; what it was like back then."

Cord seemed to relax a bit, settling back into the car seat. At first he said nothing, gazing out the passenger window, reaching into his flannel shirt pocket for a pouch of tobacco and some papers. With an unconscious, surprisingly swift motion he pinched out a measure of tobacco and rolled it into the paper with one hand; with the other hand, he procured a book of wooden matches, and lit the hand-rolled cigarette like an act of history. Staring at some point on the distant horizon, he began to speak.

At first the words rolled out slowly, sparingly. He told Kris that he had come up to Alaska during the war, and Kris gently prodded him with questions: what was the country like then? Was there much of anything in Fairbanks: things that he might recognize now? What was he doing with the military there? This latter question got Cord into a low-key account of piloting a bush plane into tiny Alaskan communities, in order to scope the airstrips and deliver supplies—and about how they had always made him feel like Santa Claus in those places, delivering mail and news from Outside, and of course gifts around Christmastime.

Then, a hint of animation came into Cord's even voice as he told Kris how, after the war ended, he realized that he wanted somehow to keep his relationship with those remote communities going, and so he began playing a sort of bush-pilot Santa during the holiday seasons. It didn't take Mr.

Martin long to become a well-known figure in the Alaskan interior, and for him to realize that this was what he wanted to do. Therefore, somewhere around '47 or '48, he decided to relocate to the conveniently-named town of North Pole—at that time, a small hamlet about fifteen miles southeast of Fairbanks—to set up shop and let Christmas come to him year-round.

Kris had heard some elements of this story before, but never directly from the source, so he was genuinely interested. Throughout the drive from Macintosh, over the summit to Silver City and Lake Kluane, he kept Mr. Martin going with questions about the old days. How had those Bush communities changed over the years? What was it like to watch some of those children grow up, move away and come back to visit at North Pole with kids of their own? Cord patiently answered Kris' questions, still in the same measured, mildly detached voice—but seemed gradually to grow more monosyllabic in his answers, almost brusque, and Kris sensed that he was wearying.

Finally, at Kluane Wilderness Village, a few miles past Burwash, Kris decided to pull in for a refueling and rest stop. Cord insisted on pumping the gas himself, virtually shooing Kris away from the car. Kris looked at Mr. Martin for a long moment, shrugged his shoulders and entered the small general store/ café. *He's still not really easing up, letting himself relax. I wish he would—but I guess I don't really blame him.*

In a couple of minutes, Kris emerged with two cups of coffee, some doughnuts and various snacks. "Got us some treats. Ready to hit the road again?" Mr. Martin lingered on the driver's side, reaching down for the door handle before realizing that Kris had the car keys. When Kris did not make a motion to hand them over, he crossed over to the passenger's side, opened the door and sat down silently. Kris handed him the snacks before closing the door for him and coming back to the driver's side.

Mr. Martin remained quiet as Kris drove back onto the northbound highway. "Please, help yourself," he reiterated, gesturing towards the bag of snacks, which was sitting untouched in Cord's lap. Stirring as if from preoccupation, Cord peered into the bag, then pulled out a packet of Corn-Nuts.

"What in heck are **these**?"

"They're pretty good. Try them."

Cord tried a Corn-Nut and, judging from the crunching sounds over the next few minutes, also thought they were pretty good. He worked his way so enthusiastically into the bag that Kris guessed, correctly, that Cord also hadn't eaten anything for a good long while. *In fact, my guess would be that he went into this Al-Can drive so single-mindedly that he's basically forgotten to eat—or to sleep, for that matter—the whole trip. I bet he used to just bull his way through the entire drive. But at this stage of his life, he can't do that any more, and he doesn't know it. Or, won't accept it.*

Mr. Martin began to cough. At first Kris merely glanced over at him, figuring that he'd been eating too fast, had gotten something down the wrong pipe, or some such thing. But the coughing did not stop, and soon began to sound like choking. Kris, alarmed, swung the car off to the side of the road, jumped out, opened Cord's door and pulled him out. He began to pound Cord's back. Finally, the object that had been lodged in Cord's windpipe came free, and Kris led Cord, who was doubled-over from the effort, slowly back to the car.

"Look," said Kris, once they were safely on their way again, half-jokingly, half deadly-serious: "we've got to keep you alive for your daughter. So go easy on those Corn-Nuts, okay?"

Mr. Martin, perspiring, nodded in agreement, almost imperceptibly. He left the bag of snacks on the floor, though, and rested his head against the window. Kris offered his driver's sweater to Cord as a pillow; soon, the features of his face began to relax, and he finally drifted off to sleep. Kris relaxed as well, driving the rest of the way to Beaver Creek as gently as possible (given the notorious permafrost) and thinking about Mr. Martin's life and circumstances.

Sleep always takes the years away. The lines of age and confusion dissolve, to be reformed as smile lines, as the good kind of crows-feet around the eyes. Now, it's not so hard to imagine how he was way back when: the true essence.

It's as if this is the first time he's slowed down since those days. He didn't want to—they never want to. But now he can: he's got the lifetime of good will, the hard-earned capital in his hands, the family reserve in his heart, to see him through as the days get shorter.

I look around me, and I see young Mr. Martin all over the place. They've got the drive, the desire, the heart to make it here. Dyea Gary's well on the way; guys like Llary have got it in spades. Even if Llary's back in the Willamette Valley this winter, pounding nails, this place will be inside him, never far away. Maybe even Peter is heading in that direction.

All of Cord's drives up and down the Al-Can: going out and coming back, but never really leaving. The more of these "real" Alaskans I meet, the closer I feel to them. I felt kind of foreign in Ketchikan, a lot of the time; Skagway was the gateway to…something. This year I'm on the highway, and I'm not sure where it's going yet. But I have some ideas—and I want to find out.

*   *   *

Cord woke up abruptly. "Beaver Creek. I know this place. It was always a damn welcome sight, after this stretch of road."

"Some things haven't changed," said Kris.

They pulled up to the main office. The staff was already aware of the situation (news traveled fast up the highway), and they told Kris that Cord's daughter was on her way from North Pole. There was nothing to do but sit tight for a spell.

Kris, knowing that Mr. Martin's last square meal probably had been somewhere near Edmonton, led him into the main dining room. They loaded up on hot roast beef, potatoes, gravy and other fortifying ballast. Cord ate with gusto, hardly saying a word. After he'd finished, he wiped his mouth with his napkin, and smiled for the first time all day. "Reckon we've time enough for a drink and a smoke before Crystal gets here."

"'Fraid I'm fresh out of smokes. Bet we can score some cigars at the bar, though." Kris grinned and got up, and soon was back with two cheroots of antiquity. They strolled over to the Animal-Head Room, camped out beneath the fifty-year-old elk, lit up and sat back, waiting for Cord's family to come.

ACCORDING TO THE MINER'S
CALENDAR

▼

Fun Fact #357: the fireweed, Epilobium angustifolium, is perhaps the most common wildflower in Alaska, growing to heights of six feet or greater and producing a spire of purplish blooms that open from bottom to top. In north-country folklore, the fireweed is known as the Miner's Calendar: purportedly, when the uppermost blooms on the spire are spent, it is only six weeks until the first snowfall. Thus, miners, sourdoughs and others in the Bush lacking the Julian calendar can discern the approximate time of year simply by watching the fireweed.

A randomly-dispersed logjam of sleeping bags, clothing and other Driver-Guide debris littered the floor of Anderson Apartment #212. There were now seven people calling the apartment home (four of whom were presently on the road); since a number of guides had finished up for the season and left, those who remained had consolidated their lodgings for September. The net results were a tad more chaos and clutter than usual, but extremely cheap rent.

Business at the Tundra Lodge had also slowed considerably after Labor Day weekend, so Genna had taken a few days off: to spirit Kris down to

Valdez, for some sea-kayaking and relaxation at a coastal cabin, then to hang out in Fairbanks as he prepared for his final tour. One languid Sunday evening, the night before his highway departure, they were making some Clean Out The Fridge spaghetti sauce: throwing in all the meats, veggies and cheese that weren't moving, breathing or had otherwise become science projects.

They were alone in the kitchen, making occasional conversation as they prepared dinner. Genna had been lamenting the fact that, each time a driver had passed through Tok lately, she was likely seeing him or her for the last time that year: "And maybe **ever**, as a tour guide. A lot can happen in nine months."

Kris remarked that signs of departure were apparent everywhere: the Fall colors were coming in, all the way down to Skagway, and the tip-top fireweed blossoms had finally come and gone. "I'd sure like to see how accurate that six-week prediction is."

Genna allowed as to its general accuracy, and turned back to her vegetable cutting. Some very dubious-looking mushrooms had been about to crawl away unimpeded, but she caught them in time, briefly interrogated them, and deposited them safely into the trash receptacle.

But something else was happening. She felt Kris' expectant silence, looked up to see him looking her right in the eye. More silence, but with the hint of a smile on his lips, and some deeper emotion playing across his face. She put down her work. Finally, he spoke again:

BROACHING THE TOPIC

▼

"Genna—I've been wanting to ask you something. Do you remember how I've been talking about that cabin? You know, Gary's place in Dyea, and the fact that he might head south for the Winter and vacate it? Well, he's finally decided to do it; last night, he called me up and asked if I would like to take care of the place for him. I tried not to stumble over my tongue by answering 'Yes!' too quickly.

"I've always dreamed of doing something like this, especially since that first summer in Ketchikan. I want to watch the snows come in; for time to go slowly. I want the complete picture of Alaska. I want to get to know a place, get attached to it.

"But mostly I want to share this all with you. Genna, I've never met anyone like you. I never expected to find someone like you—especially in Tok, Alaska, of all places—and I can't believe my good fortune every time I look at you. I love you.

"Genna, I'm twenty-three years old, and my future is wide open. I have no reason anymore to go back down to Washington, or anywhere else Outside. I have every reason to stay here in Alaska. Will you spend the Winter with me?"

THE REPLY

▼

"Yes, honey: you've told me all about Gary's cabin. You've also hinted at the caretaking possibility: in just about every 'innocent' conversation lately. When I first noticed you were doing this, I thought, 'What are you getting at, mister?'—but I didn't really wonder very long. Subtlety isn't necessarily your strong suit, Kris.

"I know that you haven't spent a Winter here. But, have you ever holed up in very close quarters with someone else? Have you ever watched the perfect friend or lover turn into the Roommate From Hell? You would have to stare at me for days on end during those big blizzards; every morning you'd wake up next to me, with my mid-Winter pallor, grody longjohns and lutefisk breath. There'd certainly be a lack of regular shower and/or laundry facilities. And God help us if we have to live on canned chili and sauerkraut for a while.

"But I also know that love isn't always pretty. I know that your foibles are my foibles, and that your forgiveness is my forgiveness. The good times will be very good—as they already are. We can live through the tough times. There will be a lot of quiet times; I'm not afraid to be quiet with you, and you can be as quiet as you like without worrying me. I love you too, you big Norwegian nut.

"Of course I'll move in with you. I'd have come and joined you anywhere: even here. Sharing that beautiful Dyea cabin with you will be a major bonus. I can't think of anywhere else I'd rather be—or anyone else I'd rather be snowbound with."

Exchanging vows

▼

you're like a puma, a
lady cougar. you're golden, you like to
sleep in the sun and stretch, lazily. if i
wake you, you growl—but friendly-like. i want to
make you purr—it sounds so good.

   well, you're a sea otter. you like to
   float on your back amongst the waves, nibbling
   fresh seafood. you like to hunker down and get wiggly, and sometimes
   slide down riverbanks on your tummy. you're
   frequently silly. you have a goofy moustache that tickles.
   but, you're the only person i'll ever
   let kiss me when they're all wet.

PART FOUR: HUNKERING DOWN

▼

"are you ready for the country?
because it's time to go…"
—neil young

Termination Dust

▼

A lovely young woman squinted into the setting sun. The sun's low autumnal angle caused it to catch the edges of both the ridgetops and the valley haze, creating a warm golden light. Ordinary hues became extraordinary: willow and highbush cranberry dripped glowing red; quaking aspen leaves fluttered like live embers; the young woman's hair and eyes were the sun itself. She hugged herself against the chilly breeze and smiled. Warm hues notwithstanding, the temperature was dropping sharply: the Tok River valley likely would see heavy frost that night.

As the sun finally winked behind the Alaska Range, an old white car pulled off the highway, into the gravel parking lot. It glowed like a slow-moving moon in the dusk. As the car rolled up to Genna, she made a quick appraisal: peeling vinyl roof, tanklike '60s body, a little Car Cancer evident through the paint job—but no dents, good tires and the engine sounded strong. She smiled again: Kris had done all right.

Kris opened the car door and fairly leaped from the driver's seat. "Here it is, my love. A '67 Ford Falcon: picked it up for five hundred bucks, from some student who was splitting town. Gets only about ten miles to the gallon—I swear, you can see the gas gauge dip when you punch the accelerator—but it definitely has some get up and go. In fact, I've already got a name for it: the 'Millennium Falcon,' you know, after Han Solo's rustbucket Star Wars spaceship? And the heater works great, too. Should get us down the highway, through the Winter and then some."

Genna, amused at Kris' ebullience, slid her arm through his. "It looks perfect."

They spent the evening packing, and were up early the next morning. Kris traveled light: backpack, guitar, tape deck, some old cross-country skis he had picked up at the Army-Navy Surplus in Fairbanks. Genna did pretty well, considering that she was leaving her lifelong home: a duffel full of knit sweaters, quilts and blankets, art supplies, a big box of books. She hugged her mother for a long time as they stood on the cabin porch: "I'll be seeing you." The day was dawning crimson, pale blue and white as they loaded the car, hopped in and headed South.

They covered the 520 miles to Skagway in near-record time, arriving in mid-evening. There was very little traffic to worry about, and the Millennium Falcon rode the frost-heaves in stately fashion. The entire route was ablaze in color, especially around Lake Kluane. Kris and Genna lamented the fact that most tourists missed this beautiful time of year: the short, sweet, bug-free stretch of high Autumn.

Upon arriving in Skagway, they walked into the Bigger Hammer Cafe, to find Vicki the waitress wiping down the nearly-deserted tables. She greeted them warmly, gave them the keys to Gary's place, told them to stop by whenever they were in town. Kris and Genna said thanks, walked out into the middle of a perfectly-still Broadway, and decided to cancel their reservation at the Golden North Hotel, in order to get to the cabin right away. They got back into the Falcon and sped out to Dyea.

The moon glowed brightly through the trees as they pulled up to the homestead. They could clearly see the tall, spent stalks of fireweed in Gary's wildflower garden, seed pods exploding in pale parachutes. Kris, masking a brief moment of uncertainty, unlocked the cabin door and pushed it open, and turned to Genna:

"Is this where I get to carry you over the threshold?"

He saw her quick, catlike smile in the moonlight. "Well, this is my first time 'living in sin.' I believe you've earned the right, sir."

Kris easily lifted Genna into his arms, stepped over the worn threshold, and promptly smacked his head on the low doorframe (those pioneers weren't very tall people). Somehow, he staggered inside without dropping her.

They allowed themselves a morning of sleeping in after the long drive, sprawled across the tattered revolution of blankets and pillows in the loft. Then, they began to assess the cabin's condition, to see what kind of work might need to be done. Overall, it was slightly rough, in terms of aesthetic niceties (Dyea Gary's "bachelor touch" was apparent everywhere), but highly functional. There was, of course, no running water, but the rainwater cistern was clean and about half full, with replenishment from the autumn rains soon to come. The outhouse was distant enough from the cabin to be out of olfactory range, but was pretty bearable anyhow; a shovelful or two of lime would make it perfectly serviceable for the immediate future. There was an old, broken diesel-powered generator around the side of the cabin, but Kris and Genna were not inclined, mechanically or otherwise, to fix it; they figured that the woodstove, kerosene lanterns and batteries (for the ever-vital boom box) would take care of their energy needs.

After the assessment, it was right to work. Chop wood, lay in food supplies, chop wood, spruce up the cabin (Genna was in charge of the "homey" touches), try to find and fill leaks in the roof and walls, chop wood and chop wood. Kris had thought that the sauna alone required a lot of fuel—but, as everyone had reminded him, relying entirely on wood heat throughout the long winter was a different ballgame. Everything had to be done before the snows fell, as finding new wood would be next to impossible then.

"We're either turning into a couple of lumberjacks," commented Genna, after they had skidded the umpteenth load out of the woods and onto the stack, "or a couple of beavers."

For bucking the logs, Kris relied as much as possible on a vintage cross-cut handsaw; for the splitting, a double-bladed axe and heavy iron maul—he did not like to shatter the silence of the woods with anything mechanical. However, after a couple of hours as an old-time sourdough, he was increasingly inclined to fire up Gary's trusty Husqvarna chainsaw and rip through the rest of the day's work. "There are limits to my desire for historical authenticity," he muttered in his mind.

Often Kris would stop cutting, lean on his axe or saw, and look up at the mountains. Whether the skies were blue or gray, the peaks were framed in that same, peculiar low-angle light that made their features almost iridescent in their clarity. He felt as if he could just reach up and rearrange the alien alphabet message on AB Mountain.

Warm and cold sensations were simultaneously apparent. The season's colorful foliage, increasingly encountered underfoot, made Kris think of warming brandy, bright Pendleton wool lap blankets, a pan of golden biscuits pulled from the gas range. At the same time, the warmth of the sun now vanished almost instantly when it ducked behind the clouds or when Kris stepped into the shade of the woods. The crunching of leaves while walking along the Taiya River—especially early in the mornings, before the frost had vanished—reminded Kris of biting into a cold apple.

Such unmistakable seasonal hints from Ma Nature had profound effects, both physical and psychological, upon all the Alaskan critters. Kris and Genna, as resident critters, were not immune.

The first seasonal change came with the emergence, after many months in exile, of Genna's longjohns. "Look well, lover," said Genna, nekkid as a light bulb, just before she slid on her frayed, pilled but mighty comfy warmwear. "This is now my second skin. For all our bluster, us Alaskan girls hate being cold just as much as anyone. I'll take 'em off to wash 'em every so often—see how civil I am?—but that's just about it.

"In some respects, it gets much easier once the longjohns come on: easier to put on a few—or more than a few—insulating pounds, as well as camouflaging bodily hair growth. But some things get harder: in particular, it gets increasingly harder to tell the men from the women around here.

"So when you hit the bars in town to pick up somebody," she jokingly concluded, "you need to be vewy, vewy careful, to paraphrase Elmer Fudd. Your new friend might be a girl. Could be a guy. Could even be a provisioning grizzly."

Another change came with the realization that no one had to look like a "fine young man" anymore. Kris began to let his hair grow and, figuring that he would soon need all the warmth he could get, threw away his razor. After several days he had perfectly trendy pop-idol stubble, but then his beard entered that intermediate phase of mangy, gappy scruffiness.

"Just wait until a month or so has gone by," Kris reassured Genna. "You will no longer want to take a Weed-Whacker to my face."

Genna dubiously stroked the ragged bristle with her hand. "Maybe Tom Bodett's 'beard ranches' aren't such a bad idea: why not just send guys like you away for a few weeks? Anyhow, **my** face will surely thank you once it's all in: no more of this 'rug burn,' you scratchy brute!"

A day or so later, Genna brought a box of Spring bulbs back from town: tulips, daffodils, irises, crocuses, everything that the Skagway mercantile hadn't been able to sell and was on the verge of throwing out. Together she and Kris went on a bulb-planting spree, working Forest Service style: Kris sinking a shovel to the hilt in the meadow loam and working it forward; Genna following behind, dropping the bulbs into the holes with care and tucking them in with her bare feet. Kris watched admiringly as the breeze played games with her now-darkening hair, as she moved among the flowerbeds in her gunnysack flannel dress and longjohns, worn in the way that only Genna could wear them. What better investment to make together, he thought to himself, than to plant the flowers that will greet us on the other side of the approaching Winter?

"Have **you** paired-up for the hunker-down?" asked the late night DJ, whose radio signal had somehow bounced off the mountains all the way from Juneau. "Have **you** found that special someone for sharing the

Winter, warming up the bed, waking you up with those icicle feet? For, believe it or not, the Termination Dust is a-comin'."

*   *   *

Weather Notes, October 3: Genna says that this stretch of Indian Summer is the second longest she can remember. The longest one was four years ago, back in Tok: it was 70 degrees on October 1. By Thanksgiving of that year, it had already gotten down to 55° below. She says not to be lulled by all this niceness, but simply to enjoy it for what it is.

October 9: Another freezing night, another crisp, surprisingly sunny day. The last aspen and cottonwood leaves are hanging on by the barest of threads.

October 14: Three weeks past the equinox; more and more minutes are shaved off the sunlight, every day. When we went to bed the moon was bright, but getting up to pee around two o-clock, I noticed that some clouds had slid in. By the time we had woken up, all was clear again. I stepped outside and looked up at AB Mountain—and sure enough, the top was dusted in white. The famous Termination Dust: the true termination of Indian Summer.

Over the next few weeks, we will watch the snowline march down the mountainside, until it finally reaches the valley floor—and Winter will be here in earnest.

INTERVIEW

▼

Roy

[The setting: a typical evening on the Ketchikan docks; quiet, light rain, just before midnight; Roy hanging out, waiting for nothing in particular, smoking a cig.]

Q: How did you come to Alaska?

Luck of the draw. Luck of the Irish. Some kind of dumb luck: only kind I know. [*squinting/ smiling*] Uncle Sam could've sent me about anywhere in '43: Italy, north Africa, the south Pacific. Instead, I wound up on that great northern line of defense: me and about 25,000 other grunts on that hunk of rock called Kodiak, to stop the Japanese island-hopping campaign.

And, sure enough, they didn't get past us. In fact, didn't hardly see a damn soul out there but ourselves and what few Natives stayed behind. We took turns on bivouac in the Kodiak bush, for several weeks at a time. The enemy was bears and boredom; the fog was like a wet wool blanket.

But there were mountains, salmon, deer and water everywhere. It was all pretty impressive to a kid from Indiana.

Q: Why did you stay?

It's hard to explain how we felt after the war. Both Tish and I felt that everything was new. In one sense, it was strange and frightening; in another sense, the world was our oyster. All those letters to Tish, telling her what I'd seen and done here: it didn't take much convincing to get her to come on up.

My stint as an MP led me into cop work, in the first available position—right here, on this hunk of rock, in Alaska's First City. I learned that drunk fishermen weren't too different from drunk GI's.

Overall, it was the right time, and the right place, to make a commitment: to become a part of this town—then, later, to become part of a new state.

Q: What would you tell someone who is considering coming to Alaska?

[*squints into the rain, looking like the Old Man of the Sea*] Don't be fooled by that one sunshiney day in June: the day you pull into town on the ferry and can see all the way up the mountain. Know that things even out everywhere, Alaska included; you're not escaping anything. The difference is, around here, we start from the extremes. Get ready for some real lows—but some real highs, too.

Q: What makes a "real" Alaskan?

A loose cannon. A spare part. A good citizen. Someone who's ready to mess up his life by coming here.

Norm

> [*The setting: Skagway, a misty half-mountain afternoon in late Spring; no cruise ships in town, and the streets are very quiet; Norm holding*

court in a half-empty Red Onion, right below the lurid portrait of Dirty-Neck Maxine; waxing philosophical, nursing a Hot R.O.]

Q: How did you come to Alaska?

Same way you did, my friend: by walking past some job listing on a western Washington college campus; signing up, on the spur of the moment, for an interview; much to my surprise (and everyone else's), actually getting hired; learning how to drive a bus on county back roads, while simultaneously being loaded up on tour-manual trivia; arriving instate and being regarded by my very first tour passengers as a qualified Alaskan expert.

Q: Why did you stay?

First, I had to learn the roads. You start with the Fairbanks city tour; then you're itching to get all the way down to Tok (that exotic locale), then Denali, then Anchorage. Then, rather than merely driving from point A to point B, you want to attain that special familiarity with your routes: to know the stories that go along with every bump in the highway. You pit your curiosity against those long distances.

Finally, I realized that you can't even get to 99% of the state by road— plus, the non-physical aspects of Alaska take even longer to know. Since day one, I've been struck by a growing sense of space, a continuing sense of wonder. It's never stopped.

Q: What would you tell someone who is considering coming to Alaska?

Know the facts. Know the myths. Go to school on Alaska. Then, create some story-telling skills—and some stories—of your own.

Q: What makes a "real" Alaskan?

Well…*[long sip of Hot R.O.]* Alaska is a state of mind, as well as a physical place. Therefore, being a "real" Alaskan doesn't necessitate being born here. Lots of folks are Alaskans before they ever set foot in the state. And of course, a good deal of them wind up here.

Sandy

[The setting: Sandy's suburban bush hideaway, off the Farmer's Loop near Fairbanks; a sunny August morning on the cabin porch. Sandy sitting on an old couch; half a case of home brew is cooling in a tub of spring water, for any friends who may happen by later. Wisps of citronella smoke from a burning smudge keep most of the bugs away.]

Q: How did you come to Alaska?

By chasin' pipe dreams—or, I should say, pipelines. There was nothin' happenin' in Dickinson or Bismarck in the mid-70's. My husband Frank and I were tired of scratching things out: we'd been married a couple of years, and life wasn't getting any easier. Word had drifted down from Canada, about teams of men being hired in Alaska to weld pipe at forty below. Shoot, we said, we know all about that in North Dakota—but wasn't nobody making twenty-five bucks an hour doing it. We had nothing to lose, as they say; had to see if all the rumors were true. Packed up our old International truck, and up the Al-Can we went.

Well, turns out we were wrong. They were paying **fifty** bucks an hour to the pipeline gangs. My husband caught on with an outfit and soon was all over the state. I was tempted to take up a welder's torch myself. But I didn't need to, after a time: I set up shop in one of those makeshift truck stops along the new gravel haul road, slinging steaks and coffee, and was making nearly as much in tips as Frank's wages. These oil guys'd come in with these rolls of bills, slap 'em down like they were layin' pipe. Those were crazy days.

Q: Why did you stay?

Because I was tired of followin'. You know that old expression, "Unless you're the lead dog, the view never changes?" Well, after Frank split for Texas with that oilwell rigging company, there was no way I was gonna hightail down there after him. Instead, I began to look up, see where I was. And, I liked what I saw. I liked staying put for a change, even through those first couple of winters down at Paxson; I liked closing down the Grayling Room after lunch to slap on the snowshoes or skis, to enjoy those couple hours of sunlight.

After a time, my new-found lead dog instincts took me up to Fairbanks. I'm still here.

Q: What would you tell someone who is considering coming to Alaska?

[*pauses, gazing off into smudge-pot haze*] It's hard. It's hard to get through that first winter—especially if you're alone. But hang in there until Spring break-up: by then, you'll know if you're meant to stay.

Q: What makes a "real" Alaskan?

Well, someone who has the attitude, "walks the walk," from the outset. Someone who's got a lot of lead dog in him. Some raven: a bit of Trickster. A man—or woman—of many hats. And coats: **good** ones. Gloves and mukluks, too.

Genna

[*The setting: very early Fall in Tok, leaves on shrub willows showing the first hints of orange-red; Genna out back in her still-lush garden, walkin' the beans.*]

Q: How did you come to Alaska?

In utero. [*smiling*] My folks were tie-dyed-in-the-wool, capital-H Hippies, and they were on the road somewhere when I was conceived: making their way North, doing the back-to-the-land thing. My mom told me later that they'd wanted to name their kids after the places in which they became more than a glimmer in the eye: you know, kind of like Winona Ryder and Winona, Minnesota? But, in my circumstance, they weren't quite sure; could have been Montana someplace—in which case, I'd presently be named Shelby, or Livingston, or even Cut Bank. [*laughs like Rocky Mtn. snowmelt*]

Anyway, that old VW bus somehow made it up the highway; they must have had plenty of duct tape on hand, to hold things together. But can you imagine bouncing along on the pre-asphalt Al-Can, dealing with frost-heaves, mudslicks, and...morning sickness?

Q: Why did you stay?

Because it's my home: I was born here. This was the first place my folks landed once they crossed into Alaska; they'd planned only to over-winter here in Tok before moving on. They found a cabin for cheap in the woods, just west of town. When my Mom's time came, a woman from the neighboring Tanacross village, a midwife, came over. On one hand, my folks were fully into the home-birthing idea; on the other hand, they were scared shitless. But this Native woman was an old pro: things worked out just fine.

Shortly afterwards, my folks had a little post-birthing ceremony: to welcome me into the world, to bond the new family with the spirits of the land. Some hodgepodge Hindu-cum-Chippewa ritual, from what I've heard of it. Anyway, part of the ceremony was to make a stew from—I'm not kidding—the placenta from my afterbirth. So they got a little saucepan with some water going, placed the, um, stuff in there, brought it to a gentle simmer.

My Mom claims to have taken a sip of the broth—I have no idea about my father. But that was plenty: they dug a little hole out back, where the garden is now, and buried the rest of the placenta stew. So my birthing ceremony continues to hold significance, every time we dig up a spud or yank a carrot. [*hunkers down, pulls up a well-nourished carrot, wipes it off, takes a big bite*]

And, my father is buried here, too. Somewhere between McGrath and Unalakleet, where his plane went down: they never found it. Anytime I'm flying over the state, even in a big jet, I look down at the Alaskan bush and see it all as a memorial to him.

So, as you can see, it's not just the logistical problem of escaping from Tok that keeps me here. At the most basic level, I will never truly leave Alaska.

Q: What would you tell someone who is considering coming to Alaska?

Two words: **duct tape**! Bring rolls and rolls of it—at least enough to get you here. But if you run out, try to do so in a cool place, so you won't mind sticking around for a while.

Q: What makes a "real" Alaskan?

Someone who adapts. Someone who copes. Someone who grows into love.

Raven Steals The Sun: A Tlingit Fable

▼

In the early days, the world was dark. The sky held no sun, no moon, no stars—only a nighttime that graduated from midnight blue to faded black. The people who lived at that time had a cold, wet, miserable existence. They spent most of their time huddled around their fires, wrapped in furs, afraid to venture very far from home.

Raven, in the course of his travels, talked to these people in their state of misery. Deep in the minds of some, the elders, were memories of light: of sun, moon and stars. But, very long ago, the light had gone away. No one could say for sure where the light had gone, but some had heard of a great chief to the south, who held the sun, the moon and the stars captive in his possession.

Deep in his heart, Raven felt compassion. He swore to the people he met that he would do everything in his powers to restore the light to their sky. The people in turn promised him all the meager wealth they had, if he could somehow recapture the sun, the moon and the stars.

Far away to the southeast lived the Nass clan. The chief of the Nass was the most powerful chief in that part of the world: his fishing boats ranged far and wide, he had many slaves from other clans in his service, his totem poles towered among the tallest trees of the forest...and his sky had **light**. As Raven journeyed southeast, towards the land of the Nass, he heard many stories about the chief: how he lived in the largest, most ornate clan house anyone had ever seen; how he had a beautiful daughter who he kept guarded at all times; how he kept a mysterious, magical cedar box above his fire, from which all of his powers were said to emanate, and allowed no one to touch it, upon penalty of death. Raven listened with interest to all of these stories.

At length, Raven came to the main village of the Nass clan. He made himself invisible—and, in his journeys around the village, found that all of the stories he had heard were true. In the clan house of the chief, the magic box, mysteriously surrounded by light, was kept on the mantle. The chief, of course, considered the box so valuable that he kept it under a constant, heavy guard of his finest warriors.

Even more valuable in the eyes of the chief, though, was his daughter. She was young, not quite of marrying age, the only child of the chief and his deceased wife. She was extraordinarily beautiful, like a snowy stream flowing over the stones of the imagination. The chief loved his daughter very much, and also kept her under the watch of the warriors, lest anyone try to steal her away.

However, the chief's daughter had a secret. In the very early mornings, she was in the habit of going off by herself for a few minutes: down to the river, to take a drink of the delicious, clear water. Raven, in following the patterns of the village, soon learned of her secret, and determined that the best way to gain access to the chief, and to the magic box, might be through his daughter.

Raven possessed superior magical abilities, and could change into any form he chose. At first he thought about transforming his body into that of a handsome young man, to win the hand of the daughter. But, she already had more potential suitors than could be counted, and the chief was not likely to select a complete stranger, someone completely lacking in family wealth and position. Raven decided to try a more direct approach: to actually become a **part** of the Nass chief's daughter, to somehow create a physical union with her.

Early one morning, Raven jumped into the icy stream, and changed himself into a small pebble. He bounced and rolled along the riverbed, propelled by the current, and somehow managed to land directly in the girl's drinking cup as she dipped it into the water. As she brought the cup to her lips, though, she noticed the small stone sitting at the bottom of her drink, picked it out and threw it back into the stream.

Raven, foiled but not discouraged, tried again the next morning. This time, he changed himself into a hemlock needle, which was much smaller and floated on top of the water. He jumped into the stream once again, transformed himself and drifted right into the girl's cup. She raised the cup without noticing the tiny hemlock needle, and drank everything down: water, Raven and all.

Within days, the chief's daughter discovered that she was pregnant.

Her father was, of course, mystified. The chief could not figure out how someone had gotten through his loyal slave guard and impregnated his daughter. He was, nonetheless, delighted—because he was now going to be a Grandpa. The following Spring, the Nass chief's daughter gave birth to a healthy young boy—who was, of course, Raven in the disguise of a baby. The new child became the center of attention in the village, and was adored and spoiled by everyone.

A couple more years went by, and Raven grew into his "terrible twos," so to speak. The toddler began to learn how to speak: how to scream, to rant and rave, to whine, to point at things and demand them. Being a determined child, and being possessed of a doting grandfather, he generally got what he wanted. There was only one exception to this dotage: whenever the Raven-child would point and scream at the magical box, the chief would admonish him: "No, no, that's my most valuable possession; you can't play with it." The Raven would give up for the moment, but would inevitably come back time after time with a new, improved tantrum.

There came one day, towards the end of Winter, when the weather was still bad and everybody was feeling confined, irritable and out of sorts: a touch of Cabin Fever. Raven was being a particularly horrible child that day: restless, squirming, crying and yelling until he was red in the face. Nobody in the clan house could handle him: not the slaves, not his mother, not even the old chief himself. The family was gathered near the fire, and Raven went into yet another tantrum for the special box: pointing at it on the mantle, kicking on the ground, demanding that he have it, in his loudest, most obnoxious little voice. The family's nerves were so frayed, and the child was so loud, that finally the chief reached up to the mantle, took the magic, glowing box, and sat it down on the hearth before the Raven.

This was the chance that Raven had been waiting for. He immediately changed himself back into bird form, grabbed the box in his talons and began to fly up through the smokehole in the clan house ceiling. The Nass chief was paralyzed in shock, as was everyone else, but he swiftly recovered and sent his own formidable magical powers into battle with those of Raven. The two forces struggled mightily, and Raven for a time could fly no higher than the smokehole: nearly escaping, then being pulled back down, again and again (that is the reason why, to this day, the Raven's feathers are black).

Finally, Raven's powers prevailed: he broke free of the Nass chief's forces and flew upward with the magic box in his talons. He was so exhausted from the battle, though, that the box slipped out of his grasp and fell to the ground. The box broke into pieces, and there was a blinding light: the sun, moon and stars all escaped from the box, rose up and assumed their positions in the sky. This is where we see them today.

The Nass chief is no more, but there are still some who feel a need to "own" what really belongs to everyone. There are also some who, for whatever motive, selfish or otherwise—feel compelled to alter that structure of "ownership." But Raven, for all his guile and cunning, never did profit from possession of the magic box containing the sun, the moon and the stars.

EXTREMES

▼

"There are times when the wolves are silent and the moon is howling."

—Native proverb

Southeast Alaska was settling indecisively into Winter: one day, pulling a thick gray blanket up over its head; the next day, kicking off the covers to let in the dwindling daylight. The rains would settle in for a while, reminding Kris of his sodden Skagit Valley autumns, before yielding to blasts of cold Yukon air. Whenever the clouds parted, Kris saw that the snowline—no longer mere Termination Dust—had crept further down the mountainside.

"This can be a very strange time of year," cautioned Genna. "Between now and Christmas, Nature tends to get a little extreme: some real highs and lows. After New Year's, things seem to settle into a more predictable pattern—and it helps that the days are actually getting longer then. But for now, hang on for the ride."

Ice

About a mile behind the cabin was a small lake, dug out by a retreating glacier and dammed by the leftover moraine. As the weather turned colder, Kris began to monitor it on a frequent basis.

There had begun a string of clear, very cold days. On November 12, Kris saw the first chunks of ice washing up against the lakeshore. Several days later, he noticed that the chunks were not going away, but were accumulating: forming a ragged rim of ice that extended further into the lake as time went by. However, the shore remained barren and dry.

"Why is there is no snow yet?" asked Kris. "I expected to be all socked in by now. It's certainly cold enough."

Genna shrugged. "That's the way some years are. Just wait: the snow will come. Trust me."

But a strong high-pressure system had settled in over Southeast. The skies remained brilliantly blue, and the lake's edge froze into a solid crazy-quilt of icebergs. Then, on November 19, the Dyea valley received its first sub-zero night.

Kris ventured out the next morning, found that the small lake had frozen completely over. The ragged periphery resembled waves that had frozen in mid-peak, creating an image of arrested motion. However, the middle had sealed so quickly that it was not nearly as jagged as the edges; there were large expanses of clear, smooth, perfectly transparent ice.

Kris made a running start at the boundary of a clear ice patch, came to a sudden halt, skidded on his Sorel bootsoles for a satisfyingly long distance. That very same afternoon, Kris and Genna made a rare run up to Whitehorse (the Millennium Falcon's strong heater serving well in the minus-twenty Interior weather), to the Hudson's Bay department store, for two cheap pairs of ice skates. For the remainder of the dry spell, about another five days, they enjoyed a skating paradise on the small lake.

Snow

Late one morning, a strong southerly wind began to blow. While walking on the Dyea tideflats, Kris saw a towering gray storm front, advancing like the Russian Army up the Lynn Canal. He made it back to the cabin just as the first spiky Stalingrad flakes were beginning to fall.

Soon the full storm had settled in. All Kris and Genna could do was dig in and watch the premature darkness snuff out the daylight. The few crackling radio reports that they could pick up said that Ketchikan had already received fifteen inches of snow, Juneau twelve, with plenty more to come. The cabin windows reflected swirling siegelike black-and-white.

Sometime that evening, Kris decided to crack the door open a bit, to take a quick peek at conditions outside. Bad move: the howling wind blammed the door all the way open, and the blizzard elbowed its way into the living room. Genna gave a little yipe, jumped over and helped Kris slam the door shut again. Snow had dandruffed a full quarter of the cabin floor during the fifteen seconds or so that the door had been ajar.

Genna, panting, turned to Kris and raised her eyebrows to their theoretical limit. "Silly boy," she finally said.

"**Cool**," said Kris, unrepentantly. "Just like on one of those old 'Sergeant Preston of the Yukon' shows."

The storm dumped about eighteen inches of snow in the Dyea valley. Once everything had blown through, Kris and Genna pushed their door open with some difficulty, and gasped in awe at the unbroken diamond-frosting landscape.

"It's like Oz."

"It's better than Oz. But **damn**, it's cold."

Kris and Genna slapped on more clothing and ventured out to romp like otters in the winter wonderland. The snow was so light and cold that they could blow it out of their mittened hands like pixie dust; it squeaked like styrofoam packing peanuts underfoot. They stopped only after they were thoroughly soaked, and their noses had begun to turn from blue to white.

Wind

Taku Wind: a regional weather phenomenon, endemic to Southeast Alaska during the winter months. A ridge of high pressure builds up on the leeward side of the Coast Range, which in conjunction with an offshore low creates a large differential. The weather systems equalize via the narrow mountain passes, over the region's massive Taku icefields. Communities at the western, seaward ends of the valleys thus experience high velocity, frigid winds that last for days on end, send windchill factors off the scale and severely tax the physical and mental well-being of all who experience them.

Kris and Genna's frosty theme-park lasted only one day before a big Taku wind settled in. The wind stripped most of the snow from exposed areas, depositing huge drifts against trees, rocks, walls and other immovable objects. The cabin's front yard was barren, but the woodpile and Millennium Falcon were nearly submerged from view.

"The road to town is impassable," grumbled Kris, "the skiing is all screwed up, and I can hardly step outside without being blown the length of the valley. I don't even want to think about the windchill. When is this all going to end?"

Genna, huddled in a thick down comforter, looked up from her embroidery—alpine wildflowers on a field of white—and smiled mysteriously, saying nothing.

"This ancient wind knows every crack, nook and cranny in the cabin," Kris wrote in his journal one night. "It flickers the candles, drives fine snow into the eaves, tries to snuff out the woodstove. It freezes the soup overnight; it slices through all the layers of sweaters and shirts. It whistles and howls, it murmurs and creaks; it whips away, laughing."

Calm

The wind finally got bored with abusing our cabin, and went away. Genna and I peeked through the frosty window and saw that conditions had changed. We donned our heavy wool and goosedown and stepped outside for the first time in, seemingly, months. The moon was brittle but bright as we set out on foot.

The woods were so still as to be almost tense, as if the trees knew that the wind would be back, someday. They were right, of course—but they also knew that there was nothing to do about it. Their response was to be silent and meditative, cloistered in their shrouds of white. Genna and I stilled our crunching footsteps, to gaze upward at the forest canopy. There was no motion at all, save for tiny crystals drifting down from the treetops, glowing palely: reflecting perfect ice-blue moon-pictures in each prism.

"He hadn't been walking long when he noticed a strange blue light that seemed to be powder, falling through the tops of the trees, as far around as he could see. It wasn't a light he knew. All of the local deer had gathered in a clearing—bucks and does and fawns that stayed in the middle. None of them were very big. They were all covered in the blue-white dust that seemed to glow but not to glitter. They were all looking up into the sky."

—Peter Gould, **Burnt Toast**

Our quiet but too-loud human bootsteps drew us to the lake's edge. We gazed across its expanse, and were struck by the complete absence of motion. While the water was open, I had never seen it without at least some breeze diamonding the surface, even on the mellowest of summer evenings. Through the Fall, high angry waves had given way to colliding ice floes, driven by the constant glacial winds. Even when the lake finally had frozen all the way, there were always the howls and echoes of the nearby mountain bowls, or the death-rattles of the final frozen leaves, or...some kind of sound.

Now, all was silent and glassy. The wind had blown off most of the snow, except around the lake's edge. We walked a number of yards out from the shore, stilled our footsteps, hushed our breathing, and entered a profound silence.

Many people believe that they have encountered true silence. A lonely country road, a moonlit forest pond, the prairie at midnight, and other places of the heart can offer a modicum of peace and solitude. But there is always **some** sound: *the call of an animal, the riverine sound of a distant highway, the stirrings of the night wind. From our vantage on the lake ice, there was no sound, motion, or sense of life to be discerned. We listened: no wind, not even among the high surrounding peaks. No lapping water, no dripping trees. No nocturnal animals making their social rounds. All was locked in a silence that, in its singularity, filled our senses.*

Genna and I had stepped into a Winter still-life: the silver solitude of the ice-encased birches; the deep purple-black of the towering mountains; the bright stars, blinking in a million languages. I wondered at the masterful strokes—and the masterful artist—that had created the tableau.

After many minutes, however, we gradually perceived a subtle, very deep vibration: the softest of sounds, so low on the tonal register as to be nearly imperceptible. The sound seemed to grow in the void, and finally we realized its source: the ice beneath us. The frozen lake was still shifting, ever so slightly: solid in its mass, but bending, groaning, stirring at a level almost beyond cognition. There was not complete silence, after all. And it became clear to me:

Winter in the Alaskan woods is a state of sleep, not death. If one listens very closely, one may hear the sounds of its slumber.

My reverie was interrupted by the realization that my toes were extremely cold. I shuffled my feet; Genna glanced over at me; the spell was broken. Slowly, as if awakening from a dream, we made our way back to the cabin.

Cold

Dyea Gary's Winter Survival Tip #7: Styrofoam Outhouse Seats.
"When Nature calls, it doesn't check on the weather first. Those 25-yard dashes to the privy are bad enough when it's below zero, but the real character-building part comes when you have to sit down. Unless you do what I do: before it begins to get really chilly, get yourself a slab of styrofoam, saw it into the approximate shape of the throne seat, and install it right away. Not only will nether parts near and dear fail to adhere, but those seats warm up almost instantly. I swear, I've sat on a styro shitter at fifty below, and haven't suffered a nip of frostbit buns.
"Just one of those little things to make your Winter bush experience a little less bushy."

Warmth

"A long time ago—back when I was about your age, in fact—I used to go up to the Boundary Waters during the Winter: weekends of snowshoeing, ice-fishing and general havoc with my college buddies, within spitting distance of the Minnesota-Canada border. It was usually so cold that, if you had in fact tried to spit at the border, it would have frozen in mid-air, about a foot away from your bearded, icicle-encrusted face. Naturally, you were forced to utilize every available means of keeping warm. One of our favorite means was, after an afternoon outdoors, to come inside for Snowshoes: sloe gin and peppermint Schnapps. A couple of Snowshoes, and you were as warm as you ever cared to be.

"Of course, the Snowshoe was invented by necessity. The booze selection up around Ely in those days was, shall we say, rather limited: Schmidt's beer, Old Crow-Gut whiskey and other delights. Sloe gin was cheap—although not so cheap as to make you go blind from drinking it—strong enough to pack a decent wallop, and just shy of being too sweet to mix with other things. The peppermint Schnapps was something we had plenty of around the cabin anyway, as a mouthwash and general anesthetic. Anyhow, one day push came to shove: somebody picked up a magnum of sloe gin, found it too nasty to drink straight, decided to cut it with the Schnapps—and the rest was history. The resulting beverage was very unique in character, yet very warming. We called it the Snowshoe, because we didn't want to call it the Birch Log, or the Frozen Walleye, or the Drying Wool Union-Suit.

"From that time forward—whether we needed a quick warmer-upper, or had some serious thawing in mind—a snort or two of Snowshoe always did the trick.

"I don't even know if you can find sloe gin anymore, although I expect cough syrup would do just as well. But if you can, try mixing up a Snowshoe and having one for your old dad—who still wants to come up to Alaska and steal your job."

—Letter from Kris' dad, Bill

Alas, sloe gin was not to be found in the Skagway mercantile; I got a seriously-raised eyebrow when I asked for it. But peppermint Schnapps was readily available. Genna returned from town one day with a carton or two of instant Swiss Miss, and shortly thereafter turned me on to the benefits of hot cocoa and Schnapps, sipped slowly after a long, rough afternoon of cross-country skiing.

"Honey, I'm **home**," said Kris, bursting through the cabin door, tossing his black briefcase to the side, shedding his navy-blue pinstripe suit and dress Oxfords, kicking his feet up on the leatherette Laz-E-Boy.

"Oh dear, did you have a rough day at the office?" asked Genna, with a concerned, matronly look on her face, pressing a freshly-mixed cocoa and Schnapps into his waiting, outstretched hand.

Like father, like son.

Darkness

December 21—the Winter Solstice, the shortest, darkest day of the year. This morning, the sun came up just after nine o'clock; by two, it was already behind the mountains to the west, and by three the sky was pitch black. Even at "high noon," the sun was so low in the sky that, were it not for the Lynn Canal to the South—and the fact that no peaks rise from its depths—we wouldn't have seen the old orb at all.

Things could be worse. Carcross, even though it's just over Chilkoot Pass from here, does have southerly peaks, so they're only getting a midday "dusk" these days. Barrow, Alaska—flat as a pancake, but way the hell North—is completely dark until sometime in February. If I were passing the Winter as a 9-to-5 yuppie in Anchorage (God forbid), I would be going to work and coming home in the dark; I would not see the sun unless I were able to step outside for a lunch break.

As it is, I crave light. I cling to the feeble sunshine: so fragile, so poignantly doomed. It's hard to imagine the glorious excesses of mid-summer right now.

I guess two basic survival rules apply. Number one, get your ass out the door by ten or eleven, no matter what the weather, and take in as much ultraviolet as possible. Number two, obey those darkness-based urges to hibernate. Going to bed early and rising late are Nature's way to deal with the solstice blues.

—Excerpt from Kris' journal

Light

"I'll be along in just a few minutes," said Genna, only halfway into her skiwear as a fully-outfitted Kris waited by the cabin door. "Go on ahead: I'll catch up."

"Are you sure? I don't mind waiting."

"I'm sure. Besides, there just might be some Santa-type stuff that needs to be done here. Can't happen if **you're** around."

"I get the hint. I'll wait for you in the meadow."

In a few minutes, Genna skied up to Kris' side. He was intently studying some animal tracks that led into an alder thicket.

"Foxes, I think," said Kris. "One good-sized set of prints, a whole passel of tiny tracks, running circles around the larger trail."

"**Pups**," said Genna, eyes glowing. "They just can't keep still."

"Their toes get cold," said Kris. "Just like mine. Let's go to the lake and look at the stars."

The moon was a thin sliver in the clear, black Christmas Eve sky, providing just enough pale glow for Kris and Genna to make their way through the forest. But on approaching the lakeshore, the sky began, for some reason, to grow lighter. Kris felt an eerie tingle rise up his spine. Then, he raised his eyes to the northern sky and there, in all its dazzling glory, danced the aurora borealis: the Northern Lights.

as pilgrims await,
a city above the trees
bends in beckoning

The hair rose on the back of Kris' neck as he watched the shifting, colorful spectacle. "They're so beautiful—and so unexpected."

"They never fail to give me the chills, even after all the times I've seen them." Genna was transfixed in awe.

The patterns and colors of the aurora were vivid but ephemeral: continuously changing, vanishing and reappearing in unpredictable, wildly beautiful ways. Finally the whole spectacle rippled away over the mountain ridges, and the sky darkened once again.

"I swear that I could **hear** the lights leave," commented Kris, after a moment. "They were like some departing alien spaceship."

"Maybe that's what the aurora really are," said Genna.

In silence they skied back towards the cabin: back to warmth and presents, mulled wine and the familiar. And, once they had entered the meadow of home, back to another kind of light: tiny, multicolored Christmas bulbs had been strung around the cabin windows. The lights twinkled in the snow, blinking in blue, red and green. Kris stopped in his tracks and stood there, shaking his head and smiling: the scene had the mark of Santa written all over it.

Genna sidled up to Kris, seemed almost apologetic. "They're not quite the Northern Lights. But they were on sale at the Hudson's Bay. And they run on batteries. They're not too corny, are they?"

Kris looked at the girl he loved, and put his arm around her. "I think they're perfect." Genna slid her arm through his, and laid her head on his shoulder. Together they watched the winking lights.

NEWS ITEM #3

▼

HAINES, ALASKA—"Alaskan Geysers": A Haines man was surprised on New Year's morning by a large hole in his front-yard snowbank. The man went to investigate: "I put my coat on and went out into the yard and I saw a hole in the snow with a lot of vapor billowing out of it—so I said, 'it must be a bear'." Further investigation revealed that his suspicions were correct: a mother black bear and two cubs were domiciled for the winter in the man's front yard. Local experts surmise that they were "garbage bears," lured into town by abundant food but stranded there when the high snows came early.

The local man plans to move the sleeping bears, with a front-end loader, to a quieter, more private location.

Meaningful January Activities

———————▼———————

"In the summer, we'll sit in a field and watch the sun melt;
In the winter, we'll sit by the fire and watch the moon freeze…"

—Michelle Shocked

One day in early January, Kris almost lost the Millennium Falcon, not to mention his life, on the road to Dyea. He was on his way back from town, where he'd made an obligatory grocery run (and may have had a Hot Red Onion or two). Around the bend from Middle Bay, by the big rocks at the mouth of the Taiya River, the car hit an iced-over shady spot, lost control, and spun around 180 degrees. It was a place where the road was just wide enough for two cars to pass; if it had been one of the truly narrow spots, Kris and the Falcon would have plunged down the cliff, into the bay.

During the Tilt-a-Whirl, the right front corner of the Falcon had smacked a boulder, bending the wheelwell so that it scraped against the tire. After his heartbeat had slowed sufficiently, Kris went to the trunk, took out a woodsplitting maul, and hammered the wheelwell back into its approximately proper place. He restarted the car, shrugged his shoulders and went on his way, accepting the near-miss as one of the tradeoffs of his rural Alaskan lifestyle.

Such winter driving hazards—not to mention the incredible incentive to stay home—were sufficient cause for hunkering down as far as possible. Kris was not at all disappointed when he and Genna were snowed in: it gave him an opportunity to be reflective, to sleep until the late sunrise, to spend his entire mornings in his wool union suit—or less, once the fire got going. To marvel at what he and Genna were building. They were nurturing a love through the long winter; the tiny cabin in Dyea was like a greenhouse.

Kris fantasized about building a lath-house, whenever Spring arrived: to get an early start on a summer garden, if for some reason Gary decided not to come back. It was hard to imagine now, with the garden area buried under six feet of snow. Kris dreamed of hothouse tomatoes, giant zucchini, raspberries in July…maybe even get some Matanuska Thunder-Fuck seeds? Plenty of time to plan such things.

There was also time for a lot of silliness. When Cabin Fever[17] hit, there were two possible responses: sulk about in a dirty-snow, sullen funk, or go slightly crazy—but friendly-like. This latter response usually resulted in unwarranted, impromptu lunacy: turning on whatever tape was in the tunebox and dancing madly (regardless of the music: reggae, country, classical); baking biscuits out of whatever was at hand and devouring them all at once; taking up charmingly annoying habits—

> today i'll learn to
> whistle said genna,

---

17. Popularly known as "a thirty-foot stare in a twenty-foot room," in Alaska and other afflicted places.

skippin around the
cabin in red union—
suit, soundin like
cracked tutankhamen tea-kettle

The small things in life surrounded Kris and filled him with wonder. The frozen puffs of his own breath which would linger in the air and refuse to dissipate on the coldest of days. The sharp sensation as the morning air hit his lungs, making him gasp. The ice-encased buds on the birches and willows. The nighttime journeys of the moose, fox and other locals. The long, long ski excursions—and coming home.

The way that Genna moved these days: always as if to music, graceful, swaying, rhythmic. The gentle lift of her breasts as she opened the curtain on a glistening snowy morning. The flickering silhouette as she rose in the night to stoke the fire. The secret, knowing smiles that Genna tried to keep thinly veiled, but which Kris spied—especially when she danced to her favorite reggae albums:

these days of
amazed uncertainty
tulip blush on her cheek
what will full
springtime bring?

The wintertime music: Sibelius and Grieg. Frosty Scandinavians, to be enjoyed near the woodstove with shots of vodka or aquavit (literally, "water of life"), chilled bottle pulled from the snowbank outside. Sibelius' **Finlandia**, combining traditional Slavic melancholia with Baltic moodiness ("Big mood swings make for good Vikings," explained Kris). Peer Gynt, home at last, chopping wood for his fire. Edvard Grieg sitting in his little *hytta* overlooking the Bergen fjord, moved to create by the simplicity and the complexity of the snowflake.

They even had visitors, on a fairly frequent basis. The Skagway area was typical of most small Alaskan locales in Winter, in that calling upon one's neighbors was a leading pastime—but people tended to be so far-flung, and travel conditions were often so extreme, that visits could last for days at a time. It was almost a season-long, community-wide Open House at times.

Vicki the waitress liked to stop by with leftover goodies from the café. Karl frequently escaped his old double-wide and came out to split wood, regale Kris and Genna with tales of the Australian Rugby League, and fill them in on the latest town gossip. Wheatgerm showed up once, bent trombone in one hand, magnum of Old Granddad in the other, for a Lost Weekend or so. It seemed as though the town's boundaries had expanded to include them.

Even Douglas Fir came down from the Fairbanks bush, vintage VW Van chugging up Kris and Genna's snowy driveway. "These buses have, like, hardly any **heat** in them," commented Doug, wrapped in his down sleeping bag, blue face still wreathed in his typical grin of good cheer. Doug greatly appreciated the sauna, but refrained from a riverine dunk.

The social times were balanced by a quiet understanding of space. When there were no visitors, Kris or Genna would occasionally feel an urge to go off into his or her own projects and meditations; the other would sense this urge and respect it.

Genna's embroidery was a constant: it kept her hands busy, was a gateway into contemplation and daydreaming. She could even cross-stitch while she talked. Her stylized flowers, leaves and birds adorned pillows, shirts and any number of household fabrics.

Her long-term sewing project was something more substantial: a large quilt that she had been working on for the past couple of winters. The quilt cover was a deep midnight-blue, upon which she was painstakingly hand-stitching the constellations of the northern sky. The "quilt of stars," as she called it, was about halfway completed, and gave her a good reason to go skiing or snowshoeing on a clear night (as if any reason were needed), and something to do while thawing by the fireside.

Other projects weren't quite so structured. Genna's sketchbook was the perfect medium for her stream-of-consciousness artistry, which ranged from the strangely profound to the profoundly strange. Amongst the surprisingly excellent portraits of local wildlife and winter habitat was a full-page drawing of a leafless tree. Upon first glance, it was a fairly faithful rendering—until one noticed the multitude of telephones that hung like ripe fruit from every available branch: old-fashioned Ma Bell wind-em-ups, sleek '80s business phones (with answering machines attached), clunky '50s licorice-blocks. Underneath the tree, amidst fallen, decomposing phone books, was the drawing's caption: "The Dangling Conversation."

Kris' beat-up old acoustic guitar accounted for one of his major creative outlets. The guitar had been with him nearly everywhere, and when played reflected the sum of its experiences. The Alaskan angle (e.g., apolitical blues, gray-whale boogies, glacial thrash) tended to dominate these days. Kris was no particularly large talent, but he managed to give voice to these sentiments in a fairly competent way.

He also learned to express himself through creative cooking and baking. For example, the woodstove lent itself to the art of soup-making very well: all Kris had to do was chop up some ingredients into a big pot, cover them with water, put the lid on and place the pot onto the stovetop, to simmer for a few hours or a couple days. The creativity lay in the ingredients: Kris' soups featured the most eclectic selections of vegetables, meats, legumes and grains that the Skagway mercantile afforded in the Winter.

For soup dunkage, Kris utilized a housewarming gift he and Genna had received from their friend Sandy: some heirloom sourdough starter. In rural Alaska, one of the greatest status symbols going was the age of one's starter: some bushers had cultivated, on a generational basis, active strains of yeast that dated all the way back to the Gold Rush era. "I don't do this for just **anyone**, now," Sandy had said as she culled off a small portion of her reputed 1908-vintage starter and bade Kris to take good care of the yeasty lil' buggers. The net result, after months of careful nurturing, was all the delicious, dunk-worthy sourdough bread and rolls (not to mention pancakes) that Kris could bake, and he and Genna could eat.

The occasion of Genna's twenty-first birthday provided Kris with an excuse to go all-out in the kitchen. While recently in town, he had been the recipient of a large bag of frozen, chopped rhubarb. "My family is sick to death of rhubarb," the giver had explained (the stuff was incredibly prolific in Skagway summer gardens). However, she had also given Kris a recipe for rhubarb cake: delicious and easy to make, even in pioneer wood-burning ovens.

Kris strongly encouraged Genna to go to town that morning, ostensibly to blow some of her birthday-card loot. Once she was safely departed, Kris gathered his ingredients and set to work. He mixed up some flour, eggs, oil and spices, added a big dollop of plain yogurt (the key ingredient), stirred in the rhubarb and poured everything into a cake pan. He mixed some walnut pieces with brown sugar and cinnamon, sprinkled these over the batter, and finally placed everything into the well-primed oven, to bake for an hour. Soon the heavenly smell permeated the cabin; Kris was sure that, if he were to open the door, all the woodland creatures would shortly gather in the yard, sniffing in wonderment.

Then, to top off his exotic creation, Kris whipped up a fresh batch of snow ice cream. He gathered two big bowlfuls of the whitest, fluffiest snow he could find, mixed a can of sweetened condensed milk into each bowl, added Hershey's chocolate syrup to the first bowl and sliced strawberries with honey to the second. He stashed the bowls outdoors again, to chill and set up before Genna came home.

That evening, he made Genna close her eyes as he decorated the rhubarb cake with candles and lit them, fetched the ice cream, and paraded everything to the table while singing 'Happy Birthday.' Genna opened her eyes, and was stunned.

"Make a wish, now," Kris gently urged as she prepared to blow out the candles.

"What more could I wish for?" asked Genna, eyes wet but smiling radiantly.

In addition to his musical and culinary endeavors, Kris had a number of other creative inspirations. For a long time, certain writing ideas had sat in the back of his mind, waiting to be liberated from the constraints of time and structured thought. Through the Winter and into the early Spring, Kris tried to put some of his ideas onto paper: some of the impressions of Alaska and the Yukon that he had collected and transformed in his mind. The following are a few of them.

CAFE REPLICA

Me and Ilana stood on the rope bridge, watching the lake trout migrate and looking at our rippled reflections in the clear blue-grey water. It was early August; the sun was just setting even though it was about 10 p.m. The icy faces of the glacier-encrusted peaks across the lake suggested long-dead Canadian premiers.

"You know," said Ilana, "it's a shame. What with these tour buses comin' through in the summer and all. They go right past my cabin, and none of 'em ever stop by. I like visitors. It's a shame." Ilana lived in a small log cabin on the shore of Lake Bennett, one of several left over from the Klondike Gold Rush. Hers had a moose rack above the door, two small windows, a table, a bed, and an old woodstove. That was just about it.

An old native man down the bridge from us snagged a lake trout. It darted like an out-of-season icicle in the water and then popped up, like Superman, out of the water and into the old man's creel. The old man smiled a toothless grin.

"You gotta give them a reason to stop by," I said. "The old railroad depot's got the gifts, curios, knickknacks, whatnots—not to mention the peanut butter ice cream. The steamboat museum's got the biffy and the free coffee. Not to mention Josey. She knows everything about those damn boats."

I could see Ilana's thoughts swimming around with the lake trout. Then, she brightened: "I got it. Carcross doesn't have a decent place to **eat**. You can get them month-old hoagies in the Caribou Hotel; other than that, you gotta sit through that goofy Gay '90s show to get a hot meal. I'll open a cafe right there on the lake, in my cabin."

"But honey, your place is about ten feet by fifteen. It's so small, you have to step outside to change your mind. You **sleep** in there. How in hell are you gonna make a restaurant out of it?"

"It's OK," Ilana smiled. "That's the way they ate 'way back when. The Stampeders didn't have any McDonald's or nothin'. People will come to my cafe 'cause it's authentic: 'cause they're **hungry**. They'll sense that something good is cooking in my cabin. Won't need any advertising; won't even need any signs. It'll spread word-of-mouth." She paused, dreaming.

"Well now, that's not too bad an idea; I've heard of worse," I teased. "So, when are you gonna start?"

"Right now," said Ilana. "I'm open for business. Stop by, have a cup of Joe, eh?"

The old native man looked up from his fishing. "You're nuts. You're fuckin' **crazy**." He grinned again, gummily.

Me and Ilana went back to her tiny cabin. We borrowed an extra table from the neighbors, fetched some potatoes, carrots, onions and venison from her storage cache, and got some water going for coffee. We were ready.

Now, it's mid-winter. The sun just went down behind the peaks, even though it's only 2 p.m. It's about thirty below outside; it hasn't gotten above freezing for a month and a half. I've seen worse.

Ilana got her first customer yesterday. "Howdy, ma'am." He entered, closing the door against the howling blizzard. A team of huskies barked outside. He bashfully removed his 1897 wool toque, cleared his throat, remembering how to speak. "Sure could use some vittles." He hung up his furs, set down his gold pans and sat down by the fire.

The Swan of Tuonela

▼

my hidden pathways are deceptively simple: sometimes leading to
scenes of destruction or glory, sometimes both; sometimes just two
tracks in the snow

at the heart of the pathway lies the land of home, to thee are we
bound, the song of our souls: the land we love to every detail. the
trees bending with snow, cowled monks lowchanting whitely;
the early chromatic sunsets, departing sunrays gilding greyhooded
sky; the animal tracks that cross my ski-trail, nightfall doings of
the winterwaltz, starlight songs that grow in intensity as the days
slowly lengthen. out of seeming silence come the dancers,
almondine eyes glowing eastern secrets: emerging to dance
victorian snowballet, then retreating to warmlair as winter lingers
a while longer

on one such journey i saw the swan: a female trumpeter, banded eyes and
white throat, circling slowly in open water above the springs; almost unbearably
lovely against minorkey winter shoreline. she circled as i knelt to drink:
slow and repetitive, circling some deeper sorrow; far deeper than my
reflection (a soldier, a sailor, others i knew long ago), into bluecold depths of
seasons distantpast:

the first thing i saw was the single
snowdrop, meltwater on the first leaflet of
spring, a bell-like note; following delicate
greenveins led me to a grotto: a place where
the water never closes, where vapor glazes
    budding branches

and i beheld the first miracle of the spring: fierce and
beautiful, so wild and strange that the lovers scarcely noticed
the thousand small miracles of the season: tulip, crocus, winking-eye
anemone, yellow-and-cream narcissus, graceful neck bent like
    the circling swan;
    their embrace was tenacious, entwining,
    lush with greenenergy of the young sapling

as the love grew into summer, they barely heeded the fireweed that
unfurled scroll-like and raced to its apogee; they barely saw the
    skymaiden blooms

    but the scent of the wildflowers, the feel of crushed incandescent
    lupine beneath the lovers' hair was a vivid oracle, even in the
    snowblue depths of the swan's pond: an oracle of foxtail,
    salmonberry, cloudberries, golden redblush and tartness; the
    bittersweet of the frosts that closely follow
        the midnight sun

the season moved swiftly, maideneye turning to seed, driftingpale umbrellas
on the winds of autumn; and one morning, she wondered where
    he had gone

    what did she dream as winter set in, as the season laid down its first
    arcticfox footfall? did she dream of news from the front, from outside?

bloodonsnow, rosepetal declarations on dying lips? news travels fast on
    light forest feet

were his dreams slowed by blizzardsnow; did his strength ebb in the
deathchill?
skis sink into whitebank, vision becomes blackness; final divergent
thoughts of
the land of home, of bulbs planted in decaying meadowloam for the
falseprophet
of spring, never to bloom; merging into minor chords of the
    swan's circling song

    but the seasons are illusory;
    the reflection ripples at
    the simplest fingertouch;
    my reality is the wandering

what seeds do i sow in my wanton way? what upland meadowvales
bear the bloom from where i lay; what mountain halls ring with my name,
voiced in tollbell anger? perhaps the echoes pass; perhaps my mark on the
world more resembles the crossing of an ocean, the tracks that swiftly fill
    with blowing snow

    my hope lies in the cabin at the end of my journey, where a
    wisp of woodsmoke rises like a prayer; where a woman waits at
    hearthside to tell me, "god bless your work"; where someday
    i will no longer see my own death in the mirrorimage
        of the pond:

        where the swan still circles,
        lovely in her solitude

Speech By The State Representative From Chicken, Alaska

▼

My fellow representatives of the Legislature of the State of Alaska: today I present an issue of great importance. Do our state symbols adequately represent this Great Land? Most of our emblems are properly indicative of the largest state in the union: the King Salmon (official state fish), the Sitka Spruce (official state tree), even the Woolly Mammoth (official state fossil). All of these represent the finest of their class. So, then: **why is the wimpy willow ptarmigan our state bird?**

True, the ptarmigan is one of the few non-migratory birds residing in our state, and therefore spends the whole year here. True, it is wide-spread, it is common—but it just represents an unsuitable image for Alaska.

Is the ptarmigan a bird of grandeur, a bird of strength and courage? Hell no. It's dumb as nails. It hardly flies, usually just scurrying along the ground like a feathered, winged gopher. Worse still, children usually think of the ptarmigan as a flat bird; i.e., "Grandpa, was that our state bird we just ran over?" It's downright embarrassing.

The ptarmigan also poses severe logistical problems. You can't see them; they camouflage in brown summer and white winter colors. It is therefore hard to decide how to officially depict them: white, brown, or molting?

They also taste too good; there is an inherent conflict of interest with respect to killing a legislatively-honored, but delicious, bird.

Finally, here's the clincher: can any of you even **spell** ptarmigan?

There is no logical reason why this ignominious grouse should be the Alaska state bird. While the other state symbols top their categories, the ptarmigan is a poor talisman for the Last Frontier, representing unwanted connotations and hatching confusion for all residents. Therefore, I propose a resolution to change our state bird: from the willow ptarmigan to *corvus corax principalis*, the distinguished **raven**.

The ubiquitous raven is a far better winged representative. As the largest member of the crow family, it is by far the most wide-spread species in the state. It is seen year-round in its distinctive black; no wimpy camouflaging. A true northern bird. It is widely regarded—although, in all probability, very few know first-hand—that they don't taste good. There would be no worry that people would eat the state emblem, despite its popular moniker as the "soul chicken."

They are creative, intelligent survivors, with loads of personality. They ride the updrafts from the mountainsides, just like the eagle; they scare away unwanted intruders, such as stray dogs and even, *en masse,* bears. Furthermore, Alaskan Native peoples, such as the Tlingit and the Haida, have long recognized the raven's importance, evidenced by the numerous legends in which the raven plays the leading role.

Finally, there is the notable difference in bird calls. Allow me to demonstrate: the ptarmigan, vis-a-vis the call of the raven. *[a weak, apathetic cooing ensues, followed by a loud, raucous **CAW**! that reverberates through the State Assembly chambers]*

In conclusion, my esteemed colleagues: the raven's spunk, character, intelligence, and physique make it an excellent avian ambassador for Alaska: one of which we can be proud. Furthermore, it does not present the complications that the piddly ptarmigan does. I implore you to enact this resolution. What will it be: the lobotomized pigeon, or the crafty crow? Come and join us, the raven-maniacs.

Next on our coalition's agenda of unworthy symbols to eradicate is the puny, forgettable state flower: the forget-me-not.

Winter Prayer

▼

i gave thanks for the
bread, the snow-bride,
the winter bower

for the ancestor who
struck stone to stone
to straw, stealing fire

for the great-uncle
who split the fir-grain
true, for the first ski

for the father who
gave me the shoul-
ders for the axeblade
and the burden

then i called on the
god of winter t keep
her from the harsh
night winds, the
draft of the door

the extinctive call of
the snow-leopard,
the fury of the
forgotten mastodons

t keep the wood-
stove goin so i can
see her stoke the
flame once more

Woodpile Reckoning

▼

Like rival alligators, the two chainsaws, one Husqvarna, one Stihl, eyed one another warily, toothily. Then, as their owners approached and yanked them to life, they growled and sputtered to one another, voicing threats and boasts: of great trees felled, magnificent firs and cedars ripped through in mere seconds, stout cordwood bucked—all at minus-forty degrees or much, much colder.

"Nice saw," said Kris to Karl, eyeing the latter's idling 24" Stihl. "Looks like you could do some serious logging with that beauty."

"No logging for this saw, yet: just a hell of a lot of firewood cutting," replied Karl, testing a sharp sawtooth with a fingertip. "In fact, Vicki thinks it's overkill: says I got this saw for the same reason that a lot of guys go out and buy Camaros—you know, to compensate for uh, certain male inadequacies."

"Chainsaw Envy: that's a new one," laughed Kris. "However, since this one is Dyea Gary's personal tool, it can't possibly be a reflection on **me**." Kris picked up the Husqvarna and gave it a couple of fierce-sounding revs before turning it off; he put on his cross-country skis and, carrying the saw, began to slide off into the snowy January woods, gesturing for Karl to follow.

Karl had shown up for yet another woodcutting session with Kris, but this time had brought Vicki the waitress—not only a mutual friend, but also Karl's new main squeeze—with him. Vicki and Genna were currently within the warm cabin, engaged in a civilized cuppa-tea ladies' visitation while Kris and Karl did the standard guy thing of whomping through pristine nature with loud machinery. However, once the noise and smoke had subsided and the work was done, the ladies would join the guys in the heating, well-provisioned (massage oils, bottle of wine) sauna.

Down by the river, the trees were mostly thick cottonwood and birch: plentiful, but not too much good in a woodstove. A little higher up, but before the slopes gave way to skinny pine, stood a mixed grove of alder, spruce and aspen, with the occasional cedar or fir mixed in. It was a downed Douglas fir that Kris and Karl, with their salivating chainsaws, were after: knocked over by the wind some time ago, and thus nice and dry, but undiscovered until one of Kris' most recent sojourns in that direction. The plan was to buck the tree into haulable lengths and skid them back to the cabin woodpile on a sled, for further sawing and splitting as needed.

They arrived at the tree, eyed it critically, and set to work. At the upper end, Kris trimmed the thinner branches until he got down to ones of sufficient thickness for firewood, while Karl, with the longer saw blade, severed the base of the tree from the ragged place where it had broken off, then started cutting the thick trunk into four-foot segments. In this manner, Kris and Karl began to move the large tree from the ridge to the river valley, piece by piece.

Of course, ordinary conversation was impossible during those times when the chainsaws were running full-force. However, during the long interludes when they were loading logs, skiing back to deposit their payload, or returning with the empty sled, Kris and Karl had plenty of time for some good, old-fashioned woodpile reckoning.

*   *   *

"I reckon," said Karl, hefting ripening firewood and grinning beneath his thick woolen toque, "I surprised you somewhat with my choice of companion today."

"What, the chainsaw? Hey, I already knew all about you two; you brag it up every chance you get...**Oh**, you must mean Vicki, right?"

"Damn straight," said Karl, ignoring Kris' goofiness for the most part (but fondly eyeing his idling Stihl). "I was going to say that you would've been about the only Skagwegian who didn't know about us, other than those living under a rock—or Dyea Gary, but of course he's a few thousand miles away." He shook his head in a fate-pondering way.

"You know, I **had** been kind of wondering how Gary would feel about this arrangement—or how he's going to feel, once he actually returns."

Karl looked Kris in the eye. "To be honest, I think he'd be pretty easy with it, at least as far as this Winter is concerned. Of course, it might be another story when he comes back—but on the other hand, I don't particularly recall any sort of vow between him and Vicki in the first place."

Kris thought of his own lack of a "formal" bond with Genna, contrasted with the ongoing incredible, gangbusters nature of their relationship—and the fact that, even in his limited experience, there were moments that felt undeniably, comfortably matrimonial. He felt that this was at odds with the seemingly free-and-easy nature of whatever was going on between Vicki and her two suitors. "It sounds as if you have the stereotypical Alaskan relationship going, Karl—you know, ten guys for every girl—but that doesn't mean I particularly understand it. Especially considering what's happening with me and Genna."

"You think **I** understand it any better? Hell, man: I **have** to go with the flow, or face an empty bed all Winter long. Been there, done that, no thanks." Karl paused, looking as philosophical as a man wrestling a heavy fir log can look. "But don't get me wrong: my type of situation doesn't mean that modern love is dead and gone in rural Alaska. Things are just different here. Always have been."

"Still, I'd like to think that Genna and I are more than just 'kids on a joyride', to quote our favorite mechanic/philosopher."

Karl visibly grimaced. "You know, I've spent entire **months** trying to get Klaus out of my head. Gee, thanks. But seriously: I can see what's happening between you two—and I can tell that she wouldn't ditch you for the first chainsaw-totin', Australian rugby-playin' stud to come around. Unlike some I could mention," he added, glancing fondly in the direction of the cabin.

"Well, congratulations on whatever it is you two have cooking: romance, survival mechanisms or whatever."

"You're too young to be a cynic, Kris: it doesn't become you." Karl laughed. "But you've hit the nail on the head about the survival part. As you've figured out by now, getting through the Winter in one piece, physically and mentally, is the name of the game. First and foremost, there are the basics to consider: staying warm, having enough food, protecting yourself. You can't just ignore them, or assume they'll be taken care of for you by some unseen hand.

"Only when you've taken care of these things can you move on to quality-of-life issues. Of course, there are plenty of people wintering in the Alaskan bush who **never** even get that far: all of their time is spent taking care of the essentials, so they simply do without any social niceties whatsoever. Some make it through the winter okay—with at least a scrap of sanity left—others don't. It depends on the individual."

Karl, taking a break from the task at hand, peeled the toque from his heavily-perspiring head and stuffed it into his back pocket. He produced a suspicious metal flask from deep within his coveralls, and took a hard pull. "But if you're so fortunate as to get beyond the basics, the sanity-keeping rule of thumb is 'Whatever It Takes'. I knew a guy who got a job one winter as the watchman for some placer mining operation, up near Fairbanks. They provided him with a shack and tons of firewood, so his basics were all taken care of. But he had to stay there from September till the following May, all winter long. And, it gets down to sixty below around there. So, this guy kept an ancient Malamute in the shack with him: the dog had to be at least fifteen years old. Over the course of the winter, he wrote a book of poetry: **Old Dog**. Had it printed up and everything. He used to try and sell 'em on his tours the next summer."

"So, did you ever catch a glimpse of this work?"

"Can't say that I did. Can't say that I'd care to. But you know, the guy was all smiles that summer, was ready to go back and do it all again—then the dog up and died on him. And, I don't think the world would be ready for a book called **Old Dead Dog**."

Karl shrugged. "Now, anywhere else, that'd all be pretty dang weird. But around here, people don't really give a rip about that sort of thing. It's the same thing with me and Vicki: if I were just about anywhere else, I'd say that's a pretty crappy thing to do to a friend like Gary—regardless of Vicki's role in the situation. But right here, in this particular Winter, I don't feel like I have to make any apologies to anyone. *Comprendé?*"

"Hey, Bud: you don't have to explain yourself to **me**. I reckon your brother Derek would say that you're beyond understanding, anyhow."

Karl grinned at this, tossing his hipflask to Kris. *Who the hell am I to judge,* Kris thought to himself as he took a hit of what seemed to be Irish whiskey. "Bushmill's?"

"Close: Jameson's. It tastes like peaches." *Maybe peaches flambé,* Kris thought—but then, in a moment, he thought more of warmed peaches over vanilla ice cream. He took another shot, then appreciatively handed the flask back to Karl: "Tasty."

After skiing down with the current load and stacking the round in the growing woodpile, they turned and headed back up the hill once more with the sled. "In any event," commented Karl, as if the prior conversation had never ended, "you're shaping up to be a fine sourdough, Kris, from the looks of things. Hell, you're even got the round worn-out spot in your jeans pocket. What are you: a Copenhagen man?"

"Actually, I'm a Carmex man: I carry it around to keep my lips from cracking and falling off. But thanks for noticing."

"Hey, the **look** is half the battle: it means they'll move over and clear a seat for you at the bar in town. Of course, your lack of shower facilities help in that regard, too." Karl chuckled, a deep rumbling sound. "So, what do you think? Could you make this a lifestyle?"

"I could make **this** a lifestyle: ready-made cabin, ready-made girlfriend in residence. As far as 'real' Alaskan backwoods homesteading is concerned: well, that might be a whole 'nother ballgame."

"I must admit, you got lucky on **all** counts. They just don't make too many like Genna: in Alaska, or anywhere else." Karl shook his head appreciatively. "But regardless, good luck even finding a piece of land like this available for basic homesteading, much less something with any kind of cabin on it."

"You know, that's about what I figured. My understanding is that actually staking a piece of land and laying claim to it is pretty near impossible anymore. Exactly why, I'm not quite clear: but my guess is that it has something to do with government entities—federal, state or tribal— owning about ninety percent of the state."

"That's my understanding, too—plus the fact that the bulk of Alaska is flat-out uninhabitable: this corner of the state is the Garden of Eden compared to all that muskeg and frozen tundra up North. Most, if not all, of the really good places are long since spoken for—and by that, I mean places where one could actually hack out some kind of living from the land. You can't eat scenery."

Karl paused in the ski trail, gazing out over a vast expanse of forest and mountains that, to his and anyone's eye, looked utterly free and unpeopled. "But it's not as if I still don't dream about that sort of thing. Every so often, I'll put in for one of those land 'lotteries' they run out of Anchorage. In those cases, the state or the BLM will release a certain parcel of public lands and hold a drawing for homestead plats, subject to the usual proving-up requirements. But the odds of winding up with a choice piece of land that way are about like those of winning a 'real' lottery: slim to none.

"And **that's** why," he concluded, grinning like a balding, grey-tinged wolf, "I'm proud to be the next best thing to a homesteader: a **squatter**."

"You know, I was wondering about your living arrangement out there: you didn't strike me as the land-baron type."

"Hey, folks have been camping out in the river flats north of town just about forever: since well before the Gold Rush, I'm sure. You see tents, old school-buses, trailers like mine—even people just sleeping under a tree when the weather's decent. I've yet to see any rangers collecting fees at the camp entrance, or private landowners chasing people off—and good luck to 'em if they ever **tried** something like that."

"Seems to me," commented Kris, sizing up Karl and realizing how tough it would be to budge him from just about anything, "that you and the others out there are living a modern-day version of the 'Alaskan Dream': you know, show up somewhere, announce 'I'm here,' and dare anyone to knock you off the land, or to stop you from where you're going. Technically, it may not be possible for most folks to homestead anymore, but the basic jist of what they're doing is not much different from what went on in the old days."

"That's pretty close," admitted Karl. "In so many words." Reaching the downed fir again, he pulled his chain saw from its dry resting place and blew a bit of corn snow from the casing. Soon the saw's off-key roar filled the woods again, and Kris' Husqvarna shortly joined in the cacophony.

The considerable weight of the tree, most of which bore down on the trunk, made Karl's cutting tricky. Using the tip of his saw, he would cut out a small wedge from the tree's underside, not quite halfway through it; then, he would cut straight down through the top side, just to the point where he could feel the weight of the tree shifting; then, he would stand back as the trunk would snap off like a toothpick. "Haven't lost a saw blade yet," he told an admiring Kris, with no particular humility.

When their heads finally began to ring from the noise, they ceased the cutting and, shutting down their saws for a breather, resumed the track of their conversation. "Speaking of town squatters and hangers-on," said

Karl, "you ever hear of the 'Ice-Bucket Pool Shark'? Here was a guy who started out from somewhere with his head on his shoulders, but lost it somewhere along the way—or maybe shortly after arriving here. Of course, he immediately fell in with the local 'marmot brigade': you know, the bushwhackers who were making a go of it out here in Dyea, which of course included our friend Gary. Well, this new guy threw together a little shack around here somewhere, and spent most of his time just runnin' around the woods barefoot, summer and winter. He fit right in.

"Whenever he got to feelin' too bushy, he would walk or hitch onto town, still barefoot—rain, shine or snow—and would inevitably wind up at the Onion. If you ever wanted to go catch some 'local color' at the bar, as a tourist or as an alternative to television, he was it: the real deal.

"One of his favorite things to do was to challenge someone to a friendly game of pool: usually someone he hadn't seen before, who might've made some comment about his particular lack of footwear. Therefore, the catch to the game was that both contestants not only had to play barefoot, but also with one of their feet in a bucket of **ice** water. To even things up, I guess.

"I can hardly remember a funnier thing than to see some big out-of-towner—someone who likely came to Skagway figuring himself to be a real bad-ass—whimpering, with his foot turning blue in a five-gallon bucket, begging for mercy while his opponent oh-so-slowly cleared the balls from the table."

"You know," said Kris, laughing at the image, "I've **heard** of stuff like that happening around here, but I've yet to see it. I guess I picked a pretty tame winter to hang around Skagpatch. So, what ever happens to guys like that? Why don't you see them around anymore?"

"Well, sometimes you do, actually: this story isn't finished yet. Mr. Ice-Bucket may be seen to this day: in fact, he went on to become 'Hizzoner' himself: the mayor of Skagway."

"You've got to be kidding."

"I'm not kidding. Turns out that this crazed coot was a well-educated one: engineering degree from some Eastern school, reasonably articulate when he wasn't howlin' at the moon. Like a lot of people, he just had some wild 'n wooly to work out of his system. But, in his case, it never **did** work out all the way—just enough to prepare him for a promising political career."

"Alaskan politics seems full of folks like that," commented Kris. "Where else could a self-declared 'bush rat' such as Jay Hammond get elected governor? And, I'm sure that plenty more bona-fide Alaskan char- acters are spread out all across the spectrum of elective office statewide."

"And across the spectrum of 'extreme', too. In the state legislature, on the city and town councils, in any place where a warm body or two gets together to decide something of public significance, you'll more often than not see an improbable, seemingly incompatible mix of politics: the most unabashed tree-huggers jammed together with square-headed logger/survivalists. Academic dropouts rubbing worn-out leather elbow patches with transplanted big-city suits—not to mention your suburban Volvo and Subaru-types. They're plenty vocal about their differences, make no mistake, but somehow they all co-exist—and sometimes manage even to get things done. Statewide, the only common political link seems to be **independence**: not only as a personal trait, but even as a goal unto itself."

"I've actually heard something about people who want to take that independence thing to a real extreme: I mean, to the point of actually wanting Alaska to secede from the rest of the country. What do you know about that?"

"One of my favorite subjects. You've been warned." Karl paused, looked around him; saw the extent of downed fir that remained, and realized that there was still far too much to cut and drag away in one afternoon. "This tree isn't going anywhere for a while, is it?" Kris, catching his drift, allowed that it was likely to stay put for some time;

he laid aside his saw and pulled up a stump, within easy reach of Karl's proffered booze flask.

Karl, clearing his throat, began to speak once more: "Well now. The Alaskan Independence Party. Run by a guy named Joe Vogler, who is about what you would expect: a curmudgeon among curmudgeons; a guy who makes William Burroughs look like Richard Simmons. He and his buddies—miners and trappers, mostly—had been carping for years about how the federal government had been taking away their God-given right, as they saw it, to take a living from the land. Not just from the sheer ownership standpoint—you know, all the parks, national forests and whatnot—but by how the attempts to administer everything came from thousands of miles away: from persons who'd never set foot in Alaska, much less understood it."

"Well, harking back to my college education, for what it's worth—God, it seems like a long time ago, anymore—that sounds like just the thing any garden-variety libertarian might talk about: you know, a far-distant, ineffectual seat of power necessitating localized means of practical decision-making, thereby fostering self-determination as to **all** public matters."

"**Whew**: I'm just a simple rugby player, Kris—but I think I know what you're saying. My reckoning is that, historically, Alaska more or less unofficially ran itself, as far as practical matters were concerned. In the territorial days, there was a perception of this Great White Father out there, somewhere—but real federal control was catch-as-catch-can. And of course, there was no state structure to fill in the gaps until 1959. However, even after statehood, the mood in Juneau seemed to be of a laissez-faire bent: aside from encouraging the multi-nationals in their widespread plundering of natural resources, they mostly left the far-flung reaches to their own business.

"Eventually, into this lack of state action stepped an increasingly pervasive and activist federal government: this would have been the late

'60s, of course. And, from that time forward, the largest single pieces of legislation that have directly impacted the way of life in rural Alaska—ANSCA and ANILCA,[18] to name a couple—have all been federal."

"For a simple rugby player, you seem to know an awful lot about this, Karl."

"It's all the time I've spent hanging around the fringes of the Bigger Hammer: anything you'd care to know about Alaskan politics, you can learn there. Anyhow, in a nutshell: while Alaska's state politicians were off squabbling in a town, Juneau, that they couldn't even drive out of, the Feds, in the name of active government, began doing things like flying over BLM land and trying to drive out Bush squatters and would-be homesteaders: in some cases, folks who had been out there for years.

"Which brings us back to Vogler. A few years back, he helped round up a fair amount of his curmudgeonly energy into a more-or-less political organization: the Alaskan Independence party. The key plank of their platform, from day one, has been secession: no half-assed territorial or commonwealth status, but totally independent nationhood."

"**Wow**."

"That's what a lot of people would say, if they thought it had a realistic chance of succeeding, or if they took Vogler half-seriously. But a surprising amount of voters do—or they at least go for the secession concept, if they don't quite embrace the movement's figurehead. The AIP has regularly pulled double figures in elections statewide, including the governorship. That's pretty exciting: name me another political third party that's managed to pull **that** off recently."

---

18. The Alaska Native Claims Settlement Act (1971) distributed large portions of Alaska's land, both state and federal, to various Native regional groupings, as well as creating the present-day structure of Native "corporations"; the Alaska National Interest Lands Conservation Act (1980) set aside very large tracts of "public interest" land for parks and other federally administered units. Among the immediate effects of ANILCA was the quadrupling in size of Denali National Park.

"I take it, then, that you might be somewhat favorably disposed towards this idea?"

"Damn betcha: I've put in my vote for 'em every time I've had the opportunity. Just think about it: how great it would be if Alaskans could call the shots on all the big issues. Fisheries. Forests. And the big one: land use and development."

"How about international relations? Not to get all Political Science-y on you again, but it seems to me that, in the event of secession, Alaska would have way more in common with the Russian far east, Scandinavia and other trans-polar lands than it would with the Lower 48. Climate, indigenous cultures, the social issues endemic to a far-flung, winter-chilled population: there's a lot there. Hell, Anchorage is on almost the exact same latitude as Oslo, Stockholm, Helsinki, St. Petersburg. That says quite a lot for commonalties right there."

"And, don't forget that Alaska is only about three miles away from the Soviet Union, at the Diomede Islands. That's the big hang-up, in my mind: do you think that the U.S. is going to break out of that Cold War mind-set any time soon, and give up a piece of land as strategic as Alaska without a fight?"

"Well, I s'pose the Russians could try giving America's money back: you know, the $7.2 million."[19]

"Very funny. But consider this: Alaska also has a hell of a lot of nukes sitting on its soil. Ever read the book 'Ecotopia': you know, the ultimate '70s granola manifesto? The Pacific Northwest secedes from the U.S. to form its own politically correct, eco-groovy society—but they actually use

---

19. In 1867, Alaska was purchased by the United States from the Russians for the amazingly paltry sum of $7.2 million. However, this bargain was strongly ridiculed at the time by the American public, who dubbed the acquisition "Seward's Folly" (for Secretary if State William Henry Seward, who engineered the purchase).

nuclear blackmail to achieve this end. Not that I would actually **suggest** such a thing, but…"

"You're a dangerous radical, Karl. But somebody also told me once that, if North Dakota were to secede from the United States, it would instantly become the world's third-largest nuclear superpower. Tell you what: the day that Fargo becomes a seat of world domination, I'd be strongly inclined to support Alaska's efforts to do the same."

"We can always use another good soldier, Kris: you're absolutely welcome in the revolution." Karl curled his meaty fist in a vintage power salute, then leaned back against the tree truck and laughed, taking another hit of burning-peach whiskey.

Kris, wondering at the direction that the day's woodpile replenishing had taken, laughed as well. *Hmmm, Karl as revolutionary leader: a pan-Arctic, considerably bulked-up Che Guevara? We could do far worse, I suppose.* He was lost in thought for a long moment before speaking again: "Well, whomever ends up running Alaska would do well to live out here in the country for a time—for a winter, at least. I just don't see how you could responsibly run the state—or the independent commonwealth, or whatever—without understanding what makes 99% of the place tick: its **natural** rhythms. All of that international intrigue makes for fine discussion fodder, but in the end what matters most about Alaska is its essential, wild nature. That's what the future leaders, whomever they might turn out to be, must fight to keep, above everything else."

"Uh oh," rejoined Karl, "do I smell an emerging eco-warrior?"

"I don't know. All I know is that I've become acquainted with this little patch of woods like no other place. I feel that I personally know every tree, every rock, every fox den in the neighborhood—and I've only been here a few months. That knowledge would just keep growing—and my love for the place surely would as well—the longer I stayed here. Just imagine how attached the 'real' homesteaders get to their land, over a lifetime of getting to know it in every detail, in every season.

"And, you can bet that, with very few exceptions, they feel a high degree of **responsibility** for the land: as the ones with the greatest capacity to move it and shake it, and of course to wreck it as well. Every move they make to 'live off' the land must be informed by this knowledge: if they ruin it, they ruin a central part of themselves. It's not just ethics, it's common sense. And it's **personal**." Kris leaned towards Karl. "Now, what if everyone, somehow, could take responsibility like that…"

"'C'mon people now, smile on your brother'," quoted Karl from ancient memory. "I'm afraid that I've seen way too many greedy bastards out in the Bush to share all of your enthusiasm. Too many cases of 'use it up, throw it out'. But you're right, in principle: a widespread sense of personal responsibility, however it might happen, would have to help Alaska in the long run." He paused, looking Kris in the eye. "You know, charity begins at home, buddy. What will **you** do after you leave here: turn your tours into your own environmental education forum?"

"Actually, that's not a bad idea. But, I don't really **know** how my tours will turn out now. They've always been shaped primarily by personal experience, so I'm sure that a lot of this particular adventure will sneak out next summer, one way or another. However, I've also heard any number of warnings, both official and unofficial, about turning a tour-bus microphone into a bully pulpit: you're bound to offend someone, and if word gets out to management that you're bucking the company line— well, game over, man."

"How well I know," said Karl. "That's one of the big reasons why I got out of the business. Hell, as 'local color', I get to shoot my mouth off all I want. It's great."

"That **is** an advantage," agreed Kris. "But you know, speaking of getting in trouble: I bet the ladies back home are wondering whether a tree fell on us, or what."

"In **my** case," said Karl, "some might consider that an improvement." Standing and stretching, he retrieved his chainsaw, secured it to the day's final load of logs with a bungee cord, and strapped on his ski gear; Kris did the same. As they hit the ski trail again, towards the sauna and warmth and waiting girlfriends, Karl, after a prolonged stretch of silence, spoke once more:

"I don't mean to rain on your optimism, Kris. I've just been around the block a few more times than you: albeit the same block sometimes, and for far too long. Actually, you've got a fair amount of perspective for someone your age: definitely more than I did, back when I was knocking heads together for a living. So, don't let an old fart like me screw up your thinking too much."

Karl looked thoughtful, and a little wistful. "You know, I can remember, back when I was about your age, Neil Young's song 'Old Man' coming out: 'Old man, look at my life, I'm a lot like you were...'. At the time, I couldn't even begin to imagine what it'd be like to be pushing forty, looking back and taking stock of my life. I couldn't see, like Neil could, myself thinking that way: about myself getting older. And now—without my hardly noticing it—I **am** that age..."

How To Take A Snow Bath

▼

"February is the month carved entirely from Mickey Mouse's snout."

—Tom Robbins

Q: What did the Alaskan say to the Pillsbury Doughboy?
A: Nice tan!

—Alaskan wintertime joke

It was a cold, gray early-February afternoon: temperatures mired in the single digits, spiky ice crystals spitting from the sky. Not a day to spend outdoors. The snow was high, about halfway up the windows. It had been this way for about a week—and things were getting a little close in the cozy Dyea cabin.

"Here, moosie moosie," commented Genna as she caught a whiff of Kris walking past.

"Yeah, right," replied Kris, testily. "And **you**, of course, are as fresh as a daisy."

Genna came up behind Kris, put her hands on his shoulders, spoke into his ear. "I'm starting to get that '30-foot stare,' my man." Her hands slipped up around his neck, gave it a few loving throttles. "I'd say it's definitely time for a snow bath."

"Huh? Is this another one of your wacky Alaskan customs? Are you **kidding?**"

"Yes and no. It is customary, primarily amongst us plumbing-free, sub-Arctic types. Yes, it is wacky. No, I'm not kidding: it really does get you clean. And rejuvenated, besides."

Ordinarily, Kris and Genna bathed when they were saunaing: a bucket of river water brought into the cedar hut for warming, a few quick rinses outside the door. However, the sauna took a couple of hours to heat up—as well as burning a lot of fuel. Even though the woodpile had looked like the Alamo back in the Fall, by mid-February it was looking rather finite, with a lot of Winter yet to go. Saunas were now a treat, rather than an everyday luxury.

Genna seemed surprisingly eager to be the Snowbath Instructor. She noted that, unlike most ordinary bathing, this was strictly a two-person enterprise: "It'll foster **togetherness.**" With some trepidation, Kris consented to being the bathee.

1) Fill bucket, teapot, large can or other heatable water receptacle; warm on stovetop until the water is a comfortable bathing temperature.

Kris and Genna always kept a container of water warming on the woodstove: primarily for washing dishes and adding humidity to the cabin air. They fetched this water from the river (fast-moving portions of which, surprisingly, stayed open through the Winter), in a vintage, World War II-surplus jerry can, inherited from Dyea Gary.

Due to the stretch of cold weather, the woodstove had been cranking away at high power for quite some time. The jerry can was humming perky sounds to itself.

**2) Fetch shampoo, soap, rubber duck and other bathing imple-
ments; while still inside cabin, strip nekkid—except for thick socks
and mukluks, to avoid adhering to frozen footpaths.**

Kris quickly got down to basics. Genna amusedly pointed out the
instantaneous shrinkage problem: frequently, attributable to cold
and/or fear.

"Okay okay **okay**." Kris pulled on his oversized, fuzzy mukluks by the
door. "So remind me: why do I have to wear **these?**"

"Try this barefoot sometime, Bubba. You'll find out why."

**3) Once nekkid, fling open cabin door; sprint for the nearest clean
(i.e., non-yellow) snowbank. Have your friend bring the water (take it
easy, now; don't want to spill any).**

Arctic air hit Kris and his various appendages—which he dearly loved,
and hoped would not freeze and fall off. Cupping his hands in a protective
position, he made a Chaplin-esque dash towards the woodpile:

"Yi, yi, yi, yi, **yipe!**"

Genna followed with shampoo and jerry can, walking much too slowly.

**4) Upon reaching snowbank, stop—but keep shuffling feet, so they
do not adhere to the ground. Have your friend pour warm water over
your head and body: enough to wet everything. Lather up, quickly.**

Kris shuffled all the way to Buffalo and back. Nonetheless, his mukluks
did the Velcro Fly on the packed snow. The soles of his feet were already
going numb.

Then, Genna poured the warm (maybe a mite too hot) water over his
head. It cascaded, steaming, down his winter-white body—and, amazingly, did not form instant icicles. Genna picked up the shampoo and
squeezed a generous splort onto Kris' head.

"Lather up!"

5) For maximum scrubbing effect, grab handfuls of snow; scour body hard enough to induce tingling and severe bodily pinkness—but not blood. Once lathered and scrubbed, have your friend douse you with enough water to rinse away all the bubbles and whatnot.

Kris grumbled though his sudsy Afro and beard. "My God: **whose** idea was this, anyway?"

"Isn't this **great**? Think I'll join you." In a twinkling, Genna was out of her Winter layers: seemingly, for the first time since early November (most bodily functions—peeing, nookie, *et cetera*—being convenienced by trapdoors). Kris' smart-ass rejoinder about "shrinkage problems" remained frozen in his mouth as Genna thrust the jerry can into his hands and implored him to pour, **now**.

Genna lathered up, grabbed a handful of snow, formed an impromptu scrubber and raked it down Kris' back. Kris quickly reached down and did the same, but planted his snow-scrubber on top of Genna's head. Genna grabbed the jerry can and more or less upturned it onto both of them.

A nearby raven sat transfixed in a tree crotch, flabbergasted at the spectacle of white, whooping, lathering humans. For once, he was at a loss for words.

6) For maximum bodily attention-getting effect, jump into the snowbank (if soft enough), roll around a few times.

"Wait, we're not through yet." Genna's voice was a brave squeak. She peered around at the high, white heaps and banks like a snowbound marmot. "That one looks large and fluffy enough. Don't think we stashed any wood under there. Sure hope not."

Genna grabbed Kris' hand, and before he had time to think or object, they had plunged into the fresh snowbank.

FWOOOMP!!

(brief, very cold whiteness)

"**Yipe**! Yi yi yi yi!"

7) Sprint, screaming, back indoors: to a dry, fluffy towel and warm fireside. Remove socks and/or mukluks, once they have thawed sufficiently.

They leaped from the snowbank and dashed back towards the cabin, bathing supplies momentarily forgotten. The cabin door slammed.

They cleared all remaining snow from their bodies and parked themselves before the stove. They did little shivering dances as their bodies thawed from blue to white. But then, pinkness took over—along with an incredible, tingling sensation that radiated sweetly from head to toe, as if their whole bodies were applauding them.

For a time, they enjoyed the sensation in silence. Then, Genna spoke up with a laugh:

"When you came up out of the snowbank, Kris, you looked just like the Bumble: you know, the Abominable Snowman from the old 'Rudolph the Red-Nosed Reindeer' TV special. Frosty, hairy and **very** white."

"Well, 'Bumbles **bounce**,' as Yukon Cornelius once said. I sure as hell bounced right up from that snow." Kris shook his head, but could not get rid of the big, full-body grin that had crept up on him along with the tingles. "And by the way: I noticed even **you** were screaming during the snowbank part, Alaska Woman."

"Well, uh, yeah. It's therapeutic, a release: part of the *gestalt* of the whole experience, you know?"

Genna was utterly unconvincing—but glowing so pinkly, with radiant good health, that Kris instantly forgave this and all future transgressions.

JOURNAL ENTRY: 2/15/89 (24TH BIRTHDAY)

▼

"In February, it will be
my snowman's anniversary..."

—Maurice Sendak, **Chicken Soup With Rice**

what can you do but fall
in love as your woman
kneads the morning bread: you kiss the back of
her neck as her hands play like dolphins
in the dough-bowl
    as she stokes the woodstove,
    late at night when all the lights are out,
    flickering shadows off the
    curves of her body reminiscent of
    fantastic natural architecture:
        the forest cathedral,
        the deerness of the deer
I know, she said, tonight we'll have a party: you bring
the firewood, i'll bring the warmth and

the wild and the life inside;
we'll laugh and love and
dance till the cookies are done

Café Society

▼

The usual motley assemblage of local color filled the Bigger Hammer Café one fine Saturday morning in late February. All manner of flannel, fur and holy denim sprawled with Rive Gauche *nonsouciance* across the booths; there was not an empty spot in the house. Vicki the waitress floated and darted like Muhammad Ali in his prime; the fry cook, a huge Samoan (also the café owner), executed his short and long orders with the speed and deftness of a surgeon.

Holding forth at an honorary window booth, tending to vital city business, was Hizzoner himself, "Mr. Ice-Bucket." He was arguing some arcane point of governance with Wheatgerm, stabbing his hash-browns for emphasis as the rest of the entourage looked on, bemused and ketchup-spotted. Not too far away, a table of four church ladies tsk-tsked under their breath, but didn't allow the roar and flutter to ruin their tea-and-toast service. Huddled at the luncheon counter, grinning furrily like the co-conspirators they were, were Karl and his new-found friend, Douglas Fir. Doug had remained in the area after his visitation with Kris and Genna—not only because he enjoyed the area, but also to avoid re-subjecting his moose-brown VW Van (and frequent residence), Bullwinkle, to the sub-zero climes of the Fairbanks bush. Having fashioned a sort of yurt in the woods upstream of town, he was now a neighbor and co-slacker of Karl's.

Karl, gigantic in his New Zealand All-Blacks shirt, coatless and clean-shaven—he tended to be a furnace, even in the most inclement weather—was enjoying a tofu scramble and hot Lemon Zinger; Doug, hirsute as Lon Chaney in a full moon, potato-like nose evidencing latent frostbite, was sawing into a chicken-fried steak, with a side of gravy-smothered biscuits. Karl was telling Doug about one Winter in the rugby leagues Down Under, when he'd had a Korean girlfriend, and had gotten into the habit of eating a big bowl of *kimchee* right before games, then huffing the fumes into the queasy faces of the opposition as they were about to scrum. "My most successful season," he declared.

Doug countered with a story of how, deep in the wilds of some Humboldt County evening, he'd enjoyed some local combustibles, concluded that he loved everybody, and circled the room giving heartfelt, soulful hugs—until, amidst one tofu-scrambling embrace, he'd heard an awful crunching sound; he'd collapsed to the floor in tears, convinced that he'd broken someone's ribs—before someone pointed out the goldfish-cracker crumbs dusting from his down-vest pocket. "Takes one to know one," he concluded amiably.

At a well-worn booth along the rear wall, the special Tour Guide spot of summers past, sat Kris and Genna. Genna was wearing her long flannel gunny-sack dress, the one she sometimes used as a nightgown, topped off by an old-fashioned, Canadian Army surplus earflap toque, which she fondly called her "fool's cap." Indeed, on just about anyone else, the flaps-down look would have been highly foolish, but on Genna it was downright cute, in a "Rocky the Flying Squirrel" way.

Kris wasn't particularly *en costume* for the occasion, having simply pulled on some Carhartt coveralls and boots over his long skivvies. However, he'd had a sauna bath and river-dunk that very morning; his hair was combed; his beard was free of leaves, twigs and other detritus;

overall, he was of more than sufficient respectability to make the social visit to town.

He and Genna had taken to coming into Skagpatch every Saturday morning, as roads and weather allowed. It was mighty pleasant to drop by the Bigger Hammer, chat with Vicki, enjoy a magnum or two of coffee and a leisurely breakfast while watching the entire town go by, more or less.

"It's like a river," said Kris. "It's like the salmon; it's like a busy corner in Manhattan."

Genna had never been to New York, had never evidenced any particular desire to go there, but allowed as to the aptness of Kris' metaphor. She had brought a bag of knitting, and was just working on the final toe reinforcement for one of two moosey-sized wool socks. Kris, and just about everyone on Genna's gift list, had already been the beneficiary of some lovely snowflake-pattern mittens that Winter; he was happy to spring for more yarn and whatnot, whenever he swung by the mercantile.

Meanwhile, over his blueberry sourdough hotcakes, Kris was sorting through their weekly stack of mail. Among the contents were: the latest newsletter from KRBD-FM, Kris' radio *alma mater* in Ketchikan; a cruise brochure from the touring company; a funding solicitation, from Kris' university ("They assume that I'm already a financial success," commented Kris, with some amusement); the March 1989 issues of National Geographic, Mother Earth News and Volleyball Digest; catalogs from L.L. Bean and Territorial Seeds; finally, an artfully-lettered envelope from Genna's mom, which Kris promptly handed over to his breakfast companion.

"Another typical Winter in Tok," remarked Genna after paging through the contents. "Ice fog and frozen fuel lines; a collection of stranded travelers, over-Wintering in the Airstream trailer; fresh moose tracks in the morning; the best Northern Lights in years, viewed at fifty below; plenty of gossip-worthy social doings. Mom misses me, though."

"Well, you're her girl: always were, always will be. I'm just thankful she relinquished her exclusive rights."

"'Relinquished', my fur-lined patootie." Genna bumped her muddy Sorels against Kris' shins. "You're just a more practical choice for the Winter, that's all. You're better at warming up the bed, scaring away predators. Only thing that separates you from the grizzlies these days, in fact, is that you take **out** the garbage."

Kris took this affirmation of love for what it was, chewed his reindeer sausage in appreciation. *Look at us: we're like an old married couple.*

As Genna buzzed and cooed over the Nat Geo cover—aptly, a full-on portrait of a lovely female sea otter, with pups aboard—Kris leafed through the company cruise brochure. "You know, just one more summer of tour-guiding, and I get a free cruise. Excuse me, **we** get a cruise: the freebie comes with guest provisions, of course. Can you imagine, though, at this time next year, us sailing through the waters of Barbados or Martinique?"

Genna studied her Cajun hashbrowns for a moment, took a bite. "To be honest," she said, chewing, "that **is** a little hard for me to visualize; in my mind, I could just about as easily cruise the lovely seas of Venus." She set down her fork. "But the bigger question, my well-traveled sweetie, is this: where do we see ourselves a year from now? Will we still be in some kind of position where we'll be able to just pick up and go somewhere in mid-Winter, for a couple weeks of sloth and decadence?"

"Sloth and decadence, I'm good at. But you have a point: who knows what exactly will happen this Summer, much less next February. And, I'm afraid I just don't do much living in the future anymore—or, by extension, living in the past."

"What do you mean?"

"Another damn good question. What I think I'm trying to say is that, in the past, I was governed to a large extent by all these self-imposed expectations about my life, all these specific future goals. I'd graduate from college, start down some highly meaningful career path, and by some self-designated age would have a certain amount of success—income, job title, academic publication, whatever. Wife and kids, I suppose, too."

"Sounds like your parents talking there."

"Well, it was all I really knew, in terms of trying to visualize my future. But since coming to Alaska—and most particularly, spending all this **slow** time with you—I tend to live for the day, the moment. Yes, there are longer-term issues we'll have to face eventually, some sooner than later: what we'll do for a living, where we'll reside. But this morning, I'm enjoying a delicious breakfast, with someone I love..." Here, Kris could not resist an affectionate handsqueeze. "And, everything else will come in time."

Genna's face flushed, just a little bit. She took another small sip of English Breakfast. "You're right. Especially that some things will come sooner than later: Vicki tells me that rumblings have been heard from Dyea Gary. He might be on his way North again soon."

"To, ahem, reclaim his territory? I trust that Karl has been properly alerted." Kris, glancing over at his massive friend, was not particularly worried. *However, such an event stands to roust our cozy existence, as well...*

During this conversation, an old Ford half-ton pickup truck, with a fine homemade canopy over the long bed, had cruised south down Broadway, almost as unhurriedly as a Slow Bicycle Racer. It had drawn the admiring attention of some of the mayor's entourage, but had passed by with minimal comment. Now, a minute or so later, it reappeared, on the opposite side of the street, just across from the Bigger Hammer. The observers at the window heard the truck door slam: a solid sound.

Then, moments later, a fisher-person walked through the café door. He looked the part through and through, as if sent by Alaskan Central Casting: oiled boots, blue jeans, hooded sweatshirt cut off at the sleeves; a head of thick, curly blonde hair. He scanned the room side to side, front to back, as if trying to find someone. His reddish, Viking-looking beard split into a smile as he spotted Genna, then a broad grin as he saw Kris. He waved and quickly strode across the room, and Kris' jaw dropped in sudden recognition.

"Peter. Peter Helgeson. I'll be damned."

Cockpit Buddhism

▼

Even amidst the hubbub of the Bigger Hammer Café, the reunion was noticeably joyful and chaotic—causing the big Samoan fry-cook briefly to glance in Kris and Peter's direction before gathering the gist of things. Kris had not seen Peter since the latter's departure from Fairbanks, the summer before, and they had somehow slipped from all forms of contact since then. Kris and Genna, sequestered in their snowy locale, could only guess that Peter had ultimately left Alaska, for travel or work Outside, but had no real way of knowing. However, from the look of things, Peter had never left, and had in fact gotten into a new and adventurous situation.

"You have a **lot** of explaining to do," said Genna as she gave Peter a big flannel hug. Procuring another magnum of coffee, the threesome retired once again to the backwall booth, for some serious story-telling.

*　　　　　*　　　　　*

After I left Fairbanks, I tracked down Kim, who had just given notice at the Captain Cook. True to our original plans, we spent some time camping on the Kenai—the Homer Spit, Russian River, Skilak Lake—before winding up in

*Seward. After maybe a week there, I discerned that the commercial fishing scene on the peninsula wasn't quite as easy to break into as advertised, so I left Kim behind at her cousin's—it wasn't easy to leave—and hoofed it out to the airstrip, to catch one of those puddle-jumper flights to Kodiak. It wasn't even really a commercial airline—some kind of charter service that was making deliveries to Homer and Seldovia before making it out to the island. Of course, we weren't exactly jumping puddles—more like glaciers, jagged mountains, the Cook Inlet and the Gulf of Alaska. And, it was a **training** run.*

"It's all yours now." The flight instructor turned over the headset to the pilot, a tall, lanky young man of twenty or so. "This is a pretty standard takeoff," the instructor assured Peter. "You don't run out of land for a good half-mile down this direction. He'll want to hug the shoreline for a while, get as far south as he can before cutting straight over to Homer. It's best to avoid flying over the Exit Glacier: you'd give the tourists a thrill as you roller-coaster over the turbulence."

The young pilot nodded to the instructor, intent on getting a hundred and one details right while keeping a straight course onto the runway. He set up, the instructor said "Go," the plane accelerated in a more or less straight direction, and the Cessna grabbed onto some air and chinned itself up.

The mountains were leapfrogged in about an hour. At the base of the Kenai Peninsula, a long, thin tongue of land taste-tested the sea. A dirt road petered out among a group of shabby buildings and then looked somewhat sheepish. The Homer Spit.

Then, like a leaf out of the sky, another plane fluttered into Peter's vision. It settled into a descent just in front of them, so that Peter could nearly read the logo on the pilot's flight jacket. Peter's pilot sat bolt upright in his seat; the flight instructor's neck veins were the Alyeska Pipeline.

"He's too close...this never should have happened...he's way too close..." The two planes touched down within seconds of each other, like synchronized swimmers. It was probably a very nice exhibition for observers on the ground. The flight instructor said a few encouraging words to the rookie pilot as they braked at the end of the Homer runway, and few very choice words to the pilot of the other plane. The other pilot simply shrugged in apology: "That's the berries, eh." Everyone helped to load up more goods, to be flown across the final leg to Kodiak.

Peter was in need of encouragement, too, as the journey resumed. The flight instructor turned to him: "There's this inherent adventure to flying in Alaska, more so than just about anywhere else. How do we deal with it? Well, you know that old idea about 'foxhole Christians?' Around here, there are a lot of 'cockpit Buddhists': oftentimes the attitude before takeoff is, 'Well, see you in another lifetime.' There's only so much you can do about nature, weather, fate..." There was a lurch as the plane hit yet another cold-air surge.

"Well, um, yeah. I think back to the famous expression: 'In Alaska, there are old pilots, and bold pilots—but no old and bold pilots'..."

"You've got it."

After a considerable stretch above choppy waters, a chain of islands rose from the blue-gray. "Look, there's Afognak," said the flight instructor, "no one down there but a bunch of horny loggers. Just past it, the one where the trees quit, the one that looks like it's got a monk's haircut—that's Kodiak."

That first view of Kodiak made me think of Scotland—misty green hills, occasional evergreens, high and lonely. Stepping off the plane, the chill, wet wind felt like November on the North Sea, off the Shetlands or somewhere. It made me comprehend at last the northern end of the Pacific Ocean: from here on out it's Bristol Bay, the Bering Sea and finally the Arctic Ocean. The rest of Alaska is like this, for more than a thousand miles: closer to Japan than to Seattle, nearly its own nation, and a world apart.

"My theory," said the man at the urinal next to Peter's, "is that people fly into Kodiak, do whatever they need to do, come back here to the airport but discover that their flight out has been cancelled, due to bad weather. They check back in a couple hours, learn that things are still socked in; check again later, same thing. They have to stay the night, maybe in town, maybe on the airport floor; they wake up early, discover that it's pea soup again. They keep checking, and checking, and checking. Eventually, they give up, and just **stay** here. That's how Kodiak gets it population: from permanently stranded airline passengers."

Peter, taking the wholly unsolicited theory for what it was worth, zipped up, grabbed his backpack, and stepped outside into the wind and drizzle, to thumb a ride into town.

The downtown boat harbor was, of course, pure Alaska, albeit a corner I'd never seen before that day. Walking on the docks and past the canneries, I was surrounded by "real" Alaskans, in the standard uniform of beards, ponytails, flannel shirts and rubber boots. Soon, I knew I would be one of them.

600 Pounds Of Sin

▼

"So you left the girlfriend behind in Seward, to run off to Kodiak."
Genna shook her head. "You ditched Kim for a bunch of slimy halibut
and flounder."

"Hey, she'd been there, done that: a thousand times over. That's what
she grew up doing, for God's sake: all her childhood summers were spent
in one fish camp or another. So, she was perfectly content to let me go off
and have my adventure." Peter stroked his Wolf Larsen beard. "Doesn't
seem to have hurt our relationship, anyhow. We're still going strong; we
have plenty to talk about. Lots of shared experiences now."

*   *   *

*Upon entering the main floor of Trident Seafoods for the first time, I felt as
if I were crashing some fraternity party from Hell: well after midnight, everyone three sheets to the wind (or on the back side of forty), oblivious to the noise
and the stink, reaching way down inside for whatever it was that kept them
going. This particular "party" would end only when they ran out of fish: no
one would run down to the 7-11 for more.*

The foreman looked Peter up and down briefly, a glint of surprise faintly visible through the glazed expression. "They need another guy down on the slime line. You're it. Grab your gear and get your ass down there."

Learning the job required very little intellectual effort. Guide a monstrous, half-frozen, unspeakably slimy halibut down the conveyor belt; steer it towards the relentlessly sharp heading knives; brace the nonplused bottom-feeder as it entered the machine's gaping maw and lost its head. Repeat for twelve to eighteen hours. He eventually realized that this situation was not necessarily Hell: more like a chilly, smelly Purgatory.

Peter reached a stage where the work became purely automatic, almost intuitive. It was only then that he realized how much else was going on at the plant aside from the alleged work objective. Gossip was incessant, frequently nasty, and omnipresent: in the break room, in the shed where Native and Filipino women assembled boxes, on the landing where the boats unloaded onto the scales. So-and-so's romantic rendezvous behind the boiler room. Post-slime line, under the bar-stool braggadocio. Vicious squirt-gun ambushes, often escalating into Rambo-esque skirmishes. Plans to get the hell out of this place as soon as the necessary funds accumulated or the fog lifted, whichever came first. The surreptitious circulation of choice seafood morsels: the incidental catches of salmon and crab that would go skittering across the plant floor into someone's safekeeping (for a later feast) rather than being discarded, per the rules.

During the eleventh hour of one slime-line day, Peter's ruminations were interrupted by the sight and sound of a large tanner crab, speeding like a slapshot on its back, right at him. He was narrowly missed by the crustacean's flailing claws as it was expertly fielded by the worker next to him and stashed into a burlap sack.

The worker turned to Peter and smiled sheepishly. "Dinner," he said. "You're invited. My name's Frank. Bring beer."

Many hours later, Peter stepped off the freshly hosed plant floor, in a peculiarly euphoric, beyond-exhaustion state. He shortly joined other scungy-looking people in line at the market for a six-pack, and walked back through the light grey rain to the workers' dorms.

The crab was briskly boiling in a large dented pot, on a woodstove made from a 55-gallon oil drum. Fresh sourdough bread, piping hot and ripped into rough chunks, lay on a plate. Some newspapers were laid out on a wooden bench, in lieu of place settings, and Frank, Peter and several other newfound friends settled back for a feast. For a while they simply tended to the business of digging in. A little later, the normal all-night conversation ensued.

I don't even remember what most of the talk was all about: lost in the debris of another wasted evening. But there was one point made which I still find kind of poignant:

"Never thought I'd be able to look seafood in the face again, after my first day on the job," commented Peter. "But **damn**, this is good. Feel like I've earned it."

Frank's voice was quiet and deliberate. "I saw some ad for Red Lobster in the Anchorage paper a while back that said something like, 'Now, you don't have to suffer to taste Alaska.' What I wonder about is, do they even think about **who** does the suffering? Does one reach a point where one, with a clear conscience, can pay to avoid suffering in the cold and rain to enjoy fresh salmon and halibut?

"Do the fishermen consider themselves to be suffering? Do we, on the slime line, fit into this equation? Is the flavor of the fish somehow made more poignant by knowing of such hardship? What kind of 'suffering' do tourists, and everybody else, go through just to get to Alaska, or even to stay here—to realize their dreams?"

For the remainder of the job, Peter, with Frank's help, utilized two routes of escape: the Grateful Dead, and good old Matanuska Thunder-Fuck. While work conditions were conducive to some form of substance abuse—in some cases, to an alarming degree—Peter found that the herb relaxed him, without making him lose all his faculties, as well as placing the whole adventure into some kind of silly perspective. Certain vintage

Dead tunes and albums further enhanced these sensibilities: in particular, **Workingman's Dead**. "Dire Wolf," for example, was a cheerful, boingy little pedal-steel tune with an inexplicable story line (the Big Bad Wolf?) and the incongruous chorus, "Oh, please don't murder me..." After sixteen hours or more on the slime line, Peter was so tired that he could barely lift his arms, using his hips to push the fish into the blades. In the frequent hallucinatory moments, Peter saw the chorus line of headless halibut singing the refrain, in their goopy baritone voices: "I beg ya, please don't **mur**-der **meee**..."

Late at night in the bunkhouse, after several good hits of Matanuska Thunder-Fuck, Peter adapted his breathing to the shuffling beat of **Workingman's Dead**. Blue-collar breathing exercises: the Grateful Dead were doing the work for him.

> *"When I awoke the Dire Wolf, 600 pounds of sin*
> *was grinning at my window, all I said was 'come on in'..."*

INTO THE MYSTIC

▼

Kris was mildly amazed, and considerably amused, by Peter's vivid storytelling. "Slime-lines and substance abuse. You've been leading quite a different life, friend."

"Different from Seattle, that's for sure," Peter admitted. "Different from college: it all seems so long ago now. But not at all different from the way that a good number of people live on Kodiak. Or any other place in coastal Alaska, for that matter."

"Well, whatever you've been doing has served you well, if appearances are any indication. I'd say you've got the 'native' look down to a T." Kris paused, thinking of their friend Randy, whom they had visited in Haines during the Skagway summer—and Randy's startling evolution from Fine Young Man to local color. *Peter was always the one who used to joke about 'going native', and who didn't quite feel as though he were really in Alaska, or a part of it. Now look at him.* "Yeah: I guess we're **all** official sourdoughs now."

*   *   *

As is invariably the case on Kodiak, I came to a certain crossroads. I finally reached a point of no return regarding work in the packing plant: a point where one has either made a few friends in the area and/or on the boats, and realizes that other, more lucrative, less demoralizing fisheries employment exists—or one is fed up with the whole thing, cashes in and hopefully has enough for airfare off the island. Fortunately, through Frank I had met some locals, who not only offered me a house-sitting gig, but also a chance to crew for a while on a little purse-seiner. I gratefully chose this situation over the cannery—didn't really have enough savings to head home, even if I'd wanted to— gleefully told the line boss to 'take this job and shove it,' and never looked back. Moved in with Pat and Roger, and went fishing.

Suburban Kodiak: the homes were new and the streets were muddy; signs of recent prosperity were everywhere. Grass grew between heaps of netting and stacked crab pots in the front yards. Peter walked into a front door foyer, set his duffel bag on top of a violently shaking washing machine, stepped over a pile of yellow rubber outerwear, and called out his arrival.

Roger, nineteen years old, about three-quarters Koniag, returned his greeting, from the direction of the kitchen. In the sink he was busily gutting a chum salmon, a task which displaced a truckload of long-dirty dishes. "Got the smoker fired up," said Roger. "Still haven't decided what to make: cold-smoke it with that sweet stuff, the Indian sugar, or cook it down into jerky."

"I'd pass on the jerky," said Pat, coming into the room. "You need an oilier fish for that. Your chum'll turn into belt leather if you try to make squaw candy."

Pat's home was decorated in late-70's well-to-do divorcee fisherman: veneer walls, some fairly nice but already-thrashed furniture, Playboy calendar on the wall. Pat, although just in his early thirties, had bought the place outright several years back, with two seasons of Bering Sea crabbing earnings. "Never again," he had said. "Screw it, I'm set." These days, he drove a fuel-oil truck around the eastern end of the island, a fairly lucrative but laid-back job. In recent years, Pat had crossed between extremes of outlook and lifestyle: from the routine terror of winter seas to the mystic and fog and cool of Kodiak Island.

In fact, he had embraced the New Age. The pivotal conversation at the Mecca Bar between Peter, Frank and Pat had involved the malignant karma of Russian fur trappers; the Harmonic Convergence, as observed above town on Pillar Mountain ("the place we went to escape the tsunamis from the '64 quake"), the ups and downs of the crystal market around Anchorage, and Pat's upcoming return journey to Peru—to explore Macchu Picchu with some South American friends. Talk of the impending trip had led to the house-sitting offer, which Peter quickly accepted. "Okay. I like the look of you," Pat had said, smiling. He smiled a lot these days, as the rain and gurry-saturated streets of town had a tendency in his mind to dry up into steep Andean foot trails and llama byways.

Pat dodged the mess in the sink, made himself a peanut butter/banana sandwich, and drifted out the door, mumbling something about visiting his girlfriend, whom he called "Yummy." Peter and Roger gathered the pellucid chum flesh in a large Baggie and toted it out back. "This is 'bout the only thing to do with a chum: **smoke** the puppy," pronounced Roger as he loaded the fish and stoked the low flame. Similar smells wafted around the neighborhood; in lieu of backyard barbecues, suburbanites in Kodiak tended to congregate around their smokers on pleasant evenings. "But that ain't what we're gonna fish tomorrow. The silvers are coming in around Anton Larsen Bay. We'll go over early in the morning, do a couple sets. That should keep us in beer for a while."

As we rounded the northeast cape of Kodiak at about five the next morning, the dense spruce stands dwindled and dwindled, until by the time we came to Anton Larsen Bay, there were no trees at all. In a westerly direction, one would encounter the next native trees on Kamchatka or Sakhalin. The hills were as bright and golden as those of northern California. Way up on shore, I saw some old homesteader's place, with junk still in the yard, and a couple of Sitka blacktail deer browsing among the ruins.

Roger steered the boat into a tiny cove of the bay, with a small stream trickling into its head. There was just enough room remaining for a pod of Beluga whales to park, straight-in only. Peter, somewhat awkwardly, shifted the net into position. Roger anchored, climbed into the small dinghy and putted off with one end of the net, shouting out last-minute instructions to Peter:

"Now grab the plunger, and start popping when I've almost completed my loop. And remember: you ain't sucking out a stopped-up head. You're **smacking** the water, to get them silvers into the net. Pop that sucker: scare 'em.'"

The tranquility of the bay was broken by the loud noise of the plunger. Peter popped the water with all his might. The true pros, of course, would have made more noise with far less strain (as Roger told him later), but his effort was adequate; the water boiled with subsurface activity as Roger completed his circle with the dinghy. They closed the ends of the purse seine and hitched the net to the ancient winch. The payload began slowly to climb over the gunwales.

"**Damn** skookum!" shouted Roger as the net sagged with flashing silver color. He and Peter spilled the intelligent metal onto the deck and danced their catch into the lower hold.

A few more sets, and I had made my summer profit margin—and never had so much fun. Money never looked so beautiful, or gave you such a rush, rising up out of the water like that. You don't have to bust your balls and high-line. If you're like Roger, and have known these fish all your life, you can make your rent and a little more if you work at the exact right time. Not a bad lifestyle; Roger was about the most easy-going guy I've met in Alaska. Anyway, I felt like quite the stud fisherman around town, but didn't have much to do until a couple days before Pat took off for Peru—when he asked me to "host" a video of Kodiak he was shooting for his friends there. That was fun, too.

Peter stood on the windswept western ridge of Near Island. Before him, a winding dirt road led down to a small boat harbor. Behind him spread sixteen fish processing plants, the old blue-domed Russian Orthodox

Church, various stores, saloons, derelict ships and ghosts of all kinds. Pat stood by, video camera mounted and ready on a tripod. Peter gave a thumbs-up.

"Okay. Having crossed the $2.5 million 'Bridge to Nowhere' (so named for a broken development promise; notice the conspicuous lack of condos on Near Island), we are now enjoying a sweeping panorama of Kodiak town. About six thousand people now live here, making it the sixth largest city in Alaska—people from nearly all walks, swims and flounders of life. Ratio of bars to churches: formerly way out-of-line, now about dead-even. Note how, interestingly, the rise above downtown boasts the more vintage architecture, while below is all new-ish: namely, the modestly-upscale center mall, the commercial boat docks and the waterfront park and memorial. This is due to that great urban renewal project known as the Good Friday Earthquake of 1964."

"It was no joking matter," interjected Pat from behind the camera. "Imagine the whole harbor sucking dry, then a hundred-foot surge of water smashing back into town, knocking every low-lying building into flotsam or off its foundation, carrying a small boat onto an inland **lake**. You should walk around this part of town sometime, take note of the high-water marks on the second stories."

"Were you here for it?"

"I was five years old. I don't remember much, except for the end of the world, and a cold night up on the mountain. They get such life-and-death mayhem in Peru, I'm sure: they're a part of that same Rim of Fire."

"Anyway," resumed Peter, "everything in the central city's layout points towards the harbor. The harbor points towards the bald, stormy hills of the Aleutians. Cone-shaped blips on the blue horizon, stretching out for a thousand miles west of here. Note the 'termination dust,' the new snow, on the far islands, barely in view."

*On the slime line it's hard to look up from one's work and **see** the town. It really does have a spectacular setting, but everything is very pragmatically* *geared for the major local industry...and, it does not take long at all to get into some real boondocks.*

The camera rolled as the van (borrowed from Pat's brother) left the main highway out of Kodiak and bumped along a gravel road. At the foot of Mt. Barometer, through the middle of a moss-covered colony of old U.S. Army bunkers, was a beautifully wild salmon river, the Buskin.

"Some pertinent numbers: about 25,000 U.S. troops stationed on Kodiak alone during World War II; over one hundred natural spawning rivers on the island. Kodiak was supposed to be the last line of defense for mainland Alaska if the Japanese were successful in island-hopping through the Aleutians. It never happened, but nonetheless a lot of GIs spent some cold, wet, lonely months out here in the island bush. Meanwhile, the salmon, lured and fed by the incredible volumes of water emanating from Kodiak, kept on doing their timeless thing, virtually unmolested. In the one hundred-odd rivers, most of which are isolated and virtually inaccessible, they still do.

"How many fish are there in the streams and rivers of Kodiak? You've got to be kidding. But we are about to meet a man who is attempting to answer that very question."

The van stopped by a low bridge. Peter and Pat got out; Pat set up the tripod on the bridge while Peter walked down to a nylon mesh fence spanning the width of the river, with a single portal in the middle. Standing in hip-waders by the portal, busily at work, was the Buskin River fish-counter.

"How's it going?"

The fish counter leaned on his pitchfork. "They're not just going: they're **coming**, too. Going up through this gate, past me and my counting gadget," —CLICK, CLICK—"going to their spawning grounds, and then coming right back: dead, of course, after they've spawned out. They just wash back downstream and get hung up on the fence. Sometimes, this job is more like bucking hay bales back on the farm than your standard fisheries gig."

With an endlessly practiced motion, a spent, degenerated humpie was skewered on the pitchfork and flung back over the fence, to wash up against a sand bar in another quarter-mile or so. Grizzly aperitifs. Eagle elevensies.

"And so, do you like your work?"

"Well, the advent of modern technology has made it much more enjoyable. Used to be, I would have to bring a little tape recorder out with me into the river and speak into it as the salmon were fighting by, and I would try **verbally** to count them. You know, 'one, one, three, five, a thousand.' That method worked fine when I was counting sea otters; then it was just 'one, one, one.' But since I got my little doodad, my vocal cords, and my sanity, have been spared. I'm sure developing some dandy thumb muscles, though, from all this clicking."

Peter turned to the camera, in his best National Geographic documentary tones. "Men at work: in the wilds of the Buskin riparian corridor. Cold feet, wet trousers, huge thumbs. Someone's gotta do it. Next, we turn to the question of bears. Back to you, Pat?"

A short piece downriver lay the headquarters of the National Park Service, administrators to the outlying three-fourths of the island. The several Native villages lay outside their jurisdiction, the substantial population of Kodiak bears within. A mounted specimen of the latter stood in the doorway, grinning like eleven or twelve hundred pounds of sin.

"The gigantic Kodiak bear: fact or fiction?"

"Peter Helgeson, famous documentarist: Man or Myth?"

"Pat Fitzmorris: Zen archer or banana slug?"

Cindy the Park Service ranger bravely stood amidst the dense verbiage, fending it off. "Well, to answer your first question: what makes people grow up big and strong? And, how do we explain the size differential between us and, say, the Green Bay Packers offensive line? It's **food**. Compared to other food sources for bears, the Kodiak bush is like an NFL training table: an endless supply of protein-rich goodies delivered down every stream and rivulet. Fat, rain-fed blueberries and salmonberries, stretching up every hillside. No steroids, or dumpsters, necessary. Only a few Big White Hunters to interrupt chow time. The natural conditions here are so optimal, it's no wonder that Kodiak has the world's largest bears."

The natural history is incredibly vivid on Kodiak. Back on the eastern part of the island is a place where the spruces grow tall and gnarled, and are covered with phenomenal layers of moss. The reason why it is so thick has to do with the 1912 eruption of Mt. Katmai, on the Alaska Peninsula: twelve inches of ash fell on Kodiak as a result. You couldn't see the sun for three days. People loaded into boats and went out to sea, thinking that the end of the world had come—only to realize it hadn't as soon as they were clear of the ash cloud. Anyway, the ash stuck to these trees, and the moss quickly grew over it; all those minerals, it's quite fertile stuff. Strip away the moss on any of those trees, and you get a first-hand look at 1912.

Anyway, the human history is also fascinating, and moss-covered, on that part of Kodiak. There are more of those lonely-looking bunkers, gazing out to sea at Ft. Abercrombie. Unlike the ones at the Buskin, they do not seem remotely connected to any sort of war or battle or event within our memory; coming upon them is a bit like discovering Mayan ruins on the Yucatan.

"…Or Incan ruins: Macchu Picchu," cried out Pat as the van crept past the bunkers, camera rolling.

Also out in the woods is something that is not a historical ruin, but rather a historical tribute: a very special amphitheater, where one may learn all about…

"The 'Wild Ram.' That was what the Russian settlers called their leader, Alexander Baranov. Baranov gave his considerable strength and abilities, his soul, ultimately his life, for this outpost on the frontier of the Russian Empire: an empire too far-flung, too wildly improbable, to survive for long before collapsing and receding like a riptide. This amphitheater alternately celebrates and curses the life and times of Lord Baranov, via an epic play enacted every August. 'The Cry Of The Wild

Ram' is primarily a local production, keeping the citizens of Kodiak in touch with their rich and scandalous heritage as much as any other people have a right to claim."

The northern road finally ended at Monashka Bay, a place teeming with life and silence (not the quiet kind) and stillness (not the motionless kind). A short walk from the gravel parking lot led to a horseshoe-shaped beach: a place where water dripped from sandstone cliffs, gulls wheeled in a nonsensical circle game and the mystic lived like Robinson Crusoe (not Gilligan). One of probably hundreds of such places on Kodiak Island— but the only one you could drive to. Peter took the camera and aimed it towards Pat, seated on a piece of driftwood, lost in reverie.

"At first," said Pat, "I would come out here in my truck, all alone, and crank up some music in the tape deck—as a social alternative to another night in the bars. I'd just sit in the front seat, play my favorite tapes, loud, all by myself, and stare out the windshield at the waves and birds.

"Then, I began to leave the tapes at home. I'd open the doors and windows, breathe the salt air, listen to a different kind of music."

A beatific smile, a fade-out: the conclusion of the Kodiak video.

LETTER: 3/10/89

▼

Dear Dad:

Greetings from the tag end of my first Alaskan winter. While we can still expect more snow or slush, and plenty of mud, the bulk of the season is behind us: the days are getting noticeably longer, and the sub-zero temperatures are a thing of the past. Genna and I are still together, and still head-over-heels about each other: no small feat, from what I've heard, after spending such a lengthy period in close confines. Around here, the "Spring Break-up Season" refers to more than just river ice.

Peter Helgeson—remember him?—was here last week. He'd been traveling down the Al-Can, decided to take that scenic detour to Skagway, and dropped into town, out of the blue. He was on his way Outside for a couple weeks, to gather the bulk of his personal belongings and haul them back to Seward, where he's been spending the fishing offseason. I think he and Kim, his girlfriend, were ready for a little break from that rainy South Central weather: she actually went to Hawaii with her family for the month (top vacation destination for winter-weary Alaskans: you can spot 'em on the beach by their snowy-white sunglare). Anyway, Pete ended up staying with us at the Dyea cabin for a few days before hitting the road again. You might see him soon: don't be too surprised if a scruffy, mildly disreputable Viking-type shows up on your doorstep around suppertime. I swear, you'd hardly recognize him.

Would **you** recognize me? Would Mom make a quick grab for the rolling pin if I were to appear on the front porch? On one hand, my life is very different now, and I guess my north-woodsy look reflects that. On the other hand, I think this is the type of future you could have predicted for me, when you think about the things that interested me while I was growing up. All that fishing and hiking; all those books of far-away adventure; all your stories about winter camping with your friends in the Boundary Waters. See, you're at least in part to blame! But I think that Alaska was in me all along.

That being said and done, there is the continuing issue of how I'll get by up here. I don't really see going back to being a tour guide, as nice (and as lucrative) as it's been. It seems to me that tourism necessarily involves a superficial examination of a particular place: standardized and at least mildly homogenized. Some experiences are clearly more authentic than others, but ultimately they're skin-deep. Over three years of touring, I always tried to inject my own personal touch, tried to learn and understand as much as I could about the places we were visiting. I also think, as a result, that it was worthwhile for those who had sought out such an experience: those who had come from such long distances, and paid so much, for the likes of my tours. But all the factoids and anecdotes in the world cannot communicate what it's like to **live** here in Alaska: not as a visitor, but as a **part** of it. So I think I've outgrown that particular line of work.

The lack of continued free tours notwithstanding, I hope that you and Mom, and whoever else, will want to come visit us, wherever we may be. It's almost certain now that Gary (whom you met a couple summers ago), the owner of this cabin, will be returning soon. Genna and I have begun to explore the options for our next homestead. One possibility for the summer is her family cabin near Valdez, where there's the added bonus of abundant work: fisheries, river guiding, Alaska Pipeline tours (ha!). After that, it's wide open: maybe we'll get lucky and find a nice piece of land of our own, in one bushy locale or another. The way I feel, home is wherever she is—and she is an Alaskan through and through.

Come up and see us, any time.

Love, your son, Kris

Otters

▼

Sea Otter: Enhydra lutris, largest member of the weasel family, weighing up to 90 pounds; an aquatic mammal with thick brown fur, webbed feet and a long-flattened tail; found in the North Pacific, from subarctic Alaska to the California coast.

"How I love otters," said Genna, placing the March issue of National Wildlife into a partially-packed wicker basket. "They're my absolute favorite. The river otters are way cool: I love how they slide down the riverbanks on their tummies into the open water, even in the Winter. But the sea otters are the champions of playtime, the winners of the Ultimate Lifestyle award…"

Playing

"In the Ideal Otter Lifestyle, there is no clear line dividing Work and Play."

—Conventional Otter Wisdom

One unusually balmy afternoon last Fall, Genna and I went sea-kayaking in the Lynn Canal. We were eyeball-to-eyeball with a variety of marine critters: the Orca-like Dall porpoises, who accepted us as their own, following our boats' wake; the tiny puffins, struggling mightily to lift their pot-bellies from the water, looking embarrassed when all that flapping didn't quite make it; and of course the sea otters. They seemed to wave at us as they went about their otter business—which consisted mainly of rolling, diving, rolling, nibbling, scratching, playing with their moustaches, rolling and rolling.

I pointed out that the nibbling and rolling helped groom their fur, keeping it clean and working in enough air bubbles to insulate them from the cold sea water.

"Does there have to be a purpose?" *countered Genna, her eyes fixed on a single otter that had been tumbling and spinning in the swells the whole time we were there. When we left some time later, it was still stuck in the tumble-and-spin cycle.*

"Hackysack," said Llary, pulling out his hack from a flannel-shirt pocket, "is the most **pointless** game ever invented." The momentarily-idle Driver/Guides were the spokes of a wheel in the Tok Tundra Lodge parking lot. Genna drifted over, was immediately accepted into the circle.

I shanked the hackysack off into the dust. "Uh, **sorry**," *I muttered as I moved to fetch it. But Genna beat me to it; with surprising strength and accuracy she hurled the hack into my chest. Oops—the "S" word.*

"By the time this Summer is over, Kris," vowed Genna, "I will have cured you of **all** your good manners."

Just last night, I was floating there in the easy chair, treading water when the silken sea whispered in my ear, "Just think, Kris: we've been lovers for nine months. I could've had your **child** by now." *She slid away thru the laughing waves.*

"Similarly, the otter's distinction between Love and Play is also blurred."

—*Ibid.*

languid august dog-day, sky
thick with honey, haze, dragonflies; genna
stands up on front porch, does slow kitty-
stretch and kicks off a sandal, walks
ten feet away, kicks off the other sandal;
walks fifteen feet away sheds ohmygod her
cutoff jeans, she is on forest's edge now
pulls off t-shirt, drops it on ground, looks over
bare shoulder, smiles, pads into the trees
> *i follow her wake into kelp-forest*
> *lair, no sign until i spy panties on low*
> *birch limb, sudden movement aha i caught you as lithe*
> *blonde figure lunges, takes me down in*
> *deep-sea fern grotto, wrestling breathing hard i'm*
> *soon mercifully pinned; the victor rides high and straddling*
> *runs a hand up my shirt says this is a special*
> *place i've always wanted to take you;*
> > *just watch out*
> > > *for that*
> > > > *devil's club*

"Look at those two otters together," said Genna, pointing from her kayak. "They've been wrestling and nipping each other for about ten minutes now. Look: the smaller one just slapped the other upside the head!" She pivoted her boat. "Best to leave 'em to their own devices now, I guess."

Eating

The sea otter enjoys a diet that would be the envy of any seafood gourmand—provided that such a gourmand was not averse to whole, very fresh (i.e., live) sushi. She uses her Olympic diver's

body to plunge after squid, crab, clams and sea urchins; she flags
down sea-run trout and young salmon with swift paddling strokes.
After this brief burst of energy, the otter lolls on her back, floating
like a cork; she lays out the seafood spread, right where her bib
should be; she briefly considers and rejects Cordon Bleu aesthetics
before tearing into chowtime with sharp teeth. If clams are on the
menu, she also will have brought up a small rock, for bashing the
stubborn shells. If she has young pups, they'll climb right on board
and partake as well: picnic on Mom's tummy! They eat long and
well: up to 25% of their body weight per day. Day in and day out,
nothin' but…

"Seafood…" muttered Genna, in mock exasperation. "Seafood everywhere. A whole fridge full of leftover seafood…what in the **world** are we
to do?"

*I took Genna's agitation for the ruse that it was—for the word "cioppino"
had passed her lips repeatedly over the past 24 hours. It was late September,
and we both had been liberated from the tour season; upon arriving at the
Valdez coastal cabin, we had been confronted with a freezerful of various fishy
leftovers—not enough of any one thing for a whole meal, but, cumulatively,
plenty for some down-home, honest-to-God, Mediterranean seafood stew.*

"One halibut steak," counted Genna, taking inventory of freezer contents. "Some mystery fish: looks like rock cod. A bag of mussels: where did
they come from? Scallops, a few oysters. Some tanner crab legs, judging
from the wingspan. Cioppino: it's the **only** answer."

"I think I saw some tomato sauce back in the pantry there, Kris. Also
saw a bunch of Italian spices: thank God our hosts weren't spice-impaired,
like you Norwegians!"

I protested: "Hey, I'm getting better. If I hadn't met you, I'd still be cooking generic mac 'n cheese. And remember how I ordered from the **two**-star
menu last time we were at the Thai House? But admittedly, if it were up to
my forebears, they'd just boil up all of this bounty to a paste and find

something **white** to slather all over it." *The water came to a boil; I popped in the goodies and a heavenly, primal aroma steamed the cabin windows.*

"Amanda smelled like the leftovers from an Eskimo picnic. John Paul was inflamed."

—Tom Robbins

"No clams!" Genna emerged from the freezer with a start. "Check the tide book, Kris: we need to do some digging if we're to have proper cioppino."

The stones on the beach below the cabin were uniformly black, small and wafer-thin, pounded first by the glaciers, then by the relentless waves. Kris felt as if he were walking on poker chips.

"There's one!" said Genna, pointing instinctively. As Kris and Genna tiptoed over to the mini-volcano in the casino sand, the telltale spurt of water revealed the reclusive, tasty mollusk.

Soon, a bucket of fresh butter clams joined the spicy, garlicky melange of sea critters stewing in a pot on the old gas stove. While the cioppino cooked, Kris and Genna sipped Hearty Burgundy and fed each other sneak previews of the warmed sourdough loaf, dipped in basil-flavored olive oil. At length, large tureens were procured and filled (all those mollusk shells took up lots of bowl-space), the bread and wine were transferred to tableside, and Kris and Genna fell to dinner. Scarce a word was said for some time, in lieu of shell-cracking and munching sounds.

Afterwards, they lolled on the front porch, absorbing the late alpenglow off the peaks across Valdez Arm, intertwined like the sea-bed kelp.

Sleeping

When sleepy-time arrives, most otters would just as soon stay at home in the sea. Remaining afloat while asleep is no problem; of greater concern is waking up somewhere off Kamchatka. Thus, the otter often will swim into a raft of seaweed and secure herself for the night. She rolls up in the giant green strands; she can be as much of a blanket-hog as she desires. Her cozy kelp bed quells the restless sea swells into a gentle, sleep-inducing rocking.

I remember our first night together. It was sometime in late June; we'd had our first date, at Sandy's party, but I didn't really know Genna very well yet. I had just driven down to Tok from Fairbanks. There had been the usual volleyball, and afterwards I walked her back to her cabin, said good night and went out to the drivers' Airstream trailer. I had drawn the curtains, put on one of my going-to-sleep tapes and was just sliding into bed when the screen door rustled. In the half-dusk I saw Genna peering thru the screen, then in a quiet instant she was next to me. She sat down on the edge of the bed—made a gentle shushing motion, finger to lips—and put her arms around me. "I just want to snuggle," she whispered, giving my ear a little kiss.

I heard her clothes fall to the floor, piece by piece; I felt her slip into bed next to me, naked and warm. She moored herself to me as we rocked into deep-blue sleep.

And in fact, all we did that night was snuggle. I woke up first in the morning; Genna stirred, looked up at me with golden eyes and smiled. She slid out of bed, back into her flannel shirt and jeans in a twinkling, and went to serve breakfast at the motel cafe.

Genna has been much the same way these late-winter nights. We may kiss, we may even make love—but mostly we snuggle. Her breathing is easy, angelic, just inches away.

"Wrong," Genna whispers at the weather report. "I believe we'll have a **warm** night." She snuggles closer.

Sometimes she holds me tightly, as if she fears she will drift away. And she loves to steal the covers.

THE SALMON WHO LIVED

▼

affirming life
in a baritone smile, he will
swim past his spawned brothers,
stiff-eyed and
green in the rain;
he will pass beneath the circling
call of the raven;
he will pass the doe-eyed
woman on the shore, upon whom
the scent of cedar rests lightly
    his long silver song will
     flow like a beard to the sea

About the Author

Tim Rundquist spent eight seasons as a professional tour guide in Alaska, covering territory from Ketchikan to Prudhoe Bay. He currently resides in rural Minnesota with his wife, Heather.